# HEALTHIER COOKING
## ANNUAL RECIPES

## Taste of Home

RDA ENTHUSIAST BRANDS, LLC • MILWAUKEE, WI

# HEALTHIER COOKING
## ANNUAL RECIPES

73

22

© 2021 RDA Enthusiast Brands, LLC.
1610 N. 2nd St., Suite 102, Milwaukee WI 53212-3906

Visit us at **tasteofhome.com** for other Taste of Home books and products.

**ISBNs:**
D 978-1-62145-724-4
U 978-1-62145-725-1
**Component Numbers:**
D 117900102H
U 117900100H
**ISSN:** 1944-7736

**Executive Editor:** Mark Hagen
**Senior Art Director:** Raeann Thompson
**Editor:** Christine Rukavena
**Art Director:** Maggie Conners
**Designer:** Arielle Anttonen
**Deputy Editor, Copy Desk:** Dulcie Shoener
**Copy Editor:** Ann Walter
**Senior Food Editor:** Peggy Woodward, RDN

**Cover Photographer:** Mark Derse
**Senior Set Stylist:** Melissa Franco
**Food Stylist:** Josh Rink

**Pictured on front cover:**
Coconut-Crusted Turkey Strips, p. 166;
So-Easy Succotash, p. 118.

**Pictured on title page:**
Kale & Bacon Salad with Honey-Horseradish Vinaigrette, p. 81.

**Pictured on back cover:**
Creamy Avocado Manicotti, p. 151; Edamame & Soba Noodle Bowl p. 137; Spice-Rubbed Salmon, p. 181; Blackberry Daiquiri Sherbet, p. 241; Simple Guacamole, p. 34.

Printed in USA
1 3 5 7 9 10 8 6 4 2

To find a recipe: *tasteofhome.com*
To submit a recipe: *tasteofhome.com/submit*
To find out about other *Taste of Home*
products: *shoptasteofhome.com*

**f** LIKE US facebook.com/tasteofhome

**🐦** TWEET US twitter.com/tasteofhome

**📷** FOLLOW US @tasteofhome

**📌** PIN US pinterest.com/taste_of_home

# Contents

Eating healthy just got a whole lot easier. Dig into 366 better-for-you
dishes that are perfect for your active lifestyle.

60

# A Plant-Rich Diet Makes a Healthier You

We're here to help with delicious ways to eat your fruits and veggies.

Eating less meat has been growing in popularity for some time now, but over the last couple of years, it's made a subtle shift. The focus used to be removing meat from meals, but now the importance of adding more plant-based foods has taken center stage, and this is a good thing!

Eating a wider variety of plants at most meals means more vitamins, nutrients, fiber and overall health benefits. Centering meals around a single animal-based protein, while still common, is giving way to main dishes that incorporate plant-based sources of protein like legumes, nuts and seeds instead of, or in addition to, meat.

**WE'RE ON BOARD**
You will see that trend in recipes throughout this edition of *Healthier Cooking Annual Recipes* like **CHICKEN WITH CURRY ROASTED SQUASH (P. 155)** and **ONE-PAN TUSCAN RAVIOLI (P. 141).** We've also continued to use our power-packed icon to highlight recipes that are especially packed full of nutrients, most of which are also in line with plant-forward eating.

Even breakfast foods like **PUMPKIN AND CHICKEN SAUSAGE HASH (P. 23)** can be loaded with veggies to start your day off right. And dessert doesn't have to mean empty calories; **CREAMY COCONUT RICE PUDDING PARFAITS (P. 244)** will satisfy your sweet tooth, but they also include a whole grain, two kinds of fruit, crunchy almonds and nutrient-rich dairy. That's a win-win.

Happy Cooking,

*Peggy*

Peggy Woodward, RDN
Senior Food Editor

155

244

# About Our Nutrition Facts

*Healthier Cooking Annual Recipes* offers a variety of recipes to fit today's healthy lifestyles. Here is how we arrive at the nutritional information found at the end of each recipe.

- Whenever a choice of ingredients is given (such as ½ cup sour cream or plain yogurt), we use the first ingredient in our calculations.

- When a range is given for an ingredient, we calculate using the first amount.

- Only the amount of a marinade absorbed is calculated.

- Optional ingredients are not included in our calculations.

- Sugars provided in the Nutrition Facts represent both added and naturally occurring sugars.

\* **HEALTH TIP** \* Peggy shares her best secrets to help you make healthy eating choices throughout the week.

**SPECIAL INDICATORS**

**Power-Packed** Each dish contains a whole grain or legume, a lean protein, and a healthy dose of fruits or vegetables.

**Meatless** Indicates breakfast, lunch, dinner and snack-time options that don't use meat or meat products.

**Fast Fix** Dishes are table-ready in 30 minutes or less.

**Slow Cooker** Dozens of slow-simmered recipes use the favorite appliance.

**Small-Batch** recipes are perfect for 2.

# Tricks for Making Satisfying Meatless Dishes

**1 Go Meaty with Mushrooms.** With their rich taste and meaty texture, mushrooms make vegetarian meals that are wonderfully satisfying. Sliced portobello and shiitake mushrooms create a rich stew in Iben Ravn's **MUSHROOM & SWEET POTATO POTPIE.** Though mushroom stems can be woody and tough, they're packed with flavor. Rinse them well to remove dirt, coarsely chop, and simmer the stems in a homemade vegetable broth. **P. 148**

**2 Load Up on Veggies & Low-Fat Dairy.** Go ahead and let the vegetables shine! This healthy strategy can help you get all of the recommended servings of produce each day. **ZUCCHINI ROLL-UPS** from Kansas' Courtney Stultz feature summer garden favorites and 4 grams of fiber per serving. Plus, low-fat ricotta cheese adds stick-to-your-ribs protein. **P. 176**

**3 Get To Know Tofu.** Also called soybean curd or bean curd, tofu is made from soy milk the same way cheese is made from dairy milk. Soy milk is mixed with calcium or magnesium salt to create curds. The more liquid (whey) that is pressed from the curd, the firmer the tofu will be. Its neutral taste is a blank canvas for soy sauce, pepper flakes and garlic in Emily Steers' simple **ASIAN TOFU.** Also try tofu in veggie-rich stir-fries and soups, or blend it in with your morning smoothie. **P. 166**

**4 Reach for Lentils, Beans & Other Legumes.** They're a major food source throughout the Americas, Caribbean, Mediterranean and parts of Asia, and billions of people rely on these plants as a meatless source of protein. **CURRIED LENTIL SOUP** from Michigan's Christina Till is packed with satisfying lentils. Calorie for calorie, lentils produce only 2.5% as much carbon dioxide (a greenhouse gas) as beef and 10% as much as tofu. That means lentils are one of the leanest, greenest crops around. **P. 61**

**5 Add an Egg.** The protein powerhouse adds richness to Amy McDonough's on-trend breakfast, **POACHED EGG BUDDHA BOWLS.** Also consider adding an egg to your breakfast potatoes, ramen noodle soup, pad thai or even a vegetarian burger. **P. 19**

**6 Season with Smoked Peppers.** Smoked paprika adds rich complexity to Geraldine Hennessey's **SPICY VEGGIE & LENTIL SOUP.** It and other smoked spices like anchos and ground chipotle pepper lend sweetness, heat and smoky notes to your dishes. They let you enjoy a bacony taste without the unwanted calories, fat or meat. **P. 71**

## Popular Protein Sources in Vegetarian Dishes

A good rule of thumb for calculating your daily protein need is to multiply your body weight in pounds by 0.4 gram. For example, a 150-pound person needs about 60 grams of protein daily. Here are some popular meatless sources of protein.

| PROTEIN SOURCE | GRAMS OF PROTEIN |
|---|---|
| 1 cup cooked black beans | 15g |
| 1 cup cooked chickpeas | 12g |
| 1 cup cooked lentils | 18g |
| 1 cup cooked quinoa | 8g |
| 4 oz. tofu | 10g |
| 1 large egg | 7g |
| 1 cup cottage cheese | 24g |
| 1 cup flavored Greek yogurt | 18g |
| 1 cup dairy milk | 8g |
| 1 cup plain soy milk | 7g |
| 1 oz. cheddar cheese | 7g |
| 1 oz. almonds | 6g |
| 2 Tbsp. peanut butter | 7g |

# GOOD MORNINGS

"These pancakes are a favorite at my house. If I don't make them every Saturday or Sunday, the family won't believe it's the weekend! My son's friends often spend the night, and I think it's because they like the pancakes so much. The stacks of jacks are extra delicious served with maple syrup."
—Sharon Bickett, Chester, SC

## HAM & SPINACH PIE

(PICTURED ON P. 6)

*With the exception of the phyllo dough, which I always have on hand, this ham and spinach pie recipe is made entirely from Easter dinner leftovers. One of my neighbors traded me four freshly caught trout for a piece!*
—Teena Petrus, Johnstown, PA

**Prep:** 30 min. • **Bake:** 45 min. + cooling
**Makes:** 8 servings

- 3 Tbsp. butter, divided
- 1 medium onion, halved and sliced
- 8 oz. sliced fresh mushrooms
- 1 garlic clove, minced
- 1 pkg. (10 oz.) frozen chopped spinach, thawed and squeezed dry
- 6 sheets phyllo dough (14x9 in.)
- 2 cups finely chopped fully cooked ham
- 1 cup shredded mozzarella cheese
- 3 large eggs, beaten
  Optional: Salt and pepper to taste

**1.** Preheat oven to 350°. In a large skillet, heat 1 Tbsp. butter over medium heat. Add onion; cook and stir 6-8 minutes or until transparent. Add mushrooms and garlic; cook and stir until mushrooms are browned, about 6 minutes longer. Add spinach; cook until heated through.
**2.** In a microwave, melt remaining butter; stir until smooth. Place 1 sheet of phyllo dough on a work surface; brush with butter. Layer with 3 additional phyllo sheets, brushing each layer. Transfer to a lightly greased 11x7-in. baking dish, letting ends extend up sides. (Keep remaining phyllo covered with a damp towel to prevent it from drying out.)
**3.** Layer dish with the ham, cheese and spinach mixture; pour eggs over filling. If desired, sprinkle with salt and pepper. Top with remaining phyllo dough. Fold dough ends over filling; pinch edges to seal. Brush with the remaining butter. Cut slits in the top. Bake until browned, 40-45 minutes. Cool for 20 minutes before cutting.

**1 piece:** 195 cal., 11g fat (6g sat. fat), 113mg chol., 633mg sod., 9g carb. (2g sugars, 2g fiber), 16g pro. **Diabetic exchanges:** 2 fat, 1 lean meat, ½ starch.

## FRESH STRAWBERRY BREAKFAST TACOS

*When our son was growing up, this was one of his favorite breakfasts. I've used lower-fat ingredients in this recipe with good results, too.*
—Joan Hallford, North Richland Hills, TX

**Takes:** 30 min. • **Makes:** 6 servings

- 2 Tbsp. butter
- 6 flour tortillas (6 in.)
- ⅓ cup cream cheese, softened
- 1 Tbsp. honey
- ½ tsp. ground cinnamon
- ⅓ cup vanilla yogurt
- 1¾ cups quartered fresh strawberries

**1.** In a large skillet, heat 1 tsp. butter over medium-low heat. Add 1 tortilla; cook each side until light golden, 1-2 minutes. Transfer to wire rack. Repeat with the remaining butter and tortillas.
**2.** Beat together cream cheese, honey and cinnamon; slowly mix in yogurt until blended. Spread tortillas with cream cheese mixture; top with strawberries.

**1 taco:** 225 cal., 12g fat (6g sat. fat), 24mg chol., 280mg sod., 25g carb. (8g sugars, 2g fiber), 4g pro.

**FRESH STRAWBERRY BREAKFAST TACOS**

**RUSTIC VEGETABLE FRITTATA**

## BRAIN FOOD SMOOTHIE

*My grandson refuses fruits and vegetables almost completely. After he and our son moved home, I tried everything to improve his diet. This smoothie was one of the only ways I could sneak him something nutritious, and he loves it!*
—Sandra Roberts, Dexter, MO

**Takes:** 15 min. • **Makes:** 6 servings

- 1½ cups fat-free vanilla Greek yogurt
- ½ cup 2% milk
- 2 medium ripe avocados, peeled and pitted
- 2 cups halved fresh strawberries
- 1 cup sliced ripe banana
- 1 cup fresh raspberries or frozen unsweetened raspberries, thawed
- 1 cup fresh baby spinach
- 1 cup fresh blueberries
- ½ cup fresh or frozen blackberries, thawed
- ¼ cup unflavored whey protein powder

Place all ingredients in a blender; cover and process until smooth.

**1 cup:** 215 cal., 8g fat (1g sat. fat), 3mg chol., 65mg sod., 29g carb. (17g sugars, 7g fiber), 10g pro.

## RUSTIC VEGETABLE FRITTATA

*I love that this veggie-loaded frittata combines seriously nutritious ingredients into a filling dish I can serve as breakfast, lunch or dinner—and even the leftovers are delicious!*
—Deborah Jamison, Austin, TX

**Takes:** 30 min. • **Makes:** 4 servings

- 1 medium sweet potato, peeled and cut into ¼-in. slices
- 2 Tbsp. water
- 7 large eggs
- 3 Tbsp. fat-free milk
- ¼ tsp. salt
- ⅛ tsp. pepper
- 6 center-cut bacon strips, coarsely chopped
- 1 small green pepper, chopped
- ½ cup chopped red onion
- 2 cups coarsely chopped fresh kale

**1.** Preheat oven to 375°. Place sweet potato and water in a microwave-safe bowl; microwave, covered, on high until potato is just tender, 5-6 minutes; drain.

**2.** Meanwhile, whisk together the eggs, milk, salt and pepper. In a 10-in. oven-safe skillet, cook bacon over medium heat until crisp, stirring occasionally. Using a slotted spoon, remove bacon to paper towels. Remove all but 1 Tbsp. drippings from pan.

**3.** In drippings, saute green pepper, onion and kale over medium heat until tender, 4-5 minutes. Reduce heat to low. Stir in egg mixture; add potato and bacon. Cook until eggs are partially set, 1-2 minutes.

**4.** Transfer to oven; bake until eggs are set, 5-7 minutes. Cut into wedges.

**1 wedge:** 259 cal., 14g fat (5g sat. fat), 340mg chol., 448mg sod., 16g carb. (7g sugars, 2g fiber), 17g pro. **Diabetic exchanges:** 2 medium-fat meat, 1 starch.

> **TEST KITCHEN TIP**
>
> Finishing the frittata in the oven instead of on the stovetop will keep the bottom from getting too dark.

FESTIVE CRANBERRY
FRUIT SALAD

## FESTIVE CRANBERRY FRUIT SALAD

*This fruit salad is a tradition on my Christmas table. It goes together quickly, which is a plus on such a busy day.*
—Rousheen Arel Wolf, Delta Junction, AK

- - - - - - - - - - - - - - - - - - - - - - - - - - - - - - - -

**Takes:** 25 min. • **Makes:** 14 servings

- 1 pkg. (12 oz.) fresh or frozen cranberries
- ¾ cup water
- ½ cup sugar
- 5 medium apples, diced
- 2 medium firm bananas, sliced
- 1½ cups fresh or frozen blueberries, thawed
- 1 can (11 oz.) mandarin oranges, undrained
- 1 cup fresh or frozen raspberries, thawed
- ¾ cup fresh strawberries, halved

**1.** In a large saucepan, combine the cranberries, water and sugar. Cook and stir over medium heat until berries pop, about 15 minutes. Remove from the heat; cool slightly.

**2.** In a large bowl, combine the remaining ingredients. Add cranberry mixture; stir gently. Refrigerate until serving.

**¾ cup:** 105 cal., 0 fat (0 sat. fat), 0 chol., 2mg sod., 27g carb. (21g sugars, 4g fiber), 1g pro.

## EGGS FLORENTINE CUPS

*I'm always looking for creative ways to use up the baby spinach I have in my fridge. I'm also a fanatic about making sure my children get a nutritious breakfast. So I make these up the night before, bake them in the morning and breakfast is done! If there are any leftovers, I reheat them for a quick lunch or dinner.*
—Jan Charles, Greeneville, TN

- - - - - - - - - - - - - - - - - - - - - - - - - - - - - - - -

**Prep:** 20 min. • **Cook:** 15 min.
**Makes:** 6 servings

- 6 slices deli ham, ⅛-in. thick
- ¼ cup finely chopped onions
- 1 Tbsp. butter
- 6 cups fresh spinach
- 6 Tbsp. half-and-half cream
- 6 tsp. grated Parmesan cheese
- ¾ tsp. salt
- ¾ tsp. pepper
- 6 large eggs

**1.** Preheat oven to 350°. Press the ham slices into 6 greased foil muffin cup liners; set aside.

**2.** In a large skillet, saute the onions in butter until tender. Add spinach; cook 3-4 minutes longer or until wilted. Divide spinach mixture among ham cups. Top each with 1 Tbsp. of cream, 1 tsp. of cheese and a dash of salt and pepper. Break 1 egg into each cup.

**3.** Bake until eggs are set, 15-17 minutes.

**1 muffin cup:** 148 cal., 9g fat (4g sat. fat), 209mg chol., 690mg sod., 4g carb. (2g sugars, 1g fiber), 12g pro.

## MINI HAM & CHEESE QUICHES

*We bake mini quiches for breakfast or brunch with ham and cheddar in muffin pans. Salad croutons are a simple stand-in for crust.*

—Lois Enger, Colorado Springs, CO

- - - - - - - - - - - - - - - - - - - - - - - - -

**Takes:** 30 min. • **Makes:** 1 dozen

- 1 cup salad croutons
- 1 cup shredded cheddar cheese
- 1 cup chopped fully cooked ham
- 4 large eggs
- 1½ cups 2% milk
- 1½ tsp. dried parsley flakes
- ½ tsp. Dijon mustard
- ¼ tsp. salt
- ⅛ tsp. onion powder
  Dash pepper

**1.** Preheat oven to 325°. Divide the croutons, cheese and ham among 12 greased muffin cups. In a large bowl, whisk remaining ingredients until blended. Divide egg mixture among prepared muffin cups.

**2.** Bake until a knife inserted in the center comes out clean, 15-20 minutes. Let stand 5 minutes before removing from pan. Serve warm.

**1 mini quiche:** 107 cal., 6g fat (3g sat. fat), 81mg chol., 328mg sod., 4g carb. (2g sugars, 0 fiber), 8g pro.

## SPICY BREAKFAST PIZZA
(PICTURED ON P. 6)

*Eggs and hash browns have extra pizazz when they're served up on a pizza pan. My family requests this fun breakfast quite often, and it's a snap to make with ready-to-use pizza crust. I adjust the heat index of the toppings to suit the taste buds of my diners.*

—Christy Hinrichs, Parkville, MO

- - - - - - - - - - - - - - - - - - - - - - - - -

**Takes:** 30 min. • **Makes:** 6 servings

- 2 cups frozen shredded hash brown potatoes
- ¼ tsp. ground cumin
- ¼ tsp. chili powder
- 2 Tbsp. canola oil, divided
- 4 large eggs
- 2 Tbsp. 2% milk
- ¼ tsp. salt
- 2 green onions, chopped
- 2 Tbsp. diced sweet red pepper
- 1 Tbsp. finely chopped jalapeno pepper
- 1 garlic clove, minced
- 1 prebaked 12-in. thin pizza crust
- ½ cup salsa
- ¾ cup shredded cheddar cheese

**1.** Preheat the oven to 375°. In a large nonstick skillet, cook the hash browns, cumin and chili powder in 1 Tbsp. oil over medium heat until golden. Remove and keep warm.

**2.** In a small bowl, beat the eggs, milk and salt; set aside. In same skillet, saute the onions, peppers and garlic in remaining 1 Tbsp. oil until tender. Add egg mixture. Cook and stir over medium heat until almost set. Remove from heat.

**3.** Place crust on an ungreased round 14-in. cast-iron griddle or pizza pan. Spread salsa over crust. Top with egg mixture. Sprinkle with hash browns and cheese. Bake until the cheese is melted, 8-10 minutes.

**1 slice:** 320 cal., 16g fat (5g sat. fat), 138mg chol., 605mg sod., 31g carb. (2g sugars, 1g fiber), 13g pro.

**MINI HAM & CHEESE QUICHES**

**FRENCH TOAST CASSEROLE**

## BLACKBERRY MUFFINS

*Take advantage of delicious summer blackberries by adding them to these muffins. They are very easy to prepare and disappear as soon as they're served.*
—Candy Woelk, Lexington, MO

**Prep:** 15 min. • **Bake:** 20 min.
**Makes:** 1 dozen

- ¼ cup butter, softened
- ½ cup sugar
- 1 large egg, room temperature, lightly beaten
- ¾ cup 2% milk
- ¼ tsp. vanilla extract
- 1¾ cups plus 1 Tbsp. all-purpose flour, divided
- 2½ tsp. baking powder
- ¼ tsp. salt
- 1 cup fresh blackberries
  Honey, optional

**1.** Preheat oven to 400°. In a bowl, cream the butter and sugar. Add the egg and mix well. Beat in the milk and vanilla until almost smooth, about 1 minute. Combine 1¾ cups flour, baking powder and salt; stir into creamed mixture just until combined (batter will be thick). Toss blackberries with the remaining flour until coated; fold into batter.

**2.** Fill greased or paper-lined muffin cups half full. Bake at until muffins are golden brown, 20-25 minutes. Serve warm, with honey if desired.

**1 muffin:** 156 cal., 5g fat (3g sat. fat), 30mg chol., 184mg sod., 25g carb. (10g sugars, 1g fiber), 3g pro. **Diabetic exchanges:** 1½ starch, 1 fat.

## FRENCH TOAST CASSEROLE

*I sprinkle a cinnamon-sugar topping on my easy oven version of French toast. I love the fact that I can assemble it the previous night and save time in the morning.*
—Sharyn Adams, Crawfordsville, IN

**Prep:** 15 min. + chilling
**Bake:** 45 min.
**Makes:** 12 servings

- 1 loaf (1 lb.) French bread, cut into 1-in. cubes
- 8 large eggs, lightly beaten
- 3 cups 2% milk
- 4 tsp. sugar
- 1 tsp. vanilla extract
- ¾ tsp. salt
  TOPPING
- 2 Tbsp. butter
- 3 Tbsp. sugar
- 2 tsp. ground cinnamon
  Maple syrup, optional

**1.** Place bread cubes in a greased 13x9-in. baking dish. In a large bowl, whisk the eggs, milk, sugar, vanilla and salt. Pour over bread. Cover and refrigerate for 8 hours or overnight.

**2.** Remove from refrigerator 30 minutes before baking. Preheat oven to 350°. Dot with the butter. Combine the sugar and cinnamon; sprinkle over the top.

**3.** Cover and bake 45-50 minutes or until a knife inserted in the center comes out clean. Let stand for 5 minutes. Serve with maple syrup if desired.

**1 serving:** 223 cal., 7g fat (3g sat. fat), 151mg chol., 484mg sod., 29g carb. (9g sugars, 1g fiber), 11g pro.

### TEST KITCHEN TIP

Cinnamon comes in two basic types: Ceylon and cassia. Ceylon cinnamon's delicate, complex flavor is ideal for ice creams and simple sauces. The spicy, bolder cassia cinnamon (often labeled simply as cinnamon) is preferred for baking.

BLACKBERRY
MUFFINS

## BLUEBERRY PANCAKE SMOOTHIE

*My family loves this pancake smoothie in the morning. I don't normally measure the blueberries, so go crazy! If you have fresh blueberries, I would recommend freezing the banana ahead of time.*
—Kailey Thompson, Palm Bay, FL

**Takes:** 5 min. • **Makes:** 2 servings

- 1 cup unsweetened almond milk
- 1 medium banana
- ½ cup frozen unsweetened blueberries
- ¼ cup instant plain oatmeal
- 1 tsp. maple syrup
- ½ tsp. ground cinnamon
  Dash sea salt

Place the first 6 ingredients in a blender; cover and process until smooth. Pour into 2 chilled glasses; sprinkle with sea salt. Serve immediately.
**1 cup:** 153 cal., 3g fat (0 sat. fat), 0 chol., 191mg sod., 31g carb. (13g sugars, 5g fiber), 3g pro. **Diabetic exchanges:** 2 starch.

BREAKFAST GRANOLA

## BREAKFAST GRANOLA

*This is one of my family's favorite breakfasts. It gives them the energy they need to get through the day's chores.*
—Wilma Beller, Hamilton, OH

**Prep:** 20 min. • **Bake:** 20 min.
**Makes:** 8 cups

- 4 cups old-fashioned oats
- ⅓ cup honey or molasses
- ¼ cup canola oil
- 1 tsp. vanilla extract
- 1 cup chopped nuts
- ¾ cup uncooked oat bran cereal
- 1 cup sweetened shredded coconut
- 1 cup raisins
- 1 cup chopped dates
  Optional: Yogurt and fresh fruit

**1.** Spread rolled oats on a 15x10x1-in. baking pan. Bake at 350° for 5 minutes. Stir; bake 5 minutes longer or until toasted. Meanwhile, combine honey and oil in a small saucepan. Cook and stir over medium heat for 2-3 minutes or until heated through. Remove from the heat; stir in vanilla. Remove oats from oven; toss with nuts, bran and coconut.

**2.** Pour hot honey mixture over oat mixture; toss well. Return to the oven and bake 20-25 minutes, stirring every 6 minutes. Remove from oven. Stir in the raisins and dates. Cool. Store in an airtight container. Serve with yogurt and fresh fruit of your choice if desired.
**½ cup:** 275 cal., 12g fat (3g sat. fat), 0 chol., 18mg sod., 41g carb. (20g sugars, 4g fiber), 6g pro.

## VEGETABLE SCRAMBLED EGGS

*I like to have friends and family over for a special Sunday brunch, especially when there's a big game on television. I make several batches of these colorful eggs— they go perfectly with sausage, toasted English muffins and fresh fruit.*
—Marilyn Ipson, Rogers, AR

- - - - - - - - - - - - - - - - - - - - - - - - - - - - -

**Takes:** 10 min. • **Makes:** 2 servings

- 4    large eggs, lightly beaten
- ¼    cup fat-free milk
- ½    cup chopped green pepper
- ¼    cup sliced green onions
- ¼    tsp. salt
- ⅛    tsp. pepper
- 1    small tomato, chopped and seeded

In a small bowl, combine the eggs and milk. Add green pepper, onions, salt and pepper. Pour into a lightly greased skillet. Cook and stir over medium heat until eggs are nearly set, 2-3 minutes. Add tomato; cook and stir until eggs are completely set.

**¾ cup:** 173 cal., 10g fat (3g sat. fat), 373mg chol., 455mg sod., 7g carb. (4g sugars, 2g fiber), 15g pro. **Diabetic exchanges:** 2 medium-fat meat, 1 vegetable.

## TURKEY SAGE SAUSAGE PATTIES

*Eat smart, starting with this homemade turkey sausage. If you like garlic, try substituting it for the sage.*
—Janice Wuertzer, Dubuque, IA

- - - - - - - - - - - - - - - - - - - - - - - - - - - - -

**Prep:** 10 min. + chilling • **Cook:** 15 min.
**Makes:** 6 patties

- 1    small onion, finely chopped
- ¼    cup dry bread crumbs
- 1    tsp. rubbed sage
- ½    tsp. salt
- ½    tsp. paprika
- ¼    tsp. pepper
- 1    lb. lean ground turkey
- 2    tsp. canola oil

**1.** In a large bowl, combine the first 6 ingredients. Crumble turkey over mixture; mix lightly but thoroughly. Shape into 6 patties. Refrigerate, covered, for 2 hours.

**2.** In a large nonstick skillet, heat oil over medium heat. Add patties; cook until a thermometer reads 165°, 6-7 minutes on each side.

**1 patty:** 150 cal., 8g fat (2g sat. fat), 60mg chol., 307mg sod., 4g carb. (1g sugars, 0 fiber), 14g pro. **Diabetic exchanges:** 2 lean meat, ½ fat.

**VEGETABLE SCRAMBLED EGGS**

# ROLLED BUTTERMILK BISCUITS

*I scribbled down this recipe when our family visited The Farmers' Museum in Cooperstown, New York, more than 25 years ago. I must have gotten it right, because these biscuits turn out fantastic every time.*
—Patricia Kile, Elizabethtown, PA

**Prep:** 20 min. • **Bake:** 15 min.
**Makes:** 8 biscuits

- 2 cups all-purpose flour
- 3 tsp. baking powder
- ½ tsp. baking soda
- ¼ tsp. salt
- 3 Tbsp. cold butter
- ¾ to 1 cup buttermilk
- 1 Tbsp. fat-free milk

**1.** Preheat oven to 450°. In a large bowl, combine the flour, baking powder, baking soda and salt; cut in butter until mixture resembles coarse crumbs. Stir in enough buttermilk just to moisten dough.
**2.** Turn onto a lightly floured surface; knead 3-4 times. Pat or roll to ¾-in. thickness. Cut with a floured 2½-in. biscuit cutter. Place in a large ungreased cast-iron or other ovenproof skillet.
**3.** Brush with milk. Bake until golden brown, 12-15 minutes.

**1 biscuit:** 162 cal., 5g fat (3g sat. fat), 12mg chol., 412mg sod., 25g carb. (1g sugars, 1g fiber), 4g pro. **Diabetic exchanges:** 1½ starch, 1 fat.

ROLLED BUTTERMILK BISCUITS

# FRESH FRUIT BOWL

*The glorious colors used here make this a festive salad. Slightly sweet and served chilled, it makes a nice accompaniment to almost any brunch spread.*
—Marion Kirst, Troy, MI

**Prep:** 15 min. + chilling
**Makes:** 16 servings

- 8 cups fresh melon cubes
- 1 to 2 Tbsp. corn syrup
- 1 pint fresh strawberries, halved
- 2 cups fresh pineapple chunks
- 2 oranges, sectioned
  Fresh mint leaves, optional

In a large bowl, combine melon cubes and corn syrup. Cover and refrigerate overnight. Just before serving, stir in remaining fruit. Garnish with fresh mint leaves if desired.

**¾ cup:** 56 cal., 0 fat (0 sat. fat), 0 chol., 14mg sod., 14g carb. (11g sugars, 2g fiber), 1g pro.
**Diabetic exchanges:** 1 fruit.

BANANA OAT
BREAKFAST COOKIES

## BLUEBERRY CORNMEAL PANCAKES

*Blueberry cornmeal pancakes are one of my family's favorite breakfasts. No time to make flapjacks from scratch? No problem! My grandmother's standby of store-bought muffin mix makes quick work of the job.*
—Carolyn Eskew, Dayton, OH

**Takes:** 30 min. • **Makes:** 10 pancakes

- 1 pkg. (8½ oz.) cornbread/muffin mix
- 1 cup fresh or frozen blueberries
- ⅓ cup canned white or shoepeg corn
  Maple syrup

In a large bowl, prepare the muffin mix according to package directions. Gently stir in blueberries and corn. Lightly grease a griddle; warm over medium heat. Pour batter by ¼ cupfuls onto griddle; flatten slightly. Cook until bottoms are golden brown. Turn; cook until second sides are golden brown. Serve with syrup.

**2 pancakes:** 251 cal., 7g fat (2g sat. fat), 39mg chol., 454mg sod., 41g carb. (14g sugars, 4g fiber), 6g pro.

## BANANA OAT BREAKFAST COOKIES

*I used to buy name-brand breakfast cookies from the supermarket, but since I found this recipe I've enjoyed making my cookies more than buying them.*
—Linda Burciaga,
*Taste of Home* Online Community

**Prep:** 20 min. • **Bake:** 15 min./batch
**Makes:** 1 dozen

- 1 cup mashed ripe bananas (about 2 medium)
- ½ cup chunky peanut butter
- ½ cup honey
- 1 tsp. vanilla extract
- 1 cup old-fashioned oats
- ½ cup whole wheat flour
- ¼ cup nonfat dry milk powder
- 2 tsp. ground cinnamon
- ½ tsp. salt
- ¼ tsp. baking soda
- 1 cup dried cranberries or raisins

**1.** Preheat oven to 350°. Beat bananas, peanut butter, honey and vanilla until blended. In another bowl, combine next 6 ingredients; gradually beat into wet mixture. Stir in dried cranberries.

**2.** Drop dough by ¼ cupfuls 3 in. apart onto greased baking sheets; flatten to ½-in. thickness.

**3.** Bake the cookies until golden brown, 14-16 minutes. Cool on pans 5 minutes. Remove to wire racks. Serve warm or at room temperature. To reheat, microwave each cookie on high just until warmed, 15-20 seconds.

**1 cookie:** 212 cal., 6g fat (1g sat. fat), 0 chol., 186mg sod., 38g carb. (25g sugars, 4g fiber), 5g pro.

**POACHED EGG
BUDDHA BOWLS**

## POACHED EGG BUDDHA BOWLS

*My husband and I celebrate the arrival of spring with this dish, enjoying it in the backyard. I often include fresh peas and other spring delights.*
—Amy McDonough, Carlton, OR

**Prep:** 10 min. • **Cook:** 65 min.
**Makes:** 2 servings

¾ cup wheat berries
3½ cups water, divided
2 Tbsp. olive oil
2 Tbsp. lemon juice
1 Tbsp. thinly sliced fresh mint leaves
¼ tsp. salt
⅛ tsp. freshly ground pepper
½ cup quartered cherry tomatoes
½ cup reduced-fat ricotta cheese
2 Tbsp. sliced Greek olives
2 large eggs
Optional: Additional olive oil and pepper

**1.** Place the wheat berries and 2½ cups water in a large saucepan; bring to a boil. Reduce the heat; simmer, covered, until tender, about 1 hour. Drain; transfer to a bowl. Cool slightly.
**2.** Stir in oil, lemon juice, mint, salt and pepper; divide between 2 bowls. Top with tomatoes, ricotta cheese and olives.
**3.** To poach each egg, place ½ cup water in a small microwave-safe bowl or glass measuring cup. Break an egg into water. Microwave, covered, on high 1 minute. Microwave in 10-second intervals until white is set and yolk begins to thicken; let stand 1 minute.
**4.** Using a slotted spoon, transfer egg to 1 of the bowls. Repeat. If desired, drizzle with additional olive oil and sprinkle with more pepper.
**1 serving:** 526 cal., 24g fat (5g sat. fat), 201mg chol., 563mg sod., 58g carb. (5g sugars, 10g fiber), 21g pro.

### TEST KITCHEN TIP

Wheat berries are whole kernels of wheat. They cook up to a chewy texture with a hint of buttery flavor. Look for wheat berries near other whole grains; they're usually in the baking aisle in small packages.

**STRAWBERRY FRENCH TOAST**

## STRAWBERRY FRENCH TOAST

*These strawberry French toast kabobs are great for a buffet—and kids love them.*
—Mavis Diment, Marcus, IA

**Takes:** 20 min. • **Makes:** 4 servings

2 large eggs
¼ cup 2% milk
¼ tsp. salt
½ cup strawberry preserves
8 slices day-old white or whole wheat bread
Optional: Confectioners' sugar and halved strawberries

**1.** In a shallow bowl, whisk together the eggs, milk and salt. Spread preserves on 4 slices of bread; top with remaining bread. Trim crusts; cut each sandwich into 3 strips.
**2.** Preheat griddle over medium heat. Lightly grease griddle. Dip both sides of strips in egg mixture; place on griddle. Cook 2 minutes per side or until golden brown. If desired, cut into squares and alternately thread onto skewers with halved strawberries. Dust with confectioners' sugar if desired.
**3 strips:** 298 cal., 5g fat (1g sat. fat), 94mg chol., 474mg sod., 56g carb. (28g sugars, 2g fiber), 9g pro.

BERRY-TOPPED
PUFF PANCAKE

## BERRY-TOPPED PUFF PANCAKE

*Impressive to look at and even better to taste, this gorgeous pancake is surprisingly simple to make.*

—Marie Cosenza, Cortlandt Manor, NY

- - - - - - - - - - - - - - - - - - - - - - - - -

**Prep:** 20 min. • **Bake:** 15 min.
**Makes:** 4 servings

- 2 **Tbsp. butter**
- 2 **large eggs, room temperature**
- ½ **cup 2% milk**
- ½ **cup all-purpose flour**
- 2 **Tbsp. sugar**
- ¼ **tsp. salt**

**TOPPING**

- ⅓ **cup sugar**
- 1 **Tbsp. cornstarch**
- ½ **cup orange juice**
- 2 **tsp. orange liqueur**
- 1 **cup sliced fresh strawberries**
- 1 **cup fresh blueberries**
- 1 **cup fresh raspberries**
  **Confectioners' sugar, optional**

**1.** Preheat oven to 425°. Place butter in a 9-in. pie plate. Bake until butter is melted, 4-5 minutes. Meanwhile, in a large bowl, whisk eggs and milk. In another bowl, combine the flour, sugar and salt. Whisk into egg mixture until blended. Pour into prepared pie plate. Bake until sides are crisp and golden brown, 14-16 minutes.

**2.** Meanwhile, in a small saucepan, combine the sugar and cornstarch. Gradually stir in the orange juice and liqueur. Bring to a boil over medium heat, stirring constantly. Cook and stir until thickened, 1-2 minutes longer. Remove from heat.

**3.** Spoon the berries over pancake and drizzle with sauce. Dust with confectioners' sugar if desired.

**1 piece:** 320 cal., 9g fat (5g sat. fat), 123mg chol., 239mg sod., 54g carb. (35g sugars, 4g fiber), 7g pro.

## OVERNIGHT HAM & EGG CASSEROLE

*I love how easy it is to assemble this savory breakfast casserole. Putting it together the night before really frees up my time the next morning.*
—Jennifer Howell, Fort Collins, CO

- - - - - - - - - - - - - - - - - - - - - - - -

**Prep:** 10 min. + chilling • **Bake:** 1 hour
**Makes:** 9 servings

- 4 cups frozen shredded hash brown potatoes, thawed
- 1 cup cubed fully cooked ham
- 1 can (4 oz.) chopped green chiles
- ½ cup shredded Monterey Jack cheese
- ¼ cup shredded cheddar cheese
- 6 large eggs
- 1 can (12 oz.) evaporated milk
- ¼ tsp. pepper
  Salsa, optional

**1.** In a greased 8-in. square baking dish, layer the hash browns, ham, chiles and cheeses. In a large bowl, whisk the eggs, milk and pepper; pour over the casserole. Cover and refrigerate overnight.
**2.** Remove from refrigerator 30 minutes before baking. Preheat oven to 350°. Bake, uncovered, until a knife inserted in center comes out clean, about 1 hour. Let stand 5-10 minutes. Serve with salsa if desired.

**1 piece:** 203 cal., 11g fat (6g sat. fat), 175mg chol., 407mg sod., 11g carb. (5g sugars, 1g fiber), 14g pro. **Diabetic exchanges:** 2 lean meat, ½ starch, ½ fat.

## BROWN SUGAR OATMEAL PANCAKES

**(PICTURED ON P. 7)**

*These pancakes are a favorite at my house. If I don't make them every Saturday or Sunday, the family won't believe it's the weekend! My son's friends often spend the night, and I think it's because they like the pancakes so much. The stacks of jacks are extra delicious served with maple syrup.*
—Sharon Bickett, Chester, SC

- - - - - - - - - - - - - - - - - - - - - - - -

**Takes:** 15 min. • **Makes:** about 10 pancakes

- ½ cup plus 2 Tbsp. quick-cooking oats
- ¼ cup whole wheat flour
- ½ cup all-purpose flour
- ½ tsp. baking soda
- ½ tsp. salt
- ⅓ cup packed brown sugar
- 1 large egg, room temperature
- 2 Tbsp. vegetable oil
- 1 cup buttermilk

**1.** In a small bowl, combine the oats, flours, baking soda, salt and sugar. In another small bowl, beat the egg, oil and buttermilk. Stir into dry ingredients just until moistened.
**2.** Pour the batter by ⅓ cupfuls onto a greased hot griddle. Turn when bubbles form on top; cook until the second side is golden brown.

**Freeze option:** Freeze cooled pancakes between layers of waxed paper in a freezer container. To use, place pancakes on an ungreased baking sheet, cover with foil and reheat in a preheated 375° oven for 5-10 minutes. Or place a stack of 3 pancakes on a microwave-safe plate and microwave on high 1¼-1½ minutes or until heated through.

**2 pancakes:** 263 cal., 8g fat (1g sat. fat), 44mg chol., 433mg sod., 42g carb. (17g sugars, 3g fiber), 7g pro.

**OVERNIGHT HAM & EGG CASSEROLE**

## LEMON & CORIANDER GREEK YOGURT

*You'll be surprised how easy it is to make homemade Greek yogurt. Flavored with lemon and coriander, it's simply amazing.*
—*Taste of Home* Test Kitchen

**Prep:** 5 min. + chilling
**Cook:** 20 min. + standing
**Makes:** about 3 cups

- 2 qt. pasteurized whole milk
- 2 Tbsp. plain yogurt with live active cultures
- 2 tsp. grated lemon zest
- 1 tsp. ground coriander
  Honey, optional

**1.** In a Dutch oven, heat milk over medium heat until a thermometer reads 200°, stirring occasionally to prevent scorching. Remove from heat; let stand until a thermometer reads 112°-115°, stirring occasionally. (If desired, place pan in an ice-water bath for faster cooling.)
**2.** Whisk 1 cup warm milk into the yogurt until smooth; return all to pan, stirring gently. Stir in lemon zest and coriander. Transfer mixture to warm, clean jars, such as 1-qt .canning jars.
**3.** Cover jars; place in oven. Turn on oven light to keep mixture warm, about 110°. Let stand, undisturbed, 6-24 hours or until yogurt is set, tilting jars gently to check. (Yogurt will become thicker and more tangy as it stands.)
**4.** Refrigerate, covered, until cold. Store in refrigerator up to 2 weeks. If desired, serve with honey.
**½ cup:** 203 cal., 11g fat (6g sat. fat), 33mg chol., 142mg sod., 16g carb. (16g sugars, 0 fiber), 10g pro.

## PRESSURE-COOKER POTATO-CHEDDAR FRITTATA

*I like to serve this protein-packed frittata with toasted rustic bread. You can also use your own leftover potatoes instead of the prepackaged potatoes with onions.*
—Donna-Marie Ryan, Topsfield, MA

**Prep:** 15 min. + standing
**Cook:** 30 min. + releasing
**Makes:** 4 servings

- 1 Tbsp. canola oil
- 1½ cups refrigerated diced potatoes with onion
- 8 large egg whites
- 4 large eggs
- ½ cup fat-free milk
- 2 green onions, chopped
- 2 tsp. minced fresh parsley
- ¼ tsp. salt
- ¼ tsp. pepper
- ½ cup shredded cheddar cheese

**1.** In a large skillet, heat oil over medium-high heat. Add the potatoes; cook and stir until lightly browned, 4-6 minutes. Transfer to a greased 1½-qt. baking dish. Whisk next 7 ingredients; stir in shredded cheese. Pour egg mixture over potatoes. Loosely cover baking dish with foil.
**2.** Place trivet insert and 1 cup water in a 6-qt. electric pressure cooker. Fold an 18x12-in. piece of foil lengthwise into thirds, making a sling. Use sling to lower dish onto trivet. Lock lid; close pressure-release valve. Adjust to pressure-cook on high 30 minutes.
**3.** Let the pressure release naturally for 10 minutes; quick-release any remaining pressure. Using foil sling, carefully remove baking dish. Let stand 10 minutes.
**1 wedge:** 241 cal., 13g fat (5g sat. fat), 201mg chol., 560mg sod., 11g carb. (2g sugars, 1g fiber), 18g pro. **Diabetic exchanges:** 2 medium-fat meat, 1 fat, ½ starch.
**\* HEALTH TIP \*** Replacing some of the whole eggs with egg whites keeps this dish on the light side. If you prefer to use all whole eggs, use 8 eggs total.

**PRESSURE-COOKER POTATO-CHEDDAR FRITTATA**

**PUMPKIN & CHICKEN SAUSAGE HASH**

## UPSIDE-DOWN PEAR PANCAKE

*There's a pear tree in my yard that inspires me to bake with its fragrant fruit. My upside-down pancake works best with a firm pear, not fully ripe.*
—Helen Nelander, Boulder Creek, CA

**Takes:** 30 min. • **Makes:** 2 servings

- ½ cup all-purpose flour
- ½ tsp. baking powder
- 1 large egg, room temperature
- ¼ cup 2% milk
- 1 Tbsp. butter
- 1 tsp. sugar
- 1 medium pear, peeled and thinly sliced lengthwise
  Confectioners' sugar

**1.** Preheat oven to 375°. In a large bowl, whisk flour and baking powder. In a separate bowl, whisk egg and milk until blended. Add to dry ingredients, stirring just until combined.

**2.** Meanwhile, in a small ovenproof skillet, melt butter over medium-low heat. Sprinkle with sugar. Add pear slices in a single layer; cook 5 minutes. Spread prepared batter over pears. Cover and cook until top is set, about 5 minutes.

**3.** Transfer pan to oven; bake until edges are lightly brown, 8-10 minutes. Invert onto a serving plate. Sprinkle with confectioners' sugar. Serve warm

**½ pancake:** 274 cal., 9g fat (5g sat. fat), 111mg chol., 197mg sod., 41g carb. (12g sugars, 4g fiber), 8g pro. **Diabetic exchanges:** 2 starch, 1½ fat, 1 medium-fat meat, ½ fruit.

## PUMPKIN & CHICKEN SAUSAGE HASH

*I like to serve this hash topped with poached or fried eggs.*
—Valerie Donn, Williamsburg, MI

**Prep:** 15 min. • **Cook:** 25 min.
**Makes:** 4 servings

- 2 Tbsp. olive oil
- 2 cups cubed fresh pumpkin or butternut squash
- ¼ tsp. salt
- ¼ tsp. pepper
- ½ cup chopped onion
- 1 pkg. (12 oz.) fully cooked apple chicken sausage links or flavor of your choice, cut into ½-in. slices
- 1 cup sliced fresh mushrooms
- ½ cup chopped sweet red pepper
- ½ cup chopped green pepper
- 1 tsp. garlic powder
- ¼ cup minced fresh parsley

In a large skillet, heat oil over medium heat. Add pumpkin; sprinkle with salt and pepper. Cook and stir until crisp-tender, 8-10 minutes. Add onion; cook 3 minutes longer. Add sausage, mushrooms, red and green peppers and garlic powder. Cook and stir until pumpkin is tender, 10-12 minutes. Top with parsley.

**1 serving:** 260 cal., 14g fat (3g sat. fat), 60mg chol., 634mg sod., 19g carb. (13g sugars, 2g fiber), 16g pro. **Diabetic exchanges:** 2 lean meat, 1½ fat, 1 starch.

## BERRY SMOOTHIE BOWL

*We turned one of our favorite smoothies into a smoothie bowl and topped it with even more fresh fruit and a few toasted almonds and chia seeds for crunch.*
—*Taste of Home* Test Kitchen

**Takes:** 5 min. • **Makes:** 2 servings

- 1 cup fat-free milk
- 1 cup frozen unsweetened strawberries
- ½ cup frozen unsweetened raspberries
- 3 Tbsp. sugar
- 1 cup ice cubes
  Optional: Sliced fresh strawberries, fresh raspberries, chia seeds, fresh pumpkin seeds, unsweetened shredded coconut and sliced almonds

Place the milk, berries and sugar in a blender; cover and process until smooth. Add ice cubes; cover and process until smooth. Divide mixture between 2 serving bowls. Add optional toppings as desired.

**1½ cups:** 155 cal., 0 fat (0 sat. fat), 2mg chol., 54mg sod., 35g carb. (30g sugars, 2g fiber), 5g pro.

AUNT EDITH'S
BAKED PANCAKE

## AUNT EDITH'S BAKED PANCAKE

*My aunt made a mighty breakfast that revolved around The Big Pancake. I always enjoyed watching as she poured the batter into her huge iron skillet, then baked the confection to perfection in the oven.*
—Marion Kirst, Troy, MI

**Prep:** 15 min. • **Bake:** 20 min.
**Makes:** 4 servings

- 3 large eggs, room temperature
- ½ tsp. salt
- ½ cup all-purpose flour
- ½ cup 2% milk
- 2 Tbsp. butter, softened
  Confectioners' sugar
  Lemon wedges

**1.** In a bowl, beat eggs until very light. Add salt, flour and milk; beat well. Thoroughly rub bottom and sides of a 10-in. cast-iron or other heavy skillet with butter.

**2.** Pour batter into skillet. Bake at 450° for 15 minutes. Reduce heat to 350° and bake until set, 5 minutes longer. If desired, remove pancake from the skillet and place on a large hot platter. Dust the pancake with confectioners' sugar and serve immediately with lemon.

**1 piece:** 180 cal., 10g fat (5g sat. fat), 158mg chol., 407mg sod., 14g carb. (2g sugars, 0 fiber), 7g pro.

**READER REVIEW**

*"In my family we call these Dutch babies. I divide the batter between two smaller pans, baking individual ones for my husband and me. (Seriously, you will want half of one, not just a quarter!)"*

—LADY FINGERS, TASTEOFHOME.COM

## HAWAIIAN HASH

*I like the combination of ginger, pineapple and macadamia nuts. This dish brings back memories of an island vacation.*

—Roxanne Chan, Albany, CA

**Prep:** 20 min. • **Cook:** 15 min.
**Makes:** 6 servings

2 tsp. canola oil
1 tsp. sesame oil
4 cups cubed peeled sweet potatoes (about 1 lb.)
1 cup chopped onion
½ cup chopped sweet red pepper
1 tsp. minced fresh gingerroot
¼ cup water
1 cup cubed fully cooked ham
1 cup cubed fresh pineapple or unsweetened pineapple tidbits, drained
¼ cup salsa verde
1 tsp. soy sauce
½ tsp. black sesame seeds
Chopped fresh cilantro
Chopped macadamia nuts, optional

**1.** In a large cast-iron or other heavy skillet, heat oils over medium-high heat. Add sweet potatoes, onion, pepper and gingerroot; cook and stir 5 minutes. Add water. Reduce heat to low; cook, covered, until potatoes are tender, 8-10 minutes, stirring occasionally.

**2.** Stir in next 5 ingredients; cook and stir over medium-high heat until heated through, about 2 minutes. Top servings with cilantro and, if desired, chopped macadamia nuts.

**¾ cup:** 158 cal., 4g fat (1g sat. fat), 14mg chol., 440mg sod., 26g carb. (8g sugars, 4g fiber), 7g pro. **Diabetic exchanges:** 1½ starch, 1 lean meat, ½ fat.

**HAWAIIAN HASH**

# STARTERS
# & SNACKS

"Frozen raspberries lend fruity flavor and lovely color to this pretty iced tea that's good year-round. The recipe calls for just a few common ingredients and offers make-ahead convenience."
—Lois McGrady, Hillsville, VA

## MUSHROOM CAPONATA

*This is a lovely appetizer when served with crostini, pita bread, bagel chips or crackers. I've also used it as a topping over a salad of mixed greens. This mushroom version of a caponata is a twist on the traditional eggplant one.*
—Julia Cotton, Chalfont, PA

**Prep:** 40 min. • **Cook:** 10 min.
**Makes:** 6 cups

- 2   large green peppers, chopped
- 1   large onion, chopped
- 2   Tbsp. butter, divided
- 2   Tbsp. olive oil, divided
- 2   lbs. fresh mushrooms, coarsely chopped
- ½   cup pitted Greek olives, chopped
- ¼   cup balsamic vinegar
- ¼   cup tomato paste
- 1   Tbsp. sugar
- 1   tsp. dried oregano
- ½   tsp. salt
- ¼   tsp. coarsely ground pepper
     Bagel chips or lightly toasted French bread baguette slices

**1.** In a large cast-iron or other heavy skillet, saute green peppers and onion in 1 Tbsp. butter and 1 Tbsp. oil for 10 minutes or until golden brown.
**2.** Add half the mushrooms and the remaining butter and oil; saute until tender. Remove onion mixture and set aside. Saute the remaining mushrooms until tender. Return all to the pan. Cover and simmer over medium-high heat for 2 minutes.
**3.** Add the olives, vinegar, tomato paste, sugar, oregano, salt and pepper. Reduce heat; simmer, uncovered, until thickened, about 10 minutes.
**4.** Serve warm or at room temperature with bagel chips or baguette slices.
**¼ cup:** 53 cal., 3g fat (1g sat. fat), 3mg chol., 107mg sod., 6g carb. (3g sugars, 1g fiber), 2g pro. **Diabetic exchanges:** ½ starch, ½ fat.

## GREEN OLIVE TAPENADE

*Here's a tasty tapenade, made a bit different with green olives instead of black. Besides serving it as an appetizer, you can also use it to punch up your favorite deli sandwich.*
—Teresa Spencer, Oconomowoc, WI

**Takes:** 10 min. • **Makes:** 1¾ cups

- ⅓   cup olive oil
- 1½  tsp. lemon juice
- 2   anchovy fillets
- 1   garlic clove, peeled
- ¼   tsp. pepper
     Dash sugar
     Dash salt
- 2   cups pimiento-stuffed olives
- 14  slices French bread (½ in. thick), toasted

In a food processor, combine the first 7 ingredients; cover and process until smooth. Add olives; cover and pulse until coarsely chopped. Serve with toasted French bread.
**2 Tbsp.:** 116 cal., 9g fat (1g sat. fat), 0 chol., 512mg sod., 8g carb. (0 sugars, 0 fiber), 1g pro.

**GREEN OLIVE TAPENADE**

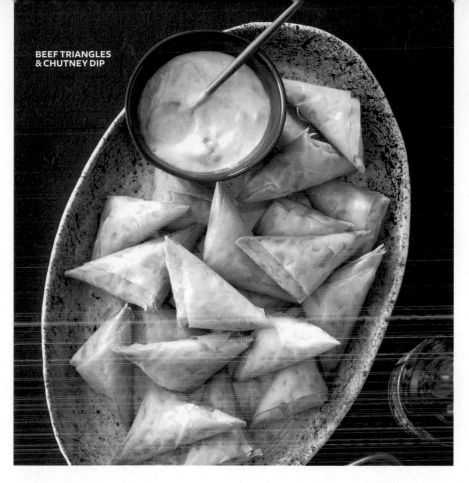

BEEF TRIANGLES
& CHUTNEY DIP

## GARLIC GARBANZO BEAN SPREAD

*My friends and family always ask me to make this. I guarantee you'll be asked for the recipe. You can serve it as an appetizer or a filling for wraps and pitas.*
—Lisa Moore, North Syracuse, NY

**Takes:** 10 min. • **Makes:** 1½ cups

- 1 can (15 oz.) garbanzo beans or chickpeas, rinsed and drained
- ½ cup olive oil
- 2 Tbsp. minced fresh parsley
- 1 Tbsp. lemon juice
- 1 green onion, cut into 3 pieces
- 1 to 2 garlic cloves, peeled
- ¼ tsp. salt
    Assorted fresh vegetables and baked pita chips

In a food processor, combine the first 7 ingredients; cover and process until blended. Transfer to a bowl. Refrigerate until serving. Serve with vegetables and pita chips.

**2 Tbsp.:** 114 cal., 10g fat (1g sat. fat), 0 chol., 96mg sod., 6g carb. (1g sugars, 1g fiber), 1g pro. **Diabetic exchanges:** 2 fat, ½ starch.

## BEEF TRIANGLES & CHUTNEY DIP

*When I brought these crisp, golden brown triangles to a friend's housewarming party, they disappeared in minutes. The spices in the beef make them unusual and delicious.*
—Carla DeVelder, Mishawaka, IN

**Prep:** 45 min. • **Bake:** 10 min./batch
**Makes:** 56 appetizers (1 cup sauce)

- 1 lb. ground beef
- 1 small onion, finely chopped
- ⅓ cup dried currants
- ½ tsp. salt
- ½ tsp. ground cumin
- ¼ tsp. ground cinnamon
- ¼ tsp. ground nutmeg
- ⅛ tsp. cayenne pepper
- ⅛ tsp. pepper
- 1 Tbsp. cornstarch
- ½ cup water
- 28 sheets phyllo dough (14x9 in.)
    Butter-flavored cooking spray
- ½ cup plain yogurt
- ½ cup chutney

**1.** In a large skillet, cook beef and onion over medium heat until the meat is no longer pink; drain. Stir in currants and seasonings. Combine cornstarch and water until smooth; gradually stir into the beef mixture. Bring to a boil; cook and stir for 2 minutes or until thickened. Remove from the heat.

**2.** Place 1 sheet of phyllo dough on a work surface with a short end facing you; spray sheet with butter-flavored spray. Place another sheet of phyllo on top and spritz with spray. (Keep remaining phyllo covered with a damp towel to prevent it from drying out.) Cut the 2 layered sheets into four 14x2¼-in. strips.

**3.** Place a rounded teaspoon of filling on lower corner of each strip. Fold dough over filling, forming a triangle. Fold the triangle up, then over, forming another triangle. Continue folding, like a flag, until you come to the end of the strip. Spritz end of dough with spray and press onto triangle to seal. Turn triangle and spritz top with spray. Repeat with remaining phyllo and filling.

**4.** Place the triangles on baking sheets coated with cooking spray. Bake at 400° for 8-10 minutes or until golden brown. Combine yogurt and chutney. Serve with warm appetizers.

**1 triangle with ¾ tsp. sauce:** 41 cal., 1g fat (0 sat. fat), 4mg chol., 51mg sod., 5g carb. (2g sugars, 0 fiber), 2g pro.

FESTIVE TURKEY MEATBALLS

## FESTIVE TURKEY MEATBALLS

*Turkey gives a different twist to these slightly sweet and spicy meatballs. For the holidays, I serve them on a tray lined with parsley and garnished with red pepper or pimientos.*
—Audrey Thibodeau, Gilbert, AZ

**Prep:** 25 min. • **Bake:** 30 min.
**Makes:** about 3½ dozen

- 1 large egg, beaten
- ½ cup dry bread crumbs
- ¼ cup finely chopped onion
- ½ tsp. curry powder
- ¼ tsp. ground ginger
- ¼ tsp. ground cinnamon
- ¼ tsp. salt
- ¼ tsp. pepper
- 1 lb. ground turkey

**SAUCE**

- 1 cup honey
- ¼ cup Dijon mustard
- ½ tsp. curry powder
- ½ tsp. ground ginger

**OPTIONAL ADDITIONS**

- Fresh basil leaves
- Fresh cilantro leaves
- Fresh mint leaves
- Lime wedges

**1.** Preheat oven to 350°. Combine first 8 ingredients. Add turkey; mix lightly but thoroughly. Shape into 1-in. balls. Place on greased rack in a 15x10-in. baking pan. Bake, uncovered, until cooked through and juices run clear, 20-25 minutes.
**2.** Meanwhile, combine sauce ingredients in a small saucepan; whisk over medium heat until heated through. Brush the meatballs with ¼ cup sauce; return to oven for 10 minutes. Serve meatballs with remaining sauce for dipping and, if desired, fresh herbs and lime wedges.
**1 meatball:** 46 cal., 1g fat (0 sat. fat), 11mg chol., 61mg sod., 7g carb. (6g sugars, 0 fiber), 2g pro.

## SAUSAGE WONTON CUPS

*Here's a tasty hot appetizer for all those parties that feature fun finger foods. I've made this recipe several times, and the bites always disappear fast. I love how easy these are to make.*
—Shirley Van Allen, High Point, NC

-------------------------------------

**Takes:** 30 min. • **Makes:** 2 dozen

- 1 lb. Italian turkey sausage links, casings removed
- 1 can (15 oz.) tomato sauce
- ½ tsp. garlic powder
- ½ tsp. dried basil
- 24 wonton wrappers
- 1 cup shredded Italian cheese blend

**1.** In a large skillet, cook sausage over medium heat until no longer pink; drain. Stir in the tomato sauce, garlic powder and basil. Bring to a boil. Reduce heat; simmer, uncovered, until thickened, 8-10 minutes.

**2.** Meanwhile, press wonton wrappers into miniature muffin cups coated with cooking spray. Bake at 350° until lightly browned, 8-9 minutes.

**3.** Spoon sausage mixture into cups. Sprinkle with cheese. Bake until cheese is melted, 5-7 minutes longer. Serve warm.

**Freeze option:** Cool appetizers; freeze them in freezer containers, separating layers with waxed paper. To use, reheat wonton cups in coated muffin pans in a preheated 350° oven until crisp and heated through.

**1 wonton cup:** 68 cal., 3g fat (1g sat. fat), 15mg chol., 270mg sod., 6g carb. (0 sugars, 0 fiber), 5g pro. **Diabetic exchanges:** ½ starch, ½ fat.

## PARISIAN CHICKEN BITES
**(PICTURED ON P. 26)**

*When a friend of mine returned from a trip to Paris, she raved about the food she had and described one of her favorite meals. Her story inspired me to create a similar hors d'oeuvre.*
—Noelle Myers, Grand Forks, ND

-------------------------------------

**Takes:** 30 min. • **Makes:** 4 dozen

- ½ lb. boneless skinless chicken breasts, cut into ¼-in. cubes
- ¼ tsp. salt
- ¼ tsp. pepper
- ½ cup chopped fennel bulb
- 2 tsp. olive oil
- 1 Tbsp. chopped green onion
- ½ tsp. minced fresh rosemary
- 1 medium apple, chopped
- ¼ cup chopped pecans
- 1 Tbsp. minced fresh parsley
- 1 Tbsp. lime juice
- 3 heads Belgian endive, separated into leaves
- 1 cup dark chocolate chips
- ⅓ cup seedless blackberry spreadable fruit
- ¼ cup balsamic vinegar

**1.** Sprinkle chicken with salt and pepper. In a large skillet, saute chicken and fennel in oil until chicken is no longer pink. Add green onion and rosemary; cook 1 minute longer. Remove from the heat.

**2.** In a large bowl, combine the apple, pecans, parsley and lime juice. Stir in chicken mixture. Spoon filling into the endive leaves.

**3.** In a microwave, melt chocolate chips; stir until smooth. Stir in spreadable fruit and vinegar. Drizzle over appetizers.

**1 appetizer:** 40 cal., 2g fat (1g sat. fat), 3mg chol., 23mg sod., 5g carb. (4g sugars, 1g fiber), 2g pro.

**SAUSAGE WONTON CUPS**

**MARINATED SHRIMP**

## SOFT GIANT PRETZELS

*My husband, friends and family love these soft, chewy pretzels. Let your machine mix the dough; then all you have to do is shape and bake these fun snacks.*
—Sherry Peterson, Fort Collins, CO

**Prep:** 20 min. + rising • **Bake:** 10 min.
**Makes:** 8 pretzels

- 1 cup plus 2 Tbsp. water (70° to 80°), divided
- 3 cups all-purpose flour
- 3 Tbsp. brown sugar
- 1½ tsp. active dry yeast
- 2 qt. water
- ½ cup baking soda
  Coarse salt

**1.** In a bread machine pan, place 1 cup water and next 3 ingredients in order suggested by manufacturer. Select dough setting. Check dough after 5 minutes of mixing; add 1 to 2 Tbsp. water or flour if needed.
**2.** When cycle is completed, turn dough onto a lightly floured surface. Divide the dough into 8 balls. Roll each into a 20-in. rope; form into pretzel shape.
**3.** Preheat oven to 425°. In a large saucepan, bring 2 qt. water and the baking soda to a boil. Drop the pretzels into boiling water, 2 at a time; boil for 10-15 seconds. Remove with a slotted spoon; drain on paper towels.
**4.** Place pretzels on greased baking sheets. Bake until golden brown, 8-10 minutes. Spritz or lightly brush with remaining 2 Tbsp. water. Sprinkle with salt.

**1 pretzel:** 193 cal., 1g fat (0 sat. fat), 0 chol., 380mg sod., 41g carb. (5g sugars, 1g fiber), 5g pro.

**READER REVIEW**

*"So I don't have a bread maker. No big deal. Mix first 4 ingredients, knead for 5 minutes and let rise in a covered bowl for an hour. It is SO WORTH IT!"*

—EDIECZ, TASTEOFHOME.COM

## MARINATED SHRIMP

*My husband's aunt shared this recipe with me ages ago. Not only is it a Christmas Eve tradition in my home, but in the homes of our grown children as well.*
—Delores Hill, Helena, MT

**Prep:** 10 min. + marinating • **Cook:** 10 min.
**Makes:** about 3 dozen

- 2 lbs. uncooked jumbo shrimp, peeled and deveined
- 1 cup olive oil
- 2 garlic cloves, minced
- 4 tsp. dried rosemary, crushed
- 2 tsp. dried oregano
- 2 bay leaves
- 1 cup dry white wine or chicken broth
- ¾ tsp. salt
- ⅛ tsp. pepper

**1.** In a bowl, combine the shrimp, oil, garlic, rosemary, oregano and bay leaves. Cover and refrigerate for 2-4 hours.
**2.** Pour shrimp and marinade into a large deep skillet. Add wine or broth, salt and pepper. Cover and cook over medium-low heat for 10-15 minutes or until shrimp turn pink, stirring occasionally. Discard bay leaves. Transfer with a slotted spoon to a serving dish.

**1 piece:** 40 cal., 2g fat (0 sat. fat), 31mg chol., 42mg sod., 0 carb. (0 sugars, 0 fiber), 4g pro.

SOFT GIANT PRETZELS

## SIMPLE GUACAMOLE

*Because avocados can brown quickly, it's best to make this guacamole just before serving. If you do have to make it a little in advance, place the avocado pit in the guacamole until serving.*
—Heidi Main, Anchorage, AK

**Takes:** 10 min. • **Makes:** 1½ cups

- 2   medium ripe avocados
- 1   Tbsp. lemon juice
- ¼   cup chunky salsa
- ⅛ to ¼ tsp. salt

Peel and chop avocados; place in a small bowl. Sprinkle with lemon juice. Add the salsa and salt; mash coarsely with a fork. Refrigerate until serving.

**2 Tbsp.:** 53 cal., 5g fat (1g sat. fat), 0 chol., 51mg sod., 3g carb. (0 sugars, 2g fiber), 1g pro.

## MINI PIZZA CUPS

*Served hot or cold, these little pizzas are wonderful. Their small size makes them ideal for an after-school snack or kid-friendly party. Plus, they're so easy to make, little ones can help you in the kitchen!*
—Jane Jones, Cedar, MN

**Prep:** 25 min. • **Bake:** 15 min.
**Makes:** 32 appetizers

- 2   tubes (8 oz. each) refrigerated round crescent rolls
- 1   can (8 oz.) pizza sauce
- ¼   cup finely chopped onion
- ⅓   cup finely chopped green pepper
- 2   oz. sliced turkey pepperoni, chopped
- 1   cup shredded part-skim mozzarella cheese

**1.** Separate tubes of dough into 8 rolls each; halve the rolls. Press dough onto the bottom and up the sides of miniature muffin cups coated with cooking spray.
**2.** Spoon pizza sauce into each cup. Sprinkle with onion, green pepper, pepperoni and cheese. Bake at 375° until the crusts are browned and cheese is melted, 15-18 minutes.
**1 pizza cup:** 75 cal., 4g fat (2g sat. fat), 4mg chol., 193mg sod., 7g carb. (1g sugars, trace fiber), 3g pro.

**SIMPLE GUACAMOLE**

NUTTY STUFFED
MUSHROOMS

## LEMON THYME GREEN TEA

*Fresh sprigs of lemon thyme make this
citrusy tea so refreshing—it's like sipping
summer from a cup. My family enjoys it so
much, it's quickly become a staple on our
Southern front porch.*
—Melissa Pelkey Hass, Waleska, GA

- - - - - - - - - - - - - - - - - - - - - - - - - - - - - - -

**Takes:** 20 min. • **Makes:** 8 servings

- 2 qt. water
- 8 individual green tea bags
- 12 fresh lemon thyme sprigs or
  8 fresh thyme sprigs plus
  ½ tsp. grated lemon zest
- ¼ cup honey
- 3 Tbsp. lemon juice
  Sugar, optional

In a large saucepan, bring water to a boil;
remove from heat. Add tea bags and
lemon thyme sprigs; steep, covered,
3 minutes. Discard the tea bags; steep,
covered, 3 minutes longer. Strain tea.
Add honey and lemon juice; stir until
honey is dissolved. Stir in sugar if desired.
Serve immediately.
**1 cup:** 33 cal., 0 fat (0 sat. fat), 0 chol., 0 sod.,
9g carb. (9g sugars, 0 fiber), 0 pro.

## NUTTY STUFFED
## MUSHROOMS

*Basil, Parmesan cheese and mushrooms
blend together well, while buttery pecans
give these little treats unexpected crunch.
Our children, grandchildren and great-
grandchildren always ask for them!*
—Mildred Eldred, Union City, MI

- - - - - - - - - - - - - - - - - - - - - - - - - - - - - - -

**Takes:** 30 min. • **Makes:** 20 servings

- 20 large fresh mushrooms
- 3 Tbsp. butter
- 1 small onion, chopped
- ¼ cup dry bread crumbs
- ¼ cup finely chopped pecans
- 3 Tbsp. grated Parmesan cheese
- ¼ tsp. salt
- ¼ tsp. dried basil
  Dash cayenne pepper

**1.** Preheat oven to 400°. Remove stems
from mushrooms; set caps aside. Finely
chop stems. In a large skillet, heat butter
over medium heat. Add the chopped
mushrooms and onion, saute until the
liquid has evaporated, about 5 minutes.
Remove from heat; set aside.
**2.** Meanwhile, combine the remaining
ingredients; add mushroom mixture.
Stuff firmly into mushroom caps. Bake,
uncovered, in a greased 15x10x1-in.
baking pan until tender, 15-18 minutes.
Serve warm.
**1 stuffed mushroom:** 44 cal., 3g fat (1g sat.
fat), 5mg chol., 67mg sod., 3g carb. (0 sugars,
0 fiber), 2g pro.

## SO-EASY SNACK MIX

*I eat this tasty treat just as much as (if not more than) the kids! Have fun with it by adding other goodies into the mix, like nuts, cereal, pretzels and more.*
—Jeff King, Duluth, MN

**Takes:** 5 min. • **Makes:** 4 qt.

- 4 cups Goldfish cheddar crackers
- 4 cups golden raisins
- 4 cups dried cherries
- 2 cups yogurt-covered raisins
- 2 cups miniature pretzels

Place all ingredients in a large bowl; toss to combine. Store in airtight containers.
**½ cup:** 195 cal., 3g fat (1g sat. fat), 1mg chol., 104mg sod., 42g carb. (29g sugars, 2g fiber), 2g pro.

CAULIFLOWER CEVICHE

## CAULIFLOWER CEVICHE

*My 87-year-old mom showed me how to make this delicious vegetarian recipe that tastes so much like seafood ceviche. I like to serve it with crackers on the side.*
—Beatriz Barranco, El Paso, TX

**Prep:** 20 min. + chilling
**Makes:** 10 servings

- 1 medium head cauliflower, finely chopped
- 1 cup ketchup
- 1 cup orange juice
- 3 medium tomatoes, chopped
- 1 medium onion, finely chopped
- ½ cup minced fresh cilantro
- ¼ tsp. salt
- ¼ tsp. pepper
- 3 medium ripe avocados, peeled and cubed
  Optional: Lemon wedges, tortilla chip scoops and hot pepper sauce

**1.** In a large skillet, bring 1 cup water to a boil. Add cauliflower; cook, uncovered, 5-8 minutes or just until crisp-tender. Remove with a slotted spoon; drain and pat dry. Meanwhile, stir together ketchup and orange juice.
**2.** In a large bowl, combine cauliflower with tomatoes and onion. Add ketchup mixture, cilantro, salt and pepper; toss to coat. Refrigerate, covered, at least 1 hour.
**3.** Stir in avocado cubes. If desired, serve with lemon wedges, tortilla chip scoops and hot pepper sauce.
**1 serving:** 129 cal., 7g fat (1g sat. fat), 0 chol., 387mg sod., 18g carb. (11g sugars, 5g fiber), 3g pro.

**TEST KITCHEN TIP**

This ceviche-style dish has a hint of sweetness. If you like things more savory, use tomato sauce instead of ketchup. You may also spice it up with a minced jalapeno or chipotle pepper.

## EASY SMOKED SALMON

*I found this in a magazine years ago, and it quickly became a favorite. It's so elegant!*
—Norma Fell, Boyne City, MI

- - - - - - - - - - - - - - - - - - - - - - - - -

**Prep:** 10 min. + marinating
**Bake:** 35 min. + chilling
**Makes:** 16 servings

1 salmon fillet (about 2 lbs.)
2 Tbsp. brown sugar
2 tsp. salt
½ tsp. pepper
1 to 2 Tbsp. liquid smoke
    Optional: Capers and lemon slices

**1.** Place salmon, skin side down, in an 11x7 in. baking pan coated with cooking spray. Sprinkle with brown sugar, salt and pepper. Drizzle with liquid smoke. Cover and refrigerate for 4-8 hours.

**2.** Drain salmon, discarding liquid. Bake, uncovered, at 350° until fish flakes easily with a fork, 35-45 minutes. Cool to room temperature. Cover and refrigerate for 8 hours or overnight. If desired, serve with capers and lemon slices.

**1½ oz. cooked salmon:** 95 cal., 5g fat (1g sat. fat), 28mg chol., 324mg sod., 2g carb. (2g sugars, 0 fiber), 10g pro.

## ICED RASPBERRY TEA

**(PICTURED ON P. 27)**

*Frozen raspberries lend fruity flavor and lovely color to this pretty iced tea that's good all year round. The recipe calls for just a few common ingredients and offers make-ahead convenience.*
—Lois McGrady, Hillsville, VA

- - - - - - - - - - - - - - - - - - - - - - - - -

**Prep:** 10 min. + chilling
**Makes:** 16 servings (4 qt.)

1½ cups sugar
4 qt. water
1 pkg. (12 oz.) frozen unsweetened raspberries
10 tea bags
¼ cup lemon juice
    Optional: Fresh raspberries and lemon slices

**1.** In a Dutch oven over high heat, bring sugar and water to a boil. Remove from heat; stir until sugar is dissolved. Add raspberries, tea bags and lemon juice. Steep, covered, for 3 minutes. Strain; discard berries and tea bags.

**2.** Transfer tea to a large container or pitcher. Refrigerate until chilled. Serve over ice. If desired, serve with raspberries and lemon slices.

**1 cup:** 87 cal., 0 fat (0 sat. fat), 0 chol., 8mg sod., 22g carb. (20g sugars, 0 fiber), 0 pro.

**EASY SMOKED SALMON**

POMEGRANATE
GINGER SPRITZER

## POMEGRANATE GINGER SPRITZER

*A pitcher of this non-alcoholic beverage can conveniently be made hours before your guests arrive. Add the club soda just before serving.*
—*Taste of Home* Test Kitchen

**Prep:** 10 min. + chilling • **Makes:** 7 servings

- ½ cup sliced fresh gingerroot
- 1 medium lime, sliced
- 3 cups pomegranate juice
- ¾ cup orange juice
- 3 cups chilled club soda
  Optional: Lime wedges, pomegranate seeds and ice

**1.** Place ginger and lime slices in a pitcher; stir in pomegranate and orange juices. Refrigerate overnight.
**2.** Just before serving, strain and discard ginger and lime. Stir club soda into juice mixture. Garnish as desired.
**1 cup:** 80 cal., 0 fat (0 sat. fat), 0 chol., 35mg sod., 20g carb. (17g sugars, 0 fiber), 1g pro.

## SOUTHWEST SPANAKOPITA BITES

*I'm a big fan of the Southwest-style egg rolls served at restaurants and wanted to re-create them without the fat of deep frying. Phyllo dough was the solution! For a main dish, I fill small flour tortillas with the filling and bake them.*
—Marianne Shira, Osceola, WI

**Prep:** 40 min. • **Bake:** 10 min.
**Makes:** 2 dozen (½ cup sauce)

- 2 Tbsp. finely chopped sweet red pepper
- 1 green onion, finely chopped
- 1 tsp. canola oil
- 1 pkg. (10 oz.) frozen chopped spinach, thawed and squeezed dry
- ¾ cup shredded reduced-fat Monterey Jack cheese or Mexican cheese blend
- ½ cup frozen corn, thawed
- ½ cup canned black beans, rinsed and drained
- 1 Tbsp. chopped seeded jalapeno pepper
- ½ tsp. ground cumin
- ½ tsp. chili powder

**SOUTHWEST SPANAKOPITA BITES**

- ¼ tsp. salt
- 8 sheets phyllo dough (14x9 in.)
  Butter-flavored cooking spray

**SAUCE**
- ⅓ cup cubed avocado
- ¼ cup reduced-fat mayonnaise
- ¼ cup reduced-fat sour cream
- 1½ tsp. white vinegar

**1.** In a small skillet, saute red pepper and onion in oil until tender. Transfer to a large bowl; stir in ½ cup spinach (save the rest for another use). Stir in the cheese, corn, beans, jalapeno, cumin, chili powder and salt.
**2.** Place 1 sheet of phyllo dough on a work surface with a short end facing you. (Keep remaining phyllo covered with a damp towel to prevent it from drying out.) Spray sheet with butter-flavored spray; cut into three 14x3-in. strips.

**3.** Place a scant Tbsp. of filling on lower corner of each strip. Fold dough over filling, forming a triangle. Fold triangle up, then over, forming another triangle. Continue folding, like a flag, until you come to the end of the strip.
**4.** Spritz end of dough with spray and press onto triangle to seal. Turn triangle and spritz top with spray. Repeat with remaining phyllo and filling.
**5.** Place triangles on baking sheets coated with cooking spray. Bake at 375° until golden brown, 10-12 minutes. Mash avocado with the mayonnaise, sour cream and vinegar; serve sauce with warm appetizers.
**Note:** Wear disposable gloves when cutting hot peppers; the oils can burn skin. Avoid touching your face.
**1 appetizer with 1 tsp. sauce:** 50 cal., 3g fat (1g sat. fat), 4mg chol., 103mg sod., 5g carb. (1g sugars, 1g fiber), 2g pro. **Diabetic exchanges:** ½ starch, ½ fat.

## POLYNESIAN MEATBALLS

*With pretty bits of pineapple, these meatballs are sure to attract attention—and the sweet-tart sauce brings people back for seconds.*
—Carol Wakley, North East, PA

**Prep:** 30 min. • **Cook:** 15 min.
**Makes:** about 6 dozen

- 1 can (5 oz.) evaporated milk
- ⅓ cup chopped onion
- ⅔ cup crushed saltines
- 1 tsp. seasoned salt
- 1½ lbs. lean ground beef

SAUCE
- 1 can (20 oz.) pineapple tidbits
- 2 Tbsp. cornstarch
- ½ cup cider vinegar
- 2 Tbsp. soy sauce
- 2 Tbsp. lemon juice
- ½ cup packed brown sugar

**1.** In a bowl, combine the milk, onion, saltines and seasoned salt. Crumble the beef over mixture and mix lightly but thoroughly. With wet hands, shape into 1-in. balls. In a large skillet over medium heat, brown meatballs in small batches, turning often. Remove with a slotted spoon and keep warm. Drain skillet.
**2.** Drain pineapple, reserving juice; set pineapple aside. Add enough water to the juice to measure 1 cup. In a bowl, combine the cornstarch, juice mixture, vinegar, soy sauce, lemon juice and brown sugar until smooth. Add to skillet. Bring to a boil; cook and stir until thickened, about 2 minutes. Add meatballs. Reduce heat; cover and simmer for 15 minutes. Add the pineapple; heat through.
**1 meatball:** 37 cal., 1g fat (1g sat. fat), 9mg chol., 61mg sod., 4g carb. (3g sugars, 0 fiber), 3g pro.

## APPLE CARTWHEELS

*Stuff apples with a yummy filling, then slice the fruit into rings to make eye-appealing after-school snacks. The fun filling is an irresistible combination of creamy peanut butter, sweet honey, miniature chocolate chips and raisins.*
—Miriam Miller, Thorp, WI

**Prep:** 20 min. + chilling
**Makes:** about 2 dozen

- ¼ cup peanut butter
- 1½ tsp. honey
- ½ cup miniature semisweet chocolate chips
- 2 Tbsp. raisins
- 4 medium unpeeled Red Delicious apples, cored

**1.** In a small bowl, combine peanut butter and honey; fold in miniature chocolate chips and raisins.
**2.** Fill centers of apples with peanut butter mixture; refrigerate for at least 1 hour. Cut into ¼-in. rings.
**1 piece:** 50 cal., 3g fat (1g sat. fat), 0 chol., 13mg sod., 7g carb. (6g sugars, 1g fiber), 1g pro.

**POLYNESIAN MEATBALLS**

BAKED EGG ROLLS

## ROASTED BUFFALO CAULIFLOWER BITES

*Try these savory bites for a kickin'*
*appetizer that's healthy, too!*
—Emily Tyra, Traverse City, MI

- - - - - - - - - - - - - - - - - - - - - - - - - - - - - -

**Takes:** 25 min. • **Makes:** 8 servings

  1   **medium head cauliflower (about
      2¼ lbs.), cut into florets**
  1   **Tbsp. canola oil**
  ½  **cup Buffalo wing sauce
      Blue cheese salad dressing**

**1.** Preheat oven to 400°. Toss cauliflower with oil; spread in a 15x10x1-in. pan. Roast 20-25 minutes or until tender and lightly browned, stirring once.
**2.** Transfer to a bowl; toss with wing sauce. Serve with dressing.
**⅓ cup:** 39 cal., 2g fat (0 sat. fat), 0 chol., 474mg sod., 5g carb. (2g sugars, 2g fiber), 2g pro.

## BAKED EGG ROLLS

*These egg rolls are low in fat but the
crispiness from baking will fool your taste
buds into thinking they were fried!*
—Barbara Lierman, Lyons, NE

- - - - - - - - - - - - - - - - - - - - - - - - - - - - - -

**Prep:** 30 min. • **Bake:** 10 min.
**Makes:** 16 servings

  2   **cups grated carrots**
  1   **can (14 oz.) bean sprouts, drained**
  ½  **cup chopped water chestnuts**
  ¼  **cup chopped green pepper**
  ¼  **cup chopped green onions**
  1   **garlic clove, minced**
  2   **cups finely diced cooked chicken**
  4   **tsp. cornstarch**
  1   **Tbsp. water**
  1   **Tbsp. light soy sauce**
  1   **tsp. canola oil**
  1   **tsp. brown sugar**
      **Pinch cayenne pepper**
 16  **egg roll wrappers
      Cooking spray**

**1.** Coat a large skillet with cooking spray; heat pan over medium heat. Add the first 6 ingredients; cook and stir until vegetables are crisp-tender, about 3 minutes. Add chicken; heat through.
**2.** In a small bowl, combine cornstarch, water, soy sauce, oil, brown sugar and cayenne until smooth; stir into the chicken mixture. Bring to a boil. Cook and stir for 2 minutes or until thickened; remove from the heat.
**3.** Spoon ¼ cup chicken mixture on the bottom third of 1 egg roll wrapper; fold sides toward center and roll tightly. (Keep remaining wrappers covered with a damp paper towel until ready to use.) Place roll seam side down on a baking sheet coated with cooking spray. Repeat.
**4.** Spritz tops of egg rolls with cooking spray. Bake at 425° for 10-15 minutes or until lightly browned.
**Freeze option:** Freeze cooled egg rolls in a freezer container, separating layers with waxed paper. To use, reheat rolls on a baking sheet in a preheated 350° oven until crisp and heated through.
**1 egg roll:** 146 cal., 2g fat (0 sat. fat), 18mg chol., 250mg sod., 22g carb. (1g sugars, 1g fiber), 9g pro. **Diabetic exchanges:** 1½ starch, 1 lean meat, ½ fat.
**\* HEALTH TIP \*** A deep-fried chicken egg roll has more than 200 calories and 10 grams of fat per serving. This baked version is packed with veggies and lean protein and comes in at just 146 calories and 2 grams of fat per roll.

## SESAME-GARLIC PUMPKIN SEEDS

*This "everything" mix of pumpkin seeds with other seeds and seasoning is a fun treat—a lively way to use the seeds left over from carving your fall pumpkin.*
—Danielle Lee, West Palm Beach, FL

**Prep:** 10 min. • **Bake:** 35 min.
**Makes:** 2 cups

- 1 **large egg white**
- 1 **Tbsp. canola oil**
- 2 **cups fresh pumpkin seeds**
- 1 **tsp. sesame seeds**
- 1 **tsp. poppy seeds**
- 1 **tsp. dried minced onion**
- 1 **tsp. dried minced garlic**
- ¾ **tsp. kosher salt**
- ½ **tsp. caraway seeds**

**1.** Preheat oven to 325°. In a small bowl, whisk egg white and oil until frothy. Add pumpkin seeds and toss to coat. Stir in sesame seeds, poppy seeds, onion, garlic, salt and caraway seeds. Spread in a single layer in a parchment-lined 15x10x1-in. baking pan.

**2.** Bake 35-40 minutes or until dry and golden brown, stirring every 10 minutes.

**¼ cup:** 95 cal., 5g fat (1g sat. fat), 0 chol., 190mg sod., 9g carb. (0 sugars, 3g fiber), 4g pro. **Diabetic exchanges:** 1 fat, ½ starch.

**MANDARIN CHICKEN BITES**

## MANDARIN CHICKEN BITES

*Instead of a big Christmas meal, our family enjoys nibbling on an all-day appetizer buffet. Each year we present tempting new dishes alongside our favorites. This is one of those tried-and-true dishes that's a must each year.*
—Susannah Yinger, Canal Winchester, OH

**Takes:** 30 min. • **Makes:** 15 servings

- 1 **cup all-purpose flour**
- ½ **tsp. salt**
- ¼ **tsp. pepper**
- 1 **lb. boneless skinless chicken breasts, cut into 2-in. cubes**
- 2 **Tbsp. butter**
- 1 **can (11 oz.) mandarin oranges, drained**
- ⅔ **cup orange marmalade**
- ½ **tsp. dried tarragon**

**1.** In a large bowl, combine the flour, salt and pepper. Add chicken, a few pieces at a time, and turn to coat.

**2.** In a skillet, brown the chicken in butter until no longer pink. In a small saucepan, combine the oranges, marmalade and tarragon; bring to a boil. Pour over the chicken; stir gently to coat. Serve warm with toothpicks.

**1 piece:** 124 cal., 2g fat (1g sat. fat), 21mg chol., 115mg sod., 19g carb. (12g sugars, 0 fiber), 7g pro.

## VEGGIE DILL DIP

*I like to keep this good-for-you dip and a variety of cut-up veggies on hand for an easy snack.*

—Hazel Baber, Yuma, AZ

**Prep:** 10 min. + chilling • **Makes:** 2½ cups

- 2 cups 1% cottage cheese
- 3 Tbsp. fat-free milk
- ¾ cup fat-free mayonnaise
- 1 Tbsp. dried minced onion
- 1 Tbsp. dried parsley flakes
- 1 tsp. dill weed
- 1 tsp. seasoned salt
- ¼ tsp. garlic powder

In a blender, blend cottage cheese and milk until smooth. Stir in the remaining ingredients and mix well. Chill overnight. Serve with raw vegetables.

**2 Tbsp.:** 37 cal., 0 fat (0 sat. fat), 2mg chol., 303mg sod., 3g carb. (2g sugars, 0 fiber), 5g pro.

## TOMATO BASIL SNACKERS

*Fresh basil, summer-ripe tomatoes and melted mozzarella cheese cover toasted English muffins in this fabulous afternoon pick-me-up. You can even double up the serving size for a light meatless lunch.*

—*Taste of Home* Test Kitchen

**Takes:** 15 min. • **Makes:** 4 servings

- 2 English muffins, split and toasted
- 2 Tbsp. reduced-fat mayonnaise
- 3 plum tomatoes, cut into ¼-in. slices
- 6 fresh basil leaves, thinly sliced
- ⅛ tsp. pepper
- ½ cup shredded part-skim mozzarella cheese

Place muffin halves on an ungreased baking sheet; spread with mayonnaise. Top with the tomatoes, basil, pepper and cheese. Broil 4 in. from the heat for 3-4 minutes or until cheese is melted.

**1 English muffin half:** 146 cal., 6g fat (2g sat. fat), 12mg chol., 268mg sod., 17g carb. (3g sugars, 1g fiber), 7g pro. **Diabetic exchanges:** 1 starch, ½ fat.

**VEGGIE DILL DIP**

**WALNUT BALLS**

## PEPPY PEACH SALSA

*Garden-fresh salsas are one of my favorite condiments. So when I saw a recipe for peach salsa in the newspaper, I couldn't think of anything that sounded better.*
—Jennifer Abbott, Moraga, CA

- - - - - - - - - - - - - - - - - - - - - - - - - - - - -

**Takes:** 20 min. • **Makes:** 1¼ cups

- 2 Tbsp. lime juice
- 1 Tbsp. honey
- ½ tsp. minced garlic
- ⅛ tsp. ground ginger
- 2 fresh peaches, peeled and diced
- ½ green serrano chile pepper, seeded and minced
- ½ red serrano chile pepper, seeded and minced
- ½ small yellow chile pepper, seeded and minced
- 2 tsp. minced fresh cilantro
  Tortilla chips

In a small bowl, combine the lime juice, honey, garlic and ginger; let stand for 5 minutes. Stir in peaches, peppers and cilantro. Serve with chips.

**¼ cup:** 30 cal., 0 fat (0 sat. fat), 0 chol., 1mg sod., 8g carb. (6g sugars, 1g fiber), 0 pro.

## WALNUT BALLS

*Most of my family members don't eat meat, so I've made these appetizers for special occasions ever since a friend shared them with me. The moist bites and tangy sauce are always well received.*
—Bonnie Young, Desert Hot Springs, CA

- - - - - - - - - - - - - - - - - - - - - - - - -

**Prep:** 30 min. • **Bake:** 25 min.
**Makes:** 8 servings

- 2 large eggs, lightly beaten
- 3 large egg whites, lightly beaten
- 1 small onion, finely chopped
- 3 Tbsp. minced fresh parsley
- 1½ tsp. poultry seasoning
- 2 garlic cloves, minced
- ½ tsp. salt
- 1¼ cups finely crushed reduced-sodium saltine crackers
- ¾ cup ground walnuts
- ¾ cup shredded reduced-fat cheddar cheese

**APRICOT BARBECUE SAUCE**
- ¾ cup apricot spreadable fruit
- ½ cup ketchup
- ¼ cup lemon juice
- 2 Tbsp. brown sugar
- 2 Tbsp. finely chopped onion
- 1 Tbsp. canola oil
- ½ tsp. salt
- ½ tsp. dried oregano

**1.** In a large bowl, combine the first 7 ingredients. Stir in crackers, walnuts and cheese. Coat hands with cooking spray; shape mixture into 1-in. balls. Place in a 13x9-in. baking dish coated with cooking spray.
**2.** In a small saucepan, combine sauce ingredients. Bring to a boil. Pour over walnut balls. Bake, uncovered, at 350° for 25 minutes or until a thermometer reads 160°.

**4 pieces:** 265 cal., 12g fat (3g sat. fat), 61mg chol., 585mg sod., 34g carb. (0 sugars, 1g fiber), 8g pro.

### Peel Peaches
1. **Blanch.** Place peaches in a large pot of boiling water for 10-20 seconds or until skin begins to split.
2. **Ice.** Remove with a slotted spoon. Immediately place in an ice water bath to cool peaches and stop the cooking process.
3. **Peel.** Use a paring knife to peel the skin, which should easily peel off. If stubborn areas of skin won't peel off, return fruit to the boiling water for a few more seconds.

PHOTO CREDIT: NANCY MOCK

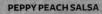

## APPLE PROSCIUTTO BRUSCHETTA

*This is a simple but delicious holiday appetizer. I use Honeycrisp apples, but you can use whatever apples you have handy.*
*For parties, I add a splash of cream sherry wine for an extra special flavor.*
—Nancy Heishman, Las Vegas, NV

**Prep:** 20 min. • **Bake:** 10 min./batch
**Makes:** 3 dozen

- 1 **cup finely chopped peeled apple**
- 1 **cup grated Asiago cheese**
- 2 **oz. finely chopped prosciutto**
- 1 **tsp. minced fresh oregano**
- 1 **tsp. minced fresh thyme**
- ¼ **tsp. ground cinnamon**
- ⅛ **tsp. coarsely ground pepper**
- 1 **tsp. cream sherry or apple juice, optional**
- 36 **slices French bread baguette (¼ in. thick)**

**1.** Preheat oven to 375°. For topping, combine the first 7 ingredients and, if desired, sherry.
**2.** Place baguette slices on foil-lined baking sheets. Top each with 1 rounded Tbsp. topping. Bake until lightly browned and cheese is melted, 8-10 minutes.

**1 appetizer:** 36 cal., 1g fat (1g sat. fat), 4mg chol., 88mg sod., 5g carb. (0 sugars, 0 fiber), 2g pro.

> **TEST KITCHEN TIP**
>
> Instead of making bruschetta, you can spoon this filling into ready-to-bake mini phyllo tart shells. Then just heat as directed in the recipe. So easy!

## TOMATO-ONION PHYLLO PIZZA

*With a delicate crust and lots of lovely tomatoes on top, this dish is a special one to serve to guests. I make it often when fresh garden tomatoes are in season. It freezes well unbaked, so I can keep one on hand to pop in the oven for a quick dinner.*
—Neta Cohen, Bedford, VA

**Prep:** 20 min. • **Bake:** 20 min.
**Makes:** 28 slices

- 5 **Tbsp. butter, melted**
- 14 **sheets phyllo dough (14x9 in.)**
- 7 **Tbsp. grated Parmesan cheese, divided**
- 1 **cup shredded part-skim mozzarella cheese**
- 1 **cup thinly sliced onion**
- 1 **lb. plum tomatoes, sliced**
- 1½ **tsp. minced fresh oregano or ½ tsp. dried oregano**
- 1 **tsp. minced fresh thyme or ¼ tsp. dried thyme**
  **Salt and pepper to taste**

**1.** Brush a 15x10x1-in. baking pan with some of the melted butter. Unroll phyllo dough; cut the stack into a 10½x9-in. rectangle. Discard scraps.
**2.** Line bottom and sides of prepared pan with 2 sheets of phyllo dough (sheets will overlap slightly). Brush with butter and sprinkle with 1 Tbsp. Parmesan cheese. Repeat layers 5 times. (Keep the dough covered with a damp towel until ready to use to prevent it from drying out.)
**3.** Top with layers of the remaining phyllo dough; brush with the remaining butter. Sprinkle with mozzarella cheese; arrange onion and tomatoes over cheese. Sprinkle with oregano, thyme, salt, pepper and the remaining Parmesan cheese. Bake at 375° until edges are golden brown, 20-25 minutes.

**1 slice:** 54 cal., 3g fat (2g sat. fat), 9mg chol., 87mg sod., 4g carb. (1g sugars, 0 fiber), 2g pro.

**TOMATO-ONION PHYLLO PIZZA**

**FALL FRUIT SALSA
WITH CINNAMON CHIPS**

## BBQ CHICKEN BITES

*Chicken bites wrapped in bacon get a kick from Montreal steak seasoning and sweetness from barbecue sauce. We love the mix of flavors and textures.*
—Kathryn Dampier, Quail Valley, CA

**Takes:** 25 min. • **Makes:** 1½ dozen

- 6 bacon strips
- ¾ lb. boneless skinless chicken breasts, cut into 1-in. cubes (about 18)
- 3 tsp. Montreal steak seasoning
- 1 tsp. prepared horseradish, optional
- ½ cup barbecue sauce

**1.** Preheat oven to 400°. Cut bacon crosswise into thirds. Place bacon on a microwave-safe plate lined with paper towels. Cover with additional paper towels; microwave on high 3-4 minutes or until partially cooked but not crisp.
**2.** Place chicken in a small bowl; sprinkle with steak seasoning and toss to coat. Wrap a bacon piece around each chicken cube; secure with a toothpick. Place on a parchment-lined baking sheet.
**3.** Bake 10 minutes. If desired, add horseradish to barbecue sauce; brush over wrapped chicken. Bake until the chicken is no longer pink and bacon is crisp, 5-10 minutes longer.
**1 appetizer:** 47 cal., 2g fat (0 sat. fat), 13mg chol., 249mg sod., 3g carb. (3g sugars, 0 fiber), 5g pro.

## FALL FRUIT SALSA WITH CINNAMON CHIPS

*For a fun treat that's sure to be requested at all your parties, try this appetizer. The salsa offers good-for-you fruits, and the crunchy home-baked chips are healthy alternative to commercial snacks.*
—Courtney Fons, Brighton, MI

**Prep:** 25 min. • **Bake:** 10 min.
**Makes:** 12 servings

- 3 Tbsp. sugar
- 1 tsp. ground cinnamon
- 6 flour tortillas (8 in.)
  Cooking spray

**SALSA**
- 4 cups finely chopped tart apples (about 2 large)
- 1 medium ripe pear, finely chopped
- ½ cup quartered seedless red grapes
- ½ cup chopped celery
- ¼ cup chopped walnuts
- 2 tsp. grated orange zest
- 3 Tbsp. orange juice
- 1 Tbsp. brown sugar

**1.** Preheat oven to 350°. Mix sugar and cinnamon. Spritz both sides of tortillas with cooking spray; sprinkle with sugar mixture. Cut each tortilla into 8 wedges. Spread in a single layer on baking sheets. Bake until lightly browned, 10-12 minutes, rotating pans as needed.
**2.** Place salsa ingredients in a large bowl; toss to combine. Serve with chips.
**1 serving:** 154 cal., 4g fat (1g sat. fat), 0 chol., 123mg sod., 28g carb. (12g sugars, 3g fiber), 3g pro. **Diabetic exchanges:** 1 starch, 1 fruit, ½ fat.

**PEANUT BUTTER
GRANOLA PINWHEELS**

## PEANUT BUTTER GRANOLA PINWHEELS

*I came across this easy and delicious snack while searching online for healthy munchies for kids. It's really quick to make and filling enough to hold the kids over until dinner.*

—Mary Haluch, Ludlow, MA

- - - - - - - - - - - - - - - - - - - - - - - - - - - - -

**Takes:** 10 min. • **Makes:** 16 pinwheels

| | |
|---|---|
| 4 | Tbsp. creamy peanut butter |
| 2 | flour tortillas (8 in.) |
| 2 | tsp. honey |
| ½ | cup granola without raisins |

Spread peanut butter over each tortilla; drizzle with honey and sprinkle with granola. Roll up; cut into slices.

**1 piece:** 60 cal., 3g fat (1g sat. fat), 0 chol., 48mg sod., 7g carb. (2g sugars, 1g fiber), 2g pro.

---

**READER REVIEW**

*"I change this up a bit to match my kids' tastes! Here are some ideas: jelly, raisins, chocolate chips, nuts, marshmallows, banana slices, apple slices ...try anything they enjoy eating with peanut butter! If I serve them right away, I microwave the tortillas for 20-30 seconds so they are more pliable and easier to roll."*

— DACIAKENNEDY, TASTEOFHOME.COM

---

## CITRUS SPICED OLIVES

*Lemon, lime and orange bring a burst of sunny citrus flavor to marinated olives. You can even blend the olives and spread the mixture onto baguette slices. Set them out for snacking at holiday buffets.*

—Ann R. Sheehy, Lawrence, MA

- - - - - - - - - - - - - - - - - - - - - - - - - - - - -

**Prep:** 20 min. + chilling • **Makes:** 4 cups

| | |
|---|---|
| ½ | cup white wine |
| ¼ | cup canola oil |
| 3 | Tbsp. salt-free seasoning blend |
| 4 | garlic cloves, minced |
| ½ | tsp. crushed red pepper flakes |
| 2 | tsp. each grated orange, lemon and lime zest |
| 3 | Tbsp. each orange, lemon and lime juices |
| 4 | cups mixed pitted olives |

In a large bowl, combine the first 5 ingredients. Add the citrus zest and juices; whisk until blended. Add olives and toss to coat. Refrigerate, covered, at least 4 hours before serving.

**¼ cup:** 74 cal., 7g fat (1g sat. fat), 0 chol., 248mg sod., 3g carb. (1g sugars, 1g fiber), 0 pro.

## QUICK PICANTE SAUCE

*Hot pepper sauce and a jalapeno pepper give this snappy sauce just the right amount of zip. It makes a great dip for tortilla chips or a tangy sauce for tacos and fajitas. This is always a big hit at parties and office gatherings. I even make it for my mother when she needs to bring a dip to a party.*
—Barbara Sellers, Shreveport, LA

**Takes:** 5 min. • **Makes:** 5 servings

- 1 can (14½ oz.) diced tomatoes, drained
- ½ cup coarsely chopped onion
- ½ cup minced fresh cilantro
- 1 jalapeno pepper, seeded and halved
- 3 Tbsp. lime juice
- 1 Tbsp. chili powder
- 1 garlic clove, halved
- ½ tsp. salt
- ¼ tsp. grated lime zest
- 5 drops hot pepper sauce
  Tortilla chips

In a blender, combine the first 10 ingredients; cover and process until smooth. Serve with tortilla chips.
**Note:** Wear disposable gloves when cutting hot peppers; the oils can burn skin. Avoid touching your face.
**¼ cup:** 32 cal., 0 fat (0 sat. fat), 0 chol., 415mg sod., 7g carb. (4g sugars, 2g fiber), 1g pro.

**AVOCADO SALSA**

## AVOCADO SALSA

*I first set out this recipe at a party, and it was an absolute success. People love the garlic, corn and avocado combination.*
—Susan Vandermeer, Ogden, UT

**Prep:** 20 min. + chilling
**Makes:** about 7 cups

- 1⅔ cups (about 8¼ oz.) frozen corn, thawed
- 2 cans (2¼ oz. each) sliced ripe olives, drained
- 1 medium sweet red pepper, chopped
- 1 small onion, chopped
- 5 garlic cloves, minced
- ⅓ cup olive oil
- ¼ cup lemon juice
- 3 Tbsp. cider vinegar
- 1 tsp. dried oregano
- ½ tsp. salt
- ½ tsp. pepper
- 4 medium ripe avocados, peeled
  Tortilla chips

**1.** Combine corn, olives, red pepper and onion. In another bowl, mix the next 7 ingredients. Pour over corn mixture; toss to coat. Refrigerate, covered, overnight.
**2.** Just before serving, chop avocados; stir into salsa. Serve with tortilla chips.
**¼ cup:** 82 cal., 7g fat (1g sat. fat), 0 chol., 85mg sod., 5g carb. (1g sugars, 2g fiber), 1g pro. **Diabetic exchanges:** 1½ fat.

# CHICKEN POT STICKERS

*Chicken and mushrooms make up the filling in these pot stickers, a traditional Chinese dumpling. Greasing the steamer rack makes it easy to remove them once they're steamed.*
—Jacquelynne Stine, Las Vegas, NV

- - - - - - - - - - - - - - - - - - - - - - - - - - - - - - -

**Prep:** 50 min. • **Cook:** 5 min./batch
**Makes:** 4 dozen

- 1 **lb. boneless skinless chicken thighs, cut into chunks**
- 1½ **cups sliced fresh mushrooms**
- 1 **small onion, cut into wedges**
- 2 **Tbsp. hoisin sauce**
- 2 **Tbsp. prepared mustard**
- 2 **Tbsp. Sriracha chili sauce or**
  1 **Tbsp. hot pepper sauce**
- 1 **pkg. (10 oz.) pot sticker or gyoza wrappers**
- 1 **large egg, lightly beaten**

**SAUCE**
- 1 **cup reduced-sodium soy sauce**
- 1 **green onion, chopped**
- 1 **tsp. ground ginger**

**1.** In a food processor, combine the uncooked chicken, mushrooms, onion, hoisin sauce, mustard and chili sauce; cover and process until blended.
**2.** Place 1 Tbsp. chicken mixture in the center of 1 wrapper. (Until ready to use, keep remaining wrappers covered with a damp towel to prevent them from drying out.) Moisten entire edge with egg. Fold wrapper over filling to form a semicircle. Press edges firmly to seal, pleating the front side to form several folds.
**3.** Holding sealed edges, place each dumpling on an even surface; press to flatten bottom. Curve ends to form a crescent shape. Repeat with remaining wrappers and filling.

**4.** Working in batches, arrange the pot stickers in a single layer on a large greased steamer basket rack; place in a Dutch oven over 1 in. of water. Bring to a boil; cover and steam until filling juices run clear, 5-7 minutes. Repeat with remaining pot stickers.
**5.** Meanwhile, in a small bowl, combine the sauce ingredients. Serve with pot stickers. Refrigerate leftovers.
**Freeze option:** Cover and freeze uncooked pot stickers in a single layer on waxed paper-lined sheets until firm. Transfer to freezer containers; return to freezer. To use, steam pot stickers as directed until heated through and juices run clear.

**1 pot sticker with 1 tsp. sauce:** 43 cal., 1g fat (0 sat. fat), 11mg chol., 374mg sod., 5g carb. (0 sugars, 0 fiber), 3g pro.

CHICKEN POT STICKERS

# SOUPS & SANDWICHES

> "The Yukon Gold potatoes my daughter shares from her garden make this soup incredible. Add some cheddar cheese and crisp croutons, and it's just heavenly. It's total comfort with the simplicity of good, wholesome ingredients!"
> —Cindi Bauer, Marshfield, WI

## ITALIAN SAUSAGE & FENNEL SOUP

*Years ago, I watched chef and TV personality Mario Batali make an Italian soup that had fennel, garlic and bread as the base. My dietary restrictions don't allow me to eat bread, so I made my own version by omitting the bread and adding sausage for protein. This soup is hearty and irresistible on a cold night. It can feed a crowd or provide plenty of leftovers. If you find yourself missing the bread, serve it on the side to round out your meal.*
—Suzanne Clark, Fort Dodge, IA

**Prep:** 20 min. • **Cook:** 30 min.
**Makes:** 12 servings (3 qt.)

- 2   Tbsp. olive oil, divided
- 1   pkg. (12 oz.) fully cooked Italian or spicy chicken sausage links, halved and sliced ¾ in. thick
- 1   medium fennel bulb, cut into ¾-in. pieces (2 cups)
- 3   medium carrots, cut into ½-in. slices
- 1   medium onion, coarsely chopped
- 3   garlic cloves, thinly sliced
- ¾   lb. red potatoes (about 3 medium), cut into ¾-in. cubes
- 1   can (15 oz.) cannellini beans, rinsed and drained
- 1   carton (32 oz.) chicken broth
- 4   cups water
- 1   can (14½ oz.) diced tomatoes, drained
- ½   tsp. salt
- ½   tsp. pepper

**1.** In a 6-qt. stockpot, heat 1 Tbsp. oil over medium-high heat; saute sausage until lightly browned, 2-3 minutes. Remove sausage, reserving drippings in pot.
**2.** In same pot, heat remaining oil over medium heat; saute fennel, carrots and onion 8 minutes. Add the garlic; cook and stir 1 minute. Add potatoes, beans, broth and water; bring to a boil. Reduce heat; simmer, covered, 10 minutes.
**3.** Stir in the tomatoes, salt, pepper and sausage; return to a boil. Reduce heat; simmer, uncovered, until vegetables are tender, about 5 minutes.

**1 cup:** 140 cal., 5g fat (1g sat. fat), 23mg chol., 707mg sod., 16g carb. (4g sugars, 4g fiber), 8g pro. **Diabetic exchanges:** 1 starch, 1 lean meat, ½ fat.

## TANGY PULLED PORK SANDWICHES

*The slow cooker not only makes this an easy meal, but it keeps the pork tender, moist and loaded with flavor. The sandwiches are so comforting, they seem anything but light.*
—Beki Kosydar-Krantz, Mayfield, PA

**Prep:** 10 min. • **Cook:** 4 hours
**Makes:** 4 servings

- 1   pork tenderloin (1 lb.)
- 1   cup ketchup
- 2   Tbsp. plus 1½ tsp. brown sugar
- 2   Tbsp. plus 1½ tsp. cider vinegar
- 1   Tbsp. plus 1½ tsp. Worcestershire sauce
- 1   Tbsp. spicy brown mustard
- ¼   tsp. pepper
- 4   rolls or buns, split and toasted Coleslaw, optional

**1.** Cut the tenderloin in half; place in a 3-qt. slow cooker. Combine ketchup, brown sugar, vinegar, Worcestershire sauce, mustard and pepper; pour over the pork.
**2.** Cover and cook on low for 4-5 hours or until meat is tender. Remove meat; shred with 2 forks. Return to slow cooker; heat through. Serve on toasted rolls or buns, with coleslaw if desired.

**1 sandwich:** 402 cal., 7g fat (2g sat. fat), 63mg chol., 1181mg sod., 56g carb. (18g sugars, 2g fiber), 29g pro.

**TANGY PULLED PORK SANDWICHES**

**BEEFY MUSHROOM SOUP**

## CALIFORNIA ROLL WRAPS

*I love the California rolls I get at sushi bars and wanted to capture those flavors in a sandwich I could take to work. I started with the standard ingredients, then added a few others and came up with a hit.*
—Mary Pax-Shipley, Bend, OR

- - - - - - - - - - - - - - - - - - - - - - - - - - -

**Takes:** 20 min. • **Makes:** 6 wraps

½ cup wasabi mayonnaise
6 whole wheat tortillas (8 in.)
2 pkg. (8 oz. each) imitation crabmeat
1 medium ripe avocado, peeled and thinly sliced
1½ cups julienned peeled jicama
1 medium sweet red pepper, julienned
1 small cucumber, seeded and julienned
¾ cup bean sprouts

Divide wasabi mayonnaise evenly among the the 6 tortillas and spread to within ½ in. of edges. Layer with crab, avocado, jicama, pepper, cucumber and sprouts. Roll up tightly.

**1 wrap:** 365 cal., 18g fat (3g sat. fat), 10mg chol., 647mg sod., 39g carb. (2g sugars, 7g fiber), 13g pro. **Diabetic exchanges:** 2 starch, 2 fat, 1 vegetable, 1 lean meat.

---

**TEST KITCHEN TIP**

If you can't find wasabi mayo, or don't like the spicy kick, use regular mayo instead.

## BEEFY MUSHROOM SOUP

*Here's a tasty way to use leftover roast or steak and to get a delicious supper on the table in about half an hour. The warm, rich taste of this mushroom soup is sure to please.*
—Ginger Ellsworth, Caldwell, ID

- - - - - - - - - - - - - - - - - - - - - - - - - - -

**Takes:** 30 min. • **Makes:** 3 cups

1 medium onion, chopped
½ cup sliced fresh mushrooms
2 Tbsp. butter
2 Tbsp. all-purpose flour
2 cups reduced-sodium beef broth
⅔ cup cubed cooked roast beef
½ tsp. garlic powder
¼ tsp. paprika
¼ tsp. pepper
⅛ tsp. salt
Dash hot pepper sauce
Shredded part-skim mozzarella cheese, optional

**1.** In a large saucepan, saute the onion and mushrooms in butter until onion is tender; remove with a slotted spoon and set aside. In a small bowl, whisk flour and broth until smooth; gradually add to the pan. Bring to a boil; cook and stir until thickened, 1-2 minutes.
**2.** Add the roast beef, garlic powder, paprika, pepper, salt, pepper sauce and onion mixture; cook and stir until heated through. Garnish with cheese if desired.

**1 cup:** 180 cal., 9g fat (5g sat. fat), 52mg chol., 470mg sod., 9g carb. (3g sugars, 1g fiber), 14g pro. **Diabetic exchanges:** 2 lean meat, 2 fat, 1 vegetable.

CABBAGE BARLEY SOUP

## CABBAGE BARLEY SOUP

*My neighbor had an abundance of cabbage, so a group of us had a contest to see who could come up with the best cabbage dish. My vegetarian cabbage soup was the clear winner.*
—Lorraine Caland, Shuniah, ON

- - - - - - - - - - - - - - - - - - - -

**Prep:** 15 min. • **Cook:** 6¼ hours
**Makes:** 8 servings (3 qt.)

- 1 cup dried brown lentils, rinsed
- ½ cup medium pearl barley
- 3 medium carrots, chopped
- 2 celery ribs, chopped
- ½ tsp. poultry seasoning
- ¼ tsp. pepper
- 1 bottle (46 oz.) V8 juice
- 4 cups water
- 8 cups shredded cabbage (about 16 oz.)
- ½ lb. sliced fresh mushrooms
- ¾ tsp. salt

**1.** Place first 8 ingredients in a 5- or 6-qt. slow cooker. Add cabbage. Cook, covered, on low until lentils are tender, 6-8 hours.
**2.** Stir in mushrooms and salt. Cook, covered, on low until mushrooms are tender, 15-20 minutes.
**Freeze option:** Freeze cooled soup in freezer containers. To use, partially thaw in refrigerator overnight. Heat through in a saucepan, stirring occasionally; add water if necessary.
**1½ cups:** 197 cal., 1g fat (0 sat. fat), 0 chol., 678mg sod., 39g carb. (7g sugars, 9g fiber), 11g pro. **Diabetic exchanges:** 2½ starch, 1 lean meat.

> **TEST KITCHEN TIP**
> Salt can prevent lentils from softening, so it's added toward the end of cooking.

## MINT-CUCUMBER TOMATO SANDWICHES

*I jazzed up the quintessential tea-time cucumber sandwich to suit my family's tastes. This was my absolute go-to sandwich last summer. It hits all the right spots!*
—Namrata Telugu, Terre Haute, IN

- - - - - - - - - - - - - - - - - - - -

**Takes:** 15 min. • **Makes:** 4 sandwiches

- 3 Tbsp. butter, softened
- 8 slices sourdough bread
- 1 large cucumber, thinly sliced
- 2 medium tomatoes, thinly sliced
- ¼ tsp. salt
- ⅛ tsp. pepper
- ¼ cup fresh mint leaves

Spread butter over 4 slices of bread. Layer with cucumber and tomatoes; sprinkle with salt, pepper and mint. Top with remaining bread. If desired, cut each sandwich into quarters.
**1 sandwich:** 286 cal., 10g fat (6g sat. fat), 23mg chol., 631mg sod., 42g carb. (5g sugars, 3g fiber), 9g pro.

## DILLY CHICKPEA SALAD SANDWICHES

*This chickpea salad is super flavorful and contains less fat and cholesterol than chicken salad. These sandwiches are delightful for a picnic.*
—Deanna Wolfe, Muskegon, MI

**Takes:** 15 min. • **Makes:** 6 servings

- 1 can (15 oz.) chickpeas or garbanzo beans, rinsed and drained
- ½ cup finely chopped onion
- ½ cup finely chopped celery
- ½ cup reduced-fat mayonnaise or vegan mayonnaise
- 3 Tbsp. honey mustard or Dijon mustard
- 2 Tbsp. snipped fresh dill
- 1 Tbsp. red wine vinegar
- ¼ tsp. salt
- ¼ tsp. paprika
- ¼ tsp. pepper
- 12 slices multigrain bread
  Optional: Romaine leaves, tomato slices, dill pickle slices and sweet red pepper rings

Place chickpeas in a large bowl; mash to desired consistency. Stir in onion, celery, mayonnaise, mustard, dill, vinegar, salt, paprika and pepper. Spread over each of 6 bread slices; layer with toppings of your choice and remaining bread.

**1 sandwich:** 295 cal., 11g fat (2g sat. fat), 7mg chol., 586mg sod., 41g carb. (9g sugars, 7g fiber), 10g pro.

**DILLY CHICKPEA SALAD SANDWICHES**

## SALMON SWEET POTATO SOUP

(PICTURED ON P. 52)

*I created this recipe as a healthier alternative to whitefish chowder, which is a favorite in the area where I grew up. The salmon and sweet potatoes boost the nutrition, and the slow cooker makes my soup convenient. It's especially comforting on a cold fall or winter day!*
—Matthew Hass, Ellison Bay, WI

**Prep:** 20 min. • **Cook:** 5½ hours
**Makes:** 8 servings (3 qt.)

- 1 Tbsp. olive oil
- 1 medium onion, chopped
- 1 medium carrot, chopped
- 1 celery rib, chopped
- 3 garlic cloves, minced
- 2 medium sweet potatoes, peeled and cut into ½-in. cubes
- 1½ cups frozen corn, thawed
- 6 cups reduced-sodium chicken broth
- 1 tsp. celery salt
- 1 tsp. dill weed
- ½ tsp. salt
- ¾ tsp. pepper
- 1½ lbs. salmon fillets, skin removed and cut into ¾-in. pieces
- 1 can (12 oz.) fat-free evaporated milk
- 2 Tbsp. minced fresh parsley

**1.** In a large skillet, heat oil over medium heat. Add the onion, carrot and celery; cook and stir until tender, 4-5 minutes. Add the garlic; cook 1 minute longer. Transfer to a 5-qt. slow cooker. Add the next 7 ingredients. Cook, covered, on low 5-6 hours or until sweet potatoes are tender.
**2.** Stir in salmon, milk and parsley. Cook, covered, until fish just begins to flake easily with a fork, 30-40 minutes longer.
**1½ cups:** 279 cal., 10g fat (2g sat. fat), 45mg chol., 834mg sod., 26g carb. (13g sugars, 3g fiber), 22g pro. **Diabetic exchanges:** 3 lean meat, 1½ starch, ½ fat.

## HEARTY PORK BEAN SOUP

*It's wonderful to come home to this pork bean soup dinner simmering away in a slow cooker, especially on a busy weeknight. It is simple to throw together in the morning before work. When you get home, just add a few ingredients, and in half an hour dinner is ready! Do not put the tomatoes in for the first 8 hours of cooking, or the beans won't become soft.*
—Colleen Delawder, Herndon, VA

**Prep:** 20 min. + soaking • **Cook:** 6¼ hours
**Makes:** 12 servings (4 qt.)

- 1 pkg. (16 oz.) dried great northern beans, rinsed and drained
- 1 large sweet onion, chopped
- 3 medium carrots, chopped
- 3 celery ribs, chopped
- 1 pork tenderloin (1 lb.)
- 1 tsp. garlic powder
- 1 Tbsp. fresh minced chives or 1 tsp. dried chives
- 1 tsp. dried oregano
- ½ tsp. dried thyme
- 1 tsp. pepper
- 1 carton (32 oz.) reduced-sodium chicken broth
- 1 can (14½ oz.) reduced-sodium chicken broth
- 1 bottle (12 oz.) extra pale ale
- 1 can (14½ oz.) diced tomatoes, drained
- 5 oz. fresh spinach
- 1½ to 2 tsp. salt

**1.** Place beans in a large bowl; add cool water to cover. Soak 5 hours or overnight. Drain beans, discarding water; rinse with cool water.
**2.** In a 6-qt. slow cooker, layer the beans, onion, carrots, celery and pork. Add the seasonings, broth and ale. Cook, covered, on low for 6-8 hours or until beans and pork are tender.
**3.** Remove pork; shred with 2 forks. Stir in tomatoes, spinach and salt. Return pork to slow cooker. Cook, covered, on low for 15-20 minutes or until heated through.

**1⅓ cups:** 207 cal., 2g fat (1g sat. fat), 21mg chol., 695mg sod., 30g carb. (5g sugars, 9g fiber), 18g pro. **Diabetic exchanges:** 2 starch, 2 lean meat.

**FRENCH DIP SANDWICHES**

## FRENCH DIP SANDWICHES

*I found this recipe in one of our local publications. It's perfect for an easy weeknight meal, since the meat cooks all day without any attention.*
—Dianne Joy Richardson, Colorado Springs, CO

**Prep:** 15 min. • **Cook:** 10 hours
**Makes:** 12 sandwiches

- 1 beef sirloin tip roast (3 to 4 lbs.)
- ½ cup reduced-sodium soy sauce
- 1 tsp. beef bouillon granules
- 1 bay leaf
- 3 to 4 whole peppercorns
- 1 tsp. dried crushed rosemary
- 1 tsp. dried thyme
- 1 tsp. garlic powder
- 12 French rolls, split

**1.** Cut roast in half. Place in a 5-qt. slow cooker. Combine the soy sauce, bouillon and seasonings; pour over roast. Add water to almost cover roast, about 5 cups. Cover and cook on low for 10-12 hours or until meat is very tender.
**2.** Remove roast; cool slightly. Discard bay leaf. Shred meat with 2 forks and return to slow cooker; heat through. Serve on rolls with broth.

**1 sandwich:** 318 cal., 8g fat (2g sat. fat), 72mg chol., 792mg sod., 31g carb. (1g sugars, 1g fiber), 29g pro. **Diabetic exchanges:** 3 lean meat, 2 starch.

HEARTY PORK
BEAN SOUP

# CRANBERRY TURKEY WRAPS

*Fruity and flavorful, these grab-and-go wraps are quick to assemble, easy to handle and low in calories.*
—Bobbie Keefer, Byers, CO

**Takes:** 15 min. • **Makes:** 8 servings

- 1 can (11 oz.) mandarin oranges, drained
- 1 medium tart apple, peeled and diced
- 3 Tbsp. dried cranberries
- ¾ cup fat-free plain yogurt
- 2 Tbsp. fat-free mayonnaise
- 8 flour tortillas (8 in.)
- 8 lettuce leaves
- 1½ lbs. thinly sliced deli turkey
- 8 slices (1 oz. each) part-skim mozzarella cheese
- 2 Tbsp. chopped pecans, toasted

In a small bowl, combine the oranges, apple and cranberries. In another bowl, combine yogurt and mayonnaise; spread over tortillas. Layer each with lettuce, turkey, cheese, fruit mixture and pecans. Roll up tightly.

**1 wrap:** 374 cal., 12g fat (4g sat. fat), 54mg chol., 1477mg sod., 40g carb. (9g sugars, 1g fiber), 27g pro.

**CHORIZO & CHICKPEA SOUP**

# CHORIZO & CHICKPEA SOUP

*The chorizo sausage adds its own spice to the broth, creating delicious flavor with no need for more seasonings. And while it's cooking, the whole house smells delicious.*
—Jaclyn McKewan, Lancaster, NY

**Prep:** 15 min. • **Cook:** 8¼ hours
**Makes:** 1½ qt.

- 3 cups water
- 2 celery ribs, chopped
- 2 fully cooked Spanish chorizo links (3 oz. each), cut into ½-in. pieces
- ½ cup dried chickpeas or garbanzo beans
- 1 can (14½ oz.) petite diced tomatoes, undrained
- ½ cup ditalini or other small pasta
- ½ tsp. salt

Place the water, celery, chorizo and chickpeas in a 4- or 5-qt. slow cooker. Cook, covered, on low until beans are tender, 8-10 hours. Stir in the tomatoes, pasta and salt; cook, covered, on high until pasta is tender, 15-20 minutes.

**Freeze option:** Freeze cooled soup in freezer containers. To use, partially thaw in refrigerator overnight. Heat through in a saucepan, stirring occasionally; add water if necessary.

**1 cup:** 180 cal., 8g fat (3g sat. fat), 18mg chol., 569mg sod., 23g carb. (3g sugars, 6g fiber), 9g pro. **Diabetic exchanges:** 1½ starch, 1 high-fat meat.

**\* HEALTH TIP \*** Chorizo is very flavorful, but it's also high in fat. Using just a small amount, as in this dish, is a smart way to boost flavor without creating a soup that's overly high in fat.

## FALL VEGETABLE SLOPPY JOES

*I make this dish in the fall and sneak grated vegetables into the sloppy joe mixture. It's especially good when you're serving kids who don't like to eat their vegetables! Just walk away until the end of the day and let the slow cooker do all the work. Also delicious: Top the filling with a little shredded cheese before serving.*
— Nancy Heishman, Las Vegas, NV

**Prep:** 30 min. • **Cook:** 4 hours
**Makes:** 18 servings

- 8   bacon strips, cut into 1-in. pieces
- 2   lbs. lean ground beef (90% lean)
- 1   medium onion, chopped
- 2   garlic cloves, minced
- 2   cups shredded peeled butternut squash
- 2   medium parsnips, peeled and shredded
- 2   medium carrots, peeled and shredded
- 1   can (12 oz.) cola
- 1   can (8 oz.) tomato paste
- 1   cup water
- ⅓   cup honey mustard
- 1½  tsp. ground cumin
- 1¼  tsp. salt
- 1   tsp. ground allspice
- ½   tsp. pepper
- 18  hamburger buns, split

**1.** In a large skillet, cook the bacon over medium heat until crisp, stirring occasionally. Remove with a slotted spoon; drain on paper towels. Discard drippings. In the same skillet, cook beef, onion and garlic over medium heat until beef is no longer pink and onion is tender, 10-12 minutes, breaking up beef into crumbles, drain.

**2.** Transfer to a 5- or 6-qt. slow cooker. Stir in the squash, parsnips, carrots, cola, tomato paste, water, mustard and seasonings. Cook, covered, on low until vegetables are tender, 4-5 hours. Stir in bacon. Serve on buns.

**Freeze option:** Freeze cooled meat mixture in freezer containers. To use, partially thaw in refrigerator overnight. Heat through in a saucepan, stirring occasionally; add water if necessary.

**1 sandwich:** 275 cal., 8g fat (3g sat. fat), 35mg chol., 526mg sod., 35g carb. (9g sugars, 3g fiber), 17g pro. **Diabetic exchanges:** 2 starch, 2 lean meat.

## CURRIED LENTIL SOUP

*Curry gives a different taste sensation to this chili-like soup. It's delicious with a dollop of sour cream. My family welcomes it with open arms—and watering mouths.*
—Christina Till, South Haven, MI

**Prep:** 15 min. • **Cook:** 8 hours
**Makes:** 10 servings (2½ qt.)

- 4   cups water
- 1   can (28 oz.) crushed tomatoes
- 3   medium potatoes, peeled and diced
- 3   medium carrots, thinly sliced
- 1   cup dried lentils, rinsed
- 1   large onion, chopped
- 1   celery rib, chopped
- 4   tsp. curry powder
- 2   bay leaves
- 2   garlic cloves, minced
- 1¼  tsp. salt

In a 4- or 5-qt. slow cooker, combine the first 10 ingredients. Cover and cook on low for 8 hours or until vegetables and lentils are tender. Stir in salt. Discard the bay leaves.

**1 cup:** 148 cal., 1g fat (0 sat. fat), 0 chol., 462mg sod., 31g carb. (6g sugars, 5g fiber), 7g pro. **Diabetic exchanges:** 1½ starch, 1 vegetable.

**FALL VEGETABLE SLOPPY JOES**

## TEXAS BLACK BEAN SOUP

*This hearty meatless soup is quick to prep with canned items. It's perfect for spicing up a family gathering on a cool day. It requires so little time and attention.*
—Pamela Scott, Garland, TX

- - - - - - - - - - - - - - - - - - - - - - - - - -

**Prep:** 5 min. • **Cook:** 4 hours
**Makes:** 10 servings (2½ qt.)

- 2 cans (15 oz. each) black beans, rinsed and drained
- 1 can (14½ oz.) stewed tomatoes or Mexican stewed tomatoes, cut up
- 1 can (14½ oz.) diced tomatoes or diced tomatoes with mild green chiles
- 1 can (14½ oz.) chicken broth
- 1 can (11 oz.) Mexicorn, drained
- 2 cans (4 oz. each) chopped green chiles
- 4 green onions, thinly sliced
- 2 to 3 Tbsp. chili powder
- 1 tsp. ground cumin
- ½ tsp. dried minced garlic

In a 3-qt. slow cooker, combine all ingredients. Cover and cook on high for 4-6 hours or until heated through.
**1 cup:** 91 cal., 0 fat (0 sat. fat), 0 chol., 609mg sod., 19g carb. (6g sugars, 4g fiber), 4g pro.

**SNAPPY TUNA MELTS**

## SNAPPY TUNA MELTS

*I lightened up a tuna melt by substituting creamy balsamic vinaigrette for the mayonnaise. Children and adults all go for this quick-cook meal hero.*
—Christine Schenher, Exeter, CA

- - - - - - - - - - - - - - - - - - - - - - - - - -

**Takes:** 15 min. • **Makes:** 4 servings

- 1 pouch (11 oz.) light tuna in water
- 1 hard-boiled large egg, coarsely chopped
- 2 Tbsp. reduced-fat creamy balsamic vinaigrette
- 1 Tbsp. stone-ground mustard, optional
- 4 whole wheat hamburger buns, split
- 8 slices tomato
- 8 slices reduced-fat Swiss cheese

**1.** In a small bowl, mix the tuna, egg, vinaigrette and, if desired, mustard. Place buns on an ungreased baking sheet, cut side up. Broil 4-6 in. from heat until golden brown, 1-2 minutes.
**2.** Spread tuna mixture over buns; top with tomato and cheese. Broil until cheese is melted, 2-3 minutes longer.
**2 open-faced sandwiches:** 341 cal., 13g fat (5g sat. fat), 105mg chol., 557mg sod., 27g carb. (6g sugars, 4g fiber), 35g pro. **Diabetic exchanges:** 4 lean meat, 2 starch, 1 fat.

## MEXI-STRONI SOUP

*If you're a fan of classic minestrone but love bold Mexican flavors, this soup's for you! It's pumped up with spices, veggies, and pasta for a fill-you-up bowl of fun.*
—Darlene Island, Lakewood, WA

**Prep:** 25 min. • **Cook:** 7½ hours
**Makes:** 10 servings (3¾ qt.)

1½ lbs. beef stew meat (1-in. pieces)
1½ cups shredded carrots
½ cup chopped onion
1 jalapeno pepper, seeded and minced, optional
1 tsp. ground cumin
1 tsp. chili powder
¾ tsp. seasoned salt
½ tsp. Italian seasoning
2 cans (10 oz. each) diced tomatoes and green chiles, undrained
2 cups spicy hot V8 juice
1 carton (32 oz.) reduced-sodium beef broth
1 medium zucchini, halved and thinly sliced
2 cups finely shredded cabbage
2 celery ribs, thinly sliced
1 can (16 oz.) kidney beans, rinsed and drained
1 can (15 oz.) black beans, rinsed and drained
1 cup small pasta shells
¼ cup chopped fresh cilantro

**1.** Place first 11 ingredients in a 6- or 7-qt. slow cooker. Cook, covered, on low until meat is tender, 7-9 hours.

**2.** Stir in the zucchini, cabbage, celery, beans and pasta. Cook, covered, on high until vegetables and pasta are tender, 30-45 minutes, stirring occasionally. Stir in cilantro.

**1½ cups:** 249 cal., 5g fat (2g sat. fat), 44mg chol., 816mg sod., 29g carb. (5g sugars, 6g fiber), 21g pro. **Diabetic exchanges:** 2 starch, 2 lean meat.

### TEST KITCHEN TIP

The V8 and diced tomatoes with green chiles add nice heat. If you like it spicier still, go ahead and add the optional jalapeno.

MEXI-STRONI SOUP

SALSA BLACK BEAN
BURGERS

## SALSA BLACK BEAN BURGERS

*Meatless meals will be so tasty when these hearty bean burgers are on the menu. Guacamole and sour cream make them seem decadent.*
—Jill Reichardt, St. Louis, MO

---

**Takes:** 20 min. • **Makes:** 4 servings

- 1 can (15 oz.) black beans, rinsed and drained
- ⅔ cup dry bread crumbs
- 1 small tomato, seeded and finely chopped
- 1 jalapeno pepper, seeded and finely chopped
- 1 large egg
- 1 tsp. minced fresh cilantro
- 1 garlic clove, minced
- 1 Tbsp. olive oil
- 4 whole wheat hamburger buns, split
  Optional: Reduced-fat sour cream and guacamole

**1.** Place the beans in a food processor; cover and process until blended. Transfer to a large bowl. Add the bread crumbs, tomato, jalapeno, egg, cilantro and garlic. Mix until combined. Shape into 4 patties.
**2.** In a large nonstick skillet, cook the patties in oil over medium heat until lightly browned, 4-6 minutes on each side. Serve on buns. If desired, top with sour cream and guacamole.
**Note:** Wear disposable gloves when cutting hot peppers; the oils can burn skin. Avoid touching your face.
**1 burger:** 323 cal., 8g fat (1g sat. fat), 53mg chol., 557mg sod., 51g carb. (6g sugars, 9g fiber), 13g pro.

CREAM OF POTATO & CHEDDAR SOUP

## CREAM OF POTATO & CHEDDAR SOUP

*The Yukon Gold potatoes my daughter shares from her garden make this soup incredible. Add some cheddar cheese and crispy croutons, and it's just heavenly. It's total comfort with the simplicity of good, wholesome ingredients!*
—Cindi Bauer, Marshfield, WI

---

**Prep:** 25 min. • **Cook:** 7½ hours
**Makes:** 11 servings (2¾ qt.)

- 8 medium Yukon Gold potatoes, peeled and cubed
- 1 large red onion, chopped
- 1 celery rib, chopped
- 2 cans (14½ oz. each) reduced-sodium chicken broth
- 1 can (10¾ oz.) condensed cream of celery soup, undiluted
- 1 tsp. garlic powder
- ½ tsp. white pepper
- 1½ cups shredded sharp cheddar cheese
- 1 cup half-and-half cream
  Optional toppings: Salad croutons, crumbled cooked bacon, chives and additional shredded sharp cheddar cheese

**1.** Combine the first 7 ingredients in a 4- or 5-qt. slow cooker. Cover and cook on low for 7-9 hours or until potatoes are tender.
**2.** Stir in cheese and cream. Cover and cook 30 minutes longer or until cheese is melted. Garnish servings with toppings of your choice.
**1 cup:** 212 cal., 8g fat (5g sat. fat), 28mg chol., 475mg sod., 27g carb. (4g sugars, 3g fiber), 8g pro. **Diabetic exchanges:** 2 starch, 1½ fat.

## BEEF & VEGETABLE SOUP

*On cool nights, it's heartwarming to enjoy a bowl of hot homemade soup. You can opt for chicken and chicken broth instead of beef and substitute your favorite veggies for your own version of this versatile, easy soup.*
—*Taste of Home* Test Kitchen

**Prep:** 20 min. • **Cook:** 30 min.
**Makes:** 6 servings

- 1 lb. lean ground beef (90% lean)
- ⅓ cup chopped onion
- ⅓ cup chopped green pepper
- 2 cans (14½ oz. each) reduced-sodium beef broth
- 1 can (14½ oz.) diced tomatoes, undrained
- 1 cup cubed peeled potatoes
- ¾ cup fresh or frozen cut green beans
- ½ cup chopped carrot
- ½ cup water
- 1 garlic clove, minced
- 1 tsp. Italian seasoning
- ⅛ tsp. pepper

**1.** In a Dutch oven, cook the beef, onion and green pepper over medium heat until meat is no longer pink; drain. Stir in the remaining ingredients. Bring to a boil. Reduce the heat; cover and simmer for 30 minutes or until vegetables are tender.
**2.** Serve soup immediately or transfer to freezer containers. May be frozen for up to 3 months.
**3.** To use frozen soup: Thaw in the refrigerator overnight. Transfer to a saucepan. Cover and cook over medium heat until heated through.

**1⅓ cups:** 173 cal., 6g fat (2g sat. fat), 40mg chol., 394mg sod., 13g carb. (5g sugars, 3g fiber), 17g pro. **Diabetic exchanges:** 2 lean meat, 1 starch.

## ROAST PORK SOUP

*This well-seasoned, satisfying soup has a rich full-bodied broth brimming with tender chunks of pork, potatoes and navy beans. It has been a family favorite for years. Served with cornbread, it's one of our comfort foods in winter.*
—Sue Gulledge, Springville, AL

**Prep:** 15 min. • **Cook:** 55 min.
**Makes:** 9 servings (2¼ qt.)

- 3 cups cubed cooked pork roast
- 2 medium potatoes, peeled and chopped
- 1 large onion, chopped
- 1 can (15 oz.) navy beans, rinsed and drained
- 1 can (14½ oz.) Italian diced tomatoes, undrained
- 4 cups water
- ½ cup unsweetened apple juice
- ½ tsp. salt
- ½ tsp. pepper
- Minced fresh basil

In a soup kettle or Dutch oven, combine the first 9 ingredients. Bring to a boil. Reduce heat; cover and simmer until vegetables are crisp-tender, about 45 minutes. Sprinkle with basil.

**1 cup:** 206 cal., 5g fat (2g sat. fat), 42mg chol., 435mg sod., 23g carb. (6g sugars, 4g fiber), 18g pro. **Diabetic exchanges:** 1 starch, 1 vegetable, 1 meat.

**ROAST PORK SOUP**

**CHICKEN CORDON BLEU STROMBOLI**

## BEEF BARLEY LENTIL SOUP

*I serve this soup often to family and friends on cold nights, along with homemade rolls and a green salad. For variety, you can substitute jicama for the potatoes.*
—Judy Metzentine, The Dalles, OR

- - - - - - - - - - - - - - - - - - - - - - - - - -

**Prep:** 20 min. • **Cook:** 8 hours
**Makes:** 10 servings (about 3¾ qt. )

- 1 lb. lean ground beef (90% lean)
- 1 medium onion, chopped
- 2 cups cubed red potatoes (¼-in. pieces)
- 1 cup chopped celery
- 1 cup chopped carrots
- 1 cup dried lentils, rinsed
- ½ cup medium pearl barley
- 8 cups water
- 2 tsp. beef bouillon granules
- 1 tsp. salt
- ½ tsp. lemon-pepper seasoning
- 2 cans (14½ oz. each) stewed tomatoes, coarsely chopped

**1.** In a nonstick skillet, cook beef and onion over medium heat until meat is no longer pink; drain.

**2.** Transfer to a 5-qt. slow cooker. Layer with the potatoes, celery, carrot, lentils and barley. Combine the water, bouillon, salt and lemon pepper; pour over the vegetables. Cover and cook on low for 6 hours or until vegetables and barley are tender.

**3.** Add tomatoes; cook 2 hours longer.

**1½ cups:** 232 cal., 4g fat (2g sat. fat), 28mg chol., 603mg sod., 33g carb. (6g sugars, 6g fiber), 16g pro. **Diabetic exchanges:** 2 lean meat, 1½ starch, 1 vegetable.

## CHICKEN CORDON BLEU STROMBOLI

*If chicken cordon bleu and stromboli had a baby, this would be it. Serve with some jarred Alfredo sauce, homemade Alfredo sauce or classic Mornay sauce on the side if desired.*
—Cyndy Gerken, Naples, FL

- - - - - - - - - - - - - - - - - - - - - - - - - -

**Takes:** 30 min. • **Makes:** 6 servings

- 1 tube (13.8 oz.) refrigerated pizza crust
- 4 thin slices deli ham
- 1½ cups shredded cooked chicken
- 6 slices Swiss cheese
- 1 Tbsp. butter, melted
  Roasted garlic Alfredo sauce, optional

**1.** Preheat oven to 400°. Unroll pizza dough onto a baking sheet. Layer with the ham, chicken and cheese to within ½ in. of edges. Roll up jelly-roll style, starting with a long side; pinch seam to seal and tuck ends under. Brush with melted butter.

**2.** Bake until crust is dark golden brown, 18-22 minutes. Let stand 5 minutes before slicing. If desired, serve with Alfredo sauce for dipping.

**1 slice:** 298 cal., 10g fat (4g sat. fat), 53mg chol., 580mg sod., 32g carb. (4g sugars, 1g fiber), 21g pro.

**TEST KITCHEN TIP**

Don't let this stand too long before slicing and eating, or the underside of the crust will get soft.

## SPICY CHICKEN TOMATO SOUP

*Cumin, chili powder and cayenne pepper give my slow-cooked specialty its kick. I serve bowls of it with crunchy tortilla strips that bake in no time. Leftover soup freezes well for nights I don't feel like cooking.*
—Margaret Bailey, Coffeeville, MS

**Prep:** 20 min. • **Cook:** 4 hours
**Makes:** 8 servings

- 2 cans (14½ oz. each) chicken broth
- 3 cups cubed cooked chicken
- 2 cups frozen corn
- 1 can (10¾ oz.) tomato puree
- 1 can (10 oz.) diced tomatoes and green chiles
- 1 large onion, finely chopped
- 2 garlic cloves, minced
- 1 bay leaf
- 1 to 2 tsp. ground cumin
- ½ tsp. salt
- ½ to 1 tsp. chili powder
- ⅛ tsp. pepper
- ⅛ tsp. cayenne pepper
- 4 white or yellow corn tortillas (6 in.), cut into ¼-in. strips

**1.** In a 5-qt. slow cooker, combine the first 13 ingredients. Cover and cook on low for 4 hours.
**2.** Place the tortilla strips on an ungreased baking sheet. Bake at 375° for 5 minutes; turn. Bake 5 minutes longer. Discard bay leaf from soup. Serve soup with crunchy tortilla strips.
**1 serving:** 196 cal., 5g fat (1g sat. fat), 49mg chol., 800mg sod., 19g carb. (3g sugars, 3g fiber), 19g pro.

GREEK BEEF PITAS

## GREEK BEEF PITAS

*A local restaurant that's famous for pitas inspired me to make my own Greek-style sandwiches at home. Feel free to add olives if you'd like.*
—Nancy Sousley, Lafayette, IN

**Takes:** 25 min. • **Makes:** 4 servings

- 1 lb. lean ground beef (90% lean)
- 1 small onion, chopped
- 3 garlic cloves, minced
- 1 tsp. dried oregano
- ¾ tsp. salt, divided
- 1 cup reduced-fat plain Greek yogurt
- 1 medium tomato, chopped
- ½ cup chopped peeled cucumber
- 1 tsp. dill weed
- 4 whole pita breads, warmed

**Optional: Additional chopped tomatoes and cucumber**

**1.** In a large skillet, cook beef, onion and garlic over medium heat 8-10 minutes or until beef is no longer pink and vegetables are tender, breaking up the beef into crumbles; drain. Stir in oregano and ½ tsp. salt.
**2.** In a small bowl, mix yogurt, tomato, cucumber, dill and remaining salt. Spoon ¾ cup beef mixture over each pita bread; top with 3 Tbsp. yogurt sauce. If desired, top with additional chopped tomatoes and cucumbers. Serve with the remaining yogurt sauce.
**1 pita:** 407 cal., 11g fat (4g sat. fat), 74mg chol., 851mg sod., 40g carb. (5g sugars, 2g fiber), 34g pro.

# FRESH PUMPKIN SOUP

*This appealing soup harvests the autumn flavors of just-picked pumpkins and tart apples. It's sure to warm you up on a crisp day. I top the creamy soup with a sprinkling of toasted pumpkin seeds.*

—Jane Shapton, Irvine, CA

**Prep:** 50 min. • **Cook:** 8 hours
**Makes:** 9 servings (2¼ qt.)

8  cups chopped fresh pumpkin (about 3 lbs.)
4  cups chicken broth
3  small tart apples, peeled and chopped
1  medium onion, chopped
2  Tbsp. lemon juice
2  tsp. minced fresh gingerroot
2  garlic cloves, minced
½  tsp. salt

**TOASTED PUMPKIN SEEDS**
½  cup fresh pumpkin seeds
1  tsp. canola oil
⅛  tsp. salt

**1.** In a 5-qt. slow cooker, combine the first 8 ingredients. Cover and cook on low for 8-10 hours or until pumpkin and apples are tender.

**2.** Meanwhile, toss pumpkin seeds with oil and salt. Spread onto an ungreased 15x10x1-in. baking pan. Bake at 250° for 45-50 minutes or until golden brown. Set aside.

**3.** Cool soup slightly; process in batches in a blender. Transfer to a large saucepan; heat through. Garnish with the toasted pumpkin seeds.

**1 cup:** 102 cal., 2g fat (1g sat. fat), 0 chol., 567mg sod., 22g carb. (0 sugars, 3g fiber), 3g pro. **Diabetic exchanges:** 1 starch, ½ fruit.

**FRESH PUMPKIN SOUP**

LIME NAVY BEAN CHILI

## LIME NAVY BEAN CHILI

*I love using my slow cooker for tasty soups like this one. Just fill it in the morning and come home later to a wonderful, warm meal—no matter how busy the day!*
—Connie Thomas, Jensen, UT

- - - - - - - - - - - - - - - - - - - - - - - - - - - -

**Prep:** 15 min. + soaking • **Cook:** 5 hours
**Makes:** 6 servings

1¼  cups dried navy beans
3  cups water
2  bone-in chicken breast halves (7 oz. each), skin removed
1  cup frozen corn
1  medium onion, chopped
1  can (4 oz.) chopped green chiles
4  garlic cloves, minced
1  Tbsp. chicken bouillon granules
1  tsp. ground cumin
½  tsp. chili powder
2  Tbsp. lime juice
   Minced fresh cilantro, optional

**1.** Sort beans and rinse with cold water. Place beans in a large saucepan; add water to cover by 2 in. Bring to a boil; boiling for 2 minutes. Remove from the heat; cover and let soak until beans are softened, 1-4 hours. Drain and rinse beans, discarding liquid.
**2.** In a 3-qt. slow cooker, combine the beans, water, chicken, corn, onion, chiles, garlic, bouillon, cumin and chili powder. Cover and cook on low for 5-6 hours, until a thermometer reads 170° and beans are tender.
**3.** Remove chicken breasts; set aside until cool enough to handle. Remove meat from bones; discard bones. Cut chicken into bite-sized pieces; return to slow cooker. Stir in the lime juice just before serving. If desired, serve with minced fresh cilantro.
**1 cup:** 250 cal., 2g fat (1g sat. fat), 30mg chol., 532mg sod., 37g carb. (5g sugars, 12g fiber), 22g pro. **Diabetic exchanges:** 3 lean meat, 2 starch, 1 vegetable.

## SPICY VEGGIE & LENTIL SOUP

**(PICTURED ON P. 53)**

*I enjoy this recipe because it's meatless, easy on the pocket and simply delicious! You can substitute any vegetables you like—it's all a matter of preference. Serve warm pita bread on the side.*
—Geraldine Hennessey, Glendale, NY

- - - - - - - - - - - - - - - - - - - - - - - - - - - -

**Prep:** 15 min. • **Cook:** 6½ hours
**Makes:** 8 servings (2 qt.)

2  cups halved fresh green beans
2  cups fresh cauliflowerets
1  cup dried lentils, rinsed and drained
1  cup fresh baby carrots, halved diagonally
1  medium onion, chopped
1  jalapeno pepper, seeded and finely chopped
2  garlic cloves, minced
4  cups vegetable stock
2  bay leaves
2  tsp. smoked paprika
1  tsp. dried oregano
¼  tsp. pepper
1  tsp. salt
1  can (14½ oz.) diced tomatoes with spicy red pepper, undrained

**1.** In a 4-qt. slow cooker, combine the first 12 ingredients. Cook, covered, on low until vegetables and lentils are tender, 6-8 hours.
**2.** Discard the bay leaves. Stir in the salt and diced tomatoes; cook, covered, for 30 minutes longer.
**Note:** Wear disposable gloves when cutting hot peppers; the oils can burn skin. Avoid touching your face.
**1 cup:** 146 cal., 1g fat (0 sat. fat), 0 chol., 693mg sod., 27g carb. (7g sugars, 5g fiber), 10g pro. **Diabetic exchanges:** 1½ starch, 1 lean meat.
**\* HEALTH TIP \*** Lentils are a healthy and inexpensive way to add a boost of nutrition to soups and stews. They are a good source of fiber, protein, potassium, iron and vitamin B6.

VEGAN CREAM OF
BROCCOLI SOUP

## VEGAN CREAM OF
## BROCCOLI SOUP

*Pureed potatoes help give this vegan
cream of broccoli soup a silky texture
without the cream! It's a great trick to
make dairy-free soups super creamy.*
—*Taste of Home* Test Kitchen

Prep: 20 min. . • Cook: 25 min.
Makes: 8 servings (2 qt.)

3  medium onions, chopped
2  celery ribs, chopped
2  Tbsp. canola oil
4  cups plus ½ cup vegetable broth
4  medium russet potatoes, peeled
   and cubed (about 4 cups)
6  cups chopped fresh broccoli (about
   3 small heads)
1  tsp. salt
¼  tsp. pepper

1. In a large saucepan, saute onions and
celery in oil until tender. Add 4 cups broth
and potatoes; bring to a boil. Reduce the
heat; cover and simmer for 15-20 minutes
or until potatoes are tender.
2. Cool slightly. In a blender, process soup
in batches until smooth. Return to pan;
add the remaining broth and bring to a
boil. Add the broccoli, salt and pepper.
Reduce heat; simmer, uncovered, for
8-10 minutes or until broccoli is tender.
1 cup: 142 cal., 4g fat (0 sat. fat), 0 chol.,
409mg sod., 24g carb. (5g sugars, 4g fiber),
4g pro. Diabetic exchanges: 1½ starch,
1 vegetable, ½ fat.

## HEARTY BEAN SOUP

*This soup is convenient to simmer all day
in a slow cooker—your family will love it.*
—*Alice Schnoor, Arion, IA*

Prep: 10 min. • Cook: 6 hours
Makes: 10 servings (2½ qt.)

3  cups chopped parsnips
2  cups chopped carrots
1  cup chopped onion
1½  cups dried great northern beans
5  cups water
1½  lbs. smoked ham hocks
2  garlic cloves, minced
2  tsp. salt
½  tsp. pepper
⅛ to ¼ tsp. hot pepper sauce

1. In a 5-qt. slow cooker, place parsnips,
carrots and onion. Top with beans. Add
water, ham, garlic, salt, pepper and hot
pepper sauce. Cover and cook on high
for 6-7 hours or until beans are tender.
2. Remove meat and bones from slow
cooker. When cool enough to handle, cut
meat into bite-sized pieces and return to
slow cooker; heat through.
1 cup: 161 cal., 2g fat (0 sat. fat), 8mg chol.,
686mg sod., 29g carb. (4g sugars, 9g fiber),
10g pro. Diabetic exchanges: 2 starch,
1 lean meat.

## ASIAN PULLED PORK SANDWICHES

*My pulled pork is a happy flavor mash-up of Vietnamese pho noodle soup and a banh mi sandwich. It's one seriously delicious slow-cooker dish!*
—Stacie Anderson, VA Beach, VA

**Prep:** 15 min. • **Cook:** 7 hours
**Makes:** 18 servings

- ½ cup hoisin sauce
- ¼ cup seasoned rice vinegar
- ¼ cup reduced-sodium soy sauce
- ¼ cup honey
- 2 Tbsp. tomato paste
- 1 Tbsp. Worcestershire sauce
- 2 garlic cloves, minced
- 4 lbs. boneless pork shoulder roast
- 18 French dinner rolls (about 1¾ oz. each), split and warmed

Optional toppings: Shredded cabbage, julienned carrot, sliced jalapeno pepper, fresh cilantro or basil, and Sriracha chili sauce

**1.** In a small bowl, whisk first 7 ingredients until blended. Place roast in a 4- or 5-qt. slow cooker. Pour sauce mixture over top. Cook, covered, on low until the pork is tender, 7-9 hours.
**2.** Remove roast; cool slightly. Skim fat from cooking juices. Coarsely shred pork with 2 forks. Return pork to slow cooker; heat through. Using tongs, serve pork on rolls, adding toppings as desired.
**Freeze option:** Freeze cooled meat mixture in freezer containers. To use, partially thaw in refrigerator overnight. Heat through in a saucepan, stirring occasionally; add broth if necessary. Serve as directed.
**1 sandwich:** 350 cal., 12g fat (4g sat. fat), 60mg chol., 703mg sod., 35g carb. (8g sugars, 1g fiber), 23g pro.

## ITALIAN CHICKEN SOUP

*Fennel, thyme, basil and orzo pasta add a taste of Italy to chicken soup. If you don't start with a low-sodium or sodium-free stock, you might want to decrease the amount of salt you use.*
—*Taste of Home* Test Kitchen

**Prep:** 10 min. • **Cook:** 45 min.
**Makes:** 4 servings

- 1 fennel bulb, chopped
- ½ cup chopped onion
- 2 tsp. olive oil
- 2 cups hot water
- 4 cups reduced-sodium chicken broth
- 1½ cups chopped carrots
- ¼ tsp. dried thyme
- ¼ tsp. dried basil
- ¼ tsp. salt
- ¼ tsp. pepper
- 2 cups cubed cooked chicken breast
- ½ cup uncooked orzo pasta
- 2 Tbsp. finely chopped fennel fronds

**1.** In a Dutch oven, saute the fennel bulb and onion in oil until fennel is tender. Add the next 7 ingredients. Bring to a boil. Reduced heat; cover and simmer for 15 minutes.
**2.** Stir in chicken and orzo. Cover and cook for 20 minutes or until orzo is tender. Stir in fennel fronds.
**1½ cups:** 279 cal., 5g fat (1g sat. fat), 54mg chol., 829mg sod., 30g carb. (7g sugars, 4g fiber), 28g pro. **Diabetic exchanges:** 3 lean meat, 1½ starch, 1 vegetable.

ASIAN PULLED PORK SANDWICHES

## SLOW-COOKED MEXICAN BEEF SOUP

*My family loves this soup, and I'm happy to make it since it's so simple! You can serve it with cornbread instead of corn chips to make it even more satisfying.*
—Angela Lively, Conroe, TX

**Prep:** 15 min. • **Cook:** 6 hours
**Makes:** 6 servings (2 qt.)

- 1  lb. beef stew meat (1¼-in. pieces)
- ¾  lb. potatoes (about 2 medium), cut into ¾-in. cubes
- 2  cups frozen corn (about 10 oz.), thawed
- 2  medium carrots, cut into ½-in. slices
- 1  medium onion, chopped
- 2  garlic cloves, minced
- 1½ tsp. dried oregano
- 1  tsp. ground cumin
- ½  tsp. salt
- ¼  tsp. crushed red pepper flakes
- 2  cups beef stock
- 1  can (10 oz.) diced tomatoes and green chiles, undrained
   Optional: Sour cream and tortilla chips

In a 5- or 6-qt. slow cooker, combine the first 12 ingredients. Cook, covered, on low until meat is tender, 6-8 hours. If desired, serve with sour cream and chips.
**1⅓ cups:** 218 cal., 6g fat (2g sat. fat), 47mg chol., 602mg sod., 24g carb. (5g sugars, 3g fiber), 19g pro. **Diabetic exchanges:** 2 lean meat, 1½ starch.

## 🌶 🌶 SPICY BUFFALO CHICKEN WRAPS

*This recipe has a real kick and is one of my husband's favorites. It's ready in a flash, is easily doubled and is the closest thing to restaurant Buffalo wings I've ever tasted in a light version.*
—Jennifer Beck, Meridian, ID

**Takes:** 25 min. • **Makes:** 2 servings

- ½  lb. boneless skinless chicken breast, cubed
- ½  tsp. canola oil
- 2  Tbsp. Louisiana-style hot sauce
- 1  cup shredded lettuce
- 2  flour tortillas (6 in.), warmed
- 2  tsp. reduced-fat ranch salad dressing
- 2  Tbsp. crumbled blue cheese

**1.** In a large nonstick skillet, cook chicken in oil over medium heat for 6 minutes; drain. Stir in hot sauce. Bring to a boil. Reduce heat; simmer, uncovered, until sauce is thickened and chicken is no longer pink, 3-5 minutes.
**2.** Place lettuce on tortillas; drizzle with ranch dressing. Top with chicken mixture and blue cheese; roll up.
**1 wrap:** 273 cal., 11g fat (3g sat. fat), 70mg chol., 453mg sod., 15g carb. (1g sugars, 1g fiber), 28g pro. **Diabetic exchanges:** 3 lean meat, 1½ fat, 1 starch.

**SPICY BUFFALO CHICKEN WRAPS**

## AVOCADO EGG SALAD TOAST

*After purchasing far too many unripe avocados for an event, I had a surplus of ripe ones each day in my kitchen for the week after! I was making some egg salad sandwiches for lunch one day and had the idea to use avocado to bind it together instead of traditional mayo. Not only was this version unbelievably delicious, the healthy fats in the avocado make this a better option that the traditional mayo-laden version.*
—Shannon Dobos, Calgary, AB

**Takes:** 20 min. • **Makes:** 4 servings

- 1   medium ripe avocado, peeled and cubed
- 6   hard-boiled large eggs, chopped
- 1   green onion, finely chopped
- 1   tsp. lemon juice
- ¼   tsp. salt
- ⅛   tsp. pepper
- 4   large slices sourdough bread, halved and toasted

In a large bowl, mash avocado to desired consistency. Gently stir in eggs, green onion, lemon juice, salt and pepper. Spread over toast. Serve immediately.

**2 pieces:** 367 cal., 15g fat (4g sat. fat), 280mg chol., 671mg sod., 41g carb. (4g sugars, 4g fiber), 18g pro.

## VEGETARIAN PEA SOUP

*This recipe is my version of several online recipes—and a real favorite when I was a vegetarian for health reasons. Even my meat-loving husband asked for seconds!*
—Corrie Gamache, Palmyra, VA

**Prep:** 15 min. • **Cook:** 7 hours
**Makes:** 8 servings (2 qt.)

- 1   pkg. (16 oz.) dried green split peas, rinsed
- 1   medium leek (white portion only), chopped
- 3   celery ribs, chopped
- 1   medium potato, peeled and chopped
- 2   medium carrots, chopped
- 1   garlic clove, minced
- ¼   cup minced fresh parsley
- 2   cartons (32 oz. each) reduced-sodium vegetable broth
- 1½   tsp. ground mustard
- ½   tsp. pepper
- ½   tsp. dried oregano
- 1   bay leaf

In a 5-qt. slow cooker, combine all the ingredients. Cover and cook on low for 7-8 hours or until peas are tender. Discard bay leaf. Stir before serving.

**1 cup:** 248 cal., 1g fat (0 sat. fat), 0 chol., 702mg sod., 46g carb. (7g sugars, 16g fiber), 15g pro.

# SALADS

*"This protein-rich dish is a light meatless entree. The basmati rice adds a unique flavor and the vinaigrette dressing gives it a bit of a tang."*
—Janelle Lee, Appleton, WI

**Shaved Fennel Salad** (p. 97) **Black-Eyed Pea Tomato Salad** (p. 85) **Spinach-Orzo Salad with Chickpeas** (p. 94)
**Ginger-Apricot Tossed Salad** (p. 88) **Cool Beans Salad** (p. 81) **Zucchini Panzanella Salad** (p. 78)

## ZUCCHINI PANZANELLA SALAD

(PICTURED ON P. 77)

*I learned how to make panzanella from a dear friend's grandmother. This is a version I crave during the summer. It's a tasty way to use day-old bread and your garden's bounty of zucchini.*
—Felicity Wolf, Kansas City, MO

**Prep:** 20 min. • **Bake:** 40 min.
**Makes:** 14 cups

- 3 medium zucchini, cut into ¼-in. slices
- ¼ cup olive oil, divided
- 1 French bread baguette (10½ oz.), cubed
- 1½ cups heirloom mini or cherry tomatoes, halved
- 1 medium green pepper, coarsely chopped
- ½ medium red onion, thinly sliced
- ¼ cup balsamic vinegar
- 1 tsp. jarred roasted minced garlic
- 1 tsp. Italian seasoning
- ½ tsp. crushed red pepper flakes
- 1 tsp. kosher salt
- ½ tsp. coarsely ground pepper
- 1½ cups fresh mozzarella cheese pearls

**1.** Place zucchini in a 15x10x1-in. baking pan. Toss with 1 Tbsp. olive oil. Bake, uncovered, at 400° until tender and lightly browned, 25-30 minutes, stirring halfway. Remove from the oven and cool.
**2.** Meanwhile, in a large bowl, toss bread cubes with 1 Tbsp. olive oil. Transfer to a baking sheet. Bake bread cubes at 400° until lightly browned, 12-14 minutes, stirring occasionally.
**3.** Place the cooled zucchini, toasted bread, tomatoes, green pepper and red onion in a large bowl. In a small bowl, whisk together vinegar, garlic, seasonings and remaining oil. Drizzle over salad; toss gently to combine. Add the mozzarella and stir to combine. Serve immediately.
**1 cup:** 152 cal., 8g fat (3g sat. fat), 13mg chol., 301mg sod., 16g carb. (4g sugars, 1g fiber), 5g pro. **Diabetic exchanges:** 1½ fat, 1 starch.

> **TEST KITCHEN TIP**
>
> If the raw onion is too pungent for you, roast it with the zucchini.

## TROPICAL SWEET POTATO SALAD

*I had an abundance of sweet potatoes, so I put them to work and came up with this sweet and spicy picnic salad.*
—Crystal Jo Bruns, Iliff, CO

**Prep:** 20 min. • **Bake:** 35 min. + chilling
**Makes:** 8 servings

- 3 lbs. sweet potatoes, peeled and cut into ½-in. cubes
- 1 medium mango, peeled and cut into ½-in. cubes
- 1 medium red onion, thinly sliced
  Cooking spray
- 1½ Tbsp. chili powder
- ¼ tsp. salt
- ¼ tsp. pepper
- ½ cup Miracle Whip
- ¼ cup plain Greek yogurt
- 2 Tbsp. thawed pineapple juice concentrate
- 2 serrano peppers, seeded and finely chopped, veins removed
  Thinly sliced serrano pepper, optional

**1.** Preheat oven to 350°. Place sweet potatoes, mango and onion in a single layer in 2 foil-lined 15x10x1-in. baking pans. Spritz with cooking spray; sprinkle with chili powder, salt and pepper. Bake, turning vegetables at least twice, until tender, 35-40 minutes; cool. Transfer to a large serving bowl.
**2.** Combine the Miracle Whip, yogurt, pineapple juice concentrate and serrano peppers. Fold into the potato mixture. Refrigerate, covered, at least 1 hour. Serve cold. If desired, sprinkle with sliced serrano pepper.
**Note:** Wear disposable gloves when cutting hot peppers; the oils can burn skin. Avoid touching your face.
**¾ cup:** 240 cal., 5g fat (1g sat. fat), 3mg chol., 317mg sod., 46g carb. (17g sugars, 7g fiber), 4g pro.

**TROPICAL SWEET POTATO SALAD**

NECTARINE CHICKEN SALAD

## HONEY-MELON SALAD WITH BASIL

*Put the taste of summer in your salad! Loaded with juicy cantaloupe and honeydew and glazed with a sweet honey dressing, this will be gone in minutes. Watermelon is a great addition, too.*
—Khurshid Shaik, Omaha, NE

**Takes:** 20 min. • **Makes:** 12 servings

- 6 **cups cubed cantaloupe (about 1 medium)**
- 6 **cups cubed honeydew melon (about 1 medium)**
- ¼ **cup honey**
- 3 **Tbsp. lemon juice**
- ½ **tsp. paprika**
- ¼ **tsp. salt**
- ¼ **tsp. coarsely ground pepper**
- ¼ **cup minced fresh basil or mint Dried cranberries, optional**

**1.** In a large bowl, combine cantaloupe and honeydew. Refrigerate, covered, until serving.
**2.** Whisk honey, lemon juice, paprika, salt and pepper. Pour over melon cubes just before serving; toss to coat. Stir in basil and, if desired, dried cranberries. Serve with a slotted spoon.

**1 cup:** 68 cal., 0 fat (0 sat. fat), 0 chol., 72mg sod., 17g carb. (16g sugars, 1g fiber), 1g pro. **Diabetic exchanges:** 1 fruit.

## NECTARINE CHICKEN SALAD

*When guests are coming for lunch or dinner in the warm summer months, I like to serve this attractive, colorful salad. The dressing is refreshingly tart. A neighbor shared the recipe years ago, and I've passed it on many times.*
—Cathy Ross, Van Nuys, CA

**Takes:** 15 min. • **Makes:** 4 servings

- ¼ **cup lime juice**
- 1 **Tbsp. sugar**
- 1 **Tbsp. minced fresh thyme or 1 tsp. dried thyme**
- 1 **Tbsp. olive oil**
- 1 **garlic clove, minced**
- 6 **cups torn mixed salad greens**
- 1 **lb. boneless skinless chicken breasts, cooked and sliced**
- 5 **medium ripe nectarines, thinly sliced**

**1.** In a jar with a tight-fitting lid, combine the lime juice, sugar, thyme, oil and garlic; shake well.
**2.** On a serving platter, arrange salad greens, chicken and nectarines. Drizzle with dressing. Serve immediately.

**1½ cups:** 266 cal., 7g fat (1g sat. fat), 63mg chol., 76mg sod., 27g carb. (21g sugars, 5g fiber), 26g pro. **Diabetic exchanges:** 3 lean meat, 1½ starch, 1 vegetable, 1 fat.

HONEY MUSTARD
RED POTATO SALAD

## HONEY MUSTARD
## RED POTATO SALAD

*This summer cookout star is crunchy-delicious with a brilliant zesty dressing.*
—Brittany Allyn, Mesa, AZ

**Prep:** 20 min. • **Cook:** 20 min.
**Makes:** 16 servings

3   **lbs. baby red potatoes, unpeeled**
½   **tsp. sea salt**
2   **green onions**
1   **cup finely diced celery**
½   **cup diced red onion**
1   **medium carrot, grated**

DRESSING
¼   **cup red wine vinegar**
2   **Tbsp. honey**
2   **Tbsp. Dijon mustard**
2   **tsp. minced fresh thyme**
1   **tsp. sea salt**
½   **tsp. coarsely ground pepper**
½   **cup extra virgin olive oil**

**1.** Place potatoes and ½ tsp. salt in a Dutch oven; add water to cover. Bring to a boil. Reduce heat; cook, uncovered, until potatoes are tender, 10-12 minutes. Drain and cool.

**2.** Mince white portions of the green onions; slice green portions and reserve. Combine minced onions with celery, red onion and carrot. For the dressing, whisk together vinegar, honey, mustard, thyme, sea salt and coarsely ground pepper. Gradually whisk in oil until blended.

**3.** Cut cooled potatoes into 1-in. pieces, preserving as much peel as possible. Combine potatoes with onion mixture. Drizzle dressing over salad; toss to coat. Top with reserved green onion slices.

**¾ cup:** 138 cal., 7g fat (1g sat. fat), 0 chol., 233mg sod., 19g carb. (3g sugars, 2g fiber), 2g pro. **Diabetic exchanges:** 1½ starch, 1½ fat.

## KALE & BACON SALAD WITH HONEY-HORSERADISH VINAIGRETTE

*Totally scrumptious and packed with nutrition, this salad was my response to friends who asked how they could incorporate kale into their diets without sacrificing taste. It is also wonderful made with collard or mustard greens, prepared in the same fashion as the kale, or with a mix of spinach and arugula or watercress.*
—Elizabeth Warren, Oklahoma City, OK.

Prep: 35 min. • Makes: 8 servings

- 10 kale leaves, stems removed, thinly sliced
- ¼ cup loosely packed basil leaves, thinly sliced
- ½ cup alfalfa sprouts
- 4 bacon strips, cooked and crumbled
- ½ cup crumbled feta cheese
- ½ medium ripe avocado, peeled and thinly sliced
- 1 hard-boiled large egg, chopped
- 1 cup grape tomatoes, chopped

VINAIGRETTE
- ⅓ cup olive oil
- 3 Tbsp. lemon juice
- 2 Tbsp. prepared horseradish
- 2 Tbsp. honey
- 1½ tsp. garlic powder
- 1½ tsp. spicy brown mustard
- ¼ tsp. crushed red pepper flakes
- ⅛ tsp. pepper
  Dash salt

1. Arrange kale and basil on a serving platter. Top with sprouts, bacon, cheese, avocado, egg and tomatoes.
2. In a small bowl, whisk the vinaigrette ingredients. Drizzle over the salad; serve immediately.

**1 serving:** 236 cal., 15g fat (3g sat. fat), 34mg chol., 248mg sod., 21g carb. (6g sugars, 4g fiber), 8g pro.

## COOL BEANS SALAD
(PICTURED ON P. 77)

*This protein-rich dish is a light meatless entree. The basmati rice adds a unique flavor and the vinaigrette dressing gives it a bit of a tang.*
—Janelle Lee, Appleton, WI

Takes: 20 min. • Makes: 6 servings

- ⅓ cup olive oil
- ¼ cup red wine vinegar
- 1 Tbsp. sugar
- 1 garlic clove, minced
- 1 tsp. salt
- 1 tsp. ground cumin
- 1 tsp. chili powder
- ¼ tsp. pepper
- 3 cups cooked basmati rice
- 1 can (16 oz.) kidney beans, rinsed and drained
- 1 can (15 oz.) black beans, rinsed and drained
- 1½ cups frozen corn, thawed
- 4 green onions, sliced
- 1 small sweet red pepper, chopped
- ¼ cup minced fresh cilantro

In a large bowl, whisk first 8 ingredients. Add the remaining ingredients; toss to coat. Chill until serving.

**1⅓ cups:** 440 cal., 19g fat (3g sat. fat), 0 chol., 659mg sod., 58g carb. (5g sugars, 8g fiber), 12g pro.

**DID YOU KNOW?**

Basmati rice is grown in the foothills of the Himalayas in India and Pakistan. The cooked rice has an irresistible popcorn aroma, nutty taste, and a fluffy, fine-grained texture. We have American versions grown in California, as well as Texmati®, a hybrid of basmati and long-grain rice grown in Texas. These U.S. versions are more affordable than true basmati rice.

KALE & BACON SALAD WITH HONEY-HORSERADISH VINAIGRETTE

**FARMHOUSE APPLE COLESLAW**

*My family loves pasta salads, but usually they have too much mayonnaise or oily dressing for my liking. Using hummus gives this dish a great taste and texture, while also improving its nutritional profile. Adding chicken (store-bought rotisserie chicken works well here), makes this pasta salad a complete meal.*
—Jenny Lynch, Rock Island, IL

**Takes:** 25 min. • **Makes:** 6 servings

- 8   oz. uncooked whole wheat rotini
- ½   cup hummus
- 3   Tbsp. Italian salad dressing
- ¼   tsp. salt
- ⅛   tsp. pepper
- 4   cups fresh baby spinach
- 1   cup cubed cooked chicken breast
- 2   cups cherry tomatoes, halved
- 1   can (2¼ oz.) sliced ripe olives, drained
- ¼   cup crumbled feta cheese

**1.** Cook pasta according to the package directions for al dente. Drain and rinse with cold water.

**2.** Combine hummus, salad dressing, salt and pepper in a large bowl. Add pasta; toss to coat. Stir in spinach, chicken, tomatoes and olives. Sprinkle with feta. Serve immediately.

**1½ cups:** 263 cal., 6g fat (1g sat. fat), 20mg chol., 405mg sod., 35g carb. (3g sugars, 7g fiber), 16g pro. **Diabetic exchanges:** 2 starch, 1 lean meat, 1 fat.

**TEST KITCHEN TIP**

It's OK to chill the salad before serving, but the pasta will absorb some of the dressing. If needed, add more right before serving.

## FARMHOUSE APPLE COLESLAW

*A friend from church gave me this apple coleslaw recipe that her grandmother handed down to her. The flavors complement each other well, and the fruit creates a refreshing change of pace from the usual coleslaw.*
—Jan Myers, Atlantic, IA

**Prep:** 20 min. + chilling
**Makes:** 12 servings

- 4   cups shredded cabbage
- 1   large apple, chopped
- ¾   cup raisins
- ½   cup chopped celery
- ¼   cup chopped onion
- ¼   cup mayonnaise
- 2   Tbsp. lemon juice
- 1   Tbsp. sugar
- 1   Tbsp. olive oil
- ½   tsp. salt
- ⅛   tsp. pepper

In a serving bowl, combine the cabbage, apple, raisins, celery and onion. In a small bowl, combine the remaining ingredients. Pour over cabbage mixture and toss to coat. Cover and refrigerate for at least 30 minutes.

**⅔ cup:** 87 cal., 5g fat (1g sat. fat), 0 chol., 131mg sod., 12g carb. (8g sugars, 1g fiber), 1g pro. **Diabetic exchanges:** 1 vegetable, 1 fat, ½ starch.

## APRICOTS WITH HERBED GOAT CHEESE

*After ending up with bunches of apricots one summer, I created this quick and simple dish. My friends were blown away by its fresh taste and uniqueness.*
—Wendy Weidner, Ham Lake, MN

**Takes:** 20 min. • **Makes:** 4 servings

- 3 oz. fresh goat cheese
- 2 tsp. minced fresh basil
- 2 tsp. minced fresh chives
- 2 tsp. 2% milk
- 4 fresh apricots, sliced
- ⅛ tsp. salt
  Dash pepper
- 2 Tbsp. balsamic glaze

Place the goat cheese, minced basil and chives, and milk in a mini food processor; process until smooth. Arrange apricot slices on a serving platter. Drop goat cheese mixture by teaspoonfuls over top. Sprinkle with salt and pepper; drizzle with balsamic glaze. Garnish with additional basil leaves. Serve immediately.

**1 serving:** 71 cal., 3g fat (2g sat. fat), 14mg chol., 163mg sod., 9g carb. (6g sugars, 1g fiber), 3g pro. **Diabetic exchanges:** ½ fruit, ½ fat.

HONEYDEW & PROSCIUTTO SALAD

## HONEYDEW & PROSCIUTTO SALAD

*For parties, I turn melon and prosciutto into an easy salad with a honey mustard dressing. To add zip, stir in fresh basil and mint.*
—Julie Merriman, Seattle, WA

**Takes:** 30 min. • **Makes:** 12 servings

- ⅓ cup olive oil
- ½ tsp. grated lime zest
- 2 Tbsp. lime juice
- 2 Tbsp. white wine vinegar
- 2 Tbsp. honey
- 1 tsp. Dijon mustard
- ¼ tsp. salt
- ¾ cup fresh cilantro leaves

SALAD

- 8 cups fresh arugula or baby spinach (about 5 oz.)
- ½ medium red onion, thinly sliced
- ¼ cup thinly sliced fresh mint leaves
- ¼ cup thinly sliced fresh basil leaves
- 8 cups diced honeydew melon
- 1 pkg. (8 oz.) fresh mozzarella cheese pearls
- ¼ lb. thinly sliced prosciutto, cut into wide strips

Place the first 8 ingredients in a blender; cover and process until smooth. Place arugula, onion and herbs in a large bowl. Drizzle with ⅓ cup vinaigrette and toss lightly to coat. In large serving bowl layer with a quarter of the arugula mixture, honeydew, mozzarella cheese pearls and prosciutto. Repeat layers 3 times. Serve with remaining vinaigrette.

**1 serving:** 186 cal., 12g fat (4g sat. fat), 23mg chol., 294mg sod., 15g carb. (13g sugars, 1g fiber), 7g pro. **Diabetic exchanges:** 1 fruit, 1 vegetable, 1 medium-fat meat, 1 fat.

## COUSCOUS TABBOULEH WITH FRESH MINT & FETA

*Using couscous instead of bulgur for tabbouleh really speeds up the process of making this colorful salad. Other quick-cooking grains such as barley or quinoa work well, too.*
—Elodie Rosinovsky, Brighton, MA

**Takes:** 20 min. • **Makes:** 3 servings

- ¾ cup water
- ½ cup uncooked couscous
- 1 can (15 oz.) garbanzo beans or chickpeas, rinsed and drained
- 1 large tomato, chopped
- ½ English cucumber, halved and thinly sliced
- 3 Tbsp. lemon juice
- 2 tsp. grated lemon zest
- 2 tsp. olive oil
- 2 tsp. minced fresh mint
- 2 tsp. minced fresh parsley
- ¼ tsp. salt
- ⅛ tsp. pepper
- ¾ cup crumbled feta cheese
  Lemon wedges, optional

**1.** In a small saucepan, bring water to a boil. Stir in couscous. Remove from the heat; cover and let stand for 5-8 minutes or until water is absorbed. Fluff with a fork.
**2.** In a large bowl, combine the beans, tomato and cucumber. In a small bowl, whisk the lemon juice, lemon zest, oil and seasonings. Drizzle over bean mixture. Add couscous; toss to combine. Serve immediately or refrigerate until chilled. Sprinkle with cheese. If desired, serve with lemon wedges.

**1⅔ cups:** 362 cal., 11g fat (3g sat. fat), 15mg chol., 657mg sod., 52g carb. (7g sugars, 9g fiber), 15g pro.
**\* HEALTH TIP \*** Make this refreshing main dish salad gluten-free by replacing the couscous with about 1½ cups of cooked quinoa.

## BLACK-EYED PEA TOMATO SALAD

(PICTURED ON P. 76)

*Spending time in the kitchen with my late aunt was so much fun because she was an amazing cook and teacher. This black-eyed pea salad was one of her specialties. It's easy to make and is a nice alternative to pasta or potato salad. Add some cooked cubed chicken breast to make it a meal on its own.*
—Patricia Ness, La Mesa, CA

**Prep:** 20 min. + chilling
**Makes:** 12 servings

- 4 cans (15½ oz. each) black-eyed peas, rinsed and drained
- 3 large tomatoes, chopped
- 1 large sweet red pepper, chopped
- 1 cup diced red onion
- 4 bacon strips, cooked and crumbled
- 1 jalapeno pepper, seeded and diced
- ½ cup canola oil
- ¼ cup sugar
- ¼ cup rice vinegar
- 2 Tbsp. minced fresh parsley
- 1½ tsp. salt
- ½ tsp. pepper
- ⅛ tsp. garlic powder

**1.** Combine the first 6 ingredients. In another bowl, whisk together remaining ingredients. Add to bean mixture; toss to coat. Refrigerate, covered, at least 6 hours or overnight.
**2.** Stir just before serving.
**Note:** Wear disposable gloves when cutting hot peppers; the oils can burn skin. Avoid touching your face.
**¾ cup:** 242 cal., 11g fat (1g sat. fat), 3mg chol., 602mg sod., 29g carb. (9g sugars, 5g fiber), 9g pro. **Diabetic exchanges:** 2 starch, 2 fat.

**COUSCOUS TABBOULEH WITH FRESH MINT & FETA**

## SESAME-GINGER CUCUMBER SALAD

*I love the marinated sides and salads that come with meals at Japanese restaurants, and wanted to try some at home. After some research, I came up with this cool and crisp salad with a little Asian zing. We love it with meat hot off the grill!*
—Kimberly Ludvuck, Newburgh, NY

**Takes:** 15 min. • **Makes:** 6 servings

- 2 Tbsp. rice vinegar
- 4 tsp. soy sauce
- 1 Tbsp. olive oil
- 2 tsp. minced fresh gingerroot
- 2 tsp. sesame oil
- 1 tsp. honey
- ¼ tsp. Sriracha chili sauce
- 2 English cucumbers
- 1 tsp. sesame seeds, toasted
  Thinly sliced green onions

**1.** For dressing, mix first 7 ingredients. Trim ends and cut cucumbers crosswise into 3-in. sections. Cut the sections into julienne strips.

**2.** To serve, toss cucumbers with sesame seeds and dressing. Sprinkle with sliced green onions.

**¾ cup:** 64 cal., 4g fat (1g sat. fat), 0 chol., 293mg sod., 7g carb. (4g sugars, 1g fiber), 1g pro. **Diabetic exchanges:** 1 vegetable, 1 fat.

**POMEGRANATE SPLASH SALAD**

## POMEGRANATE SPLASH SALAD

*The sparkling pomegranate gems make this salad irresistibly beautiful. My family loves it at holiday gatherings when pomegranates are in season. Even the children can't get enough of this antioxidant-rich delight.*
—Emily Jamison, Champaign, IL

**Takes:** 15 min. • **Makes:** 8 servings

- 4 cups fresh baby spinach
- 4 cups spring mix salad greens
- ¾ cup crumbled feta cheese
- ¾ cup pomegranate seeds
- ¾ cup fresh or frozen raspberries
- ⅓ cup pine nuts, toasted

CRANBERRY VINAIGRETTE
- ½ cup thawed cranberry juice concentrate
- 3 Tbsp. olive oil
- 2 Tbsp. rice vinegar
  Dash salt

In a large bowl, combine the first 6 ingredients. In a small bowl, whisk vinaigrette ingredients. Serve with salad.

**1 cup with about 4½ tsp. vinaigrette:** 164 cal., 10g fat (2g sat. fat), 6mg chol., 140mg sod., 16g carb. (11g sugars, 2g fiber), 4g pro. **Diabetic exchanges:** 2 fat, 1 starch.

## SUMMER ORZO

*I'm always looking for fun ways to use the fresh veggies that come in my Community Supported Agriculture box, and this salad is one of my favorite creations. I like to improvise with whatever I have on hand, so feel free to do the same!*
—Shayna Marmar, Philadelphia, PA

**Prep:** 30 min. + chilling
**Makes:** 16 servings

1 pkg. (16 oz.) orzo pasta
¼ cup water
1½ cups fresh or frozen corn
24 cherry tomatoes, halved
2 cups crumbled feta cheese
1 medium cucumber, seeded and chopped
1 small red onion, finely chopped
¼ cup minced fresh mint
2 Tbsp. capers, drained and chopped, optional
½ cup olive oil
¼ cup lemon juice
1 Tbsp. grated lemon zest
1½ tsp. salt
1 tsp. pepper
1 cup sliced almonds, toasted

**1.** Cook orzo according to the package directions for al dente. Drain orzo; rinse with cold water and drain well. Transfer to a large bowl.

**2.** In a large nonstick skillet, heat water over medium heat. Add corn; cook and stir until crisp-tender, 3-4 minutes. Add to the orzo; stir in tomatoes, feta cheese, cucumber, onion, mint and, if desired, capers. In a small bowl, whisk oil, lemon juice, lemon zest, salt and pepper until blended. Pour over orzo mixture; toss to coat. Refrigerate 30 minutes.

**3.** Just before serving, stir in almonds.

**¾ cup:** 291 cal., 15g fat (4g sat. fat), 15mg chol., 501mg sod., 28g carb. (3g sugars, 3g fiber), 11g pro.

SUMMER ORZO

## GINGER-APRICOT TOSSED SALAD

(PICTURED ON P. 76)

*This dish is a nice change from ordinary green salad and is elegant enough for company. The dressing is one of my favorites. Its sweetness complements the crisp greens and crunchy green beans.*

—Trisha Kruse, Eagle, ID

- - - - - - - - - - - - - - - - - - - - - - - - - - - -

**Prep:** 25 min. • **Cook:** 10 min.
**Makes:** 6 servings (¾ cup salad dressing)

- 1   **can (16 oz.) apricot halves, drained**
- ¼   **cup rice vinegar**
- 1   **tsp. sugar**
- ½   **tsp. minced fresh gingerroot**
- 1   **garlic clove, minced**
- ¼   **tsp. salt**
- ¼   **tsp. pepper**
- 1½  **lbs. fresh green beans, trimmed and cut into 2-in. pieces**
- 5   **cups torn mixed salad greens**
- 1   **medium mango, peeled and cubed**
- 3   **Tbsp. coarsely chopped dry-roasted peanuts**

**1.** Process the first 7 ingredients in a blender until smooth. Fill a 6-qt. stockpot two-thirds full with water and bring to a boil. Add beans; cook, uncovered, until crisp-tender, 8-10 minutes.

**2.** Remove beans and immediately drop into ice water. Drain and pat dry. In a salad bowl, combine salad greens, mango and beans. Sprinkle with chopped peanuts. Serve with dressing.

**1½ cups:** 181 cal., 3g fat (0 sat. fat), 0 chol., 335mg sod., 40g carb. (30g sugars, 7g fiber), 5g pro.

## RADISH ASPARAGUS SALAD

*Lemon zest and mustard in the dressing add the perfect punch to crisp asparagus and spicy radishes in this fun spring salad. My family loves it!*

—Nancy Latulippe, Simcoe, ON

- - - - - - - - - - - - - - - - - - - - - - - - - - - -

**Takes:** 25 min. • **Makes:** 6 servings

- 1   **lb. fresh asparagus, trimmed and cut into 2-in. pieces**
- 7   **radishes, thinly sliced**
- 2   **Tbsp. sesame seeds**

DRESSING

- 2   **Tbsp. olive oil**
- 2   **Tbsp. thinly sliced green onion**
- 1   **Tbsp. white wine vinegar**
- 1   **Tbsp. lemon juice**
- 2   **tsp. honey**
- 1   **tsp. Dijon mustard**
- ¼   **tsp. garlic powder**
- ¼   **tsp. grated lemon zest**
- ¼   **tsp. pepper**

**1.** In a large saucepan, bring 6 cups water to a boil. Add asparagus; cover and boil for 3 minutes. Drain and immediately place asparagus in ice water. Drain and pat dry.

**2.** Transfer to a large bowl; add radishes and sesame seeds. Place the dressing ingredients in a jar with a tight-fitting lid; shake well. Pour over salad; toss to coat.

**⅔ cup:** 73 cal., 6g fat (1g sat. fat), 0 chol., 28mg sod., 5g carb. (3g sugars, 1g fiber), 2g pro. **Diabetic exchanges:** 1 vegetable, 1 fat.

**RADISH ASPARAGUS SALAD**

**WILTED SPINACH SALAD WITH BUTTERNUT SQUASH**

## SESAME, SUNFLOWER & CARROT SALAD

*This is such a beautiful salad to serve because of the ingredients' harmonizing colors. And it's super-healthy to eat. This versatile side salad goes with just about every main dish!*
—Jessica Gerschitz, Jericho, NY

**Prep:** 20 min. + chilling • **Makes:** 8 servings

- 6 medium carrots
- ½ cup sesame seeds, toasted
- ½ cup sunflower kernels, toasted
- ½ cup sliced almonds, toasted
- ½ cup golden raisins

**DRESSING**
- ¼ cup reduced-fat mayonnaise
- ¼ cup lemon juice
- ¼ cup olive oil
- 2 Tbsp. honey mustard
- ½ tsp. salt

Shred the carrots with a hand grater or in a food processor fitted with grating attachment. Place carrots in a large bowl with next 4 ingredients. In a small bowl, whisk dressing ingredients until blended. Pour dressing over the carrot mixture; toss to coat. Cover and refrigerate for at least 1 hour before serving.

**½ cup:** 283 cal., 21g fat (3g sat. fat), 3mg chol., 335mg sod., 22g carb. (11g sugars, 5g fiber), 6g pro.

## WILTED SPINACH SALAD WITH BUTTERNUT SQUASH

*This warm winter salad is packed with good-for-you spinach, squash and almonds. It feels so festive served at the holidays.*
—Margee Berry, White Salmon, WA

**Prep:** 20 min. • **Cook:** 25 min.
**Makes:** 4 servings

- 1 cup cubed peeled butternut squash
- ½ tsp. chili powder
- ½ tsp. salt, divided
- 4 tsp. olive oil, divided
- ⅓ cup balsamic vinegar
- 2 Tbsp. dry red wine or chicken broth
- 2 Tbsp. whole-berry cranberry sauce
- 5 cups fresh baby spinach
- 4 slices red onion
- ½ cup dried cranberries
- ⅓ cup slivered almonds, toasted
- ⅓ cup crumbled goat cheese
  Coarsely ground pepper, optional

**1.** In a small skillet, saute the squash, chili powder and ¼ tsp. salt in 2 tsp. oil until tender, 11-13 minutes. Set aside and keep warm.

**2.** In a small saucepan, bring the balsamic vinegar to a boil. Reduce heat; simmer for 4-6 minutes or until reduced to ¼ cup. Stir in the wine, cranberry sauce, and the remaining oil and salt. Bring to a boil; cook 1 minute longer.

**3.** Place spinach on a serving platter; top with the onion, cranberries and squash mixture. Drizzle with warm dressing. Sprinkle with almonds, goat cheese and, if desired, pepper. Serve immediately.

**1 serving:** 228 cal., 12g fat (3g sat. fat), 12mg chol., 382mg sod., 28g carb. (17g sugars, 4g fiber), 5g pro. **Diabetic exchanges:** 2 fat, 1½ starch, 1 vegetable.

**SPICY PORK TENDERLOIN SALAD**

## SPICY PORK TENDERLOIN SALAD

*A friend served this flavorful salad at a luncheon, and I adjusted it to fit our tastes. Since it's a meal in one, it's perfect for weeknights. And the pretty presentation makes it ideal for entertaining.*
—Pat Sellon, Monticello, WI

**Prep:** 30 min. • **Bake:** 25 min.
**Makes:** 4 servings

- ½ tsp. salt
- ½ tsp. ground cumin
- ½ tsp. ground cinnamon
- ½ tsp. chili powder
- ¼ tsp. pepper
- 1 pork tenderloin (1 lb.)
- 2 tsp. olive oil
- ⅓ cup packed brown sugar
- 6 garlic cloves, minced
- 1½ tsp. hot pepper sauce

SALAD
- 4½ tsp. lime juice
- 1½ tsp. orange juice
- 1½ tsp. Dijon mustard
- ½ tsp. curry powder
- ¼ tsp. salt
- ⅛ tsp. pepper
- 2 Tbsp. olive oil
- 1 pkg. (6 oz.) fresh baby spinach

1. Combine the salt, cumin, cinnamon, chili powder and pepper; rub over pork.
2. In a cast-iron or other ovenproof skillet, brown the pork on all sides in oil, about 8 minutes. Combine the brown sugar, garlic and hot pepper sauce; spread over the pork.
3. Bake at 350° for 25-35 minutes or until a thermometer inserted in the pork reads 145°. Let stand 5 minutes before slicing.
4. For the vinaigrette, in a large bowl, combine juices, mustard, salt and pepper; gradually whisk in oil. Toss vinaigrette with spinach. Place spinach on serving platter; top with sliced pork. If desired, drizzle with pan juices.

**1 serving:** 306 cal., 13g fat (3g sat. fat), 64mg chol., 594mg sod., 22g carb. (18g sugars, 2g fiber), 24g pro. **Diabetic exchanges:** 3 lean meat, 2 fat, 1 starch, 1 vegetable.

TANGY CILANTRO
LIME CONFETTI SALAD

## TANGY CILANTRO LIME CONFETTI SALAD

*I love standout salads that burst with flavor—the kind that make you feel as if you're splurging without having to eat that piece of chocolate cake. This is one of my very favorites, and everyone who tastes it enjoys it as well.*
—Jasey McBurnett, Rock Springs, WY

**Prep:** 25 min. + chilling • **Makes:** 6 servings

- 2 medium sweet orange peppers, chopped
- 2 medium ripe avocados, peeled and cubed
- 1 container (10½ oz.) cherry tomatoes, halved
- 1 cup fresh or frozen corn, thawed
- ½ medium red onion, finely chopped

DRESSING
- ¼ cup seasoned rice vinegar
- 3 Tbsp. lime juice
- 2 Tbsp. olive oil
- ½ cup fresh cilantro leaves
- 2 garlic cloves, halved
- 2 tsp. sugar
- ½ tsp. kosher salt
- ¼ tsp. pepper

Place the first 5 ingredients in a large bowl. Place dressing ingredients in a blender; cover and process until creamy and light in color. Pour over vegetable mixture; toss to coat. Refrigerate salad, covered, up to 3 hours.

**1 cup:** 187 cal., 12g fat (2g sat. fat), 0 chol., 526mg sod., 20g carb. (10g sugars, 5g fiber), 3g pro. **Diabetic exchanges:** 2 vegetable, 2 fat, ½ starch.

## BLACKBERRY BALSAMIC SPINACH SALAD

*This lightly dressed salad is packed with superfoods! When I have time, I make my vinaigrette from scratch.*
—Mary Lou Timpson, Colorado City, AZ

**Takes:** 15 min. • **Makes:** 6 servings

- 3 cups fresh baby spinach
- 2 cups fresh blackberries, halved
- 1½ cups cherry tomatoes, halved
- ⅓ cup crumbled feta cheese
- 2 green onions, thinly sliced
- ¼ cup chopped walnuts, toasted
- ⅓ cup balsamic vinaigrette

In a large bowl, combine the first 6 ingredients. Divide salad among 6 plates; drizzle with dressing.

**1 cup:** 106 cal., 7g fat (1g sat. fat), 3mg chol., 230mg sod., 9g carb. (4g sugars, 4g fiber), 3g pro. **Diabetic exchanges:** 1½ fat, ½ starch.
**\* HEALTH TIP \*** Blackberries are rich in anthocyanins, which give them their beautiful dark purple-black color. This phytonutrient is thought to help protect the brain from oxidative stress, Alzheimer's disease and dementia.

SPICY CAJUN POTATO SALAD

## SPICY CAJUN POTATO SALAD

*Here in the South we have quite a few get-togethers, and if you want your dish to be chosen over all of the rest, it has to have a kick! This potato salad with a hint of heat does the trick.*
—Amanda West, Shelbyville, TN

**Prep:** 20 min. • **Cook:** 10 min. + chilling
**Makes:** 20 servings

- 5 lbs. medium Yukon Gold potatoes, peeled and cut into ¾-in. cubes
- 1 large yellow onion
- ½ medium lemon
- ½ tsp. salt
- 8 hard-boiled large eggs, chopped
- 1½ cups mayonnaise with olive oil and coarsely ground pepper
- 1 cup dill pickle relish
- ¼ cup yellow mustard
- 1 to 2 Tbsp. Cajun seasoning
- ¼ cup minced fresh parsley
  Paprika

**1.** Place potatoes in a Dutch oven; add water to cover. Cut the onion in half crosswise; add half to saucepan. Bring to a boil. Add the lemon and salt to cooking water. Reduce heat; cook, uncovered, until the potatoes tender, 5-6 minutes.
**2.** Meanwhile, chop the remaining half onion. Combine with eggs, mayonnaise, dill pickle relish, yellow mustard and Cajun seasoning.
**3.** Drain potatoes; rinse under cold water. Discard onion and lemon. Add potatoes to the egg mixture; gently toss until well mixed (do not overmix, or potatoes will break down). Refrigerate, covered, for 1-2 hours. Just before serving, sprinkle the potato salad with minced parsley and paprika.

**¾ cup:** 229 cal., 10g fat (2g sat. fat), 81mg chol., 400mg sod., 31g carb. (3g sugars, 2g fiber), 5g pro.

**TEST KITCHEN TIP**

Adding lemon juice or vinegar to the water when boiling potatoes will help keep them on the firm side. This is a great tactic for potato salads, but not so much for mashed potatoes.

## CALIFORNIA CITRUS & AVOCADO SALAD

*The awesome flavors in this salad remind me of my childhood in southern California. My great-uncle had an orchard, so our family meals were filled with avocados, citrus fruits and nuts of all varieties.*
—Catherine Cassidy, Milwaukee, WI

**Takes:** 25 min.
**Makes:** 12 servings

- 10 cups torn Bibb or Boston lettuce
- 1½ cups orange sections (about 2 medium oranges)
- 1 cup ruby red grapefruit sections (about 1 medium grapefruit)
- 2 medium ripe avocados, peeled and cubed
- 3 Tbsp. ruby red grapefruit juice
- 3 Tbsp. extra virgin olive oil
- 2 tsp. honey
- ½ tsp. salt
- ¾ cup crumbled queso fresco or feta cheese
- ¼ cup pistachios, chopped

Place lettuce, oranges, grapefruit and avocados in a large bowl. In a small bowl, whisk grapefruit juice, oil, honey and salt until blended. Drizzle over salad and toss gently to coat. Sprinkle with cheese and pistachios. Serve immediately.

**1 cup:** 132 cal., 9g fat (2g sat. fat), 5mg chol., 134mg sod., 10g carb. (5g sugars, 3g fiber), 4g pro. **Diabetic exchanges:** 2 fat, 1 vegetable

## PEAS & PEPPER PASTA SALAD

*I often serve a pasta salad for a buffet. That way, there's no need for a side salad. Any leftover pasta salad is fantastic stuffed into halved and seeded plum tomatoes.*
—Ann R. Sheehy, Lawrence, MA

**Prep:** 20 min. • **Cook:** 10 min. + standing
**Makes:** 10 servings

- 1 pkg. (16 oz.) acini di pepe pasta
- 1½ cups coarsely chopped Cubanelle peppers or miniature sweet peppers
- 1 cup loosely packed fresh Italian parsley leaves
- 4 radishes, trimmed and quartered
- ½ medium red onion, coarsely chopped
- 2 green onions, cut into 1-in. pieces
- 1¾ cups frozen petite peas (about 8 oz.), thawed
- ½ cup creamy Caesar salad dressing
- ¾ tsp. salt
- ½ tsp. freshly ground pepper
  Thinly sliced radishes, optional

**1.** Cook pasta according to the package directions. Drain; rinse with cold water and drain well. Place peppers, parsley, radishes, red onion and green onions in a food processor; pulse until finely chopped, scraping the sides of food processor bowl as necessary.
**2.** In a large bowl, combine the pasta, chopped vegetables and peas. Add the dressing, salt and pepper; toss to coat. Let stand 15 minutes to allow flavors to blend. If desired, top with sliced radishes.
**¾ cup:** 255 cal., 8g fat (1g sat. fat), 5mg chol., 352mg sod., 39g carb. (4g sugars, 3g fiber), 8g pro.

CALIFORNIA CITRUS & AVOCADO SALAD

## SPINACH-ORZO SALAD WITH CHICKPEAS

**(PICTURED ON P. 77)**

*The first version of this salad was an experiment in mixing together some random ingredients I had on hand. It was a success, and several people at the party asked for the recipe—which meant I had to re-create it! It's healthy, delicious and perfect for warm-weather days.*

*—Glen White, Kissimmee, FL*

------------------------------------------

**Takes:** 25 min.
**Makes:** 12 servings

- 1   can (14½ oz.) reduced-sodium chicken broth
- 1½ cups uncooked whole wheat orzo pasta
- 4   cups fresh baby spinach
- 2   cups grape tomatoes, halved
- 2   cans (15 oz. each) chickpeas or garbanzo beans, rinsed and drained
- ¾   cup chopped fresh parsley
- 2   green onions, chopped

### DRESSING

- ¼   cup olive oil
- 3   Tbsp. lemon juice
- ¾   tsp. salt
- ¼   tsp. garlic powder
- ¼   tsp. hot pepper sauce
- ¼   tsp. pepper

**1.** In a large saucepan, bring broth to a boil. Stir in orzo; return to a boil. Reduce heat; simmer, covered, until al dente, 8-10 minutes.

**2.** In a large bowl, toss spinach and warm orzo, allowing spinach to wilt slightly. Add the tomatoes, chickpeas, parsley and green onions.

**3.** Whisk together dressing ingredients. Toss with salad.

**¾ cup:** 122 cal., 5g fat (1g sat. fat), 0 chol., 259mg sod., 16g carb. (1g sugars, 4g fiber), 4g pro. **Diabetic exchanges:** 1 starch, 1 fat.

## WATERMELON SHRIMP SALAD

*Sweet, spicy and easy to make, this salad travels well in a cooler to picnics and summer gatherings. I love the combination of flavors, the colorful presentation, and of course, I love to see the happy faces of my guests once they've tried it.*

*—Judy Batson, Tampa, FL*

------------------------------------------

**Prep:** 30 min. + chilling
**Makes:** 10 servings

- 1   seedless watermelon, cut into 1-in. cubes (about 10 cups)
- 1   medium honeydew melon, cut into 1-in. cubes (about 4 cups)
- 2   lbs. peeled and deveined cooked shrimp (31-40 per lb.)
- 2   cups green grapes, halved
- 1   large cucumber, seeded and chopped
- 1   small navel orange, peeled and sectioned
- 1   small red onion, chopped
- 1   jalapeno pepper, seeded and finely chopped
- ⅓   cup lemon juice
- 1   Tbsp. brown sugar
- ¼   tsp. crushed red pepper flakes

In a large bowl, combine the first 8 ingredients. Whisk together lemon juice, brown sugar and pepper flakes. Drizzle over shrimp mixture and toss to coat. Refrigerate at least 20 minutes before serving. Toss the salad gently before serving.

**Note:** Wear disposable gloves when cutting hot peppers; the oils can burn skin. Avoid touching your face.

**2 cups:** 309 cal., 2g fat (0 sat. fat), 138mg chol., 158mg sod., 56g carb. (50g sugars, 3g fiber), 21g pro.

**\* HEALTH TIP \*** Watermelon is a smart fruit to eat during the hot summer months because it's mainly made up of water, so it will help keep you hydrated. It also provides potassium and vitamins A and C.

**WATERMELON SHRIMP SALAD**

FESTIVE BEAN SALAD

## ZESTY STEAK SALAD

*Stir-fried steak and veggies give this hearty salad a cozy kick. Add any of your favorite salad ingredients like shredded cheese, croutons, mushrooms or cucumber.*
—Leah Carrell, Quitman, TX

**Takes:** 20 min. • **Makes:** 4 servings

- 1  lb. beef top sirloin steak, cut into strips
- ⅓  cup Worcestershire sauce
- 1  medium onion, julienned
- 1  medium green pepper, julienned
- 1  Tbsp. butter
- 6  cups shredded lettuce
- 6  to 9 cherry tomatoes, halved
   Salsa, optional

1. In a large bowl, combine sirloin and Worcestershire sauce; cover and refrigerate.
2. Meanwhile, in a large skillet, saute onion and green pepper in butter until crisp-tender, 3-4 minutes. Add sirloin; stir-fry until meat is no longer pink. Spoon meat and vegetables over lettuce; garnish with tomatoes. Serve with salsa if desired.
**1 serving:** 218 cal., 8g fat (4g sat. fat), 54mg chol., 314mg sod., 11g carb. (5g sugars, 2g fiber), 26g pro. **Diabetic exchanges:** 3 lean meat, 1 vegetable, ½ fat.

## FESTIVE BEAN SALAD

*I had experimented with all kinds of bean salads before I hit on this winner. My husband loves all the different varieties, and corn adds to the color and texture.*
— Dale Benoit, Monson, MA

**Prep:** 25 min. + chilling
**Makes:** 13 servings

- 2  cups fresh or frozen corn, thawed
- 1  can (16 oz.) kidney beans, rinsed and drained
- 1  can (16 oz.) red beans, rinsed and drained
- 1  can (15½ oz.) cannellini beans, rinsed and drained
- 1  can (15¼ oz.) lima beans, rinsed and drained
- 1  can (15 oz.) black beans, rinsed and drained
- 1  can (2¼ oz.) sliced ripe olives, drained
- 1  large green pepper, chopped
- 1  small onion, chopped
- ½  cup chili sauce
- ¼  cup olive oil
- ¼  cup red wine vinegar
- 2  garlic cloves, minced
- 2  tsp. dried oregano
- ½  tsp. pepper

1. In a large bowl, combine the first 9 ingredients. In a small bowl, whisk the chili sauce, oil, vinegar, garlic, oregano and pepper. Pour over the bean mixture; toss to coat.
2. Refrigerate salad for at least 1 hour before serving.
**¾ cup:** 199 cal., 5g fat (1g sat. fat), 0 chol., 486mg sod., 31g carb. (3g sugars, 8g fiber), 8g pro. **Diabetic exchanges:** 1½ starch, 1 lean meat, ½ fat.

SALADS

## JICAMA CITRUS SALAD

*Jicama is a crunchy Mexican vegetable I use in this easy salad with tangerines and shallots. The sweet and sour flavors, plus the crunchy texture, all add up to a yummy dish.*
—Crystal Jo Bruns, Iliff, CO

- - - - - - - - - - - - - - - - - - - - - - - - - -

**Takes:** 15 min. • **Makes:** 10 servings

- 8   tangerines, peeled, quartered and sliced
- 1   lb. medium jicama, peeled and cubed
- 2   shallots, thinly sliced
- 2   Tbsp. lemon or lime juice
- ¼   cup chopped fresh cilantro
- ½   tsp. salt
- ½   tsp. pepper

Combine all ingredients; refrigerate salad until serving.
**¾ cup:** 76 cal., 0 fat (0 sat. fat), 0 chol., 123mg sod., 19g carb. (11g sugars, 4g fiber), 1g pro.
**Diabetic exchanges:** 1 vegetable, ½ fruit.

## MEDITERRANEAN SPINACH & BEANS

*If you want to make this dish vegetarian, use soy sauce instead of Worcestershire. I like it warm or cold.*
—Becky Cuba, Spotsylvania, VA

- - - - - - - - - - - - - - - - - - - - - - - - - -

**Takes:** 30 min. • **Makes:** 4 servings

- 1   Tbsp. olive oil
- 1   small onion, chopped
- 2   garlic cloves, minced
- 1   can (14½ oz.) no-salt-added diced tomatoes, undrained
- 2   Tbsp. Worcestershire sauce
- ¼   tsp. salt
- ¼   tsp. pepper
- ⅛   tsp. crushed red pepper flakes
- 1   can (15 oz.) cannellini beans, rinsed and drained
- 1   can (14 oz.) water-packed artichoke hearts, rinsed, drained and quartered
- 6   oz. fresh baby spinach (about 8 cups)
     Additional olive oil, optional

**1.** In a 12-in. skillet, heat oil over medium-high heat; saute the onion until tender, 3-5 minutes. Add the garlic; cook and stir for 1 minute. Stir in the tomatoes, Worcestershire sauce and seasonings; bring to a boil. Reduce heat; simmer, uncovered, until the liquid is almost evaporated, 6-8 minutes.
**2.** Add beans, artichoke hearts and spinach; cook and stir until spinach is wilted, 3-5 minutes. If desired, drizzle with additional oil.
**1½ cups:** 187 cal., 4g fat (1g sat. fat), 0 chol., 650mg sod., 30g carb. (4g sugars, 6g fiber), 8g pro. **Diabetic exchanges:** 2 vegetable, 1 starch, 1 lean meat, 1 fat.

## CABBAGE & RUTABAGA SLAW

*My favorite crunchy slaw is a perfect way to use cool-weather veggies. We love it as a side with any spicy main dish.*
—Ann R. Sheehy, Lawrence, MA

**Prep:** 10 min. + chilling • **Makes:** 4 servings

- 2 cups diced peeled rutabaga
- 2 cups finely chopped cabbage
- ½ cup finely chopped red onion
- ¼ cup minced fresh Italian parsley
- ½ cup reduced-fat apple cider vinaigrette

Toss together all ingredients. Refrigerate, covered, to allow flavors to blend, about 3 hours.

**1 cup:** 126 cal., 6g fat (1g sat. fat), 0 chol., 144mg sod., 19g carb. (11g sugars, 3g fiber), 2g pro. **Diabetic exchanges:** 1 vegetable, 1 fat, ½ starch.

> **TEST KITCHEN TIP**
>
> Add a little sweetness to this salad with chopped apples or pears.

CABBAGE & RUTABAGA SLAW

## SHAVED FENNEL SALAD

(PICTURED ON P. 76)

*This salad tastes even more impressive than it looks. It's got an incredible crunch thanks to the cucumbers, radishes and apples, and the finish of fennel fronds adds just the faintest hint of licorice flavor.*
—William Milton III, Clemson, SC

**Takes:** 15 min. • **Makes:** 8 servings

- 1 large fennel bulb, fronds reserved
- 1 English cucumber
- 1 medium Honeycrisp apple
- 2 Tbsp. extra virgin olive oil
- ½ tsp. kosher salt
- ¼ tsp. coarsely ground pepper
- 2 radishes, thinly sliced

With a mandoline or vegetable peeler, cut the fennel, cucumber and apple into very thin slices. Transfer to a large bowl; toss with olive oil, salt and pepper. Top with the radishes and reserved fennel fronds to serve.

**¾ cup:** 55 cal., 4g fat (1g sat. fat), 0 chol., 138mg sod., 6g carb. (4g sugars, 2g fiber), 1g pro. **Diabetic exchanges:** 1 vegetable, 1 fat.

## SHREDDED KALE & BRUSSELS SPROUTS SALAD

*Here is a simple and delicious way to eat your superfoods! It gets even better in the fridge, so I make it ahead. I use my homemade honey mustard dressing, but any type works just fine.*
—Alexandra Weisser, New York, NY

**Takes:** 15 min. • **Makes:** 6 servings

- 1 small bunch kale (about 8 oz.), stemmed and thinly sliced (about 6 cups)
- ½ lb. fresh Brussels sprouts, thinly sliced (about 3 cups)
- ½ cup pistachios, coarsely chopped
- ½ cup honey mustard salad dressing
- ¼ cup shredded Parmesan cheese

Toss together all ingredients.

**1 cup:** 207 cal., 14g fat (2g sat. fat), 8mg chol., 235mg sod., 16g carb. (5g sugars, 4g fiber), 7g pro. **Diabetic exchanges:** 3 fat, 2 vegetable, ½ starch.

# SIDES

"I roast veggies to bring out their natural sweetness, and it works wonders with onions and cabbage. The piquant vinegar-mustard sauce makes this dish similar to a slaw."
—Ann R. Sheehy, Lawrence, MA

**Whole Wheat Refrigerator Rolls** (p. 103) **Asparagus, Squash & Red Pepper Saute** (p. 121) **Cumin Rice with Avocado** (p. 119) **Two-Tone Baked Potatoes** (p. 111) **Roasted Cabbage & Onions** (p. 100) **Veggie-Stuffed Tomatoes** (p. 114)

## ROASTED CABBAGE & ONIONS

(PICTURED ON P. 99)

*I roast veggies to bring out their natural sweetness, and it works wonders with onions and cabbage. The piquant vinegar-mustard sauce makes this dish similar to a slaw.*
—Ann R. Sheehy, Lawrence, MA

**Prep:** 10 min. • **Cook:** 30 min. + standing
**Makes:** 6 servings

- 1  medium head cabbage (about 2 lbs.), coarsely chopped
- 2  large onions, chopped
- ¼  cup olive oil
- ¾  tsp. salt
- ¾  tsp. pepper
- 3  Tbsp. minced fresh chives
- 3  Tbsp. minced fresh tarragon

DRESSING

- 2  Tbsp. white balsamic vinegar or white wine vinegar
- 2  Tbsp. olive oil
- 2  Tbsp. Dijon mustard
- 1  Tbsp. lemon juice
- ½  tsp. salt
- ½  tsp. pepper

**1.** Preheat oven to 450°. Place cabbage and onions in a large bowl. Drizzle with oil; sprinkle with salt and pepper and toss to coat. Transfer to a shallow roasting pan, spreading evenly. Roast until the vegetables are tender and lightly browned, 30-35 minutes, stirring halfway.
**2.** Transfer cabbage mixture to a large bowl. Add chives and tarragon; toss to combine. In a small bowl, whisk dressing ingredients until blended. Drizzle over cabbage mixture; toss to coat. Let stand 10 minutes to allow flavors to blend. Serve warm or at room temperature.
**¾ cup:** 183 cal., 14g fat (2g sat. fat), 0 chol., 636mg sod., 15g carb. (7g sugars, 4g fiber), 2g pro.

## CORN OKRA CREOLE

*This veggie-loaded side is a delicious representation of my region of the country, particularly the Texas-Louisiana border. The okra, corn and Creole seasonings are all cooking staples here.*
—Ruth Aubey, San Antonio, TX

**Takes:** 30 min. • **Makes:** 6 servings

- 1  cup chopped green pepper
- ½  cup chopped onion
- 3  Tbsp. canola oil
- 2  cups fresh or frozen corn or 1 can (15¼ oz.) whole-kernel corn
- 1½  cups fresh or frozen sliced okra
- 3  medium tomatoes, peeled and chopped (1½ cups)
- 1  Tbsp. tomato paste
- ¼  tsp. dried thyme
  Salt to taste
- ¼  tsp. coarsely ground pepper
- ½  tsp. hot pepper sauce, optional

**1.** In a large skillet, saute green pepper and onion in oil until tender. Add the corn and okra; cook over medium heat for 10 minutes, stirring occasionally.
**2.** Stir in the tomatoes, tomato paste, thyme, salt, pepper and, if desired, pepper sauce. Cover and simmer for 3-5 minutes, stirring occasionally.
**⅔ cup:** 147 cal., 8g fat (1g sat. fat), 0 chol., 19mg sod., 20g carb. (8g sugars, 4g fiber), 4g pro. **Diabetic exchanges:** 1½ fat, 1 starch.

> **TEST KITCHEN TIP**
>
> Dried thyme adds a lot of flavor but if you have fresh available, go ahead and use that. You'll want to use ¾ tsp. fresh thyme in place of the ¼ tsp. dried. And while you're at it, garnish with a few sprigs as well.

**CORN OKRA CREOLE**

**HONEY WHOLE WHEAT ROLLS**

## GREEN BEANS AMANDINE

*It's hard to improve on the taste Mother Nature gives to fresh green beans, but my mom has done just that for years using this simple recipe. The crunchy almonds are a super addition.*

—Brenda DuFresne, Midland, MI

- - - - - - - - - - - - - - - - - - - - - - - - - -

**Takes:** 20 min. • **Makes:** 4 servings

  - 1 lb. fresh or frozen green beans, cut into 2-in. pieces
  - ½ cup water
  - ¼ cup slivered almonds
  - 2 Tbsp. butter
  - 1 tsp. lemon juice
  - ¼ tsp. seasoned salt, optional

**1.** Place beans and water in a large skillet or saucepan and bring to a boil. Cover and cook for 10-15 minutes or until crisp-tender; drain and set aside.
**2.** In a large skillet, cook the almonds in butter over low heat. Stir in lemon juice and, if desired, seasoned salt. Add beans and heat through.

**¾ cup:** 125 cal., 9g fat (4g sat. fat), 15mg chol., 53mg sod., 10g carb. (3g sugars, 5g fiber), 4g pro. **Diabetic exchanges:** 2 fat, 1 vegetable.

## HONEY WHOLE WHEAT ROLLS

*There's nothing quite like a warm yeast roll fresh from the oven. I bake these rolls often, especially when I'm making soup or stew.*

—Celecia Stoup, Hobart, OK

- - - - - - - - - - - - - - - - - - - - - - - - - -

**Prep:** 20 min. + rising • **Bake:** 20 min.
**Makes:** 15 rolls

  - 2 pkg. (¼ oz. each) active dry yeast
  - 1 cup warm water (110° to 115°)
  - ¼ cup butter, melted
  - ¼ cup honey
  - 1 large egg, room temperature
  - ¾ cup whole wheat flour
  - ½ cup old-fashioned oats
  - 1 tsp. salt
  - 2½ to 3 cups all-purpose flour
    Additional melted butter, optional

**1.** In a small bowl, dissolve the yeast in warm water. In a large bowl, combine the melted butter, honey, egg, whole wheat flour, oats, salt, yeast mixture and 1 cup all-purpose flour; beat on medium speed until smooth. Stir in enough remaining flour to form a soft dough.
**2.** Turn dough onto a floured surface; knead 6-8 minutes or until smooth and elastic. Place in a greased bowl, turning once to grease the top. Cover and let rise in a warm place until doubled, about 1 hour.
**3.** Punch down the dough; shape into 15 balls. Place in a greased 13x9-in. pan. Cover with a kitchen towel; let rise in warm place until doubled, about 45 minutes. Preheat oven to 375°.
**4.** Bake until golden brown, about 20 minutes. If desired, brush with additional butter. Serve warm.

**1 roll:** 151 cal., 4g fat (2g sat. fat), 21mg chol., 188mg sod., 25g carb. (5g sugars, 2g fiber), 4g pro.

**BAKED BUTTERNUT SQUASH**

## BAKED BUTTERNUT SQUASH

*Make the most of fabulous fall produce and roast this scrumptious side. Lightly seasoned with cinnamon, nutmeg and brown sugar, this butternut squash could almost be dessert!*
—Heidi Vawdrey, Riverton, UT

**Prep:** 10 min. • **Bake:** 1 hour
**Makes:** 6 servings

- ¼ tsp. salt
- ⅛ tsp. ground cinnamon
- ⅛ tsp. ground nutmeg
- ⅛ tsp. pepper
- 1 small butternut squash (about 2 lbs.)
- 2 Tbsp. butter, melted
- 6 tsp. brown sugar, divided

**1.** Preheat oven to 350°. Mix seasoning ingredients. Halve squash lengthwise; remove and discard seeds. Place squash in an 11x7-in. baking dish coated with cooking spray. Brush with melted butter; sprinkle with seasonings.
**2.** Place 2 tsp. brown sugar in the cavity of each half. Sprinkle remaining brown sugar over cut surfaces.
**3.** Bake, covered, 40 minutes. Uncover; bake until the squash is tender, about 20 minutes.
**1 serving:** 120 cal., 4g fat (2g sat. fat), 10mg chol., 136mg sod., 22g carb. (9g sugars, 5g fiber), 2g pro. **Diabetic exchanges:** 1½ starch, ½ fat.

**TEST KITCHEN TIP**

Dark brown sugar contains more molasses than light or golden brown sugar. The types are generally interchangeable in recipes. But if you prefer a bolder flavor, choose dark brown sugar.

## EASY SOUTHWEST PINTO BEANS

*Want an alternative to refried beans? Try this side dish. Sometimes I top it off with a sprinkling of shredded cheese or a dollop of sour cream.*
—Lorna Nault, Chesterton, IN

**Takes:** 15 min. • **Makes:** 6 servings

- 1 small onion, chopped
- 2 tsp. minced fresh cilantro
- 1 Tbsp. canola oil
- 1 garlic clove, minced
- 2 cans (15 oz. each) pinto beans, rinsed and drained
- ⅔ cup salsa

In a large skillet or saucepan, saute onion and cilantro in oil until tender. Add garlic; cook 1 minute longer. Stir in the beans and salsa; heat through.
**½ cup:** 159 cal., 3g fat (0 sat. fat), 0 chol., 296mg sod., 26g carb. (4g sugars, 6g fiber), 7g pro. **Diabetic exchanges:** 2 starch, ½ fat.

## SOCCA

*Socca is a traditional flatbread from Nice, France. It's common to see it cooked on grills as street food, served chopped in a paper cone and sprinkled with salt, pepper or other delicious toppings. Bonus: It's gluten-free.*
—*Taste of Home* Test Kitchen

- - - - - - - - - - - - - - - - - - - - - -

**Prep:** 5 min. + standing • **Cook:** 5 minutes
**Makes:** 6 servings

1 cup chickpea flour
1 cup water
2 Tbsp. extra virgin olive oil, divided
¾ tsp. salt
  Optional toppings: Za'atar seasoning, sea salt flakes, coarsely ground pepper and additional extra virgin olive oil

**1.** In a small bowl, whisk chickpea flour, water, 1 Tbsp. oil and salt until smooth. Let stand 30 minutes.

**2.** Meanwhile, preheat broiler. Place a 10-in. cast-iron skillet in oven until hot, about 5 minutes. Add remaining 1 Tbsp. oil to the pan; swirl to coat. Pour batter into the hot pan and tilt to coat evenly.

**3.** Broil 6 in. from heat until edges are crisp and browned and center just begins to brown, 5-7 minutes. Cut into wedges. If desired, top with optional ingredients.

**1 wedge:** 113 cal., 6g fat (1g sat. fat), 0 chol., 298mg sod., 12g carb. (2g sugars, 3g fiber), 4g pro. **Diabetic exchanges:** 1 fat, ½ starch.

**To make chickpea flour:** Add dried chickpeas to food processor. Cover and process until powdery, 2-3 minutes. Sift through fine sieve into a bowl. Add larger pieces left in sieve to coffee or spice grinder; process until powdery.

**\* HEALTH TIP \*** This flatbread is not only gluten-free, but it's also egg-free and dairy-free, too. Serve it as a side or snack, or add your favorite toppings to make it a meal.

## WHOLE WHEAT REFRIGERATOR ROLLS

**(PICTURED ON P. 98)**

*I like to prepare the dough for these rolls in advance and let it rise in the refrigerator. The recipe is easy and versatile.*
—Sharon Mensing, Greenfield, IA

- - - - - - - - - - - - - - - - - - - - - -

**Prep:** 20 min. + rising • **Bake:** 10 min.
**Makes:** 2 dozen

2 pkg. (¼ oz. each) active dry yeast
2 cups warm water (110° to 115°)
½ cup sugar
1 large egg, room temperature
¼ cup canola oil
2 tsp. salt
4½ to 5 cups all-purpose flour
2 cups whole wheat flour

**1.** In a large bowl, dissolve yeast in warm water. Add the sugar, egg, oil, salt and 3 cups all-purpose flour. Beat on medium speed for 3 minutes. Stir in whole wheat flour and enough remaining all-purpose flour to make a soft dough.

**2.** Turn out onto a lightly floured surface. Knead 6-8 minutes or until smooth and elastic. Place in a greased bowl, turning once to grease top. Cover the dough and let rise until doubled or cover and refrigerate overnight.

**3.** Punch down the dough; divide into 24 portions. Divide and shape each portion into 3 balls. Place 3 balls in each greased muffin cup. Cover and let rise until doubled, about 1 hour for dough prepared the same day or 1-2 hours for refrigerated dough.

**4.** Bake at 375° until light golden brown, 10-12 minutes. Serve warm. If desired, dough may be kept up to 4 days in the refrigerator. Punch down daily.

**1 roll:** 159 cal., 3g fat (0 sat. fat), 9mg chol., 200mg sod., 29g carb. (5g sugars, 2g fiber), 4g pro.

SOCCA

**BROWN RICE WITH ALMONDS & CRANBERRIES**

## ROSEMARY WALNUT BREAD

*I received this recipe from a friend who was moving into a new apartment. To celebrate, she made this bread to share. Now I serve it at many of my family functions.*
—Robin Haas, Cranston, RI

**Prep:** 25 min. + rising • **Bake:** 20 min.
**Makes:** 1 loaf (9 slices)

1¼ tsp. active dry yeast
½ cup warm water (110° to 115°)
¼ cup whole wheat flour
1½ to 1¾ cups all-purpose flour
2 Tbsp. honey
1 Tbsp. olive oil
1½ tsp. dried rosemary, crushed
½ tsp. salt
⅓ cup finely chopped walnuts

**1.** In a small bowl, dissolve yeast in warm water. In a large bowl, mix whole wheat flour and ¼ cup all-purpose flour; stir in yeast mixture. Let stand, covered, 15 minutes. Add honey, oil, rosemary, salt and ¾ cup all-purpose flour; beat on medium speed until smooth. Stir in the walnuts and enough remaining all-purpose flour to form a soft dough.
**2.** Turn dough onto a floured surface; knead 6-8 minutes or until smooth and elastic. Place in a greased bowl, turning once to grease the top. Cover and let rise in a warm place until doubled, about 45 minutes.
**3.** Punch down dough. Turn onto a lightly floured surface; divide into thirds. Roll each into a 12-in. rope. Place ropes on a greased baking sheet and braid. Pinch ends to seal; tuck under. Cover with a kitchen towel; let rise in a warm place until almost doubled, about 30 minutes.
**4.** Preheat oven to 375°. Bake until golden brown, 20-25 minutes. Remove from pan to a wire rack to cool.
**1 slice:** 145 cal., 4g fat (0 sat. fat), 0 chol., 132mg sod., 23g carb. (4g sugars, 1g fiber), 4g pro. **Diabetic exchanges:** 1½ starch, ½ fat.

## BROWN RICE WITH ALMONDS & CRANBERRIES

*I'm always looking to switch things up during the holiday season. This easy rice dish is on the lighter side and uses ingredients I always have on hand.*
—Joan Hallford, North Richland Hills, TX

**Prep:** 35 min. • **Bake:** 1¼ hours
**Makes:** 10 servings

3 cans (14½ oz. each) beef broth
¼ cup butter, cubed
1 large onion, chopped
1 cup uncooked long grain brown rice
½ cup bulgur
½ cup slivered almonds
½ cup dried cranberries
¾ cup minced fresh parsley, divided
¼ cup chopped green onions
¼ tsp. salt
¼ tsp. pepper

**1.** Preheat oven to 375°. In a large saucepan, bring broth to a simmer; reduce heat to low and keep hot. In a large skillet, heat butter over medium heat. Add onion; cook and stir until tender, 3-4 minutes. Add rice, bulgur and almonds; cook and stir until rice is lightly browned and has a nutty aroma, 2-3 minutes.
**2.** Transfer to a greased 13x9-in. baking dish. Stir in cranberries, ½ cup parsley, green onions, salt and pepper. Stir in hot broth. Bake, covered, 45 minutes. Uncover and continue to cook until the liquid is absorbed and the rice is tender, 30-35 minutes longer. Remove from oven and fluff with a fork. Cover; let stand for 5-10 minutes. Sprinkle with remaining parsley before serving.
**¾ cup:** 207 cal., 8g fat (3g sat. fat), 12mg chol., 658mg sod., 29g carb. (7g sugars, 4g fiber), 5g pro. **Diabetic exchanges:** 2 starch, 1½ fat.
**\* HEALTH TIP \*** Brown rice is considered a whole grain because it contains the bran, germ and endosperm of the grain; white rice just contains the endosperm. Brown rice is a smart choice because it's higher in fiber, magnesium and other nutrients than white rice.

ROSEMARY WALNUT BREAD

## SWEET CARROTS

*Here's a flavorful way to dress up carrots without a lot of fuss. Simply steam the good-for-you veggies, then season with some butter, brown sugar, vinegar and a sprinkling of chives. The carrots are not only colorful, but they're tasty, too.*
—Taste of Home Test Kitchen

- - - - - - - - - - - - - - - - - - - - - - - - - -

**Takes:** 15 min. • **Makes:** 2 servings

- 1½ cups baby carrots
- 2 tsp. brown sugar
- 1 tsp. butter
- 1 tsp. white wine vinegar
- ⅛ tsp. salt
- 2 tsp. minced chives

Place carrots in a steamer basket. Place in a saucepan over 1 in. of water; bring to a boil. Cover and steam until tender, 5-8 minutes. Transfer carrots to a large bowl. Add brown sugar, butter, vinegar and salt; toss until butter is melted and carrots are coated. Sprinkle with chives.

**¾ cup:** 72 cal., 2g fat (1g sat. fat), 5mg chol., 247mg sod., 13g carb. (10g sugars, 2g fiber), 1g pro. **Diabetic exchanges:** 1 vegetable, ½ starch, ½ fat.

SPAGHETTI SQUASH CASSEROLE BAKE

## SPAGHETTI SQUASH CASSEROLE BAKE

*One of our daughters passed this delightful recipe along with squash from her first garden.*
—Glenafa Vrchota, Mason City, IA

- - - - - - - - - - - - - - - - - - - - - - - - - -

**Prep:** 25 min. • **Bake:** 1 hour
**Makes:** 6 servings

- 1 medium spaghetti squash (about 8 in.)
- 1 Tbsp. butter
- ½ lb. sliced fresh mushrooms
- 1 large onion, chopped
- 2 garlic cloves, minced
- 1 tsp. dried basil
- ½ tsp. dried oregano
- ½ tsp. salt
- ¼ tsp. dried thyme
- ¼ tsp. pepper
- 2 medium tomatoes, chopped
- 1 cup dry bread crumbs
- 1 cup ricotta cheese
- ¼ cup minced fresh parsley
- ¼ cup grated Parmesan cheese

**1.** Cut the squash in half lengthwise and scoop out the seeds. Place squash, cut side down, in a baking dish. Add ½ in. water and cover tightly with foil. Bake at 375° until squash can be easily pierced with a fork, 20-30 minutes.

**2.** Meanwhile, melt butter in a large skillet. Add the mushrooms, onion, garlic, basil, oregano, salt, thyme and pepper; saute until onion is tender. Add the tomatoes; cook until most liquid has evaporated. Set aside.

**3.** Scoop out flesh of squash, separating strands with a fork. Combine the flesh, tomato mixture, bread crumbs, ricotta cheese and parsley.

**4.** Transfer to a greased 2-qt. baking dish. Sprinkle with Parmesan cheese. Bake, uncovered, at 375° until heated through and top is golden brown, about 40 minutes.

**¾ cup:** 263 cal., 9g fat (5g sat. fat), 24mg chol., 528mg sod., 37g carb. (6g sugars, 5g fiber), 12g pro.

## ROSEMARY POTATOES WITH CARAMELIZED ONIONS

*Roasted potatoes are always amazing. Add some rosemary and caramelized onions and they become over-the-top delicious!*

—Mary Jones, Athens, OH

**Prep:** 15 min. • **Bake:** 45 min.
**Makes:** 6 servings

- 2  lbs. small red potatoes, quartered
- 2  garlic cloves, minced
- 1  Tbsp. olive oil
- 2  tsp. minced fresh rosemary or ½ tsp. dried rosemary, crushed
- ½  tsp. minced fresh thyme or ⅛ tsp. dried thyme
- ¼  tsp. salt
- ¼  tsp. pepper

**CARAMELIZED ONIONS**

- 2  large sweet onions, chopped
- 2  Tbsp. olive oil
- 1  Tbsp. sugar
- 2  tsp. balsamic vinegar

**1.** In a large bowl, combine the first 7 ingredients; toss to coat. Transfer to a greased 15x10x1-in. baking pan.
**2.** Bake at 425° for 45-50 minutes or until potatoes are tender, stirring once.
**3.** Meanwhile, in a large skillet, saute onions in oil until softened. Stir in the sugar. Reduce heat to medium-low; cook for 30-40 minutes or until deep golden brown, stirring occasionally. Stir in vinegar.
**4.** Transfer roasted potatoes to a large bowl; stir in caramelized onions.

**¾ cup:** 215 cal., 7g fat (1g sat. fat), 0 chol., 117mg sod., 35g carb., 4g fiber, 4g pro.

**ROSEMARY POTATOES WITH CARAMELIZED ONIONS**

## WHIPPED VEGETABLE TRIO

*When you only have a few potatoes and want them mashed, fill in with parsnips and carrots. The first frost of the season turns their starch to sugar, giving parsnips a subtle, sweet taste. Cook potatoes, carrots and parsnips together for a twist on garden-variety whipped potatoes.*

—LeAnn Bird, West Jordan, UT

**Prep:** 20 min. • **Cook:** 20 min.
**Makes:** 6 servings

- 8  medium potatoes, peeled and cut into 1-in. cubes
- 4  medium parsnips, peeled and coarsely chopped
- 4  medium carrots, peeled and coarsely chopped
- 8  cups water
- 2  tsp. salt
- ½  tsp. pepper
   Optional: Minced fresh chives or parsley

**1.** Place the first 4 ingredients in a Dutch oven. Bring to a boil. Reduce heat; cover and simmer for 15-18 minutes or until vegetables are tender.
**2.** Drain, reserving ½ cup cooking liquid. Place vegetables in a large bowl; add the salt, pepper and reserved cooking liquid. Mash until creamy. Garnish with chives if desired.

**¾ cup:** 258 cal., 1g fat (0 sat. fat), 0 chol., 831mg sod., 61g carb. (10g sugars, 8g fiber), 5g pro.

**READER REVIEW**

*"A great alternative to mashed potatoes. I have substituted turnips for the carrots, and it was great. Add a bit of cream for more richness."*

**—JENNIFER K, TASTEOFHOME.COM**

## ITALIAN ARTICHOKE-GREEN BEAN CASSEROLE

*My mother and I made changes to a cookbook recipe to create this family-favorite casserole. We increased the amount of vegetables significantly, and it gets rave reviews at get-togethers. It's definitely not your average green bean casserole.*
—Denise Klibert, Shreveport, LA

**Prep:** 25 min. • **Bake:** 25 min.
**Makes:** 10 servings

- 6 cups cut fresh green beans (about 1½ lbs.)
- ⅓ cup olive oil
- 1 medium onion, chopped
- 2 garlic cloves, minced
- 3 cans (14 oz. each) water-packed artichoke hearts, drained and chopped
- ½ cup minced fresh parsley
  Pinch cayenne pepper
  Pinch pepper
- 1 cup seasoned bread crumbs
- 1 cup grated Parmesan cheese, divided

**1.** Preheat oven to 350°. In a large saucepan, bring 6 cups water to a boil. Add green beans; cook, uncovered, just until crisp-tender, 3-4 minutes. Drain and set aside.
**2.** In a 6-qt. stockpot, heat the oil over medium heat. Add onion; cook and stir until tender, 3-4 minutes. Add garlic; cook 1 minute longer. Add the beans, artichoke hearts, parsley, cayenne and pepper. Stir in bread crumbs and ¾ cup cheese.
**3.** Transfer to a greased 11x7-in. baking dish. Sprinkle with the remaining cheese. Bake until lightly browned, 25-30 minutes.
**¾ cup:** 207 cal., 10g fat (2g sat. fat), 7mg chol., 616mg sod., 22g carb. (3g sugars, 2g fiber), 8g pro. **Diabetic exchanges:** 2 fat, 1 starch, 1 vegetable.

## SEASONED OVEN FRIES

*For a speedy, health-conscious side dish, try these fun wedges. They're just as tasty as the deep-fried version, but without the mess.*
—Pat Fredericks, Oak Creek, WI

**Takes:** 25 min. • **Makes:** 2 servings

- 2 medium baking potatoes
- 2 tsp. butter, melted
- 2 tsp. canola oil
- ¼ tsp. seasoned salt
  Minced fresh parsley, optional

**1.** Cut each potato lengthwise in half; cut each piece into 4 wedges. In a large shallow dish, combine the butter, oil and seasoned salt. Add potatoes; turn to coat.
**2.** Place the potatoes in a single layer on a baking sheet coated with cooking spray. Bake at 450° until tender, turning once, 20-25 minutes. If desired, sprinkle with parsley.
**8 wedges:** 263 cal., 9g fat (3g sat. fat), 10mg chol., 242mg sod., 44g carb. (3g sugars, 4g fiber), 4g pro.

**SEASONED OVEN FRIES**

**CANTINA PINTO BEANS**

## ZESTY SUGAR SNAP PEAS

Lemon-pepper seasoning and garlic make these flavorful snap peas an ideal accompaniment to a variety of entrees. You'll come to rely on this recipe that uses just a few pantry ingredients.

—*Taste of Home* Test Kitchen

**Takes:** 15 min. • **Makes:** 4 servings

- 1 lb. fresh or frozen sugar snap peas
- ½ cup water
- 1 Tbsp. butter
- 1 garlic clove, minced
- ¾ tsp. lemon-pepper seasoning
- ¼ tsp. salt

In a skillet, bring peas and water to a boil. Reduce heat. Cover and cook until tender, 6-7 minutes. Drain. Add the remaining ingredients. Cook and stir until peas are well-coated, 2-3 minutes.

**¾ cup:** 74 cal., 3g fat (2g sat. fat), 8mg chol., 267mg sod., 8g carb. (4g sugars, 3g fiber), 4g pro. **Diabetic exchanges:** 1 vegetable, ½ fat.

## CANTINA PINTO BEANS

*Cumin, cilantro and red pepper flakes lend southwestern flair to this bean dish, which was inspired by one we had at a restaurant in Dallas. The chef added chunks of ham, but my version is meatless. It makes a great Tex-Mex side or a satisfying lunch when served with cornbread.*

—L.R. Larson, Sioux Falls, SD

**Prep:** 15 min. + standing • **Cook:** 1½ hours
**Makes:** 10 servings

- 2 cups dried pinto beans (about ¾ lb.)
- 2 cans (14½ oz. each) reduced-sodium chicken broth
- 2 celery ribs, diced
- ¼ cup diced onion
- ¼ cup diced green pepper
- 1 garlic clove, minced
- 2 bay leaves
- 1 tsp. ground cumin
- ½ tsp. rubbed sage
- ¼ tsp. crushed red pepper flakes
- 2 cans (14½ oz. each) Mexican diced tomatoes, undrained
- ½ tsp. salt
  Chopped fresh cilantro

**1.** Sort and rinse beans with cold water. Place beans in a Dutch oven; add water to cover by 2 in. Bring to a boil; boil for 2 minutes. Remove from heat; let stand, covered, 1 hour.
**2.** Drain and rinse beans, discarding liquid. Return beans to pan. Stir in broth, celery, onion, green pepper, garlic and seasonings; bring to a boil. Reduce heat; simmer, uncovered, until beans are very tender, about 1 hour.
**3.** Discard the bay leaves. Stir in the tomatoes and salt. Simmer, uncovered, until heated through, 25-30 minutes, stirring occasionally. Serve with cilantro.

**¾ cup:** 162 cal., 1g fat (0 sat. fat), 0 chol., 536mg sod., 29g carb. (4g sugars, 7g fiber), 10g pro. **Diabetic exchanges:** 2 starch.

## ROASTED CAULIFLOWER

*Roasting is a simple way to prepare cauliflower. Seasoned with a wonderful blend of herbs, this side is easy enough for weeknight dinners.*
—Leslie Palmer, Swampscott, MA

**Takes:** 30 min. • **Makes:** 4 servings

- 3 cups fresh cauliflowerets
- 2 Tbsp. lemon juice
- 4½ tsp. olive oil
- 1 garlic clove, minced
- 1 tsp. dried parsley flakes
- ½ tsp. dried thyme
- ½ tsp. dried tarragon
- ¼ tsp. pepper
- ¼ cup grated Parmesan cheese

In a large bowl, combine the first 8 ingredients; toss to coat. Transfer to an ungreased 15x10x1-in. baking pan. Bake at 425° until tender, 15-20 minutes, stirring occasionally. Sprinkle with cheese.

**¾ cup:** 107 cal., 7g fat (2g sat. fat), 4mg chol., 120mg sod., 9g carb. (4g sugars, 4g fiber), 5g pro. **Diabetic exchanges:** 2 vegetable, 1 fat.

TZIMMES

## TZIMMES

*I found this tzimmes recipe a long time ago. It has become our traditional side dish for every holiday feast and is a favorite of young and old alike. It also complements chicken or turkey quite well.*
—Cheri Bragg, Viola, DE

**Prep:** 20 min. • **Bake:** 1¾ hours
**Makes:** 12 servings

- 3 lbs. sweet potatoes (about 4 large), peeled and cut into chunks
- 2 lbs. medium carrots, cut into ½-in. chunks
- 1 pkg. (12 oz.) pitted dried plums, halved
- 1 cup orange juice
- 1 cup water
- ¼ cup honey
- ¼ cup packed brown sugar
- 2 tsp. ground cinnamon
- ¼ cup dairy-free margarine or butter

**1.** Preheat oven to 350°. In a greased 13x9-in. baking dish, combine sweet potatoes, carrots and plums. Combine orange juice, water, honey, brown sugar and cinnamon; pour over vegetables.
**2.** Cover and bake for 1 hour. Uncover; dot with butter. Bake until vegetables are tender and sauce is thickened, 45-60 minutes, carefully stirring every 15 minutes.

**¾ cup:** 309 cal., 4g fat (2g sat. fat), 10mg chol., 99mg sod., 66g carb. (36g sugars, 7g fiber), 4g pro.

## WHOLESOME WHEAT BREAD

*My sister and I were in 4-H, and Mom was our breads project leader for years. Because of that early training, fresh homemade bread like this is a staple in my own kitchen.*

—Karen Wingate, Coldwater, KS

- - - - - - - - - - - - - - - - - - - - - - - - - - - - - -

**Prep:** 30 min. + rising
**Bake:** 55 min.
**Makes:** 2 loaves (16 slices each)

2 pkg. (¼ oz. each) active dry yeast
2¼ cups warm water (110° to 115°)
⅓ cup butter, softened
⅓ cup honey
3 Tbsp. sugar
1 Tbsp. salt
½ cup nonfat dry milk powder
4½ cups whole wheat flour
2¾ to 3½ cups all-purpose flour

**1.** In a large bowl, dissolve the yeast in warm water. Add butter, honey, sugar, salt, milk powder and 3 cups whole wheat flour; beat on medium speed until smooth. Stir in the remaining whole wheat flour and enough all-purpose flour to form a soft dough.

**2.** Turn dough onto a floured surface; knead until smooth and elastic, about 10 minutes. Place in a greased bowl, turning once to grease the top. Cover; let rise in a warm place until doubled, about 1 hour.

**3.** Punch down dough. Turn onto a lightly floured surface; divide into 4 portions. Roll each into a 15-in. rope. For each loaf, twist 2 ropes together; pinch ends to seal. Place in greased 9x5-in. loaf pans. Cover with kitchen towels; let rise in a warm place until doubled, about 30 minutes. Preheat oven to 375°.

**4.** Bake 25-30 minutes or until golden brown. Remove from pans to wire racks to cool.

**1 slice:** 134 cal., 2g fat (1g sat. fat), 5mg chol., 243mg sod., 25g carb. (5g sugars, 2g fiber), 4g pro. **Diabetic exchanges:** 2 starch.

## TWO-TONE BAKED POTATOES

**(PICTURED ON P. 98)**

*One potato...two potato...this recipe is doubly wonderful as far as spud lovers are concerned. I am known at home and at work for my love of trying out new recipes. Everyone is glad I took a chance on this one.*

—Sherree Stahn, Central City, NE

- - - - - - - - - - - - - - - - - - - - - - - - - - - - - -

**Prep:** 30 min. • **Bake:** 1¼ hours
**Makes:** 12 servings

6 medium russet potatoes (about 8 oz. each)
6 medium sweet potatoes (about 8 oz. each)
⅔ cup sour cream, divided
⅓ cup 2% milk
¾ cup shredded cheddar cheese
4 Tbsp. minced fresh chives, divided
1½ tsp. salt, divided

**1.** Preheat oven to 400°. Scrub russet and sweet potatoes; pierce several times with a fork. Place in foil-lined 15x10x1-in. pans; bake until tender, 60-70 minutes. Reduce oven setting to 350°.

**2.** When cool enough to handle, cut a third off the top of each russet potato (discard top or save for another use). Scoop out pulp, leaving ½ in. thick shells. In a bowl, mash pulp, adding ⅓ cup sour cream, milk, cheese, 2 Tbsp. chives and ¾ tsp. salt.

**3.** Cut a thin slice off the top of each sweet potato; discard slice. Scoop out pulp, leaving ½-in. thick shells. Mash the pulp with remaining sour cream, chives and salt.

**4.** Spoon russet potato mixture into half of each russet and sweet potato skin. Spoon sweet potato mixture into other half. Return to pans. Bake until heated through, 15-20 minutes.

**1 stuffed potato:** 237 cal., 5g fat (3g sat. fat), 11mg chol., 365mg sod., 42g carb. (11g sugars, 5g fiber), 6g pro.

WHOLESOME WHEAT BREAD

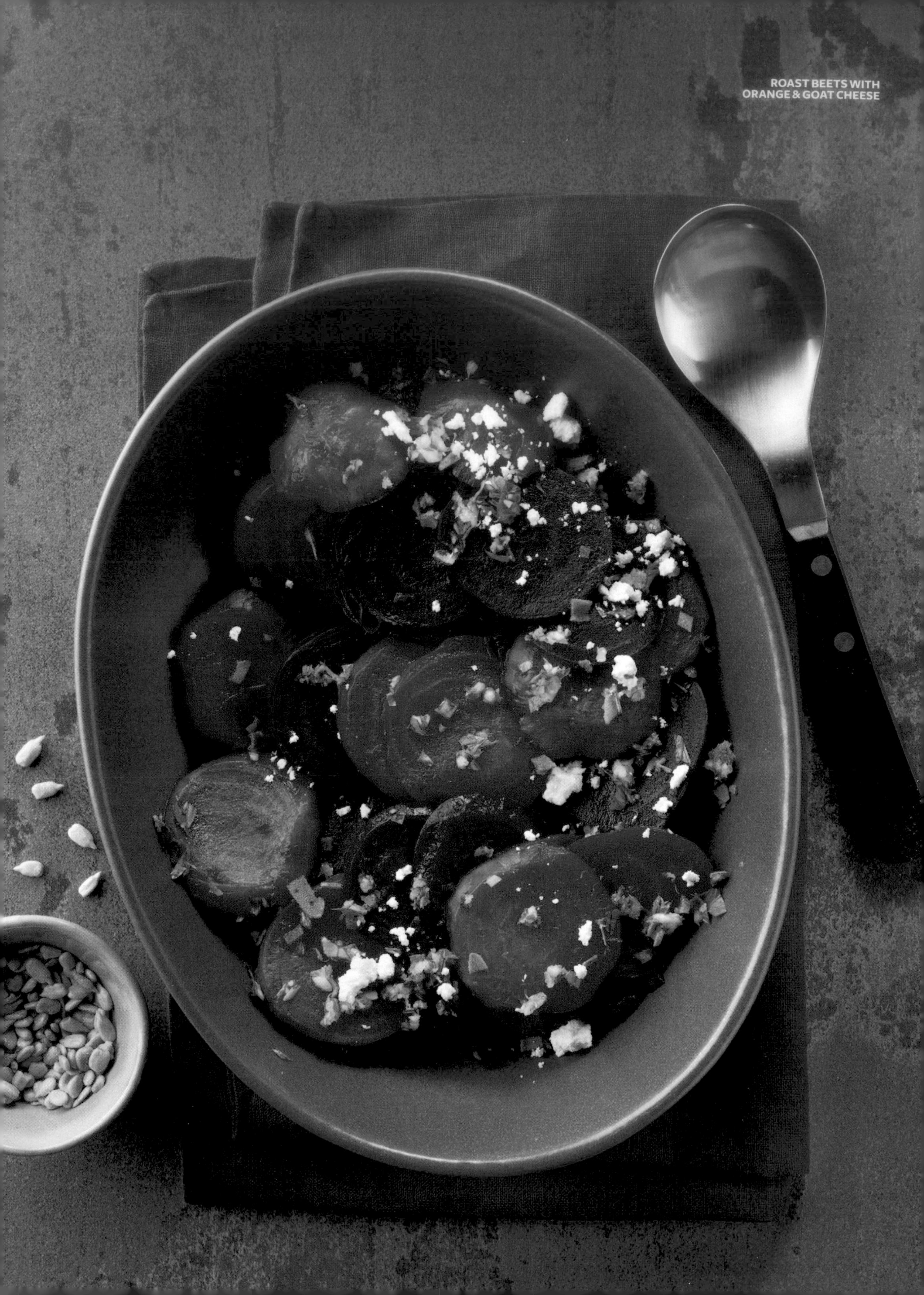
ROAST BEETS WITH
ORANGE & GOAT CHEESE

## ROAST BEETS WITH ORANGE & GOAT CHEESE

*My grandma always grew beets and then pickled or canned them, but I prefer to prepare them differently. I like these roasted beets with fresh herbs and tangy goat cheese.*
—Courtney Archibeque, Greeley, CO

- - - - - - - - - - - - - - - - - - - - - - - - - - -

**Prep:** 25 min. • **Bake:** 55 min. + cooling
**Makes:** 12 servings

- 3 medium fresh beets (about 1 lb.)
- 3 medium fresh golden beets
- 2 Tbsp. lime juice
- 2 Tbsp. orange juice
- ½ tsp. fine sea salt
- 1 Tbsp. minced fresh parsley
- 1 Tbsp. minced fresh sage
- 1 garlic clove, minced
- 1 tsp. grated orange zest
- 3 Tbsp. crumbled goat cheese
- 2 Tbsp. sunflower kernels

**1.** Preheat oven to 400°. Scrub the beets and trim tops by 1 in. Place the beets on a double thickness of heavy-duty foil (about 24x12 in.). Fold foil around beets, sealing tightly. Place on a baking sheet. Roast until tender, 55-65 minutes. Open foil carefully to allow steam to escape.
**2.** When cool enough to handle, peel, halve and slice beets; place in a serving bowl. Add lime juice, orange juice and salt; toss to coat. Combine parsley, sage, garlic and orange zest; sprinkle over beets. Top with the goat cheese and sunflower kernels. Serve warm or chilled.
**¾ cup:** 49 cal., 1g fat (0 sat. fat), 2mg chol., 157mg sod., 9g carb. (6g sugars, 2g fiber), 2g pro. **Diabetic exchanges:** 1 vegetable.

## BARLEY RISOTTO

*Low in fat, but high in fiber, this delicious dish puts a twist on typical risotto. With its nutty undertones, barley provides the perfect backdrop for lemon and parsley.*
—*Taste of Home* Test Kitchen

- - - - - - - - - - - - - - - - - - - - - - - - - - -

**Prep:** 10 min. • **Cook:** 55 min.
**Makes:** 4 servings

- 3 cups chicken broth
- ¾ cup medium pearl barley
- ¼ cup finely chopped onion
- 1 tsp. olive oil
- 1 garlic clove, minced
- ½ cup white wine or water

BARLEY RISOTTO

- 3 Tbsp. minced fresh parsley
- 2 tsp. grated lemon zest

**1.** In a small saucepan, bring broth to a simmer; keep hot.
**2.** In another small saucepan over medium-high heat, cook and stir the barley for 2-4 minutes or until lightly browned. Transfer to a small bowl. In the same saucepan, saute onion in oil for 2 minutes. Add garlic; saute 1 minute longer or until onion is tender. Stir in barley and wine. Cook and stir until all of the liquid is absorbed.
**3.** Add the hot broth, ½ cup at a time, stirring constantly and allowing the liquid to absorb between additions. Cook just until barley is almost tender (cooking time is about 45 minutes). Add parsley and lemon zest; cook and stir until heated through. Serve immediately.
**½ cup:** 184 cal., 2g fat (0 sat. fat), 4mg chol., 742mg sod., 32g carb. (2g sugars, 6g fiber), 5g pro. **Diabetic exchanges:** 2 starch, ½ fat.

HOW-TO

### Keep Parsley Fresh

Trim stems and place the bunch in a tumbler with an inch of water. Be sure no leaves are in the water. Tie a produce bag around the tumbler to trap humidity; store parsley in the refrigerator. Each time you use the parsley, change the water and turn the produce bag inside out so any moisture that has built up inside can escape. The parsley will stay fresh for up to a month.

## VEGGIE-STUFFED TOMATOES

**(PICTURED ON P. 99)**

*This recipe is my wife's favorite, and she loves when I cook it for her. The tasty meatless stuffing is perfect as a side dish, but it's also satisfying enough to turn it into a light meal.*
—Scott Szekretar, Islip, NY

**Prep:** 20 min. • **Bake:** 20 min.
**Makes:** 2 servings

- 2   medium tomatoes
- ½   small carrot
- ½   celery rib, sliced
- ½   small onion, peeled
- 1   small garlic clove, peeled
- ¼   tsp. dried oregano
- 2   tsp. olive oil
- 1   Tbsp. white wine or vegetable broth
- ⅓   cup dry bread crumbs
- 2   Tbsp. grated Parmesan cheese
- 3   to 4 fresh basil leaves, thinly sliced

**1.** Cut a thin slice off the top of each tomato. Leaving a ½-in. shell, scoop out and reserve pulp. Invert tomatoes onto paper towels to drain.
**2.** Meanwhile, in a food processor, cover and process the carrot, celery, onion, garlic and reserved pulp until finely chopped. In large skillet, saute vegetable mixture and oregano in oil until tender. Add wine or broth; simmer, uncovered, until liquid is reduced by half, about 2 minutes. Remove from the heat; cool slightly. Stir in the bread crumbs, Parmesan cheese and basil.
**3.** Stuff tomatoes; replace tops. Place in a shallow baking dish coated with cooking spray. Bake, uncovered, at 350° until heated through, 15-20 minutes.
**1 tomato:** 182 cal., 7g fat (2g sat. fat), 4mg chol., 234mg sod., 23g carb. (7g sugars, 4g fiber), 6g pro. **Diabetic exchanges:** 2 vegetable, 1½ fat, 1 starch.

## SWEET-SOUR RED CABBAGE

*The first time I bought a red cabbage, I didn't quite know what to do with it. After some experimenting, I came up with this winning recipe. Red cabbage is now my fall comfort food. This side dish is compatible with a variety of meats, but I especially like it with a pork roast or chops.*
—Karen Gorman, Gunnison, CO

**Takes:** 25 min. • **Makes:** 2 servings

- 2   Tbsp. cider vinegar
- 1   Tbsp. brown sugar
- ¼   tsp. caraway seeds
- ¼   tsp. celery seed
- 2   cups shredded red cabbage
- ½   cup thinly sliced onion
      Salt and pepper to taste

**1.** In a small bowl, combine the vinegar, brown sugar, caraway and celery seeds; set aside. Place cabbage and onion in a saucepan; add a small amount of water. Cover and steam until tender, about 15 minutes.
**2.** Add the vinegar mixture; toss to coat. Season with salt and pepper. Serve warm.
**1 serving:** 60 cal., 0 fat (0 sat. fat), 0 chol., 12mg sod., 15g carb. (12g sugars, 2g fiber), 1g pro. **Diabetic exchanges:** 1 vegetable, ½ starch.

**SWEET-SOUR RED CABBAGE**

APPLE QUINOA
SPOON BREAD

## ROASTED SWEET POTATOES WITH DIJON & ROSEMARY

*After moving to Alabama, I learned how much my friends and co-workers love sweet potatoes. I roast them with Dijon, fresh rosemary and a touch of honey.*
—Tamara Huron, New Market, AL

**Prep:** 10 min. • **Bake:** 25 min.
**Makes:** 4 servings

- 2 medium sweet potatoes (about 1½ lbs.)
- 2 Tbsp. olive oil
- 2 tsp. Dijon mustard
- 2 tsp. honey
- 1 tsp. minced fresh rosemary or ¼ tsp. dried rosemary, crushed
- ¼ tsp. salt
- ¼ tsp. pepper

Preheat oven to 400°. Peel and cut each sweet potato lengthwise into ½-in.-thick wedges; place in a large bowl. Mix the remaining ingredients; drizzle over the sweet potatoes and toss to coat. Transfer potatoes to a greased 15x10x1-in. baking pan. Roast 25-30 minutes or until tender, stirring occasionally.

**1 serving:** 170 cal., 7g fat (1g sat. fat), 0 chol., 217mg sod., 26g carb. (12g sugars, 3g fiber), 2g pro. **Diabetic exchanges:** 2 starch, 1½ fat.

## APPLE QUINOA SPOON BREAD

*My cousin is a strict vegetarian, so creating unique and satisfying veggie dishes is my yearly holiday challenge. This spoon bread can act as a side dish, but the addition of hearty, healthy quinoa and vegetables makes it a well-rounded winter casserole in its own right. It makes an amazing Thanksgiving side dish, or as a meal paired with a seasonal salad.*
—Christine Wendland, Browns Mills, NJ

**Prep:** 25 min. • **Bake:** 25 min.
**Makes:** 9 servings

- ⅔ cup water
- ⅓ cup quinoa, rinsed
- 1 Tbsp. canola oil
- 1 small apple, peeled and diced
- 1 small onion, finely chopped
- 1 small parsnip, peeled and diced
- ½ tsp. celery seed
- 1¼ tsp. salt, divided
- 1 Tbsp. minced fresh sage
- ¾ cup yellow cornmeal
- ¼ cup all-purpose flour
- 1 Tbsp. sugar
- 1 tsp. baking powder
- 1 large egg, room temperature
- 1½ cups 2% milk, divided

**1.** Preheat oven to 375°. In a small saucepan, bring water to a boil. Add quinoa. Reduce heat; simmer, covered, until liquid is absorbed, 12-15 minutes. Fluff with a fork; cool slightly.
**2.** Meanwhile, in a large skillet, heat oil over medium heat; saute apple, onion and parsnip with celery seed and ½ tsp. salt until softened, 4-5 minutes. Remove from heat; stir in sage.
**3.** In a large bowl, whisk together the cornmeal, flour, sugar, baking powder and remaining ¾ tsp. salt. In another bowl, whisk together egg and 1 cup milk. Add to cornmeal mixture, stirring just until moistened. Fold in the quinoa and apple mixture.
**4.** Transfer to a greased 8-in. square baking dish. Pour remaining milk over top.
**5.** Bake, uncovered, until the edges are golden brown, 25-30 minutes. Let stand 5 minutes before serving.

**1 serving:** 153 cal., 4g fat (1g sat. fat), 24mg chol., 412mg sod., 26g carb. (6g sugars, 2g fiber), 5g pro. **Diabetic exchanges:** 1½ starch, 1 fat.

## OLD BAY CAULIFLOWER

*Ready in 10 minutes, this bowl of veggies has three ingredients and a whole lot of flavor. It's the perfect cauliflower side dish.*
—Elizabeth Bramkamp, Gig Harbor, WA

**Takes:** 10 min. • **Makes:** 4 servings

- 1 pkg. (16 oz.) frozen cauliflower
- 1 to 2 Tbsp. butter, melted
- 1 to 2 tsp. seafood seasoning

Prepare cauliflower according to package directions; drain. Drizzle with butter; sprinkle with seafood seasoning.

**1 cup:** 53 cal., 3g fat (2g sat. fat), 8mg chol., 216mg sod., 5g carb. (3g sugars, 3g fiber), 2g pro. **Diabetic exchanges:** 1 vegetable, ½ fat.

**LEMON-PARMESAN BROILED ASPARAGUS**

## LEMON-PARMESAN BROILED ASPARAGUS

*These special spears are packed with flavor, thanks to the lemon-garlic dressing they're tossed in before roasting. It's a simple, quick side that goes with just about anything!*
—Tina Mirilovich, Johstown, PA

**Takes:** 15 min. • **Makes:** 4 servings

- ¼ cup mayonnaise
- 4 tsp. olive oil
- 1½ tsp. grated lemon zest
- 1 garlic clove, minced
- ½ tsp. pepper
- ¼ tsp. seasoned salt
- 1 lb. fresh asparagus, trimmed
- 2 Tbsp. shredded Parmesan cheese
  Lemon wedges, optional

**1.** Preheat broiler. In large bowl, combine the first 6 ingredients. Add asparagus; toss to coat. Place in a single layer on a wire rack over a foil-lined 15x10x1-in. baking pan.

**2.** Broil 5-6 in. from heat until tender and lightly browned, 5-7 minutes. Transfer to a serving platter; sprinkle with shredded Parmesan cheese. If desired, serve with lemon wedges.

**1 serving:** 156 cal., 15g fat (3g sat. fat), 3mg chol., 309mg sod., 3g carb. (1g sugars, 1g fiber), 2g pro. **Diabetic exchanges:** 3 fat, 1 vegetable.

**TEST KITCHEN TIP**

In order to keep asparagus fresh longer, place the cut stems in a container of cold water—similar to flowers in a vase. Place container in the refrigerator, changing the water at least once every 2 days.

SIDES

## SOURDOUGH DRESSING

*While we love our traditional Thanksgiving recipes, sometimes we want to change things up. This sourdough stuffing is a fun twist on an old favorite. Whenever we make it after the big feast, we like to add a cup or more of leftover cubed turkey.*
—Pat Dazis, Charlotte, NC

**Prep:** 45 min. • **Bake:** 55 min.
**Makes:** 16 servings

16 cups cubed sourdough bread
¼ cup olive oil, divided
4 garlic cloves, minced, divided
2 medium red onions, chopped
¾ cup chopped roasted sweet red peppers
1 tsp. dried oregano
1 carton (32 oz.) reduced-sodium chicken broth
1 cup cubed cooked turkey, optional
4 oz. Asiago cheese, cut into ½-in. cubes
2 large eggs, lightly beaten
4 green onions, chopped
2 Tbsp. butter

1. Preheat oven to 350°. Place the bread cubes in a large bowl. Drizzle with 2 Tbsp. oil; toss lightly. Sprinkle with half the garlic; toss to combine. Transfer bread to 2 ungreased 15x10x1-in. baking pans. Bake for 20-25 minutes or until lightly browned, turning occasionally. Let cool.

2. Meanwhile, in a large skillet, heat remaining oil over medium-high heat. Add red onions; cook and stir 5-7 minutes or until softened. Add the red peppers, oregano and remaining garlic; cook 1 minute longer. Stir in broth; bring to a boil. Remove from heat.

3. Place toasted bread in large bowl. Stir in the broth mixture, turkey if desired, cheese, eggs and green onions. Transfer to a greased 13x9-in. baking dish; dot with butter. Cover and bake for 30 minutes. Uncover; bake 25-30 minutes longer or until golden brown.

**¾ cup:** 207 cal., 8g fat (3g sat. fat), 34mg chol., 475mg sod., 24g carb. (4g sugars, 1g fiber), 8g pro. **Diabetic exchanges:** 1½ starch, 1½ fat, 1 lean meat.

**SOURDOUGH DRESSING**

## SO-EASY SUCCOTASH

*The miso paste used in this super simple recipe gives depth and a hint of savoriness to canned or fresh vegetables. To brighten the flavor profile even more, you could add a splash of your favorite white wine.*
—William Milton III, Clemson, SC

**Takes:** 20 min. • **Makes:** 6 servings

- 2 tsp. canola oil
- 1 small red onion, chopped
- 2 cans (15¼ oz. each) whole kernel corn, drained
- 1½ cups frozen shelled edamame, thawed
- ½ medium sweet red pepper, chopped (about ½ cup)
- 2 Tbsp. unsalted butter, softened
- 1 tsp. white miso paste
- 3 green onions, thinly sliced
  Coarsely ground pepper

**1.** In a large skillet, heat oil over medium-high heat. Add red onion; cook and stir until crisp-tender, about 2-3 minutes. Add corn, edamame and red pepper. Cook until vegetables reach desired tenderness, 4-6 minutes longer.
**2.** In a small bowl, mix butter and miso paste until combined; stir into pan until melted. Sprinkle with green onions and pepper before serving.
**¾ cup:** 193 cal., 9g fat (3g sat. fat), 10mg chol., 464mg sod., 20g carb. (11g sugars, 6g fiber), 8g pro.

---

**DID YOU KNOW?**

Edamame are immature green soybeans. You can purchase them still in pods or already shelled and ready to use in recipes like this.

---

## GOUDA MIXED POTATO MASH

*Can't decide what type of spuds to serve? Make both by preparing this lovely dish featuring Yukon Gold and sweet potatoes. The Gouda cheese is an unexpected twist.*
—Shelby Goddard, Baton Rouge, LA

**Prep:** 20 min. • **Cook:** 15 min.
**Makes:** 12 servings

- 6 medium Yukon Gold potatoes, peeled and cubed
- 2 medium sweet potatoes, peeled and cubed
- ½ cup 2% milk
- 1 cup shredded Gouda cheese
- 1 tsp. paprika
- ½ tsp. salt
- ½ tsp. pepper

**1.** Place Yukon Gold and sweet potatoes in a Dutch oven; add water to cover. Bring to a boil. Reduce heat; cook, uncovered, 10-15 minutes or until tender. Drain; return to pan.
**2.** Mash potatoes, gradually adding milk. Stir in cheese, paprika, salt and pepper.
**⅔ cup:** 178 cal., 3g fat (2g sat. fat), 12mg chol., 189mg sod., 33g carb. (6g sugars, 3g fiber), 6g pro. **Diabetic exchanges:** 2 starch, ½ fat.

**GOUDA MIXED POTATO MASH**

**CARROT & KALE
VEGETABLE SAUTE**

## CUMIN RICE WITH AVOCADO

*Cumin, picante sauce and avocado do
a terrific job of perking up rice in this
any-day side dish.*
—Margaret Allen, Abingdon, VA

**Prep:** 5 min. • **Cook:** 30 min.
**Makes:** 6 servings

- 2¼ cups water
- 1 Tbsp. butter
- 2 tsp. reduced-sodium chicken
  bouillon granules
- ¾ tsp. ground cumin
- 1 cup uncooked long grain rice
- ⅓ cup picante sauce
- 1 medium ripe avocado, peeled and
  cubed
- 2 green onions, sliced

**1.** Place first 4 ingredients in a large
saucepan; bring to a boil. Stir in rice;
return to a boil. Reduce the heat;
simmer, covered, until rice is tender,
20-25 minutes.
**2.** Stir in picante sauce; heat through.
Gently stir in avocado and green onions.
**⅔ cup:** 188 cal., 6g fat (2g sat. fat), 5mg chol.,
194mg sod., 31g carb. (1g sugars, 2g fiber), 3g
pro. **Diabetic exchanges:** 2 starch, 1 fat.

## CARROT & KALE VEGETABLE SAUTE

*Thanks to fresh veggie
dishes like this one, I almost
forget that I eat a wheat-
and gluten-free diet. This
gorgeous side dish is
awesome with smoky bacon.*
—Darla Andrews, Boerne, TX

**Prep:** 15 min. • **Cook:** 20 min.
**Makes:** 8 servings

- 8 bacon strips, coarsely chopped
- 4 large carrots, sliced
- 2 cups peeled cubed butternut
  squash (½-in. pieces)
- 1 poblano pepper, seeded and
  chopped
- ½ cup finely chopped red onion
- 1 tsp. smoked paprika
- ¼ tsp. salt
- ¼ tsp. pepper
- 2 plum tomatoes, chopped
- 2 cups chopped fresh kale

**1.** In a large skillet, cook bacon over
medium heat until crisp, stirring
occasionally. Using a slotted spoon,
remove bacon to paper towels. Pour
off all but 1 Tbsp. drippings.
**2.** Add carrots and squash to drippings;
cook, covered over medium heat for
5 minutes. Add poblano pepper and
onion; cook until vegetables are tender,
about 5 minutes, stirring occasionally.
Stir in seasonings. Add tomatoes and
kale; cook, covered, until kale is wilted,
2-3 minutes. Top with bacon.
**¾ cup:** 101 cal., 5g fat (2g sat. fat), 10mg
chol., 251mg sod., 11g carb. (4g sugars,
3g fiber), 4g pro. **Diabetic exchanges:**
1 vegetable, 1 fat, ½ starch.

## BALSAMIC BRUSSELS SPROUTS

*These balsamic Brussels sprouts couldn't be easier to make—and you need only a few ingredients!*
—Kallee Krong-McCreery, Escondido, CA

**Takes:** 15 min. • **Makes:** 4 servings

- 3 to 4 Tbsp. extra virgin olive oil
- 1 pkg. (16 oz.) frozen Brussels sprouts, thawed
- 2 Tbsp. balsamic vinegar
- 2 Tbsp. torn fresh basil leaves
- ½ to 1 tsp. flaky sea salt
- ½ tsp. coarsely ground pepper

In a large skillet, heat oil over medium-high heat. Add the Brussels sprouts to skillet and cook until heated through, 5-7 minutes. Transfer to a serving bowl. Drizzle with vinegar; sprinkle with basil, salt and pepper.

**⅔ cup:** 145 cal., 11g fat (2g sat. fat), 0 chol., 252mg sod., 11g carb. (2g sugars, 4g fiber), 4g pro. **Diabetic exchanges:** 2 fat, 1 vegetable.

RICE WITH COLLARD GREENS RELISH

## RICE WITH COLLARD GREENS RELISH

*This is a staple in my country of origin, Zimbabwe. It is served with sadza, a cornmeal-based stiff porridge that is used like rice or potatoes in other cultures.*
—Loveness Murinda, Upland, CA

**Prep:** 15 min. • **Cook:** 20 min.
**Makes:** 6 servings

- 1 large bunch collard greens (about 2 lbs.)
- ¼ cup finely chopped onion
- 1 garlic clove, minced
- 2 Tbsp. olive oil
- ¾ cup water
- ¾ cup crushed tomatoes
- 1 tsp. curry powder
- ½ tsp. salt
- ⅛ tsp. pepper
- 2 pkg. (8.8 oz. each) ready-to-serve long grain rice

**1.** Remove and discard center ribs and stems from collard greens. Cut leaves into 1-in. pieces. In a Dutch oven, cook onion and garlic in oil over medium heat until crisp-tender, about 2 minutes.

**2.** Stir in water, tomatoes, curry powder, salt and pepper. Bring to a boil. Add the collard greens in batches; cook and stir until they begin to wilt. Reduce heat; cover and simmer, stirring occasionally, until greens are tender, 10-15 minutes. Prepare rice according to package directions. Serve with collard greens.

**⅔ cup collards with ⅔ cup rice:** 239 cal., 7g fat (1g sat. fat), 0 chol., 279mg sod., 38g carb. (2g sugars, 8g fiber), 8g pro.

**TEST KITCHEN TIP**

If you're making the rice from scratch, start with about ¾ cup of uncooked long grain rice.

## BRAIDED MULTIGRAIN LOAF

*Use oats, rye flour, rice and sunflower seeds for a hearty holiday side. It's so robust, you could make a meal out of it just by adding a little butter!*
—Jane Thomas, Burnsville, MN

**Prep:** 40 min. + rising
**Bake:** 30 min.
**Makes:** 1 loaf (24 slices)

- 2 cups whole wheat flour
- 1 cup quick cooking oats
- ½ cup rye flour
- 2 pkg. (¼ oz. each) active dry yeast
- 2 tsp. salt
- 3 cups all-purpose flour
- 2 cups 2% milk
- ½ cup honey
- ⅓ cup water
- 2 Tbsp. butter
- 1 cup cooked long-grain rice, cooled

**TOPPING**

- 1 large egg
- 1 Tbsp. water
- ⅓ cup sunflower kernels

**1.** In a large bowl, mix whole wheat flour, oats, rye flour, yeast, salt and 1 cup all-purpose flour. In a small saucepan, heat milk, honey, water and butter to 120°-130°. Add to dry ingredients; beat on medium speed 2 minutes. Add 1 cup all-purpose flour; beat 2 minutes longer. Stir in rice and enough remaining flour to form a stiff dough.

**2.** Turn dough onto a floured surface; knead 6-8 minutes or until smooth and elastic. Place in a greased bowl, turning once to grease the top. Cover and let rise in a warm place until doubled, about 1 hour.

**3.** Punch down dough. Turn onto a lightly floured surface; divide into thirds. Cover and let rest 5 minutes. Roll each portion into an 18-in. rope. Place ropes on a greased baking sheet and braid. Shape into a ring. Pinch ends to seal; tuck under.

**4.** Cover with a kitchen towel; let rise in a warm place until doubled, about 30 minutes. Preheat oven to 375°.

**5.** For topping, in a small bowl, whisk the egg and water; brush over dough. Sprinkle with sunflower kernels. Bake 30-40 minutes or until golden brown. Remove to a wire rack to cool.

**1 slice:** 177 cal., 4g fat (1g sat. fat), 12mg chol., 231mg sod., 32g carb. (7g sugars, 2g fiber), 5g pro.

## ASPARAGUS, SQUASH & RED PEPPER SAUTE

**(PICTURED ON P. 98)**
*The appealing vegetable trio is enlivened by a wine-scented saute.*
—Deirdre Cox, Kansas City, MO

**Takes:** 30 min. • **Makes:** 4 servings

- 2 medium sweet red peppers, julienned
- 2 medium yellow summer squash, halved and cut into ¼-in. slices
- 6 oz. fresh asparagus, trimmed and cut into 1½-in. pieces
- ¼ cup white wine or vegetable broth
- 4½ tsp. olive oil
- ¼ tsp. salt
- ¼ tsp. pepper

In a large cast-iron or other heavy skillet, saute the peppers, squash and asparagus in wine and oil until crisp-tender. Sprinkle with salt and pepper.

**¾ cup:** 90 cal., 5g fat (1g sat. fat), 0 chol., 163mg sod., 8g carb. (5g sugars, 3g fiber), 2g pro. **Diabetic exchanges:** 1 vegetable, 1 fat.

**BRAIDED MULTIGRAIN LOAF**

# STOVETOP MAINS

"Here is one of my favorite ways to cook and enjoy cabbage. It has all the wonderful flavor of regular cabbage rolls, but it's a lot less bother to make. In fact, this is a one-pot recipe!"

—Bernard Snow, Lewiston, MI

## CHICKEN & BROCCOLI WITH DILL SAUCE

(PICTURED ON P. 123)

*I've had this chicken and broccoli recipe for so many years, I don't remember when I first made it. Serve it with a side of couscous or rice for a complete meal, or add sliced mushrooms or carrots for extra veggies.*
—Kallee Krong-McCreery, Escondido, CA

**Takes:** 30 min. • **Makes:** 4 servings

- 4 boneless skinless chicken breast halves (6 oz. each)
- ½ tsp. garlic salt
- ¼ tsp. pepper
- 1 Tbsp. olive oil
- 4 cups fresh broccoli florets
- 1 cup chicken broth
- 1 Tbsp. all-purpose flour
- 1 Tbsp. snipped fresh dill
- 1 cup 2% milk

**1.** Sprinkle chicken with garlic salt and pepper. In a large skillet, heat oil over medium heat; brown chicken on both sides. Remove from pan.
**2.** Add broccoli and broth to same skillet; bring to a boil. Reduce heat; simmer, covered, until broccoli is just tender, 3-5 minutes. Using a slotted spoon, remove broccoli from pan, reserving broth. Keep broccoli warm.
**3.** In a small bowl, mix flour, dill and milk until smooth; stir into broth in pan. Bring to a boil, stirring constantly; cook and stir until thickened, 1-2 minutes. Add chicken; cook, covered, over medium heat until a thermometer inserted in chicken reads 165°, 10-12 minutes. Serve with broccoli.
**1 serving:** 274 cal., 9g fat (2g sat. fat), 100mg chol., 620mg sod., 8g carb. (4g sugars, 2g fiber), 39g pro. **Diabetic exchanges:** 5 lean meat, 1 vegetable, 1 fat.

**TEST KITCHEN TIP**

If you're buying whole broccoli stalks, don't throw out the stems! Peel away the tough outer portion and chop the centers to use in soups and stir-fries or add to salads and slaws.

## MEATLESS CHILI MAC

*I came across this recipe in a newspaper years ago. It's been a hit at our house ever since. It's fast and flavorful, and it appeals to all ages.*
—Cindy Ragan, North Huntingdon, PA

**Prep:** 15 min. • **Cook:** 25 min.
**Makes:** 8 servings

- 1 large onion, chopped
- 1 medium green pepper, chopped
- 1 Tbsp. olive oil
- 1 garlic clove, minced
- 2 cups water
- 1½ cups uncooked elbow macaroni
- 1 can (16 oz.) mild chili beans, undrained
- 1 can (15½ oz.) great northern beans, rinsed and drained
- 1 can (14½ oz.) diced tomatoes, undrained
- 1 can (8 oz.) tomato sauce
- 4 tsp. chili powder
- 1 tsp. ground cumin
- ½ tsp. salt
- ½ cup fat-free sour cream

**1.** In a Dutch oven, saute onion and green pepper in oil until tender. Add garlic; cook 1 minute longer. Stir in water, macaroni, beans, tomatoes, tomato sauce, chili powder, cumin and salt.
**2.** Bring to a boil. Reduce the heat; cover and simmer for 15-20 minutes or until macaroni is tender. Top each serving with 1 Tbsp. sour cream.
**1¼ cups:** 206 cal., 3g fat (1g sat. fat), 1mg chol., 651mg sod., 37g carb. (6g sugars, 9g fiber), 10g pro. **Diabetic exchanges:** 2 starch, 1 lean meat, 1 vegetable.

MEATLESS CHILI MAC

**PEPPERY HERBED TURKEY TENDERLOIN**

## BLACK BEAN BURRITOS

*My neighbor and I discovered these fabulous low-fat burritos a few years ago. On nights my husband or I have a meeting, we can have a satisfying supper on the table in minutes.*
—Angela Studebaker, Goshen, IN

**Takes:** 10 min. • **Makes:** 4 servings

- 1 Tbsp. canola oil
- 3 Tbsp. chopped onion
- 3 Tbsp. chopped green pepper
- 1 can (15 oz.) black beans, rinsed and drained
- 4 flour tortillas (8 in.), warmed
- 1 cup shredded Mexican cheese blend
- 1 medium tomato, chopped
- 1 cup shredded lettuce
  Optional toppings: Salsa, sour cream, minced fresh cilantro and cubed avocado

**1.** In a nonstick skillet, heat oil over medium heat; saute onion and green pepper until tender. Stir in beans; heat through.

**2.** Spoon about ½ cup of vegetable mixture off center on each tortilla. Sprinkle with the cheese, tomato and lettuce. Fold sides and ends over filling and roll up. Serve with optional toppings as desired.

**1 burrito:** 395 cal., 16g fat (6g sat. fat), 25mg chol., 610mg sod., 46g carb. (2g sugars, 7g fiber), 16g pro. **Diabetic exchanges:** 2½ starch, 1 vegetable, 1 lean meat, 1 fat.

## PEPPERY HERBED TURKEY TENDERLOIN

*I won the North Carolina Turkey Cook-Off one year with these flavorful tenderloins in rich sauce. Marinating the turkey in wine, garlic, rosemary and thyme gives it a fantastic taste.*
—Virginia C. Anthony, Jacksonville, FL

**Prep:** 10 min. + marinating • **Cook:** 15 min.
**Makes:** 6 servings

- 2¼ lbs. turkey breast tenderloins
- 1 cup dry white wine or apple juice
- 3 green onions, chopped
- 3 Tbsp. minced fresh parsley
- 6 tsp. olive oil, divided
- 1 Tbsp. finely chopped garlic
- ¾ tsp. dried rosemary, crushed
- ¾ tsp. dried thyme
- 1 tsp. coarsely ground pepper
- ¾ tsp. salt, divided
- 4 tsp. cornstarch
- 1 cup reduced-sodium chicken broth

**1.** Pat tenderloins dry; flatten to ¾-in. thickness. In a small bowl, combine the wine or juice, onions, parsley, 4 tsp. oil, garlic, rosemary and thyme. Pour ¾ cup marinade into a large shallow dish; add turkey. Turn turkey to coat; cover and refrigerate for at least 4 hours, turning occasionally. Cover and refrigerate the remaining marinade.

**2.** Drain turkey, discarding marinade. Sprinkle turkey with pepper and ½ tsp. salt. In a large nonstick skillet, cook turkey in remaining oil for 5-6 minutes on each side or until a thermometer reads 165°. Remove and keep warm.

**3.** In a small bowl, combine cornstarch, broth, reserved marinade and remaining salt until smooth; pour into skillet. Bring to a boil; cook and stir for 1-2 minutes or until thickened. Slice the turkey; serve with sauce.

**6 oz. cooked turkey with 2 Tbsp. sauce:** 223 cal., 4g fat (0 sat. fat), 68mg chol., 490mg sod., 3g carb. (0 sugars, 0 fiber), 43g pro. **Diabetic exchanges:** 6 lean meat, ½ fat.

LEMON CHICKEN & RICE

## LEMON CHICKEN & RICE

*On our busy ranch, we often need meals we can put on the table in a hurry. We find this all-in-one chicken dish, with its delicate lemon flavor, an excellent go-to recipe. And it's inexpensive to boot.*

—Kat Thompson, Prineville, OR

--------------------------------------

**Takes:** 30 min. • **Makes:** 4 servings

2  **Tbsp. butter**
1  **lb. boneless skinless chicken breasts, cut into strips**
1  **medium onion, chopped**
1  **large carrot, thinly sliced**
2  **garlic cloves, minced**
1  **Tbsp. cornstarch**
1  **can (14½ oz.) chicken broth**
2  **Tbsp. lemon juice**
¼  **tsp. salt**
1  **cup frozen peas**
1½  **cups uncooked instant rice**

**1.** In a large cast-iron or other heavy skillet, heat butter over medium-high heat; saute chicken, onion, carrot and garlic until chicken is no longer pink, 5-7 minutes.

**2.** In a small bowl, mix the cornstarch, broth, lemon juice and salt until smooth. Gradually add to skillet; bring to a boil. Cook and stir until thickened, 1-2 minutes.
**3.** Stir in peas; return to a boil. Stir in rice. Remove from heat; let stand, covered, 5 minutes.
**1 serving:** 370 cal., 9g fat (4g sat. fat), 80mg chol., 746mg sod., 41g carb. (4g sugars, 3g fiber), 29g pro. **Diabetic exchanges:** 3 starch, 3 lean meat, 1½ fat.
**\* HEALTH TIP \*** Skip the salt and save 300 milligrams of sodium per serving. Use reduced-sodium broth and save about 150 milligrams more.

## TILAPIA WITH CUCUMBER RELISH

*My husband isn't big on fish, but he enjoys this mild-tasting tilapia. The relish adds garden-fresh flavor and pretty color to the lightly browned fillets.*

—Mary VanHollebeke, Wyandotte, MI

--------------------------------------

**Takes:** 15 min. • **Makes:** 4 servings

⅔  **cup chopped seeded cucumber**
½  **cup chopped radishes**

1  **Tbsp. tarragon vinegar**
1  **tsp. olive oil**
½  **tsp. salt, divided**
¼  **tsp. pepper, divided**
⅛  **tsp. sugar**
⅛  **tsp. paprika**
4  **tilapia fillets (6 oz. each)**
1  **Tbsp. butter**

**1.** In a small bowl, combine cucumber and radishes. In another small bowl, whisk the vinegar, oil, ¼ tsp. salt, ⅛ tsp. pepper and sugar. Pour over the cucumber mixture; toss to coat evenly. Combine paprika and remaining salt and pepper; sprinkle over the fillets.
**2.** In a large nonstick skillet coated with cooking spray, melt butter. Add fish; cook for 3-4 minutes on each side or until fish flakes easily with a fork. Serve with the cucumber relish.
**1 fillet with ¼ cup relish:** 181 cal., 6g fat (3g sat. fat), 90mg chol., 384mg sod., 1g carb. (1g sugars, 0 fiber), 32g pro. **Diabetic exchanges:** 4 lean meat, 1 fat.

## CAULIFLOWER ALFREDO

*My family loves this quick and healthy cauliflower Alfredo sauce on pasta.*
—Shelly Bevington, Hermiston, OR

- - - - - - - - - - - - - - - - - - - - - - - - - - -

**Prep:** 20 min. • **Cook:** 20 min.
**Makes:** 6 servings

- 2   Tbsp. extra virgin olive oil
- 3   garlic cloves, minced
- 1   shallot, minced
- 1   medium head cauliflower, chopped
- 4   cups water
- 2   vegetable bouillon cubes
- ⅔   cup shredded Parmesan cheese plus additional for garnish
- ¼   tsp. crushed red pepper flakes
- 1   pkg. (16 oz.) fettuccine
     Chopped fresh parsley

**1.** In a Dutch oven, heat oil over medium-high heat. Add garlic and shallot; cook and stir until fragrant, 1-2 minutes. Add cauliflower, water and bouillon; bring to a boil. Cook, covered, until tender, 5-6 minutes. Drain; cool slightly. Transfer to a food processor; add ⅔ cup Parmesan and the pepper flakes. Process until pureed smooth.
**2.** Meanwhile, cook fettuccine according to package directions for al dente. Drain fettuccine; place in a large bowl. Add cauliflower mixture; toss to coat. Sprinkle with parsley and additional Parmesan.

**1⅓ cups:** 371 cal., 9g fat (3g sat. fat), 6mg chol., 533mg sod., 60g carb. (5g sugars, 5g fiber), 16g pro.

CAULIFLOWER ALFREDO

## PINEAPPLE-GINGER CHICKEN STIR-FRY
(PICTURED ON P. 122)

*I found the original recipe on a can of pineapple slices in the 1980s. After making this dish for a number of years, I lightened up the ingredients and adapted it to a quick skillet meal. My family gave it a big thumbs-up, and we've enjoyed it this way ever since!*
—Sue Gronholz, Beaver Dam, WI

- - - - - - - - - - - - - - - - - - - - - - - - - - -

**Takes:** 30 min. • **Makes:** 4 servings

- 1   can (20 oz.) unsweetened pineapple chunks
- 1   Tbsp. cornstarch
- 3   Tbsp. reduced-sodium soy sauce
- 2   Tbsp. honey
- ¼   tsp. ground cinnamon
- 2   Tbsp. canola oil, divided
- 1   lb. boneless skinless chicken breasts, cut into 1-in. cubes
- 1   small onion, chopped
- 1   Tbsp. minced fresh gingerroot
- 2   garlic cloves, minced
     Hot cooked brown rice
     Minced fresh cilantro, optional

**1.** Drain pineapple, reserving juice. Mix cornstarch, soy sauce, honey, cinnamon and the reserved juice until smooth. In a skillet, heat 1 Tbsp. oil over medium-high heat; saute chicken until lightly browned, 4-6 minutes. Remove from pan.
**2.** In same pan, saute onion, ginger and garlic in remaining oil until crisp-tender, about 2 minutes. Stir cornstarch mixture; add to pan with chicken and pineapple chunks. Bring to a boil, stirring constantly; cook and stir until sauce is thickened and chicken is cooked through, 5-7 minutes.
**3.** Serve with rice. If desired, sprinkle with cilantro.

**1 cup chicken mixture:** 316 cal., 10g fat (1g sat. fat), 63mg chol., 487mg sod., 31g carb. (26g sugars, 1g fiber), 25g pro. **Diabetic exchanges:** 3 lean meat, 1½ starch, 1½ fat, ½ fruit.

**TEST KITCHEN TIP**

Cubing chicken is easier if it's slightly frozen.

## ONE-POT UNSTUFFED CABBAGE
### (PICTURED ON P. 123)

*Here is one of my favorite ways to cook and enjoy cabbage. It has all the wonderful flavor of regular cabbage rolls, but it's a lot less bother to make. In fact, this is a one-pot recipe!*
—Bernard Snow, Lewiston, MI

**Prep:** 20 min. • **Cook:** 1¼ hours
**Makes:** 6 servings

**TOMATO SAUCE**
- 1   large onion, chopped
- 1   medium head cabbage, coarsely chopped (about 8 cups)
- 1   can (28 oz.) diced tomatoes, undrained
- 1   can (8 oz.) tomato sauce
- 1   cup water
- ¼   cup lemon juice
- ⅓   cup raisins

**MEATBALLS**
- ½   cup uncooked long grain rice
- 1   tsp. Worcestershire sauce
- ½   tsp. salt
- ¼   tsp. pepper
- 1   lb. lean ground beef (90% lean)

**1.** In a large skillet, combine the sauce ingredients. Bring to a boil; reduce heat and simmer.

**2.** Meanwhile, in a large bowl, combine the rice, Worcestershire sauce, salt and pepper. Crumble beef over rice mixture; mix lightly but thoroughly. Shape into 36 balls, about 1¼ in. in diameter. Add to simmering sauce.

**3.** Cover and simmer about 45 minutes or until the cabbage is tender. Uncover and cook for 15 minutes longer or until sauce is thickened.

**1 serving:** 291 cal., 7g fat (3g sat. fat), 47mg chol., 659mg sod., 40g carb. (16g sugars, 7g fiber), 20g pro. **Diabetic exchanges:** 2½ starch, 2 lean meat.

## SUNSHINE CHICKEN

*Since it can be easily doubled and takes little time or effort to prepare, this recipe is ideal to serve for large groups. Even my husband, who usually doesn't enjoy cooking, likes to make this dish.*
—Karen Gardiner, Eutaw, AL

**Prep:** 15 min. • **Cook:** 20 min.
**Makes:** 6 servings

- 2   to 3 tsp. curry powder
- 1¼  tsp. salt, divided
- ¼   tsp. pepper
- 6   boneless skinless chicken breast halves (5 oz. each)
- 1½  cups orange juice
- 1   cup uncooked long grain rice
- ¾   cup water
- 1   Tbsp. brown sugar
- 1   tsp. ground mustard
     Chopped fresh parsley

**1.** Combine the curry powder, ½ tsp. salt and the pepper; rub over both sides of chicken. In a skillet, combine orange juice, rice, water, brown sugar, mustard and remaining salt. Add chicken; bring to a boil. Reduce heat; cover and simmer until chicken juices run clear, 20-25 minutes.

**2.** Remove from the heat and let stand, covered, until all liquid is absorbed, about 5 minutes. Sprinkle with parsley.

**1 serving:** 317 cal., 4g fat (1g sat. fat), 78mg chol., 562mg sod., 36g carb. (8g sugars, 1g fiber), 32g pro. **Diabetic exchanges:** 4 lean meat, 2 starch.

**\* HEALTH TIP \*** This one-pan dinner is easy to make and tastes special enough for company. Plus, it's free from gluten, egg and dairy, so it's allergy-friendly, too!

**SUNSHINE CHICKEN**

## MODERN TUNA CASSEROLE

*I loved tuna casserole as a kid and found myself craving it as an adult. However, the massive amounts of fat and salt in the traditional recipe were a turnoff healthwise, and it just didn't taste as good as I remembered. I reconfigured the recipe to include more vegetables, and the result was delicious.*
—Rebecca Blanton, St. Helena, CA

- - - - - - - - - - - - - - - - - - - - - - - -

**Prep:** 20 min. • **Cook:** 20 min.
**Makes:** 6 servings

- 3 Tbsp. butter, divided
- 4 medium carrots, chopped
- 1 medium onion, chopped
- 1 medium sweet red pepper, chopped
- 1 cup sliced baby portobello mushrooms
- 2 cans (5 oz. each) albacore white tuna in water, drained and flaked
- 2 cups fresh baby spinach
- 1 cup frozen peas
- 3 cups uncooked spiral pasta
- 1 Tbsp. all-purpose flour
- ⅔ cup reduced-sodium chicken broth
- ⅓ cup half-and-half cream
- ½ cup shredded Parmesan cheese
- ¾ tsp. salt
- ¼ tsp. pepper

**1.** In a large skillet, heat 1 Tbsp. butter over medium-high heat. Add the carrots, onion, red pepper and mushrooms. Cook and stir until tender, 8-10 minutes. Add tuna, spinach and peas; cook until spinach is just wilted, 2-3 minutes.
**2.** Meanwhile, cook pasta according to package directions for al dente. Drain pasta, reserving 1 cup pasta water. In a large bowl, place pasta and tuna mixture, toss to combine. Wipe skillet clean.
**3.** In the same skillet, melt the remaining butter over medium heat. Stir in the flour until smooth; gradually whisk in broth and cream. Bring to a boil, stirring constantly; cook and stir until thickened, 1-2 minutes, adding reserved pasta water if needed. Stir in cheese, salt and pepper. Pour over pasta; toss to coat.
**1¾ cups:** 372 cal., 11g fat (6g sat. fat), 47mg chol., 767mg sod., 44g carb. (7g sugars, 5g fiber), 23g pro. **Diabetic exchanges:** 3 lean meat, 2½ starch, 1½ fat, 1 vegetable.

## PORK CHOPS WITH DIJON SAUCE

*Here's a main course that tastes rich but isn't high in saturated fat. It's easy for weeknights and the creamy sauce makes it special enough for weekends.*
—Bonnie Brown-Watson, Houston, TX

- - - - - - - - - - - - - - - - - - - - - - - -

**Takes:** 25 min. • **Makes:** 4 servings

- 4 boneless pork loin chops (6 oz. each)
- ¼ tsp. salt
- ¼ tsp. pepper
- 2 tsp. canola oil
- ⅓ cup reduced-sodium chicken broth
- 2 Tbsp. Dijon mustard
- ⅓ cup half-and-half cream

**1.** Sprinkle pork chops with salt and pepper. In a large skillet coated with cooking spray, brown chops in oil for 4-5 minutes on each side or until a thermometer reads 145°. Remove and keep warm.
**2.** Stir broth into skillet, scraping up any browned bits. Stir in the mustard and half-and-half. Bring to a boil. Reduce the heat; simmer, uncovered, until thickened, 5-6 minutes, stirring occasionally. Serve with pork chops.
**1 pork chop.** 283 cal., 14g fat (5g sat. fat), 92mg chol., 432mg sod., 1g carb. (1g sugars, 0 fiber), 34g pro. **Diabetic exchanges:** 5 lean meat, 2 fat.

**STOVETOP ORANGE-GLAZED CHICKEN**

## 🕐 2

## SPICY TURKEY STIR-FRY WITH NOODLES

*I created this ground turkey stir-fry recipe when I began my journey to get fit. Healthy eating always sounds so bland and boring, so I wanted to bring life to the world of healthy eating. I think I succeeded with this spicy dish.*
—Jermell Clark, Desert Hot Springs, CA

**Takes:** 30 min. • **Makes:** 2 servings

- 2   oz. thick rice noodles
- ½   lb. lean ground turkey
- 1   small onion, chopped
- ½   cup shredded red cabbage
- ½   cup chopped fresh kale
- ¼   cup packed fresh parsley sprigs, chopped
- 1   tsp. coconut or olive oil
- ½   tsp. pepper
- ¼   tsp. salt
- 3   green onions, thinly sliced
- 1   jalapeno pepper, sliced
- 2   tsp. Sriracha chili sauce
      Thai peanut sauce, optional

**1.** Cook noodles according to package directions. Meanwhile, in a large skillet, cook turkey, onion, cabbage and kale over medium-high heat until turkey is no longer pink and the vegetables are tender, 8-10 minutes, breaking up turkey into crumbles.

**2.** Drain noodles; add to skillet. Stir in parsley, coconut oil, pepper and salt. Serve with green onions, jalapeno, chili sauce and, if desired, peanut sauce.

**Note:** Wear disposable gloves when cutting hot peppers; the oils can burn skin. Avoid touching your face.

**2 cups:** 332 cal., 11g fat (4g sat. fat), 78mg chol., 588mg sod., 32g carb. (4g sugars, 3g fiber), 25g pro. **Diabetic exchanges:** 3 lean meat, 2 starch, ½ fat.

## 🕐 2

## STOVETOP ORANGE-GLAZED CHICKEN

*I love a recipe that can put dinner on the table quickly without sacrificing flavor. This sweet and saucy dish does just that with ingredients you probably already have on hand!*
—Kallee Krong-McCreery, Escondido, CA

**Takes:** 25 min. • **Makes:** 2 servings

- ¼   cup orange juice
- 1   Tbsp. reduced-sodium soy sauce
- ½   tsp. cornstarch
- ½   tsp. Dijon mustard
- 2   Tbsp. orange marmalade
- 2   boneless skinless chicken breast halves (6 oz. each)
- ¼   tsp. garlic salt
- 1   Tbsp. olive oil

**1.** For glaze, whisk together the first 4 ingredients in a microwave-safe bowl; stir in marmalade. Microwave, covered, on high until thickened, 2½-3 minutes, stirring occasionally.

**2.** Pound chicken breasts to ½-in. thickness; sprinkle with garlic salt. In a large skillet, heat oil over medium heat; cook chicken until a thermometer reads 165°, 5-6 minutes per side. Top with glaze.

**1 chicken breast half with about 2 Tbsp. sauce:** 314 cal., 11g fat (2g sat. fat), 94mg chol., 656mg sod., 18g carb. (15g sugars, 0 fiber), 35g pro. **Diabetic exchanges:** 5 lean meat, 1½ fat, 1 starch.

### TEST KITCHEN TIP

Flattening the chicken helps it cook quickly and evenly. When flattening the chicken, cover the meat with plastic wrap and use the flat side of a meat mallet. If you don't have a meat mallet, use a rolling pin.

SPICY TURKEY STIR-FRY
WITH NOODLES

## GNOCCHI WITH PESTO SAUCE

*Perk up gnocchi and vegetables with a flavorful pesto sauce. If you don't have pine nuts for sprinkling on top, substitute sliced almonds or any nut you like.*
—Taste of Home Test Kitchen

**Takes:** 25 min. • **Makes:** 4 servings

- 1   pkg. (16 oz.) potato gnocchi
- 2   tsp. olive oil
- 1   cup diced zucchini
- ½   cup chopped sweet yellow pepper
- ¼   cup prepared pesto
- 1   cup chopped tomatoes
     Toasted pine nuts, optional

**1.** Cook gnocchi according to package directions; drain.

**2.** Meanwhile, in a large skillet, heat oil over medium-high heat; saute zucchini and pepper until zucchini is tender.

**3.** Add pesto and gnocchi, stirring gently to coat. Stir in tomatoes. If desired, top with pine nuts.

**1 cup:** 327 cal., 9g fat (2g sat. fat), 8mg chol., 682mg sod., 52g carb. (10g sugars, 4g fiber), 9g pro.

## QUICK MOROCCAN SHRIMP SKILLET

*When my niece was attending West Point, she was sent to Morocco for five months. I threw her a going-away party with Moroccan decorations, costumes and cuisine, including this saucy shrimp dish. Whenever I make it now, I think of her and I smile.*
—Barbara Lento, Houston, PA

**Takes:** 25 min. • **Makes:** 4 servings

- 1   Tbsp. canola oil
- 1   small onion, chopped
- ¼   cup pine nuts
- 1   lb. uncooked shrimp (16-20 per lb.), peeled and deveined
- 1   cup uncooked pearl (Israeli) couscous
- 2   Tbsp. lemon juice
- 3   tsp. Moroccan seasoning (ras el hanout)
- 1   tsp. garlic salt
- 2   cups hot water
     Minced fresh parsley, optional

**1.** In a large skillet, heat oil over medium-high heat; saute onion and pine nuts until onion is tender, 2-3 minutes. Stir in all remaining ingredients except parsley; bring just to a boil. Reduce the heat; simmer, covered, until shrimp turn pink, 4-6 minutes.

**2.** Remove from heat; let stand for 5 minutes. If desired, top with parsley.

**1 cup:** 335 cal., 11g fat (1g sat. fat), 138mg chol., 626mg sod., 34g carb. (1g sugars, 1g fiber), 24g pro.

**Note:** This recipe was tested with McCormick Gourmet Moroccan Seasoning (ras el hanout).

**\* HEALTH TIP \*** Shrimp are naturally high in cholesterol, but not to worry. The greatest impact on blood cholesterol comes from saturated and trans fats, and shrimp has little saturated and no trans fat.

## EASY PEPPER STEAK

*This popular beef dish is tasty as well as colorful.*
—Carolyn Butterfield, Atkinson, NE

- - - - - - - - - - - - - - - - - - - - - - - -

**Prep:** 10 min. • **Cook:** 55 min.
**Makes:** 4 servings

- 1 lb. beef top round steak, cut into ¼-in. x 2-in. strips
- 1 Tbsp. paprika
- 2 Tbsp. butter
- 1 can (10½ oz.) beef broth
- 2 garlic cloves, minced
- 2 medium green peppers, cut into strips
- 1 cup thinly sliced onion
- 2 Tbsp. cornstarch
- 2 Tbsp. reduced-sodium soy sauce
- ⅓ cup cold water
- 2 fresh tomatoes, peeled and cut into wedges
    Cooked rice

**1.** Sprinkle meat with paprika. In a large skillet, melt butter over medium-high heat. Brown beef. Add broth and garlic. Simmer, covered, for 30 minutes. Add green peppers and onion. Cover and continue to simmer for 5 minutes.

**2.** Combine cornstarch, soy sauce and water; stir into meat mixture. Cook and stir until thickened. Gently stir in tomatoes and heat through. Serve over rice.

**1 serving:** 365 cal., 4g fat (1g sat. fat), 65mg chol., 465mg sod., 48g carb. (5g sugars, 4g fiber), 32g pro.

> **TEST KITCHEN TIP**
>
> Cornstarch needs just a few minutes of boiling to thicken a sauce, gravy or dessert filling. If it cooks too long, the cornstarch will begin to lose its thickening power. Carefully follow the recipe for the best results.

## CHICKEN JAMBALAYA

**(PICTURED ON P. 123)**

*This is a great dish to serve at parties. It's just as good as, if not tastier than, most high-fat versions. And it reheats well.*
—Lynn Desjardins, Atkinson, NH

- - - - - - - - - - - - - - - - - - - - - - - -

**Prep:** 20 min. • **Cook:** 1 hour
**Makes:** 6 servings

- ¾ lb. boneless skinless chicken breasts, cubed
- 3 cups reduced-sodium chicken broth
- 1½ cups uncooked brown rice
- 4 oz. reduced-fat smoked turkey sausage, diced
- ½ cup thinly sliced celery with leaves
- ¼ cup chopped onion
- ½ cup chopped green pepper
- 2 to 3 tsp. Cajun or Creole seasoning
- 1 to 2 garlic cloves, minced
- ⅛ tsp. hot pepper sauce
- 1 bay leaf
- 1 can (14½ oz.) no-salt-added diced tomatoes, undrained
    Chopped green onions, optional

**1.** In a large skillet lightly coated with cooking spray, saute the chicken until chicken is no longer pink, 2-3 minutes. Stir in the next 10 ingredients. Bring to a boil. Reduce heat; cover and simmer until heated through, 50-60 minutes.

**2.** Stir in tomatoes; cover and simmer for 10 minutes longer or until liquid is absorbed and rice is tender. Remove from the heat; let stand for 5 minutes. Discard bay leaf. Serve with green onions if desired.

**1 cup:** 285 cal., 4g fat (1g sat. fat), 43mg chol., 654mg sod., 41g carb. (4g sugars, 4g fiber), 21g pro. **Diabetic exchanges:** 2½ starch, 2 lean meat.

EASY PEPPER STEAK

## SEARED SALMON WITH BALSAMIC SAUCE

*A friend gave me this quick and easy approach to salmon. It has a mildly sweet sauce and is such a hit, I've passed it to other fish fans.*
—Trish Horton, Colorado Springs, CO

**Takes:** 30 min. • **Makes:** 4 servings

- 4 salmon fillets (4 oz. each)
- ½ tsp. salt
- 2 tsp. canola oil
- ¼ cup water
- ¼ cup balsamic vinegar
- 4 tsp. lemon juice
- 4 tsp. brown sugar
  Coarsely ground pepper

1. Sprinkle salmon with salt. In a large nonstick skillet, heat oil over medium heat. Place salmon in skillet, skin side up; cook until fish just begins to flake easily with a fork, 4-5 minutes on each side. Remove from pan; keep warm.
2. In same skillet, combine water, vinegar, lemon juice and brown sugar. Bring to a boil; cook until liquid is reduced to about ⅓ cup, stirring occasionally. Serve salmon with sauce; sprinkle with pepper.

**1 fillet with about 1 Tbsp. sauce:** 231 cal., 13g fat (2g sat. fat), 57mg chol., 353mg sod., 9g carb. (9g sugars, 0 fiber), 19g pro. **Diabetic exchanges:** 3 lean meat, ½ starch, ½ fat.

**CHIPOTLE CITRUS-GLAZED TURKEY TENDERLOINS**

## CHIPOTLE CITRUS-GLAZED TURKEY TENDERLOINS

*This simple skillet recipe makes it easy to cook turkey on a weeknight. The combination of sweet, spicy and smoky flavors from orange, peppers and molasses is amazing.*
—Darlene Morris, Franklinton, LA

**Takes:** 30 min.
**Makes:** 4 servings (½ cup sauce)

- 4 turkey breast tenderloins (5 oz. each)
- ¼ tsp. salt
- ¼ tsp. pepper
- 1 Tbsp. canola oil
- ¾ cup orange juice
- ¼ cup lime juice
- ¼ cup packed brown sugar
- 1 Tbsp. molasses
- 2 tsp. minced chipotle peppers in adobo sauce
- 2 Tbsp. minced fresh cilantro

1. Sprinkle turkey with salt and pepper. In a large skillet, brown the turkey in oil on all sides.
2. Meanwhile, in a small bowl whisk the juices, brown sugar, molasses and chipotle peppers; add to skillet. Reduce heat and simmer for 12-16 minutes or until turkey reaches 165°. Transfer turkey to a cutting board; let rest for 5 minutes.
3. Simmer glaze until thickened, about 4 minutes. Slice turkey and serve with glaze. Top with cilantro.

**4 oz. cooked turkey with 2 Tbsp. glaze:** 274 cal., 5g fat (0 sat. fat), 56mg chol., 252mg sod., 24g carb. (22g sugars, 0 fiber), 35g pro.

## CURRIED CHICKEN SKILLET

*This protein-packed skillet dish is loaded with bright flavor. A little curry and fresh ginger make the veggies, chicken and quinoa pop.*

—Ruth Hartunian-Alumbaugh, Willimantic, CT

**Takes:** 30 min. • **Makes:** 4 servings

- 1⅓ cups plus ½ cup reduced-sodium chicken broth, divided
- ⅔ cup quinoa, rinsed
- 1 Tbsp. canola oil
- 1 medium sweet potato, diced
- 1 medium onion, chopped
- 1 celery rib, chopped
- 1 cup frozen peas
- 2 garlic cloves, minced
- 1 tsp. minced fresh gingerroot
- 3 tsp. curry powder
- ¼ tsp. salt
- 2 cups shredded cooked chicken

**1.** In a small saucepan, bring 1⅓ cups broth to a boil. Add quinoa. Reduce heat; simmer, covered, until liquid is absorbed, 12-15 minutes.

**2.** In a large skillet, heat oil over medium-high heat; saute sweet potato, onion and celery for 10-12 minutes or until potato is tender. Add the peas, garlic, ginger and seasonings; cook and stir 2 minutes. Stir in chicken and remaining broth; heat through. Stir in quinoa.

**2 cups:** 367 cal., 11g fat (2g sat. fat), 62mg chol., 450mg sod., 39g carb. (8g sugars, 6g fiber), 29g pro. **Diabetic exchanges:** 3 lean meat, 2½ starch, ½ fat.

**TEST KITCHEN TIP**

Twelve ounces of uncooked boneless chicken can be used if you don't have cooked chicken handy. Cut it into cubes or strips and saute it before cooking the vegetables. Remove the chicken while the vegetables are sauteed so it doesn't overcook.

**CURRIED CHICKEN SKILLET**

EDAMAME & SOBA
NOODLE BOWL

## EDAMAME & SOBA NOODLE BOWL

*Toothsome soba noodles are made from buckwheat flour.*
—Matthew Hass, Ellison Bay, WI

- - - - - - - - - - - - - - - - - - - - - - - - - - - - - - - -

**Takes:** 30 min. • **Makes:** 6 servings

- 1 pkg. (12 oz.) uncooked Japanese soba noodles or whole wheat spaghetti
- 2 Tbsp. sesame oil
- 2 cups fresh small broccoli florets
- 1 medium onion, halved and thinly sliced
- 3 cups frozen shelled edamame, thawed
- 2 large carrots, cut into ribbons with a vegetable peeler
- 4 garlic cloves, minced
- 1 cup reduced-fat Asian toasted sesame salad dressing
- ¼ tsp. pepper
  Sesame seeds, toasted, optional

1. In a 6 qt. stockpot, cook the noodles according to package directions; drain and return to pan.
2. Meanwhile, in a large skillet, heat oil over medium heat. Add the broccoli and onion; cook and stir 4-6 minutes or until crisp-tender. Add edamame and carrots; cook and stir until tender, 6-8 minutes. Add the garlic; cook 1 minute longer. Add vegetable mixture, dressing and pepper to noodles; toss to combine. Sprinkle with sesame seeds if desired.

**1⅓ cups:** 414 cal., 12g fat (1g sat. fat), 0 chol., 867mg sod., 64g carb. (12g sugars, 4g fiber), 18g pro.

**TEST KITCHEN TIP**

The hearty texture and slightly nutty taste of whole wheat pasta make it an ideal stand-in when you're preparing Asian recipes that call for buckwheat or soba noodles. Even if you don't enjoy the taste of whole wheat pasta in your favorite Italian recipes, don't be afraid to try it in Asian ones!

PORK TENDERLOIN WITH WINE SAUCE

## PORK TENDERLOIN WITH WINE SAUCE

*Here's a fast and easy dish that's as big on flavor as it is low in fat and calories. I like to serve it with fresh green beans and mashed potatoes.*
—Nancy LaVoice, Wexford, PA

- - - - - - - - - - - - - - - - - - - - - - - - - - - - - - - -

**Takes:** 25 min. • **Makes:** 2 servings

- 1 pork tenderloin (¾ lb.)
  Dash pepper
- 1 tsp. canola oil
- 1 tsp. butter
- ¼ cup reduced-sodium beef broth
- ¼ cup dry red wine or additional reduced-sodium beef broth
- ¼ tsp. Dijon mustard
- ¼ tsp. dried thyme
- ⅛ tsp. dried rosemary, crushed

1. Cut pork into 2-in. slices; flatten to 1½-in. thickness. Sprinkle with pepper. In a large skillet over medium heat, cook pork in oil and butter for 5 minutes on each side or until meat is no longer pink. Remove and keep warm.
2. Add the broth to the pan, scraping to loosen browned bits. Stir in the wine, mustard, thyme and rosemary. Bring to a boil. Reduce heat; simmer, uncovered, for 3 minutes, stirring occasionally. Serve with pork.

**5 oz. cooked pork:** 259 cal., 10g fat (3g sat. fat), 100mg chol., 159mg sod., 1g carb. (0 sugars, 0 fiber), 34g pro. **Diabetic exchanges:** 5 lean meat, 1 fat.

## TURKEY IN COGNAC CREAM SAUCE

*I found this recipe in a magazine and over the years have adjusted it to suit my family's taste. It is special enough for company and easy enough for any weeknight.*
—Virginia C. Anthony, Jacksonville, FL

**Prep:** 20 min. • **Cook:** 20 min.
**Makes:** 4 servings

- 1 pkg. (17.6 oz.) turkey breast cutlets
- ¼ tsp. plus ⅛ tsp. salt, divided
- ¼ tsp. coarsely ground pepper
- 2 Tbsp. mustard seeds, crushed
- 4½ tsp. olive oil, divided
- 1½ cups sliced fresh mushrooms
- 1 shallot, finely chopped
- 1 garlic clove, minced
- ⅓ cup reduced-sodium chicken broth
- 3 Tbsp. Cognac or 3 Tbsp. brandy
- 1 plum tomato, seeded and chopped
- ¼ cup half-and-half cream
- 4½ tsp. minced fresh basil

**1.** Sprinkle turkey with ¼ tsp. salt and pepper; press on mustard seeds. In a large nonstick skillet over medium heat, cook turkey in 3 tsp. oil in batches for 2-3 minutes on each side or until no longer pink. Remove and keep warm.
**2.** In the same skillet, saute mushrooms and shallot in remaining oil until tender. Add garlic; cook 1 minute longer. Remove from the heat; stir in broth and Cognac, stirring to loosen browned bits from pan. Add tomato and cream. Bring to a boil; cook until liquid is reduced by half. Stir in basil and remaining salt. Serve the sauce with turkey.

**4 oz. cooked turkey with ⅓ cup sauce:**
260 cal., 9g fat (2g sat. fat), 85mg chol., 341mg sod., 6g carb. (2g sugars, 1g fiber), 34g pro.
**Diabetic exchanges:** 4 lean meat, 1 fat, ½ starch.

## SALMON WITH TOMATO-GOAT CHEESE COUSCOUS

*This is a really simple, healthy and quick meal that tastes like it took much more time and trouble than it does. And it's easily adjusted for any number of people.*
—Toni Roberts, La Canada, CA

**Takes:** 30 min. • **Makes:** 4 servings

- 4 salmon fillets (5 oz. each)
- ¼ tsp. salt
- ¼ tsp. garlic salt
- ¼ tsp. pepper
- 1 Tbsp. olive oil
- 1 cup chicken stock
- ¾ cup uncooked whole wheat couscous
- 2 plum tomatoes, chopped
- 4 green onions, chopped
- ¼ cup crumbled goat cheese

**1.** Sprinkle salmon with salt, garlic salt and pepper. Heat oil in a large skillet over medium-high heat; add salmon skin side up and cook 3 minutes. Turn fish and cook an additional 4 minutes or until fish flakes easily with a fork. Remove from heat and keep warm.
**2.** In a large saucepan, bring stock to a boil. Stir in couscous. Remove from heat; let stand, covered, until stock is absorbed, about 5 minutes. Stir in tomatoes, onions and goat cheese. Serve with salmon.

**1 fillet with 1 cup couscous mixture:**
414 cal., 19g fat (4g sat. fat), 80mg chol., 506mg sod., 31g carb. (2g sugars, 6g fiber), 32g pro. **Diabetic exchanges:** 4 lean meat, 2 starch, 1 fat.

**TEST KITCHEN TIP**

If you can't find small pieces of salmon, buy a large fillet and cut it into 5-oz. portions.

**SALMON WITH TOMATO-GOAT CHEESE COUSCOUS**

## CREAMY CHICKEN & THYME

*Thyme gives this simple chicken dish its unique flavor. I lightened up the original recipe by using reduced-fat sour cream, but you'd never guess based on its rich, creamy flavor.*
—Harriet Johnson, Champlin, MN

**Takes:** 30 min. • **Makes:** 4 servings

- 4 boneless skinless chicken breast halves (4 oz. each)
- 1 can (14½ oz.) reduced-sodium chicken broth
- 1 Tbsp. all-purpose flour
- ½ cup reduced-fat sour cream
- ½ tsp. dried parsley flakes
- ¼ tsp. salt
- ¼ tsp. dill weed
- ¼ tsp. dried thyme
- ⅛ tsp. onion salt
- ⅛ tsp. pepper
  Hot cooked egg noodles, optional

**1.** Place chicken breasts in a large nonstick skillet. Add ½ cup of broth. Cover and simmer 10-12 minutes or until juices run clear, turning once. Remove chicken from pan; keep warm. Add the remaining broth to skillet and bring to a boil; reduce heat to low.

**2.** In a small bowl, combine the flour and sour cream. Whisk into pan. Stir in the parsley, salt, dill weed, thyme, onion salt and pepper. Simmer, uncovered, until slightly thickened, about 5 minutes. If desired, serve with hot cooked noodles.

**1 serving:** 167 cal., 5g fat (2g sat. fat), 66mg chol., 575mg sod., 4g carb. (3g sugars, 0 fiber), 27g pro. **Diabetic exchanges:** 3 lean meat, ½ fat.

CREAMY CHICKEN
& THYME

## GARLIC LEMON SHRIMP

*This shrimp dish is amazingly quick to get on the table. Serve it with crusty bread so you can soak up the luscious garlic lemon sauce.*
—Athena Russell, Greenville, SC

-------------------------------------------------

**Takes:** 20 min. • **Makes:** 4 servings

- 2　Tbsp. olive oil
- 1　lb. uncooked shrimp (26-30 per lb.), peeled and deveined
- 3　garlic cloves, thinly sliced
- 1　Tbsp. lemon juice
- 1　tsp. ground cumin
- ¼　tsp. salt
- 2　Tbsp. minced fresh parsley
　　Hot cooked pasta or rice

In a large skillet, heat oil over medium-high heat; saute shrimp 3 minutes. Add garlic, lemon juice, cumin and salt; cook and stir until shrimp turn pink. Stir in parsley. Serve with pasta.

**1 serving:** 163 cal., 8g fat (1g sat. fat), 138mg chol., 284mg sod., 2g carb. (0 sugars, 0 fiber), 19g pro. Diabetic Exchanges: 3 lean meat, 1½ fat.

**\* HEALTH TIP \*** Cooking the shrimp in olive oil instead of butter saves about 3 grams of saturated fat per serving.

**CHICKEN WITH COUSCOUS**

## CHICKEN WITH COUSCOUS

*My sister shared this recipe, and it's been a hit with me, my husband and our friends ever since. After working all day, I love that this dish is fast to prepare. Plus, it's irresistibly bright and delicious.*
—Shari Ruffalo, Watertown, NY

-------------------------------------------------

**Takes:** 25 min. • **Makes:** 4 servings

- 1½　cups fresh broccoli florets
- 1　pkg. (5.8 oz.) roasted garlic and olive oil couscous
- 1　cup water
- 1　tsp. plus 2 Tbsp. olive oil, divided
- 4　boneless skinless chicken breast halves (4 oz. each)
- ½　tsp. salt
- ½　tsp. pepper
- 2　Tbsp. lemon juice
- 2　tsp. minced garlic
- ½　tsp. dried oregano
- 1　large tomato, seeded and chopped

**1.** In a large saucepan, combine the broccoli, contents of the couscous seasoning packet, water and 1 tsp. oil. Bring to a boil. Stir in couscous. Cover and remove from the heat; let stand for 5 minutes.

**2.** Meanwhile, flatten chicken to ¼-in. thickness. Sprinkle with salt and pepper. Combine the lemon juice, garlic and oregano; rub over chicken. In a large skillet, brown chicken in remaining oil over medium heat for 8-10 minutes or until juices run clear. Stir tomato into the couscous; serve with chicken.

**1 chicken breast half with 1 cup couscous:** 357 cal., 12g fat (2g sat. fat), 63mg chol., 711mg sod., 35g carb. (3g sugars, 3g fiber), 29g pro. **Diabetic exchanges:** 3 lean meat, 2 starch, 2 fat.

## ONE-PAN TUSCAN RAVIOLI

*Sometimes I use chickpeas instead of cannellini beans, grated Asiago or provolone instead of Parmesan, and all zucchini if I don't have eggplant. Very flexible!*
—Sonya Labbe, West Hollywood, CA

- - - - - - - - - - - - - - - - - - - - - - - - - - - - - - - -

**Takes:** 25 min. • **Makes:** 4 servings

1   Tbsp. olive oil
2   cups cubed eggplant (½ in.)
1   can (14½ oz.) Italian diced tomatoes, undrained
1   can (14½ oz.) reduced-sodium chicken broth
1   medium zucchini, halved lengthwise and cut into ½-in. slices
1   pkg. (9 oz.) refrigerated cheese ravioli
1   can (15 oz.) cannellini beans, rinsed and drained
    Shredded Parmesan cheese
    Thinly sliced fresh basil

**1.** In a large skillet, heat oil over medium heat; saute eggplant until lightly browned, 2-3 minutes.
**2.** Stir in tomatoes, broth and zucchini; bring to a boil. Add the ravioli; cook, uncovered, over medium heat until the ravioli are tender, 7-9 minutes, stirring occasionally. Stir in beans; heat through. Sprinkle with cheese and basil.

**1½ cups:** 376 cal., 10g fat (4g sat. fat), 36mg chol., 1006mg sod., 56g carb. (11g sugars, 8g fiber), 16g pro.

## SWEET & SOUR SAUSAGE STIR-FRY

*Who couldn't use a stir-fry that's low in prep time, yet bursting with flavor? My quick recipe is achievable even on your busiest nights.*
—Wendy Wendler, Indian Harbour Beach, FL

- - - - - - - - - - - - - - - - - - - - - - - - - - - - - - - -

**Takes:** 30 min. • **Makes:** 4 servings

1   pkg. (14 oz.) smoked turkey sausage, cut into ½-in. slices
2   small onions, quartered and separated
1   cup shredded carrots
1   can (8 oz.) unsweetened pineapple chunks, undrained
1   Tbsp. cornstarch
½   to 1 tsp. ground ginger
⅓   cup cold water
2   Tbsp. reduced-sodium soy sauce
    Hot cooked rice, optional

**1.** Stir-fry the sausage in a large nonstick skillet for 3-4 minutes or until lightly browned. Add onions and carrots; stir-fry until crisp-tender. Drain the pineapple, reserving juice. Add the pineapple to the sausage mixture.
**2.** Combine the cornstarch and ginger. Stir in the water, soy sauce and reserved pineapple juice until smooth. Add to the skillet. Bring to a boil; cook and stir for 1-2 minutes or until thickened. Serve over rice if desired.

**1 cup:** 197 cal., 5g fat (2g sat. fat), 62mg chol., 1283mg sod., 19g carb. (13g sugars, 2g fiber), 17g pro.

**READER REVIEW**

*"Loved this. I didn't have turkey sausage, so I used the pork smoked sausage, and added some water chestnuts to the mix. Excellent, easy and economical."*
—BEEMA, TASTEOFHOME.COM

ONE-PAN TUSCAN RAVIOLI

**SMOKED SAUSAGE WITH PASTA**

## APPLES & ONION TOPPED CHOPS

*Now that my husband and I are trying to lose weight, I find it a challenge to come up with healthy dishes that are flavorful, quick and appealing to us and our young daughter. This one meets all our criteria.*
—Beverly McLain, Endicott, NY

**Takes:** 30 min. • **Makes:** 4 servings

- 4 tsp. canola oil, divided
- 4 boneless pork loin chops (5 oz. each)
- 3 cups sweet onion slices
- 2 medium Granny Smith apples, peeled and sliced
- ½ cup water
- 2 Tbsp. brown sugar
- 1 Tbsp. cider vinegar
- 1 tsp. garlic powder
- ½ tsp. salt
- ¼ to ½ tsp. pepper
- ¼ tsp. dried rosemary, crushed

**1.** In a large nonstick skillet, heat 2 tsp. canola oil over medium-high heat; cook chops until browned, about 3 minutes on each side. Remove meat; set aside and keep warm.

**2.** In same skillet, cook and stir onion in remaining 2 tsp. canola oil for 7 minutes or until golden brown. Add apple slices; cook and stir 3 minutes longer.

**3.** Combine the water, brown sugar, vinegar, garlic powder, salt, pepper and rosemary. Stir into skillet. Bring to a boil. Return meat to pan. Reduce heat; cover and cook until apples are crisp-tender, and a thermometer inserted into chops reads 145°, 6-8 minutes. Let stand 5 minutes before serving.

**1 serving:** 326 cal., 13g fat (3g sat. fat), 68mg chol., 340mg sod., 24g carb. (17g sugars, 3g fiber), 28g pro. **Diabetic exchanges:** 4 lean meat, 1 vegetable, 1 fat, ½ starch, ½ fruit.

## SMOKED SAUSAGE WITH PASTA

*Loaded with turkey sausage, mushrooms, tomatoes and basil flavor, this quick recipe satisfies the toughest critics. It's one of my husband's favorite dishes, and he has no idea it's lower in fat. Add a green salad for a delicious meal.*
—Ruth Ann Ruddell, Shelby Township, MI

**Takes:** 30 min. • **Makes:** 4 servings

- 4 oz. uncooked angel hair pasta
- ½ lb. smoked turkey kielbasa, cut into ½-in. slices
- 2 cups sliced fresh mushrooms
- 2 garlic cloves, minced
- 4½ tsp. minced fresh basil or 1½ tsp. dried basil
- 1 Tbsp. olive oil
- 2 cups julienned seeded plum tomatoes
- ⅛ tsp. salt
- ⅛ tsp. pepper
- Grated Parmesan cheese, optional

Cook pasta according to the package directions. Meanwhile, in a large nonstick skillet, saute the sausage, mushrooms, garlic and basil in oil until mushrooms are tender. Drain pasta; add to the sausage mixture. Add the tomatoes, salt and pepper; toss gently. Heat through. If desired, top with additional fresh basil and grated Parmesan cheese.

**1 cup:** 232 cal., 7g fat (2g sat. fat), 35mg chol., 639mg sod., 27g carb. (5g sugars, 2g fiber), 15g pro. **Diabetic exchanges:** 2 lean meat, 1½ starch, 1 vegetable, ½ fat.

APPLES & ONION
TOPPED CHOPS

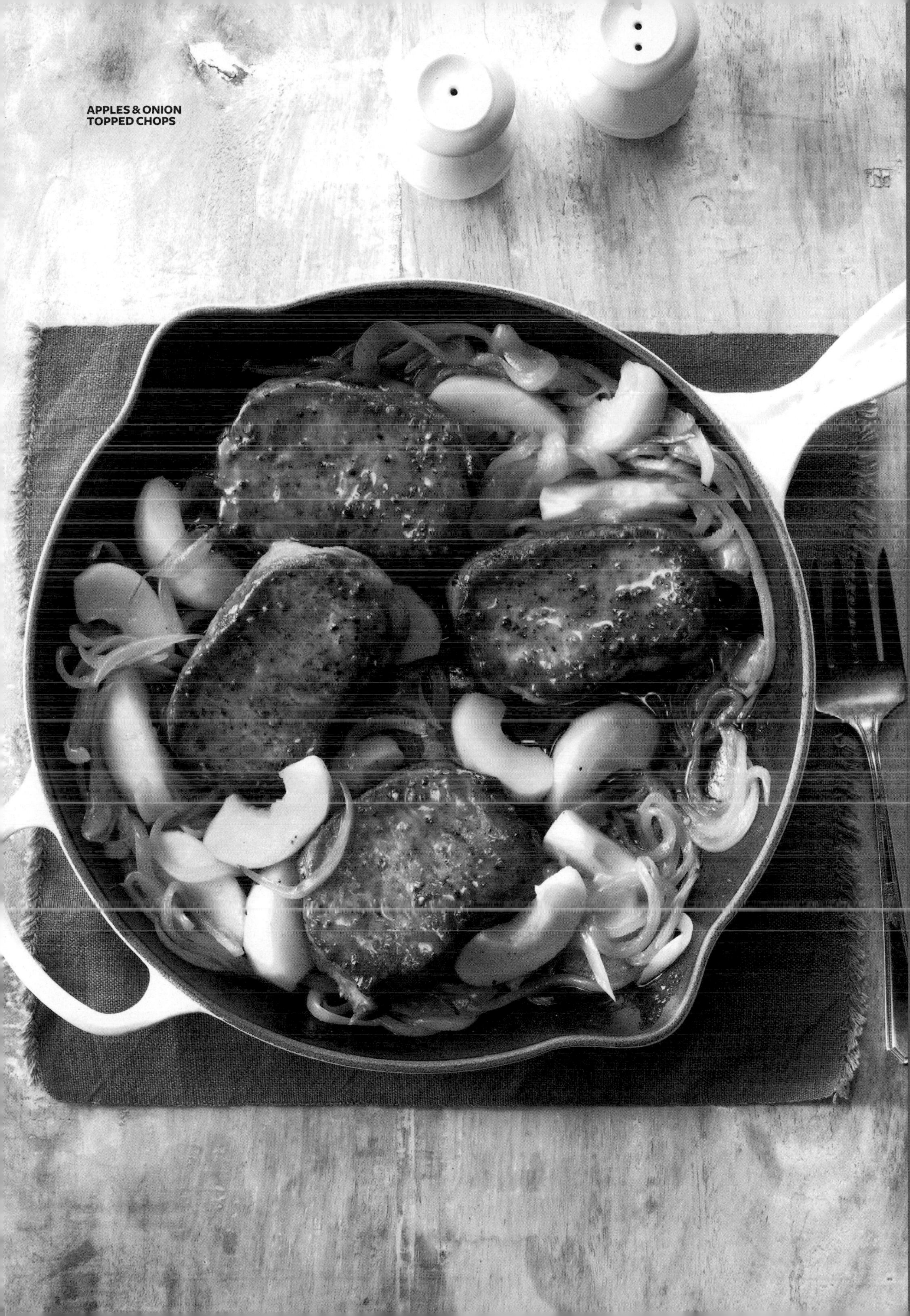

**TURKEY SALISBURY STEAKS**

## TURKEY SALISBURY STEAKS

*My mother always made Salisbury steak. When I married, I created my own version. This is one of my husband's favorites.*
—Leann Doyle, Patchogue, NY

**Prep:** 20 min. • **Cook:** 15 min.
**Makes:** 4 servings

⅔ cup seasoned bread crumbs, divided
⅓ cup finely chopped onion
2 tsp. low-sodium Worcestershire sauce
2 tsp. A.1. steak sauce
1 garlic clove, minced
½ tsp. dried basil
½ tsp. dried oregano
¼ tsp. garlic powder
¼ tsp. pepper

1 lb. extra-lean ground turkey
1½ tsp. olive oil
SAUCE
2 Tbsp. olive oil
2 Tbsp. all-purpose flour
1½ cups reduced-sodium beef broth
1 Tbsp. low-sodium Worcestershire sauce
1 Tbsp. A.1. steak sauce
1 can (4 oz.) sliced mushrooms, drained

**1.** In a large bowl, combine ⅓ cup bread crumbs, onion, Worcestershire sauce, steak sauce, garlic and seasonings. Add turkey; mix lightly but thoroughly. Shape into four ½-in.-thick oval patties. Place the remaining bread crumbs in a shallow bowl. Press patties into crumbs, patting to help coating adhere.

**2.** In a large nonstick skillet, heat 1½ tsp. oil over medium heat. Add patties; cook 3-4 minutes on each side or until a thermometer reads 165°. Remove from the pan.

**3.** In same pan, heat 2 Tbsp. oil over medium heat. Stir in flour until smooth; gradually whisk in broth, Worcestershire sauce and steak sauce. Bring to a boil, stirring constantly; cook and stir until thickened, 1-2 minutes. Stir in sliced mushrooms. Return patties to pan. Reduce heat; simmer, covered, until heated through, 2-3 minutes.

**1 patty with ⅓ cup sauce:** 291 cal., 11g fat (1g sat. fat), 47mg chol., 703mg sod., 18g carb. (5g sugars, 2g fiber), 32g pro. **Diabetic exchanges:** 3 lean meat, 2 fat, 1 starch.

## BEEF BOLOGNESE WITH LINGUINE

*After a great deal of research, tasting and tweaking, I finally came up with this recipe, based on a dish from an Italian restaurant where I worked. It's perfect for feeding a house full of holiday guests the Sunday before or after Christmas.*
—Christine Wendland, Browns Mills, NJ

**Prep:** 30 min. • **Cook:** 3½ hours.
**Makes:** 18 servings (1 cup each)

3 lbs. lean ground beef (90% lean)
⅓ cup olive oil
3 medium onions, chopped
3 large carrots, chopped
6 celery ribs, chopped
1 can (12 oz.) tomato paste, divided
9 garlic cloves, sliced
3 Tbsp. dried parsley flakes
5 tsp. kosher salt
3 tsp. dried basil
3 tsp. dried marjoram
1½ tsp. coarsely ground pepper
¼ tsp. crushed red pepper flakes
1½ cups dry red wine
3 cans (28 oz. each) diced tomatoes, undrained
1½ cups beef stock
6 bay leaves
3 cups 2% milk
¾ cup grated Parmesan cheese
Hot cooked linguine

1. In a stockpot, cook half of the beef over medium heat for 8-10 minutes or until no longer pink, breaking into crumbles. Remove beef with a slotted spoon; set aside. Pour off drippings. Repeat with remaining beef.
2. In the same pot, heat oil over medium heat. Add onions, carrots and celery; cook and stir until tender. Add 1 cup tomato paste; cook and stir 3 minutes longer. Add garlic, seasonings and beef.
3. Stir in wine. Bring to a boil; cook until almost evaporated. Add tomatoes, stock and bay leaves; return to a boil. Reduce heat; simmer, uncovered, for 3 hours or until desired consistency, stirring in milk halfway through cooking.
4. Remove bay leaves. Stir in cheese and remaining tomato paste; heat through. Serve with linguine.

**1 cup:** 270 cal., 12g fat (4g sat. fat), 53mg chol., 929mg sod., 17g carb. (10g sugars, 4g fiber), 20g pro.

**BEEF BOLOGNESE WITH LINGUINE**

## LEMON-CAPER PORK MEDALLIONS

*These pork medallions are truly something special!*
—Taste of Home Test Kitchen

**Takes:** 30 min. • **Makes:** 4 servings

1 pork tenderloin (1 lb.), cut into 12 slices
½ cup all-purpose flour
½ tsp. salt
¼ tsp. pepper
1 Tbsp. butter
1 Tbsp. olive oil
1 cup reduced-sodium chicken broth
¼ cup white wine or additional broth
1 garlic clove, minced
1 Tbsp. capers, drained
1 Tbsp. lemon juice
½ tsp. dried rosemary, crushed

1. Flatten pork slices to ¼-in. thickness. In a large shallow dish, combine the flour, salt and pepper. Add pork, a few pieces at a time, and turn to coat.
2. In a large nonstick skillet over medium heat, cook the pork in butter and oil in batches until juices run clear. Remove and keep warm. Add the broth, wine and garlic to the pan, stirring to loosen browned bits. Bring to a boil; cook until liquid is reduced by half. Stir in capers, lemon juice and rosemary; heat through. Serve with pork.

**3 medallions:** 232 cal., 10g fat (4g sat. fat), 71mg chol., 589mg sod., 7g carb. (1g sugars, 0 fiber), 24g pro. **Diabetic exchanges:** 3 lean meat, 1½ fat, ½ starch.

**HOW-TO**

### Get the Most Juice
Before squeezing, microwave the lemon 7-10 seconds. Then roll it back and forth under your palm on the counter, applying firm pressure. The fruit will be easier to squeeze and you'll get more juice.

# OVEN ENTREES

"A comforting dinner is sure to be had when flavorful Greek spaghetti is on the menu. Featuring chicken, spinach and two types of cheese, this dish is a crowd-pleaser."
—Melanie Dalbec, Inver Grove, MN

**Porcini-Crusted Pork with Polenta** (p. 169) **Broiled Shrimp Skewers** (p. 150) **Beef Cabbage Roll-Ups** (p. 155)
**Mexican-Style Meat Loaves** (p. 164) **Greek Spaghetti with Chicken** (p. 158) **Turkey Tenderloin & Root Veggie Sheet-Pan Supper** (p. 149)

**MUSHROOM &
SWEET POTATO POTPIE**

## MUSHROOM &
## SWEET POTATO POTPIE

*The last time I was in the U.S., I had an
amazing mushroom and beer potpie
at a small brew pub. It was so rich and
comforting. I tried numerous versions
when I got home and I think I've come
pretty close!*
—Iben Ravn, Copenhagen, Denmark

**Prep:** 45 min. • **Bake:** 30 min.
**Makes:** 8 servings

⅓  cup olive oil, divided
1  lb. sliced fresh shiitake mushrooms
1  lb. sliced baby portobello
    mushrooms
2  large onions, chopped
2  garlic cloves, minced
1  tsp. minced fresh rosemary, plus
    more for topping
1  bottle (12 oz.) porter or stout beer
1½  cups mushroom or vegetable
    broth, divided
2  bay leaves

1  Tbsp. balsamic vinegar
2  Tbsp. reduced-sodium soy sauce
¼  cup cornstarch
3  to 4 small sweet potatoes, peeled
    and thinly sliced
¾  tsp. coarsely ground pepper
½  tsp. salt

**1.** Preheat oven to 400°. In a Dutch oven,
heat 1 Tbsp. oil over medium heat. Add
shiitake mushrooms and cook in batches
until dark golden brown, 8-10 minutes;
remove with a slotted spoon. Repeat
with 1 Tbsp. oil and the portobello
mushrooms.

**2.** In same pan, heat 1 Tbsp. oil over
medium heat. Add onions; cook and stir
8-10 minutes or until tender. Add garlic
and 1 tsp. rosemary; cook 30 seconds
longer. Stir in the beer, 1 cup broth,
bay leaves, vinegar, soy sauce and
sauteed mushrooms.

**3.** Bring to a boil. Reduce heat; simmer,
uncovered, 10 minutes. In a small bowl,
mix cornstarch and remaining broth until
smooth; stir into mushroom mixture.

Return to a boil, stirring constantly;
cook and stir until thickened, 1-2 minutes.
Remove and discard bay leaves; transfer
the mushroom mixture to 8 greased
8-oz. ramekins. Place ramekins on a
rimmed baking sheet.

**4.** Layer sweet potatoes in a circular
pattern on top of each ramekin; brush
with remaining oil and sprinkle with
pepper, salt and additional rosemary.
Bake, covered, until sweet potatoes are
tender, 20-25 minutes. Remove cover
and bake until the potatoes are lightly
browned, 8-10 minutes. Let stand for
5 minutes before serving.

**1 serving:** 211 cal., 10g fat (1g sat. fat),
0 chol., 407mg sod., 26g carb. (10g sugars,
4g fiber), 5g pro.

**TEST KITCHEN TIP**

Instead of beer, you could use
dry red wine, marsala or
additional mushroom broth.

## PORK LOIN WITH STRAWBERRY-RHUBARB CHUTNEY

*I love strawberry rhubarb pie, so I thought the same flavor combination could work as a chutney—and it does! It makes a delicious and festive accompaniment to a succulent pork roast. The chutney can be made a day ahead and kept in the refrigerator.*
—Deborah Biggs, Omaha, NE

**Prep:** 20 min. • **Bake:** 1 hour + standing
**Makes:** 10 servings (1¾ cups sauce)

- 1  boneless pork loin roast (3 to 4 lbs.)
- 1  tsp. salt
- ½  tsp. pepper
- 2  Tbsp. canola oil
- ½  cup sugar
- ¼  cup red wine vinegar
- 1  cinnamon stick (3 in.)
- ½  tsp. grated lemon zest
- 2¼  cups chopped fresh or frozen rhubarb
- ⅔  cup sliced fresh strawberries
- 1½  tsp. minced fresh rosemary or ½ tsp. dried rosemary, crushed

**1.** Sprinkle roast with salt and pepper. In a large skillet, brown roast in oil on all sides.
**2.** Place the roast on a rack in a shallow roasting pan. Bake, uncovered, at 350° for 1-1½ hours or until a thermometer reads 145°. Remove roast to a serving platter; let stand for 15 minutes.
**3.** Meanwhile, in a large saucepan, combine the sugar, vinegar, cinnamon and lemon zest. Bring to a boil. Reduce heat; simmer, uncovered, until sugar is dissolved, about 2 minutes.
**4.** Add the rhubarb, strawberries and rosemary. Cook and stir over medium heat until rhubarb is tender and mixture is slightly thickened, 15-20 minutes. Discard cinnamon stick and serve with pork.

**4 oz. cooked pork with 3 Tbsp. chutney:**
243 cal., 9g fat (3g sat. fat), 68mg chol., 277mg sod., 13g carb. (11g sugars, 1g fiber), 27g pro.
**Diabetic exchanges:** 3 lean meat, ½ fruit, ½ fat.

## TURKEY TENDERLOIN & ROOT VEGGIE SHEET-PAN SUPPER

**(PICTURED ON P. 147)**

*My family loves turkey tenderloin, so I wanted to try using them in a sheet-pan supper. I used potatoes, carrots and onions that I had on hand as well as some bacon. Covering the ingredients with that smoked bacon really made a difference in the finished dish. The vegetables were tender and flavorful, and the turkey was tender and juicy. Use any of your favorite vegetables. Try adding turnips to the mix for a bit of sweetness.*
—Susan Bickta, Kutztown, PA

**Prep:** 15 min. • **Bake:** 30 min.
**Makes:** 6 servings

- 6  bacon strips
- 2  medium potatoes, cut into ½-in. pieces
- 4  medium carrots, peeled and cut into ½-in. pieces
- 2  medium onions, cut into ½-in. pieces
- 2  tsp. canola oil
- 1  tsp. salt, divided
- ½  tsp. pepper, divided
- 1  pkg. (20 oz.) turkey breast tenderloins
   Minced fresh parsley, optional

**1.** Preheat oven to 375°. Line a 15x10x1-in. baking pan with foil. Place bacon strips on prepared pan; bake 15 minutes.
**2.** Meanwhile, in a large bowl, toss the potatoes, carrots and onions with oil; sprinkle with ½ tsp. salt and ¼ tsp. pepper. Sprinkle remaining salt and pepper on tenderloins.
**3.** Remove the par-cooked bacon from baking pan. Transfer vegetables to pan, spreading evenly. Place tenderloins on top of vegetables; cover with bacon slices. Bake until a thermometer reads 165° and vegetables are tender, 30-35 minutes. If desired, top with parsley to serve.

**3 oz. cooked turkey with ⅔ cup vegetables:** 238 cal., 11g fat (3g sat. fat), 42mg chol., 500mg sod., 15g carb. (3g sugars, 2g fiber), 22g pro. **Diabetic exchanges:** 3 lean meat, 1 vegetable, ½ starch.

**PORK LOIN WITH STRAWBERRY-RHUBARB CHUTNEY**

## BROILED SHRIMP SKEWERS

(PICTURED ON P. 146)

*Any gathering will be special when you serve flavorful and juicy shrimp skewers. They're so easy to assemble and broil to perfection.*

—Anthony Glazik, Peotone, IL

**Prep:** 30 min. + marinating • **Cook:** 10 min.
**Makes:** 10 servings

- 1 cup chutney
- ⅓ cup minced fresh cilantro
- 2 Tbsp. lime juice
- 4 tsp. olive oil
- 2 tsp. hot pepper sauce
- 4 garlic cloves, minced
- 10-14 bacon strips
- 1½ lbs. uncooked shrimp (31-40 per lb.), peeled and deveined
- 2 medium papayas, peeled and cut into 1-in. cubes
- 30 pineapple chunks
- 30 cherry tomatoes
- 8 green onions or shallots

**1.** In a small bowl, combine the chutney, cilantro, lime juice, oil, pepper sauce and garlic. Cover and refrigerate.

**2.** Cut bacon strips in half lengthwise and widthwise. In a skillet, partially cook the bacon for 2 minutes on each side; drain. Wrap a piece of bacon around each shrimp.

**3.** On 10 metal or soaked wooden skewers, alternately thread the shrimp, papaya, pineapple, tomatoes and green onions. Brush with half the chutney mixture. Turn and brush with remaining chutney mixture. Cover and refrigerate for at least 30 minutes.

**4.** Broil skewers 4-5 in. from the heat for 5 minutes. Turn and broil until shrimp turn pink, 5-7 minutes.

**1 kabob:** 343 cal., 6g fat (1g sat. fat), 91mg chol., 523mg sod., 58g carb. (41g sugars, 3g fiber), 15g pro.

### TEST KITCHEN TIP

Instead of papaya, you can substitute cubed fresh cantaloupe or thawed mango chunks.

## CRANBERRY CHICKEN & WILD RICE

*This tender chicken in a sweet-tart cranberry sauce is delicious, and it's so easy to prepare. I love that I can do other things while it bakes.*

—Evelyn Lewis, Independence, MO

**Prep:** 10 min. • **Bake:** 35 min.
**Makes:** 6 servings

- 6 boneless skinless chicken breast halves (4 oz. each)
- 1½ cups hot water
- 1 pkg. (6.2 oz.) fast-cooking long grain and wild rice mix
- 1 can (14 oz.) whole-berry cranberry sauce
- 1 Tbsp. lemon juice
- 1 Tbsp. reduced-sodium soy sauce
- 1 Tbsp. Worcestershire sauce

**1.** Preheat oven to 350°. Place chicken in a 13x9-in. baking dish coated with cooking spray. In a bowl, mix hot water, rice mix and contents of seasoning packet; pour around chicken.

**2.** In a small bowl, mix the remaining ingredients; pour over chicken. Bake, covered, until a thermometer inserted in chicken reads 165°, 35-45 minutes.

**1 chicken breast half with ½ cup rice mixture:** 332 cal., 3g fat (1g sat. fat), 63mg chol., 592mg sod., 50g carb. (19g sugars, 2g fiber), 26g pro.

CRANBERRY CHICKEN & WILD RICE

**CREAMY AVOCADO MANICOTTI**

## PECAN PORK CHOPS

A delicate butter and brown sugar glaze and toasted pecans are a tasty topping for these broiled pork chops.
—*Taste of Home* Test Kitchen

**Takes:** 15 min. • **Makes:** 8 servings

- 8 boneless pork loin chops (4 oz. each)
- ¼ cup packed brown sugar
- 2 Tbsp. cornstarch
- ¼ tsp. salt
- ⅛ tsp. ground mustard
- 2 Tbsp. butter, softened
- 2 tsp. cider vinegar
- 3 Tbsp. chopped pecans

**1.** Broil pork chops 4-5 in. from the heat for 4 minutes. Meanwhile, in a small bowl, combine the sugar, cornstarch, salt and mustard. Stir in the butter and vinegar until smooth.

**2.** Turn pork chops over and broil for 2 minutes longer. Spoon about 2 tsp. sugar mixture over top of each chop; broil 2-3 minutes longer or until a thermometer reads 145°. Sprinkle the pecans over chops. Broil until the pecans are toasted, about 1 minute longer. Let stand for 5 minutes before serving.

**1 pork chop:** 229 cal., 11g fat (4g sat. fat), 62mg chol., 130mg sod., 9g carb. (7g sugars, 0 fiber), 22g pro.

## CREAMY AVOCADO MANICOTTI

*I am always looking for creative ways to make vegetarian dinners a little different. I grow my own basil, and avocados are a versatile favorite, so this recipe is a fantastic way to make creamy and healthy manicotti.*
—Jennifer Coduto, Kent, OH

**Prep:** 25 min. • **Bake:** 45 min.
**Makes:** 7 servings

- 1 pkg. (8 oz.) manicotti shells
- 1 small onion, finely chopped
- 1 Tbsp. olive oil
- 2 garlic cloves, minced
- 1 can (28 oz.) crushed tomatoes
- ½ cup minced fresh basil or 3 Tbsp. dried basil
- ⅓ cup dry red wine or vegetable broth
- 1 Tbsp. brown sugar
- ½ tsp. salt
- ½ tsp. pepper

FILLING

- 1 container (15 oz.) reduced-fat ricotta cheese
- 1 medium ripe avocado, peeled and mashed
- ½ cup grated Parmesan cheese
- ¼ tsp. salt
- ¼ tsp. pepper
- 1 cup shredded part-skim mozzarella cheese
- 1 medium ripe avocado, sliced, optional

**1.** Cook manicotti according to package directions. Meanwhile, in a large skillet, saute onion in oil until tender. Add garlic; cook 1 minute longer. Stir in the crushed tomatoes, basil, wine, brown sugar, salt and pepper. Bring to a boil. Reduce heat; simmer, uncovered, for 10-15 minutes, stirring occasionally.

**2.** Drain manicotti shells. In a small bowl, combine the ricotta cheese, avocado, Parmesan cheese, salt and pepper. Stuff cheese mixture into shells. Spread 1 cup sauce into a greased 13x9-in. baking dish. Arrange manicotti over sauce. Pour the remaining sauce over top.

**3.** Cover and bake at 350° for 35 minutes or until bubbly. Uncover; sprinkle with mozzarella cheese. Bake 10-15 minutes longer or until the cheese is melted. If desired, garnish with avocado slices.

**2 pieces:** 359 cal., 13g fat (5g sat. fat), 29mg chol., 625mg sod., 41g carb. (7g sugars, 5g fiber), 18g pro. **Diabetic exchanges:** 2 starch, 2 vegetable, 2 medium-fat meat, 1 fat.

**CRISPY DILL TILAPIA**

## AUTUMN PORK ROAST

*Your family will flock to the table when they smell this delicious roast. It's a hearty dish that makes everyday dinners more special. Although this meal captures the fabulous flavors of fall, don't hesitate to serve it throughout the year.*
—Kathy Barbarek, Joliet, IL

**Prep:** 20 min. • **Bake:** 2 hours + standing
**Makes:** 12 servings

- 1  bone-in pork loin roast (5 lbs.)
- 8  medium potatoes, peeled and quartered
- 8  carrots, halved lengthwise
- 2  medium onions, quartered
- 1  small pumpkin or butternut squash, peeled and cut into 1½-in. pieces
- 1  cup water
- 3  Tbsp. snipped fresh sage or 1 Tbsp. rubbed sage
- 1  tsp. salt
- ¼  tsp. pepper
- 2  Tbsp. butter
- 4  medium baking apples, quartered

**1.** Place the roast in a large baking pan. Arrange potatoes, carrots, onions and pumpkin around roast. Add water to the pan. Sprinkle meat and vegetables with sage, salt and pepper; dot the vegetables with butter.
**2.** Bake the roast, uncovered, at 400° for 15 minutes. Reduce heat to 350°; bake, uncovered, for 1 hour. Place the apples around roast; cover and bake until a thermometer inserted in pork reads 145°, 45-60 minutes, basting every 30 minutes. Let stand 10 minutes before slicing. If desired, thicken pan juices for gravy.
**1 serving:** 359 cal., 9g fat (3g sat. fat), 76mg chol., 295mg sod., 41g carb. (11g sugars, 7g fiber), 30g pro. **Diabetic exchanges:** 4 lean meat, 2½ starch.

## CRISPY DILL TILAPIA

*Every week I try to serve a new healthy fish recipe. With its fresh dill and delicious panko bread crumb and herb crust, this dish with mild tilapia is a winner.*
—Tamara Huron, New Market, AL

**Takes:** 20 min. • **Makes:** 4 servings

- 1  cup panko bread crumbs
- 2  Tbsp. olive oil
- 2  Tbsp. snipped fresh dill
- ¼  tsp. salt
- ⅛  tsp. pepper
- 4  tilapia fillets (6 oz. each)
- 1  Tbsp. lemon juice
   Lemon wedges

**1.** Preheat oven to 400°. Toss together first 5 ingredients.
**2.** Place tilapia in a 15x10x1-in. baking pan coated with cooking spray; brush with lemon juice. Top with crumb mixture, patting to help adhere.
**3.** Bake, uncovered, on an upper oven rack until fish just begins to flake easily with a fork, 12-15 minutes. Serve with lemon wedges.
**1 fillet:** 256 cal., 9g fat (2g sat. fat), 83mg chol., 251mg sod., 10g carb. (1g sugars, 1g fiber), 34g pro. **Diabetic exchanges:** 5 lean meat, 1½ fat, ½ starch.

**TEST KITCHEN TIP**

This breading would complement most types of fish. Try it on salmon if you prefer. If you don't have fresh dill, a bit of fresh thyme would be great with fish and lemon.

## PESTO HALIBUT

*The mildness of halibut contrasts perfectly with the robust flavor of pesto in this recipe. It takes only minutes to get the fish ready for the oven, so you can start quickly on your side dishes. Nearly anything goes well with this entree.*
—April Showalter, Indianapolis, IN

- - - - - - - - - - - - - - - - - - - - - - - - - -

**Takes:** 20 min. • **Makes:** 6 servings

- 2   Tbsp. olive oil
- 1   envelope pesto sauce mix
- 1   Tbsp. lemon juice
- 6   halibut fillets (4 oz. each)

**1.** Preheat oven to 450°. In a small bowl, combine oil, sauce mix and lemon juice; brush over both sides of fillets. Place in a greased 13x9-in. baking dish.
**2.** Bake, uncovered, until fish just begins to flake easily with a fork, 12-15 minutes.
**1 fillet:** 188 cal., 7g fat (1g sat. fat), 36mg chol., 481mg sod., 5g carb. (2g sugars, 0 fiber), 24g pro. **Diabetic exchanges:** 3 lean meat, 1 fat.

**NEW ENGLAND LAMB BAKE**

## NEW ENGLAND LAMB BAKE

*This hearty dish is perfect for warming up on a chilly winter evening. When you smell it baking, you'll be glad you stayed home.*
—Frank Grady, Fort Kent, ME

- - - - - - - - - - - - - - - - - - - - - - - - - -

**Prep:** 25 min. • **Bake:** 1½ hours
**Makes:** 8 servings

- 1   Tbsp. canola oil
- 2   lbs. boneless leg of lamb, cut into 1-in. cubes
- 1   large onion, chopped
- ¼   cup all-purpose flour
- 3   cups chicken broth
- 2   large leeks (white portion only), cut into ½-in. slices
- 2   large carrots, sliced
- 2   Tbsp. minced fresh parsley, divided
- ½   tsp. dried rosemary, crushed
- ½   tsp. salt
- ¼   tsp. pepper
- ¼   tsp. dried thyme
- 3   large potatoes, peeled and sliced
- 3   Tbsp. butter, melted and divided

**1.** Preheat oven to 375°. In a Dutch oven, heat oil over medium heat. Add lamb and onion; cook and stir until the meat is no longer pink. Stir in flour until blended.

Gradually add broth. Bring to a boil; cook until thickened, 1-2 minutes, stirring to loosen browned bits from pan. Add leeks, carrots, 1 Tbsp. parsley, rosemary, salt, pepper and thyme.
**2.** Spoon into a greased 13x9-in. or 3-qt. baking dish. Cover with potato slices; brush with 2 Tbsp. melted butter. Bake 1 hour; brush potatoes with remaining butter. Return to oven; bake until the meat is tender and potatoes are golden, 30 minutes to 1 hour longer. Cool briefly; sprinkle with remaining parsley.
**Freeze option:** Remove baking dish from oven; cool completely. Before adding remaining parsley, cover dish and freeze. Freeze parsley separately. To use, partially thaw lamb in refrigerator overnight. Remove from refrigerator 30 minutes before baking; thaw remaining parsley. Preheat oven to 350°. Reheat, covered, until a thermometer reads 165°, about 1 hour. Sprinkle with remaining parsley.
**1 piece:** 356 cal., 13g fat (5g sat. fat), 82mg chol., 631mg sod., 34g carb. (4g sugars, 4g fiber), 25g pro. **Diabetic exchanges:** 3 starch, 3 lean meat, 1½ fat.

## CHICKEN WITH CURRY ROASTED SQUASH

*This chicken butternut squash curry is very flavorful and full of protein, fiber and phytonutrients. The addition of apricots lends a mild sweetness to the dish.*
—Sharon Collison, Newark, DE

**Prep:** 15 min. • **Bake:** 25 min.
**Makes:** 8 servings

- 1 medium butternut squash (about 3 lbs.), cut into ¾-in. cubes
- 1 large red onion, chopped
- 2 Tbsp. olive oil, divided
- 2 tsp. curry powder
- 1 tsp. salt, divided
- ¾ tsp. pepper, divided
- 1½ cups water
- 1½ cups uncooked whole wheat couscous
- 1 can (14½ oz.) reduced-sodium chicken broth
- ¾ cup coarsely chopped dried apricots, divided
- 3 cups coarsely shredded rotisserie chicken
- 1 can (15 oz.) garbanzo beans or chickpeas, rinsed and drained Minced fresh cilantro, optional

**1.** Preheat oven to 425°. Place squash and onion in a 15x10x1-in. baking pan. Drizzle with 1 Tbsp. oil and sprinkle with curry powder and ½ tsp. each salt and pepper; toss to coat. Roast 25-30 minutes or just until squash is tender, stirring halfway.
**2.** In a small saucepan, bring water and remaining oil to a boil. Stir in couscous. Remove from heat; let stand, covered, 5 minutes or until water is absorbed. Fluff with a fork.
**3.** Meanwhile, in a 6-qt. stockpot, combine broth and ¼ cup apricots; bring to a simmer. Add the chicken, garbanzo beans, squash mixture and remaining salt and pepper; heat through, stirring gently. Serve with couscous; top with remaining apricots. Sprinkle with cilantro if desired.
**1 serving:** 463 cal., 9g fat (2g sat. fat), 62mg chol., 420mg sod., 69g carb. (12g sugars, 14g fiber), 32g pro.

## BEEF CABBAGE ROLL-UPS
### (PICTURED ON P. 147)

*Cooking up original recipes is a hobby of mine. My version of classic cabbage rolls is delicious served over rice or noodles. Other pastimes include raising flowers and tomatoes, decorating cakes and baking for my two children and five grandkids.*
—Irma Finely, Lockwood, MO

**Prep:** 30 min. • **Bake:** 30 min.
**Makes:** 6 servings

- 1 head cabbage
- 1 large potato, peeled and shredded
- 1 large carrot, shredded
- ¼ cup finely chopped celery
- ½ cup finely chopped green pepper
- ½ cup finely chopped onion
- 2 large eggs, lightly beaten
- 2 garlic cloves, minced
- ¾ tsp. salt
- ½ tsp. pepper
- 1 lb. lean ground beef (90% lean)
- 2 cans (8 oz. each) tomato sauce
- ½ tsp. dried basil
- ½ tsp. dried parsley flakes

**1.** Cook cabbage in boiling water just until the leaves fall off head. Cut out the thick vein from the bottom of 12 large leaves, making a V-shaped cut; set aside. (Refrigerate remaining cabbage for another use.)
**2.** In a large bowl, combine the potato, carrot, celery, green pepper, onion, eggs, garlic, salt and pepper. Crumble beef over mixture; mix lightly but thoroughly.
**3.** Shape into 12 logs. Place 1 log on each cabbage leaf; overlap the cut ends of leaf. Fold in sides, beginning from the cut end. Roll up completely to enclose filling. Secure with a toothpick.
**4.** Place in a greased 13x9-in. baking dish. Pour tomato sauce over roll-ups. Sprinkle with basil and parsley. Cover and bake at 350° until a thermometer reads 160° and cabbage is tender, 30-35 minutes.
**2 cabbage rolls:** 251 cal., 8g fat (3g sat. fat), 108mg chol., 584mg sod., 25g carb. (8g sugars, 6g fiber), 21g pro. **Diabetic exchanges:** 3 lean meat, 1 starch, 1 vegetable.

**CHICKEN WITH CURRY ROASTED SQUASH**

## PORK SPANISH RICE

*My family wasn't fond of pork roast until I used it in this yummy casserole.*
—Betty Unrau, MacGregor, MB

**Prep:** 20 min. • **Bake:** 20 min.
**Makes:** 4 servings

- 1 medium green pepper, chopped
- 1 small onion, chopped
- 2 Tbsp. butter
- 1 can (14½ oz.) diced tomatoes, drained
- 1 cup chicken broth
- ½ tsp. salt
- ¼ tsp. pepper
- 1¾ cups cubed cooked pork
- 1 cup uncooked instant rice
  Optional: Lime wedges and minced cilantro

**1.** In a large skillet, saute green pepper and onion in butter until tender. Stir in the tomatoes, broth, salt and pepper. Bring to a boil; stir in pork and rice.
**2.** Transfer to a greased 2-qt. baking dish. Cover and bake at 350° until rice is tender and liquid is absorbed, 20-25 minutes. Stir before serving. If desired, serve with lime wedges and top with minced cilantro.
**1 cup:** 304 cal., 12g fat (6g sat. fat), 71mg chol., 756mg sod., 29g carb. (5g sugars, 3g fiber), 21g pro. **Diabetic exchanges:** 3 lean meat, 2 starch, 1½ fat.

BAKED CHICKEN
& MUSHROOMS

## BAKED CHICKEN & MUSHROOMS

*I made up this dish years ago, and it still remains a family favorite. It's a fast and healthy weeknight meal, but the fresh mushrooms and sherry make it special enough for a weekend dinner party.*
—Lise Prestine, South Bend, IN

**Prep:** 5 min. • **Bake:** 30 min.
**Makes:** 6 servings

- 6 boneless skinless chicken breast halves (4 oz. each)
- ¼ tsp. paprika
- ½ lb. fresh mushrooms, sliced
- 1 Tbsp. butter
- ½ cup sherry or chicken broth
- 3 green onions, chopped
- 1 garlic clove, minced
- ½ tsp. salt
- ⅛ tsp. pepper
- ¾ cup shredded part-skim mozzarella cheese

**1.** Arrange chicken in a 13x9-in. baking dish coated with cooking spray. Sprinkle with paprika. Bake, uncovered, at 350° for 15 minutes.
**2.** Meanwhile, in a large nonstick skillet, saute mushrooms in butter for 5 minutes. Add the sherry or broth, green onions, garlic, salt and pepper. Bring to a boil. Pour over chicken.
**3.** Bake until a thermometer reads 165°, 10-15 minutes longer. Top with cheese. Bake for 3-5 minutes or until the cheese is melted.
**1 serving:** 215 cal., 8g fat (4g sat. fat), 77mg chol., 604mg sod., 6g carb. (2g sugars, 1g fiber), 28g pro. **Diabetic exchanges:** 4 lean meat, ½ starch, ½ fat.

## CREAMY SCALLOP CREPES

*These savory crepes feel so elegant for the holidays. I like to add ¼ teaspoon of fresh dill weed to the crepe batter before refrigerating.*
—Doreen Kelly, Hatboro, PA

**Prep:** 45 min. + chilling • **Bake:** 15 min.
**Makes:** 6 servings

- 2 **large egg whites**
- 1 **large egg**
- 1½ **cups fat-free milk**
- 1 **cup all-purpose flour**
- ½ **tsp. salt**
- 2 **Tbsp. unsalted butter, melted**

FILLING

- 1 **lb. bay scallops**
- ⅓ **cup white wine or reduced-sodium chicken broth**
- ⅛ **tsp. white pepper**
- 1 **lb. sliced fresh mushrooms**
- 4 **green onions, sliced**
- 2 **Tbsp. butter**
- ¼ **cup all-purpose flour**
- ⅔ **cup fat-free evaporated milk**
- ½ **cup shredded reduced-fat Swiss cheese**
  **Sliced green onions, optional**

**1.** In a small bowl, beat the egg whites, egg and milk. Combine flour and salt; add to milk mixture and mix well. Cover and refrigerate for 1 hour.

**2.** Brush an 8-in. nonstick skillet lightly with melted butter; heat. Stir crepe batter; pour 2 Tbsp. into center of skillet. Lift and tilt pan to coat bottom evenly. Cook until top appears dry; turn and cook 15-20 seconds longer. Remove to a wire rack. Repeat with the remaining batter, brushing skillet with melted butter as needed. When cool, stack crepes with waxed paper or paper towels in between.

**3.** In a large nonstick skillet, bring the scallops, wine and pepper to a boil. Reduce heat; simmer until scallops are firm and opaque, 3-4 minutes. Drain, reserving cooking liquid; set liquid and scallops aside.

**4.** In the same skillet, saute mushrooms and onions in butter until almost tender. Sprinkle with flour; stir until blended. Gradually stir in evaporated milk and cooking liquid. Bring to a boil; cook and stir until thickened, about 2 minutes. Remove from the heat. Stir in cheese and scallops.

**5.** Spread ⅓ cup filling down the center of each crepe; roll up and place in a 13x9-in. baking dish coated with cooking spray. Cover and bake at 350° until heated through, 12-15 minutes.

**2 crepes:** 331 cal., 10g fat (6g sat. fat), 76mg chol., 641mg sod., 33g carb. (9g sugars, 2g fiber), 24g pro. **Diabetic exchanges:** 3 lean meat, 2 starch, 2 fat.

CREAMY SCALLOP CREPES

## GREEK SPAGHETTI WITH CHICKEN

**(PICTURED ON P. 147)**

*A comforting dinner is sure to be had when flavorful Greek spaghetti is on the menu. Featuring chicken, spinach and two types of cheese, this dish is a crowd-pleaser.*
—Melanie Dalbec, Inver Grove, MN

**Prep:** 25 min. • **Bake:** 25 min.
**Makes:** 10 servings

- 1 pkg. (16 oz.) spaghetti, broken into 2-in. pieces
- 4 cups cubed cooked chicken breast
- 2 pkg. (10 oz. each) frozen chopped spinach, thawed and squeezed dry
- 2 cans (10¾ oz. each) condensed cream of chicken soup, undiluted
- 1 cup mayonnaise
- 1 cup sour cream
- 3 celery ribs, chopped
- 1 small onion, chopped
- ½ cup chopped green pepper
- 1 jar (2 oz.) diced pimientos, drained
- ½ tsp. lemon-pepper seasoning
- 1 cup shredded Monterey Jack cheese
- ½ cup soft bread crumbs
- ½ cup shredded Parmesan cheese

**1.** Cook spaghetti according to package directions; drain. Return spaghetti to saucepan. Stir in the chicken, spinach, soup, mayonnaise, sour cream, celery, onion, green pepper, pimientos and lemon pepper.
**2.** Transfer to a greased 13x9-in. baking dish (dish will be full). Top with Monterey Jack cheese, bread crumbs and Parmesan cheese. Bake, uncovered, at 350° for 25-30 minutes or until heated through.
**1⅓ cups:** 601 cal., 32g fat (10g sat. fat), 85mg chol., 850mg sod., 44g carb. (4g sugars, 4g fiber), 31g pro.

## CITRUS SALMON EN PAPILLOTE

*This salmon dish is so simple and easy to make yet so delicious, elegant and impressive.*
—Dahlia Abrams, Detroit, MI

**Prep:** 20 min. • **Bake:** 15 min.
**Makes:** 6 servings

- 6 orange slices
- 6 lime slices
- 6 salmon fillets (4 oz. each)
- 1 lb. fresh asparagus, trimmed and halved
  Olive oil-flavored cooking spray
- ½ tsp. salt
- ¼ tsp. pepper
- 2 Tbsp. minced fresh parsley
- 3 Tbsp. lemon juice

**1.** Preheat oven to 425°. Cut parchment or heavy-duty foil into six 15x10-in. pieces; fold in half. Arrange citrus slices on 1 side of each piece. Top with fish and asparagus. Spritz with cooking spray. Sprinkle with salt, pepper and parsley. Drizzle with lemon juice.
**2.** Fold parchment over fish; draw edges together and crimp with fingers to form tightly sealed packets. Place packets in baking pans.
**3.** Bake until fish flakes easily with a fork, 12-15 minutes. Open packets carefully to allow steam to escape.
**1 packet:** 224 cal., 13g fat (2g sat. fat), 57mg chol., 261mg sod., 6g carb. (3g sugars, 1g fiber), 20g pro. **Diabetic exchanges:** 3 lean meat, 1 vegetable.

**CITRUS SALMON EN PAPILLOTE**

**PEPPER-STUFFED PORK TENDERLOIN**

## CALIFORNIA ROAST LAMB

*This recipe is very easy to make and requires little attention. It's perfect for just about any occasion.*
—Ann Eastman, Santa Monica, CA

**Prep:** 10 min. • **Bake:** 2½ hours + standing
**Makes:** 12 servings

- 1 leg of lamb (4 to 5 lbs.)
- 2 to 3 garlic cloves, halved
- 1 tsp. seasoned salt
- 1 tsp. pepper
- 1 tsp. dried oregano
- 2 cans (8 oz. each) tomato sauce
- 1 cup water
  Juice of 1 lemon
- 3 to 5 large fresh artichokes, quartered
- 3 small lemons, halved, optional
  Optional: Fresh oregano and fresh thyme sprigs

**1.** Cut slits in lamb; insert garlic. Rub meat with salt, pepper and oregano. Roast at 400° for 30 minutes. Reduce heat to 350°; roast 1 hour more.
**2.** Skim off any fat in pan; pour tomato sauce, water and lemon juice over lamb. Place artichokes and, if desired, lemons around roast. Bake 1 hour longer or until meat reaches desired doneness (for medium-rare, a thermometer should read 135°; medium, 140°; medium-well, 145°). Let stand for 15 minutes before slicing. Garnish with herbs if desired.
**3 oz. cooked lamb with 1 artichoke wedge:** 152 cal., 5g fat (2g sat. fat), 68mg chol., 365mg sod., 6g carb. (1g sugars, 3g fiber), 21g pro. **Diabetic exchanges:** 3 lean meat.

## PEPPER-STUFFED PORK TENDERLOIN

*Our New Year's tradition includes eating black-eyed peas and collard greens for good fortune, along with this flavorful, easy pork tenderloin.*
—Margaret Allen, Abingdon, VA

**Prep:** 40 min. • **Bake:** 45 min. + standing
**Makes:** 8 servings

- 2 Tbsp. canola oil
- 3 small sweet red peppers, finely chopped
- 1 large onion, finely chopped
- 2 small celery ribs, finely chopped
- 1½ tsp. dried thyme
- ¾ tsp. garlic salt
- ¾ tsp. paprika
- ½ tsp. cayenne pepper
- 3 pork tenderloins (¾ lb. each)
- 4 tsp. lemon-pepper seasoning
- 4 tsp. fennel seed, crushed

**1.** Preheat oven to 325°. In a large skillet, heat oil over medium-high heat. Add red peppers, onion and celery; saute until tender, 3-4 minutes. Add thyme, garlic salt, paprika and cayenne; saute 1 minute longer. Remove from heat; set aside.
**2.** Make a lengthwise slit down the center of each tenderloin to within ½ in. of bottom. Open tenderloins so they lie flat. With a meat mallet, flatten pork to ½-in. thickness. Fill with vegetable stuffing mixture. Close tenderloins; tie at 2-in. intervals with kitchen string, securing ends with toothpicks.
**3.** Place on a rack coated with cooking spray in a shallow baking pan. Combine lemon pepper and fennel; rub over the pork tenderloins.
**4.** Bake until a thermometer inserted into pork reads 145°, 45-55 minutes. Remove tenderloins from oven; let stand 5 minutes. Discard toothpicks and string. Cut each tenderloin into 8 slices.
**3 slices:** 201 cal., 8g fat (2g sat. fat), 71mg chol., 492mg sod., 5g carb. (2g sugars, 2g fiber), 26g pro. **Diabetic exchanges:** 4 lean meat, ½ fat.

## PEPPERONI PIZZA BAKED POTATOES

*These tasty taters became a spur-of-the-moment recipe born of leftovers! It's combines two dinnertime favorites into one super fun meal.*
—Dawn Lowenstein, Huntingdon Valley, PA

**Takes:** 30 min. • **Makes:** 4 servings

- 4 medium russet potatoes (about 8 oz. each)
- 1 Tbsp. olive oil
- 1 cup sliced fresh mushrooms
- 1 small green pepper, chopped
- 1 small onion, chopped
- 1 garlic clove, minced
- 1 can (8 oz.) pizza sauce
- ⅓ cup mini sliced turkey pepperoni
- ½ cup shredded Italian cheese blend
- Optional: Fresh oregano leaves or dried oregano

**1.** Preheat oven to 400°. Scrub potatoes; place on a microwave-safe plate. Pierce several times with a fork. Microwave, uncovered, on high until potatoes are tender, 12-15 minutes.

**2.** In a large skillet, heat oil over medium-high heat; saute mushrooms, pepper and onion until tender, 6-8 minutes. Add the garlic; cook and stir 1 minute. Stir in pizza sauce and pepperoni; heat through.

**3.** Place potatoes on a baking sheet; cut an "X" in the top of each. Fluff pulp with a fork. Top with vegetable mixture; sprinkle with cheese. Bake until the cheese is melted, 5-7 minutes. If desired, sprinkle with oregano.

**1 baked potato with toppings:** 311 cal., 9g fat (3g sat. fat), 23mg chol., 515mg sod., 46g carb. (5g sugars, 6g fiber), 13g pro. **Diabetic exchanges:** 3 starch, 1 medium-fat meat, ½ fat.

> **TEST KITCHEN TIP**
>
> We used russet potatoes in this recipe. They have a slightly drier texture than other varieties and will cook up a bit fluffier. These potatoes are baked in the microwave to speed up prep. You can also bake them at 400° for 45-60 minutes.

**LEMON FETA CHICKEN**

## LEMON FETA CHICKEN

*This bright-tasting, Greek-inspired chicken has only five ingredients— it's a lifesaver on a busy day! My husband and I prepare the dish often, and it's a hit every time.*
—Ann Cain, Morrill, NE

**Takes:** 25 min. • **Makes:** 4 servings

- 4 boneless skinless chicken breast halves (4 oz. each)
- 2 to 3 Tbsp. lemon juice
- ¼ cup crumbled feta cheese
- 1 tsp. dried oregano
- ¼ to ½ tsp. pepper

**1.** Place chicken in a 13x9-in. baking dish coated with cooking spray. Pour lemon juice over chicken; sprinkle with feta cheese, oregano and pepper.

**2.** Bake chicken, uncovered, at 400° for 20-25 minutes or until a thermometer reads 165°.

**1 chicken breast half:** 143 cal., 4g fat (1g sat. fat), 66mg chol., 122mg sod., 1g carb. (0 sugars, 0 fiber), 24g pro. **Diabetic exchanges:** 3 lean meat.

**\* HEALTH TIP \*** A weeknight dinner party is easy with this chicken dinner that's special enough for company. Pair it with roasted potatoes and steamed broccoli with fresh herbs to satisfy all your guests (even those who eat gluten-free).

## ZITI BAKE

*Many of my casserole recipes have been frowned upon by my children, but they give a cheer when they hear we're having this for supper. Even the leftovers are well-liked.*
—Charity Burkholder, Pittsboro, IN

--------------------------------------------

**Prep:** 20 min. • **Bake:** 50 min.
**Makes:** 6 servings

- 3 cups uncooked ziti or small tube pasta
- 1¾ cups meatless spaghetti sauce, divided
- 1 cup 4% cottage cheese
- 1½ cups shredded part-skim mozzarella cheese, divided
- 1 large egg, lightly beaten
- 2 tsp. dried parsley flakes
- ½ tsp. dried oregano
- ¼ tsp. garlic powder
- ⅛ tsp. pepper

**1.** Cook pasta according to package directions. Meanwhile, in a large bowl, combine ¾ cup spaghetti sauce, cottage cheese, 1 cup mozzarella cheese, egg, parsley, oregano, garlic powder and pepper. Drain the pasta; stir into the cheese mixture.

**2.** In a greased 8-in. square baking dish, spread ¼ cup spaghetti sauce. Top with pasta mixture, and remaining sauce and mozzarella cheese.

**3.** Cover and bake at 375° for 45 minutes. Uncover; bake until a thermometer reads 160°, 5-10 minutes longer.

**1½ cups:** 289 cal., 8g fat (4g sat. fat), 60mg chol., 616mg sod., 37g carb. (9g sugars, 3g fiber), 18g pro.

**HERBED ROAST TURKEY BREAST**

## HERBED ROAST TURKEY BREAST

*I made this turkey breast for my first formal dinner party as a newlywed. It was such a success that it's become a standby on all my entertaining menus.*
—Lisa Mahon Fluegeman, Cincinnati, OH

--------------------------------------------

**Prep:** 10 min. • **Bake:** 2 hours + standing
**Makes:** 12 servings

- 1 bone-in turkey breast (5 to 6 lbs.)
- 5 tsp. lemon juice
- 1 Tbsp. olive oil
- 1 to 2 tsp. pepper
- 1 tsp. dried rosemary, crushed
- 1 tsp. dried thyme
- 1 tsp. garlic salt
- 1 medium onion, cut into wedges
- 1 celery rib, cut into 2-in. pieces
- ½ cup white wine or chicken broth

**1.** Preheat oven to 325°. With fingers, carefully loosen the skin from both sides of turkey breast. Combine lemon juice and oil; brush under the skin. Combine the pepper, rosemary, thyme and garlic salt; rub over turkey.

**2.** Place onion and celery in a 3-qt. baking dish. Top with turkey breast, skin side up. Pour wine into the dish.

**3.** Bake, uncovered, 2-2½ hours or until a thermometer reads 170°. (Cover loosely with foil if the turkey browns too quickly.) Cover turkey and let stand for 15 minutes before carving.

**5 oz. cooked turkey :** 285 cal., 11g fat (3g sat. fat), 102mg chol., 241mg sod., 2g carb. (1g sugars, 0 fiber), 40g pro. **Diabetic exchanges:** 5 medium-fat meat.

> **TEST KITCHEN TIP**
>
> You can often use lemon and lime juice interchangeably in recipes to get a different flavor. To substitute orange, though, you'll need to keep a little lemon or lime in the mix to spark up the flavor.

## LOADED CHICKEN CARBONARA CUPS

*Spaghetti "cupcakes" with a chicken carbonara twist make for a tasty, fun family dinner. Whole wheat pasta and reduced-fat ingredients make these little pasta cakes nutritional winners, too.*
—Jeanne Holt, Mendota Heights, MN

- - - - - - - - - - - - - - - - - - - - - - - - - - -

**Prep:** 30 min. • **Bake:** 15 min.
**Makes:** 1 dozen

- 4 oz. uncooked whole wheat spaghetti
- 1 large egg, lightly beaten
- 5 oz. frozen chopped spinach, thawed and squeezed dry (about ½ cup)
- ½ cup 2% cottage cheese
- ½ cup shredded Parmesan cheese, divided
- ¼ tsp. lemon-pepper seasoning
- 6 bacon strips, cooked and crumbled, divided
- ½ cup reduced-fat reduced-sodium condensed cream of chicken soup, undiluted
- ¼ cup reduced-fat spreadable chive and onion cream cheese
- 1 cup chopped cooked chicken breast
- ⅓ cup shredded part-skim mozzarella cheese
- ¼ cup finely chopped oil-packed sun-dried tomatoes

**1.** Preheat oven to 350°. In a large saucepan, cook spaghetti according to the package directions; drain, reserving ⅓ cup pasta water.

**2.** In a large bowl, mix the egg, spinach, cottage cheese, ¼ cup Parmesan cheese, lemon pepper and half the bacon. Add spaghetti; toss to combine. Divide among 12 greased muffin cups. Using a greased 1 bsp., make an indentation in the center of each.

**3.** In a large bowl, whisk together soup, cream cheese and reserved pasta water. Stir in chicken, mozzarella cheese and tomatoes; spoon into cups. Sprinkle with remaining bacon and Parmesan cheese.

**4.** Bake until set, about 15 minutes. Cool 5 minutes before removing from pan.

**2 pasta cups:** 266 cal., 12g fat (5g sat. fat), 74mg chol., 553mg sod., 20g carb. (4g sugars, 3g fiber), 21g pro. Diabetic Exchanges: 2 lean meat, 1½ fat, 1 starch.

## HEARTY FISH BAKE

*I've lived in Rhode Island for many years and love the fresh seafood dishes served here. This recipe from my mother-in-law is a favorite of mine.*
—Norma DesRoches, Warwick, RI

- - - - - - - - - - - - - - - - - - - - - - - - - - -

**Prep:** 25 min. • **Bake:** 20 min.
**Makes:** 4 servings

- 4 medium potatoes, peeled
- 1 tsp. all-purpose flour
- 1 small onion, sliced into rings
- ½ tsp. salt
- ¼ tsp. pepper
- ¾ cup 2% milk, divided
- 1½ lbs. cod fillets or freshwater fish (trout, catfish or pike)
- 3 Tbsp. grated Parmesan cheese, optional
- 2 Tbsp. minced fresh parsley or 2 tsp. dried parsley flakes
- ¼ tsp. paprika

**1.** Place potatoes in a saucepan and cover with water. Bring to a boil. Reduce heat; cover and simmer 15-20 minutes or until tender. Drain; cool slightly.

**2.** Slice ⅛ in. thick; place in a greased shallow 2-qt. baking dish. Sprinkle with flour. Top with the onion; sprinkle with salt and pepper. Pour half the milk over potatoes. Place the fish on top; pour remaining milk over fish. Sprinkle with Parmesan cheese if desired.

**3.** Cover and bake at 375° until fish flakes easily with a fork, 20-30 minutes. Sprinkle with parsley and paprika.

**1 serving:** 281 cal., 2g fat (1g sat. fat), 68mg chol., 414mg sod., 34g carb. (5g sugars, 2g fiber), 31g pro. **Diabetic exchanges:** 4 lean meat, 2 starch.

**LOADED CHICKEN CARBONARA CUPS**

## MEXICAN-STYLE MEAT LOAVES

**(PICTURED ON P. 146)**

*On a vacation to Arizona, I fell in love with albondigas, Latin American meatballs. After playing with a number of different spices, I came up with a version that's amazing as a meat loaf.*
—James Schend, Pleasant Prairie, WI

**Prep:** 20 min. • **Bake:** 50 min. + standing
**Makes:** 2 loaves (8 servings each)

- 3 large eggs, lightly beaten
- ⅔ cup 2% milk
- ⅔ cup thick and zesty tomato sauce
- 2 Tbsp. Worcestershire sauce
- 1 large onion, finely chopped
- 2 cans (2¼ oz. each) sliced ripe olives, drained
- ¾ cup dry bread crumbs
- ⅓ cup minced fresh cilantro
- 2½ tsp. ground cumin
- 2½ tsp. chili powder
- 1 tsp. salt
- 1 tsp. pepper
- 3 lbs. lean ground beef (90% lean)
  Optional: Salsa and additional cilantro

**1.** Preheat oven to 350°. In a large bowl, combine the first 12 ingredients. Add the beef; mix lightly but thoroughly. Transfer to 2 greased 9x5-in. loaf pans.
**2.** Bake the meat loaves 50-55 minutes or until a thermometer reads 160°. Let stand 10 minutes before slicing. If desired, top with salsa and cilantro.

**1 slice:** 196 cal., 10g fat (3g sat. fat), 89mg chol., 453mg sod., 7g carb. (2g sugars, 1g fiber), 19g pro. **Diabetic exchanges:** 3 lean meat, ½ starch.

**Freeze option:** Shape meat loaves in plastic wrap-lined loaf pans; wrap and freeze until firm. Remove from pans and wrap securely in foil; return to freezer. To use, unwrap and bake meat loaves in pans as directed, increasing the time to 1¼-1½ hours or until a thermometer inserted in center reads 160°.

## SLICED HAM WITH ROASTED VEGETABLES

*To prepare this colorful, zesty oven meal, I shop in my backyard for the fresh garden vegetables and oranges (we have our own tree!) that highlight the ham's hearty flavor. It's my family's favorite main dish.*
—Margaret Pache, Mesa, AZ

**Prep:** 10 min. • **Bake:** 35 min.
**Makes:** 6 servings

Cooking spray
- 6 medium potatoes, peeled and cubed
- 5 medium carrots, sliced
- 1 medium turnip, peeled and cubed
- 1 large onion, cut into thin wedges
- 6 slices (4 to 6 oz. each) fully cooked ham, halved
- ¼ cup thawed orange juice concentrate
- 2 Tbsp. brown sugar
- 1 tsp. prepared horseradish
- 1 tsp. grated orange zest
  Coarsely ground pepper

**1.** Grease two 15x10x1-in. baking pans with cooking spray. Add potatoes, carrots, turnip and onion; generously coat with cooking spray. Bake, uncovered, at 425° until tender, 25-30 minutes.
**2.** Arrange ham slices over the vegetables. In a bowl, combine concentrate, brown sugar, horseradish and orange zest. Spoon over ham and vegetables. Bake until the ham is heated through, about 10 minutes longer. Sprinkle with pepper.

**1 serving:** 375 cal., 5g fat (1g sat. fat), 71mg chol., 1179mg sod., 55g carb. (15g sugars, 7g fiber), 31g pro.

**SLICED HAM WITH ROASTED VEGETABLES**

**CREAMY PESTO CHICKEN**

## SPICY BEEF BRISKET

*My family fell in love with this brisket the first time I tried the recipe. The no-fuss preparation and long cooking time make it perfect to have simmering away while you take care of party preparations and other courses.*
—Mary Neihouse, Fort Smith, AR

**Prep:** 5 min. • **Bake:** 3 hours
**Makes:** 10 servings

1   fresh beef brisket (3 to 4 lbs.)
1   can (15 oz.) tomato sauce
1   can (10 oz.) diced tomatoes and green chiles, undrained
1   envelope onion soup mix
¼   tsp. garlic powder

Place the brisket on a rack in a shallow greased roasting pan. In a small bowl, combine the remaining ingredients; pour over brisket. Cover and bake at 325° for 3 hours or until meat is tender. To serve, thinly slice across the grain.

**4 oz. cooked beef:** 195 cal., 6g fat (2g sat. fat), 58mg chol., 601mg sod., 5g carb. (1g sugars, 1g fiber), 29g pro. **Diabetic exchanges:** 4 lean meat.

## ② CREAMY PESTO CHICKEN

*Basil usually takes over our garden in the middle of June, but we don't mind because we love this pesto! It's a dairy-free version but it tastes so good. We love this mixture over cauliflower rice or gluten-free pasta.*
—Courtney Stultz, Weir, KS

**Prep:** 20 min. • **Bake:** 20 min.
**Makes:** 2 servings

1   Tbsp. balsamic vinegar
1   tsp. olive oil
1   tsp. dried oregano
½   tsp. minced garlic
¼   tsp. salt
2   boneless skinless chicken breast halves (6 oz. each)
PESTO
¼   cup loosely packed basil leaves
¼   cup packed fresh parsley leaves
¼   tsp. salt
¼   cup canned coconut milk

**1.** Preheat oven to 350°. Combine the first 5 ingredients; brush over chicken. Place in a greased 8-in. square baking dish. Bake until a thermometer reads 165°, 20-25 minutes.
**2.** Meanwhile, place the basil, parsley and salt in a small food processor; pulse until chopped. While processing, gradually add coconut milk in a steady stream until mixture is pureed. Serve with chicken.

**1 chicken breast half with 2 Tbsp. pesto:** 261 cal., 11g fat (6g sat. fat), 94mg chol., 684mg sod., 4g carb. (3g sugars, 1g fiber), 35g pro. **Diabetic exchanges:** 5 lean meat, 1½ fat.

**TEST KITCHEN TIP**

It's important to get the correct coconut milk. The ones in the refrigerated dairy case have a tendency to curdle in this recipe, so be sure to grab the canned type.

ASIAN TOFU

## COCONUT-CRUSTED TURKEY STRIPS

*My granddaughter shared these turkey strips with me. With a plum dipping sauce, they're just the thing for a light supper.*
—Agnes Ward, Stratford, ON

**Prep:** 20 min. • **Cook:** 10 min./batch
**Makes:** 6 servings

  2  large egg whites
  2  tsp. sesame oil
  ½  cup sweetened shredded coconut, lightly toasted
  ½  cup dry bread crumbs
  2  Tbsp. sesame seeds, toasted
  ½  tsp. salt
 1½  lbs. turkey breast tenderloins, cut into ½-in. strips
     Cooking spray

DIPPING SAUCE
  ½  cup plum sauce
  ⅓  cup unsweetened pineapple juice
 1½  tsp. prepared mustard
  1  tsp. cornstarch

**1.** Preheat oven to 425°. In a shallow bowl, whisk egg whites and oil. In another shallow bowl, mix coconut, bread crumbs, sesame seeds and salt. Dip turkey in egg mixture, then in coconut mixture, patting to help coating adhere.
**2.** Place on baking sheets coated with cooking spray; spritz with cooking spray. Bake 10-12 minutes or until turkey is no longer pink, turning once.
**3.** Meanwhile, in a small saucepan, mix sauce ingredients. Bring to a boil; cook and stir until thickened, 1-2 minutes. Serve with turkey.

**3 oz. cooked turkey with 2 Tbsp. sauce:** 292 cal., 9g fat (3g sat. fat), 45mg chol., 517mg sod., 24g carb. (5g sugars, 1g fiber), 31g pro.
**Diabetic exchanges:** 4 lean meat, 1½ starch, ½ fat.

**Air-Fryer Coconut-Crusted Turkey Strips:** Preheat air fryer to 400°. In batches, place prepared turkey in a single layer on a greased tray in an air-fryer basket; spritz with cooking spray. Cook until golden brown, 3-4 minutes. Turn; spritz with cooking spray. Cook until golden brown and turkey is no longer pink, 3-4 minutes longer. Serve with prepared sauce.

## ASIAN TOFU

*This tasty Asian tofu was the first meatless recipe my fiance made for me. It's a tasty light protein and is so easy to pair with broiled or grilled veggies such as eggplant, asparagus or even tomatoes.*
—Emily Steers, Los Angeles, CA

**Prep:** 10 min. + marinating • **Broil:** 10 min.
**Makes:** 4 servings

  ¼  cup olive oil
  3  Tbsp. reduced-sodium soy sauce
  2  green onions, chopped
  2  garlic cloves, minced
  ¼  tsp. ground cumin
  ¼  tsp. crushed red pepper flakes
  1  pkg. (14 oz.) extra-firm tofu

**1.** Whisk together first 6 ingredients. Cut the tofu lengthwise into ⅜-in. thick slices; cut each slice in half diagonally to make triangles. Place tofu and marinade in a large shallow bowl; turn to coat. Cover and refrigerate 3-5 hours, turning occasionally.
**2.** Preheat broiler. Reserving marinade, place tofu in a 15x10x1-in. pan. Drizzle remaining marinade over tops. Broil 5-6 in. from heat until lightly browned and heated through, about 10 minutes.

**2 slices:** 208 cal., 18g fat (3g sat. fat), 0 chol., 440mg sod., 4g carb. (1g sugars, 1g fiber), 9g pro. **Diabetic exchanges:** 3 fat, 1 lean meat.

COCONUT-CRUSTED
TURKEY STRIPS

**CHICKEN QUINOA BOWLS
WITH BALSAMIC DRESSING**

## CHICKEN QUINOA BOWLS WITH BALSAMIC DRESSING

*I love this recipe because its simplicity lets me spend time with my family while not sacrificing taste or nutrition. Plus the fresh spring flavors really shine through!*
—Allyson Meyler, Greensboro, NC

**Prep:** 30 min. + cooling • **Broil:** 10 min.
**Makes:** 2 servings

¼ cup balsamic vinegar
⅔ cup water
⅓ cup quinoa, rinsed
2 boneless skinless chicken breast halves (6 oz. each)
3 tsp. olive or coconut oil, divided
¼ tsp. garlic powder
½ tsp. salt, divided
¼ tsp. pepper, divided
½ lb. fresh asparagus, trimmed
¼ cup plain Greek yogurt
½ tsp. spicy brown mustard
½ medium ripe avocado, peeled and sliced
6 cherry tomatoes, halved

**1.** Place vinegar in a small saucepan; bring to a boil. Cook until slightly thickened, 2-3 minutes. Transfer to a small bowl and cool completely.
**2.** In a small saucepan, bring water to a boil. Add quinoa. Reduce heat; simmer, covered, 10-12 minutes or until liquid is absorbed. Keep warm.
**3.** Preheat broiler. Toss chicken with 2 tsp. oil, garlic powder, ¼ tsp. salt and ⅛ tsp. pepper. Place on 1 half of a 15x10x1-in. pan coated with cooking spray. Broil 4 in. from heat for 5 minutes. Meanwhile, toss asparagus with the remaining oil, salt and pepper.
**4.** Remove pan from oven; turn chicken over. Add asparagus. Broil until a thermometer inserted in chicken reads 165° and the asparagus is tender, 3-5 minutes. Let chicken stand 5 minutes before slicing.
**5.** For dressing, stir yogurt and mustard into balsamic reduction. To serve, spoon quinoa into bowls; top with the chicken, asparagus, avocado and tomatoes. Serve with dressing.

**1 serving:** 491 cal., 21g fat (5g sat. fat), 101mg chol., 715mg sod., 35g carb. (12g sugars, 6g fiber), 42g pro.

### DID YOU KNOW?

Quinoa, an ancient South American grain, is often called the "the perfect grain." Unlike other grains, quinoa contains a complete protein. This makes it excellent for vegetarian and vegan meals, which can otherwise be low in protein.

## GINGER SALMON WITH GREEN BEANS

*I developed this flavor-packed dinner for a busy friend who wants to eat clean.*
—Nicole Stevens, Charleston, SC

**Takes:** 30 min. • **Makes:** 2 servings

- ¼ cup lemon juice
- 2 Tbsp. rice vinegar
- 3 garlic cloves, minced
- 2 tsp. minced fresh gingerroot
- 2 tsp. honey
- ⅛ tsp. salt
- ⅛ tsp. pepper
- 2 salmon fillets (4 oz. each)
- 1 medium lemon, thinly sliced

GREEN BEANS
- ¾ lb. fresh green beans, trimmed
- 2 Tbsp. water
- 2 tsp. olive oil
- ½ cup finely chopped onion
- 3 garlic cloves, minced
- ⅛ tsp. salt

**1.** Preheat the oven to 325°. Mix the first 7 ingredients.

**2.** Place each salmon fillet on an 18x12-in. piece of heavy-duty foil; fold up edges of foil to create a rim around the fish. Spoon the lemon juice mixture over salmon; top with lemon slices. Carefully fold the foil around fish, sealing tightly.

**3.** Place packets in a 15x10x1-in. pan. Bake until fish just begins to flake easily with a fork, 15-20 minutes. Open foil carefully to allow steam to escape.

**4.** Meanwhile, place green beans, water and oil in a large skillet; bring to a boil. Reduce heat; simmer, covered, 5 minutes. Stir in the remaining ingredients; cook, uncovered, until beans are crisp-tender, stirring occasionally. Serve with salmon.

**1 serving:** 357 cal., 15g fat (3g sat. fat), 57mg chol., 607mg sod., 35g carb. (18g sugars, 8g fiber), 24g pro. **Diabetic exchanges:** 3 lean meat, 1 starch, 1 vegetable, 1 fat.

GINGER SALMON WITH GREEN BEANS

## PORCINI-CRUSTED PORK WITH POLENTA

(PICTURED ON P. 146)

*Hints of rosemary and Parmesan meet earthy mushroom undertones in this restaurant-quality dish you can proudly call your own.*
—Casandra Rittenhouse, North Hollywood, CA

**Prep:** 20 min. • **Bake:** 20 min.
**Makes:** 4 servings

- 1 pkg. (1 oz.) dried porcini mushrooms
- ¼ tsp. salt
- ¼ tsp. pepper
- 4 bone-in pork loin chops (7 oz. each)
- 2 tsp. olive oil
- 1 tube (1 lb.) polenta
- ½ cup grated Parmesan cheese
- ¼ tsp. dried rosemary, crushed

**1.** Process the mushrooms in a food processor until coarsely chopped. Transfer to a shallow bowl; stir in salt and pepper. Press 1 side of each pork chop into mushroom mixture.

**2.** In a large ovenproof skillet coated with cooking spray, heat oil over medium-high heat. Place chops, mushroom side down, in skillet; cook for 2 minutes. Turn over; cook 2 minutes longer. Bake, uncovered, at 375° until at thermometer inserted in pork reads 145°, 20-25 minutes. Let stand 5 minutes before serving.

**3.** Prepare polenta according to package directions for soft polenta. Stir in cheese and rosemary. Serve with pork chops.

**1 serving:** 397 cal., 14g fat (5g sat. fat), 94mg chol., 825mg sod., 26g carb., g fiber, 38g pro.

## TLC (THANKSGIVING LEFTOVER CASSEROLE)

*Turkey, stuffing and vegetables come together into a fabulous casserole made from leftovers. There's delicious comfort in every bite.*

—Barbara Lento, Houston, PA

**Prep:** 20 min. + standing • **Bake:** 65 min.
**Makes:** 8 servings

4 cups seasoned stuffing cubes
4 cups cubed cooked turkey
2 celery ribs, finely chopped
1 cup frozen peas
1 cup fresh or frozen cranberries
½ cup chopped sweet onion
¼ cup all-purpose flour
4 large eggs
3 cups 2% milk
1 can (8¼ oz.) cream-style corn
½ tsp. salt
½ tsp. pepper
2 Tbsp. butter
⅓ cup coarsely chopped pecans

**1.** Preheat oven to 350°. Layer the first 6 ingredients in a greased 13x9-in. baking dish. In a large bowl, whisk flour, eggs and milk until smooth. Add the corn, salt and pepper; mix well. Pour over top; let stand 15 minutes. Dot with butter and sprinkle with pecans.

**2.** Cover and bake 35 minutes. Uncover and bake 30-35 minutes or until a knife inserted in the center comes out clean.

**1½ cups:** 415 cal., 15g fat (5g sat. fat), 173mg chol., 768mg sod., 38g carb. (9g sugars, 4g fiber), 32g pro. **Diabetic exchanges:** 3 lean meat, 2½ starch, 1½ fat.

**TLC (THANKSGIVING LEFTOVER CASSEROLE)**

**CRUNCHY HERBED CHICKEN BREASTS**

## SNAPPER WITH SPICY PINEAPPLE GLAZE

*Ginger and cayenne bring spice to this tangy treatment for red snapper fillets from our Test Kitchen. Sweet pineapple preserves round out the delectable combination of flavors.*
—*Taste of Home* Test Kitchen

- - - - - - - - - - - - - - - - - - - - - - - - -

**Takes:** 30 min. • **Makes:** 4 servings

- ½ cup pineapple preserves
- 2 Tbsp. rice vinegar
- 2 tsp. minced fresh gingerroot
- 2 garlic cloves, minced
- ¾ tsp. salt, divided
- ¼ tsp. cayenne pepper
- 4 red snapper fillets (6 oz. each)
- 3 tsp. olive oil

1. In a small bowl, combine the preserves, vinegar, ginger, garlic, ½ tsp. salt and cayenne; set aside. Place the fillets on a broiler pan coated with cooking spray. Rub fillets with oil; sprinkle with the remaining salt.
2. Broil fillets 4-6 in. from the heat for 5 minutes. Baste with half of the glaze. Broil 5-7 minutes longer or until the fish flakes easily with a fork. Baste with remaining glaze.

**1 fillet:** 304 cal., 6g fat (1g sat. fat), 63mg chol., 552mg sod., 27g carb. (24g sugars, 0 fiber), 35g pro. **Diabetic exchanges:** 5 lean meat, 2 starch.

## CRUNCHY HERBED CHICKEN BREASTS

*I'm always getting requests to make this simple main dish for family and friends. It might become a go-to dinner in your house, too.*
—Lucia Johnson, Massena, NY

- - - - - - - - - - - - - - - - - - - - - - - - -

**Prep:** 15 min. • **Bake:** 25 min.
**Makes:** 6 servings

- ⅔ cup panko bread crumbs
- ½ cup grated Parmesan cheese
- ½ cup grated Romano cheese
- 1 Tbsp. minced fresh oregano or 1 tsp. dried oregano
- 1 Tbsp. minced fresh basil or 1 tsp. dried basil
- 2 tsp. minced fresh parsley
- 2 garlic cloves, minced
- ½ tsp. salt
- ½ tsp. pepper
- ½ cup all-purpose flour
- 2 large eggs, lightly beaten
- 6 boneless skinless chicken breast halves (5 oz. each)
  Olive oil-flavored cooking spray

1. In a shallow bowl, mix the first 9 ingredients. Place flour and eggs in separate shallow bowls. Dip both sides of chicken in the flour, eggs, then crumb mixture, patting to help coating adhere.
2. Place on a greased baking sheet. Spritz tops with cooking spray. Bake at 375° for 25-30 minutes or until a thermometer reads 170°.

**1 chicken breast half:** 244 cal., 8g fat (3g sat. fat), 139mg chol., 333mg sod., 7g carb. (0 sugars, 0 fiber), 35g pro. **Diabetic exchanges:** 4 lean meat, ½ starch, ½ fat.

# VEGGIE PIZZA WITH HERBED TOMATO CRUST

*I love this recipe because the crust is so flavorful—tomato juice replaces most of the oil. It's one of my kids' favorite meals!*
—Karen Shipp, San Antonio, TX

- - - - - - - - - - - - - - - - - - - - - - - - - - - - - - -

**Prep:** 30 min. + rising • **Bake:** 25 min.
**Makes:** 6 servings

½   cup whole wheat flour
1½  tsp. minced fresh parsley or
     ½ tsp. dried parsley flakes
1½  tsp. minced fresh rosemary or
     ½ tsp. dried rosemary, crushed
1   tsp. active dry yeast
½   tsp. sugar
¼   tsp. salt
¼   tsp. pepper
½   cup water
½   cup tomato juice
1   tsp. olive oil
1½  to 1¾ cups all-purpose flour
TOPPINGS
1   can (8 oz.) pizza sauce
1   medium green pepper, chopped
1   cup sliced fresh mushrooms
1   small red onion, chopped
1   medium tomato, chopped
1   cup shredded part-skim
     mozzarella cheese
     Crushed red pepper flakes,
     optional

**1.** In a large bowl, combine the first 7 ingredients. In a small saucepan, heat the water, tomato juice and oil to 120°-130°. Add to dry ingredients; beat until smooth. Stir in enough all-purpose flour to form a soft dough.

**2.** Turn onto a lightly floured surface; knead until smooth and elastic, about 5 minutes. Place in a bowl coated with cooking spray, turning once to coat top. Cover and let rise until doubled, about 45 minutes.

**3.** Preheat oven to 400°. Punch dough down; roll into a 12-in. circle. Transfer to a 14-in. pizza pan coated with cooking spray; build up edge slightly.

**4.** Spread with the pizza sauce. Top with the green pepper, mushrooms, onion, tomato and cheese. Bake 25-30 minutes or until cheese is melted and edge is lightly browned. If desired, sprinkle with pepper flakes.

**1 slice:** 240 cal., 4g fat (2g sat. fat), 11mg chol., 370mg sod., 40g carb. (6g sugars, 4g fiber), 11g pro. **Diabetic exchanges:** 2 starch, 1 vegetable, 1 lean meat.

## ROASTED PORK TENDERLOIN & VEGETABLES

*There are no complicated steps to follow when preparing this medley of tender pork and veggies. Just season with herbs, then pop in the oven.*
—Diane Martin, Brown Deer, WI

**Prep:** 20 min. • **Bake:** 25 min.
**Makes:** 6 servings

- 2 pork tenderloins (¾ lb. each)
- 2 lbs. red potatoes, quartered
- 1 lb. carrots, halved and cut into 2-in. pieces
- 1 medium onion, cut into wedges
- 1 Tbsp. olive oil
- 2 tsp. dried rosemary, crushed
- 1 tsp. rubbed sage
- ½ tsp. salt
- ¼ tsp. pepper

1. Preheat oven to 450°. Place the pork in a shallow roasting pan coated with cooking spray; arrange the potatoes, carrots and onion around pork. Drizzle with oil. Combine the seasonings; sprinkle over meat and vegetables.
2. Bake, uncovered, 25-35 minutes or until a thermometer reads 145° and vegetables are tender, stirring vegetables occasionally. Remove pork from oven; tent with foil. Let stand for 5 minutes before slicing.

**1 serving:** 301 cal., 7g fat (2g sat. fat), 64mg chol., 304mg sod., 33g carb. (6g sugars, 5g fiber), 26g pro. **Diabetic exchanges:** 3 lean meat, 2 starch, 1 vegetable.

---

### READER REVIEW

*"This is a cold-weather staple at our house. I add other root vegetables, sometimes a purple turnip or two, always a sweet potato or two, and occasionally a parsnip or two. Tonight I am adding Brussels sprouts to the vegetable mix. I usually roast this for an hour."*

—STRESSIN, TASTEOFHOME.COM

SPICY OVEN-FRIED CHICKEN

## SPICY OVEN-FRIED CHICKEN

*My family adores this chicken recipe. The coating keeps the chicken nice and moist— with the taste enhanced by marinating, the results are delicious.*
—Stephanie Otten, Byron Center, MI

**Prep:** 25 min. + marinating • **Bake:** 35 min.
**Makes:** 8 servings

- 2 cups buttermilk
- 2 Tbsp. Dijon mustard
- 2 tsp. salt
- 2 tsp. hot pepper sauce
- 1½ tsp. garlic powder
- 8 bone-in chicken breast halves, skin removed (8 oz. each)
- 2 cups soft bread crumbs
- 1 cup cornmeal
- 2 Tbsp. canola oil
- ½ tsp. poultry seasoning
- ½ tsp. ground mustard
- ½ tsp. paprika
- ½ tsp. cayenne pepper
- ¼ tsp. dried oregano
- ¼ tsp. dried parsley flakes

1. Preheat oven to 400°. In a large bowl or dish, combine the first 5 ingredients. Add chicken and turn to coat. Refrigerate for 1 hour or overnight.
2. Drain chicken, discarding marinade. In a large bowl, combine the remaining ingredients. Add chicken, 1 piece at a time, and coat with crumb mixture. Place on a parchment-lined baking sheet. Bake 35-40 minutes or until a thermometer reads 170°.

**1 chicken breast half:** 296 cal., 7g fat (2g sat. fat), 103mg chol., 523mg sod., 15g carb. (2g sugars, 1g fiber), 40g pro. **Diabetic exchanges:** 6 lean meat, 1 starch, ½ fat.
**Note:** To make soft bread crumbs, tear bread into pieces and place in a food processor or blender. Cover and pulse until crumbs form. One slice of bread yields ½ to ¾ cup crumbs.
**Spicy Air-Fried Chicken:** Preheat air fryer to 375°. In batches, place the prepared chicken in a single layer in an air fryer basket coated with cooking spray. Air-fry until a thermometer reads 170°, turning chicken halfway through cooking, about 20 minutes. Repeat with the remaining chicken. When the last batch of chicken is cooked, return all chicken to basket and air-fry 2-3 minutes longer to heat through.

## QUINOA-STUFFED SQUASH BOATS

*My colorful boats with quinoa, garbanzo beans and pumpkin seeds use delicata squash, a winter squash that's cream-colored with green stripes. In a pinch, acorn squash will do.*
—Lauren McAnelly, Des Moines, IA

-------------------------------------------

**Takes:** 30 min. • **Makes:** 8 servings

- 4 delicata squash (about 12 oz. each)
- 3 tsp. olive oil, divided
- ⅛ tsp. pepper
- 1 tsp. salt, divided
- 1½ cups vegetable broth
- 1 cup quinoa, rinsed
- 1 can (15 oz.) garbanzo beans or chickpeas, rinsed and drained
- ¼ cup dried cranberries
- 1 green onion, thinly sliced
- 1 tsp. minced fresh sage
- ½ tsp. grated lemon zest
- 1 tsp. lemon juice
- ½ cup crumbled goat cheese
- ¼ cup salted pumpkin seeds or pepitas, toasted

**1.** Preheat oven to 450°. Cut each squash lengthwise in half; remove and discard seeds. Lightly brush cut sides with 1 tsp. oil; sprinkle with pepper and ½ tsp. salt. Place on a baking sheet, cut side down. Bake until tender, 15-20 minutes.

**2.** Meanwhile, in a large saucepan, combine broth and quinoa; bring to a boil. Reduce heat; simmer, covered, until liquid is absorbed, 12-15 minutes.

**3.** Stir in garbanzo beans, cranberries, green onion, sage, lemon zest, lemon juice and the remaining oil and salt; spoon into squash. Sprinkle with cheese and pumpkin seeds.

**1 stuffed squash half:** 275 cal., 8g fat (2g sat. fat), 9mg chol., 591mg sod., 46g carb. (9g sugars, 10g fiber), 9g pro. **Diabetic exchanges:** 3 starch, 1 lean meat, ½ fat

**QUINOA-STUFFED SQUASH BOATS**

ZUCCHINI ROLL-UPS

## SKILLET-ROASTED LEMON CHICKEN WITH POTATOES

*This is a meal I have my students make in our nutrition unit. It has a delicious lemon-herb flavor and is simple to make.*
—Mindy Rottmund, Lancaster, PA

**Prep:** 20 min. • **Bake:** 25 min.
**Makes:** 4 servings

- 1 Tbsp. olive oil, divided
- 1 medium lemon, thinly sliced
- 4 garlic cloves, minced and divided
- ¼ tsp. grated lemon zest
- ½ tsp. salt, divided
- ¼ tsp. pepper, divided
- 8 boneless skinless chicken thighs (4 oz. each)
- ¼ tsp. dried rosemary, crushed
- 1 lb. fingerling potatoes, halved lengthwise
- 8 cherry tomatoes
  Minced fresh parsley, optional

**1.** Preheat oven to 450°. Grease a 10-in. cast-iron or other ovenproof skillet with 1 tsp. oil. Arrange lemon slices in a single layer in skillet.
**2.** Combine 1 tsp. oil, 2 minced garlic cloves, lemon zest, ¼ tsp. salt and ⅛ tsp. pepper; rub over chicken. Place over lemon slices.
**3.** In a large bowl, combine rosemary and the remaining oil, garlic, salt and pepper. Add potatoes and tomatoes; toss to coat. Arrange over chicken. Bake, uncovered, 25-30 minutes or until the chicken is no longer pink and potatoes are tender. If desired, sprinkle with minced parsley before serving.
**2 chicken thighs with 4 oz. potatoes and 2 tomatoes:** 446 cal., 20g fat (5g sat. fat), 151mg chol., 429mg sod., 18g carb. (2g sugars, 3g fiber), 45g pro.

## ZUCCHINI ROLL-UPS

*We love lasagna, but these zucchini roll-ups are a little healthier and a lot quicker to make! Using zucchini pasta also makes the dish both gluten- and grain-free. To make zucchini strips, use a box grater or mandoline to get even slices.*
—Courtney Stultz, Weir, KS

**Prep:** 15 min. • **Bake:** 20 min.
**Makes:** 3 servings

- 1 cup part-skim ricotta cheese
- 1½ tsp. Italian seasoning, divided
- ½ tsp. salt
- ¼ tsp. pepper
- 2 medium zucchini
- 4 plum tomatoes, seeded and chopped
- 1 can (8 oz.) tomato sauce
- 1 Tbsp. tomato paste
  Shredded Parmesan cheese, optional

**1.** Preheat oven to 425°. In a small bowl, combine ricotta, ½ tsp. Italian seasoning, salt and pepper. Slice zucchini lengthwise into twelve ⅛-in.-thick slices. Top each slice with 1 rounded tablespoon cheese mixture. Roll up zucchini and secure with toothpicks; place seam side down in an ungreased 8-in. baking dish.
**2.** Combine tomatoes, tomato sauce, tomato paste and remaining 1 tsp. Italian seasoning; pour over rolls. Cover and bake until bubbly, 20-25 minutes. Remove toothpicks before serving. If desired, sprinkle with Parmesan cheese.
**4 roll-ups:** 175 cal., 8g fat (4g sat. fat), 26mg chol., 643mg sod., 16g carb. (7g sugars, 4g fiber), 13g pro. **Diabetic exchanges:** 2 vegetable, 1 medium-fat meat.

**SKILLET-ROASTED LEMON CHICKEN WITH POTATOES**

# GRILLED SPECIALTIES

"*A simple dry rub turns beef roast into a real crowd-pleaser. The slightly spicy meat is irresistible as is and as leftovers, piled on top of fresh crusty bread.*"
—Allison Ector, Ardmore, PA

**Eggplant Salad with Tomato & Goat Cheese** (p. 197) **Grilled Bruschetta** (p. 192) **Grilled Green Beans** (p. 183)
**Spinach & Mushroom Smothered Chicken** (p. 195) **Santa Maria Roast Beef** (p. 180) **Grilled Basil Chicken & Tomatoes** (p. 186)

## SANTA MARIA ROAST BEEF

(PICTURED ON P. 179)

*A simple dry rub turns beef roast into a real crowd-pleaser. The slightly spicy meat is irresistible as is and as leftovers, piled on top of fresh crusty bread.*

—Allison Ector, Ardmore, PA

- - - - - - - - - - - - - - - - - - - - - - - - -

**Prep:** 20 min. + chilling
**Grill:** 1 hour + standing • **Makes:** 6 servings

- 4 Tbsp. paprika
- 3 Tbsp. brown sugar
- 2 Tbsp. chili powder
- 1 Tbsp. garlic powder
- 1 Tbsp. white pepper
- 1 Tbsp. celery salt
- 1 Tbsp. ground cumin
- 1 Tbsp. dried oregano
- 1 Tbsp. pepper
- 2 tsp. cayenne pepper
- 1 tsp. ground mustard
- 1 beef tri-tip roast or beef sirloin tip roast (2 to 3 lbs.)
- 2 cups soaked hickory wood chips or chunks
- 2 Tbsp. canola oil

**1.** Combine the first 11 ingredients; rub desired amount over roast. Wrap and refrigerate overnight. Store the leftover dry rub in an airtight container for up to 6 months.

**2.** Remove roast from the refrigerator 1 hour before grilling. Prepare the grill for indirect heat, using a drip pan. Add soaked wood chips according to the manufacturer's directions.

**3.** Unwrap the roast and brush with oil; place over drip pan. Grill, covered, over medium-low indirect heat for 1-1½ hours or until meat reaches desired doneness (for medium-rare, a thermometer should read 135°; medium, 140°; medium-well, 145°). Let roast stand for 10-15 minutes before slicing.

**4 oz. cooked beef:** 294 cal., 16g fat (4g sat. fat), 91mg chol., 324mg sod., 5g carb. (3g sugars, 1g fiber), 32g pro. **Diabetic exchanges:** 4 lean meat, 1 fat.

## FAJITA PITAS

*I was late coming home one evening and forgot to pick up tortillas for the fajitas we planned for dinner. We used pita bread from the freezer instead. My family often requests these warm chicken-filled pockets, garnished with homemade sauce and other tasty toppings.*

—Diana Jones, Springtown, TX

- - - - - - - - - - - - - - - - - - - - - - - - -

**Prep:** 40 min. • **Bake:** 10 min.
**Makes:** 8 servings

- 1 medium tomato, finely chopped
- 1 small onion, finely chopped
- ½ jalapeno pepper, finely chopped
- 1 Tbsp. minced fresh cilantro
- 2 Tbsp. canola oil, divided
- 1 large sweet pepper, halved and seeded
- 1 large onion, cut crosswise into ½-in. slices
- 6 boneless skinless chicken breast halves (4 oz. each)
- ½ tsp. salt
- ¼ tsp. pepper
- 2 cups shredded Mexican cheese blend or cheddar cheese
- 8 pita pocket halves
  Optional: Guacamole and sour cream

**1.** Preheat oven to 325°. For the salsa, combine the first 4 ingredients; stir in 1 Tbsp. oil.

**2.** Brush pepper halves and onion slices with remaining oil. Sprinkle chicken with salt and pepper. Place the vegetables and chicken on an oiled grill rack over medium heat. Grill, covered, until vegetables are tender and a thermometer inserted in chicken reads 165°, 4-6 minutes per side.

**3.** Cut vegetables and chicken into strips; toss with cheese. Spoon into pita halves; place on a baking sheet. Bake until the cheese is melted, 5-7 minutes. Serve with the salsa and, if desired, guacamole and sour cream.

**Note:** Wear disposable gloves when cutting hot peppers; the oils can burn skin. Avoid touching your face.

**1 filled pita half:** 327 cal., 15g fat (5g sat. fat), 72mg chol., 511mg sod., 21g carb. (2g sugars, 2g fiber), 26g pro. **Diabetic exchanges:** 3 lean meat, 2 fat, 1½ starch.

**FAJITA PITAS**

**PEACH BRUSCHETTA**

## SPICE-RUBBED SALMON

*We eat this salmon a lot, along with couscous and fresh veggies. Even my 2-year-old devours it.*
—Lyndsay Rensing, Katy, TX

**Takes:** 20 min. • **Makes:** 4 servings

- 1 tsp. brown sugar
- 1 tsp. ground cumin
- ½ tsp. salt
- ½ tsp. dried parsley flakes
- ½ tsp. chili powder
- ¼ tsp. garlic powder
- ¼ tsp. ground mustard
- ¼ tsp. paprika
- ¼ tsp. pepper
- ⅛ tsp. ground cinnamon
- 4 salmon fillets (6 oz. each)
- 2 tsp. olive oil

**1.** In a small bowl, mix first 10 ingredients. Rub fillets with seasoning mixture; drizzle with oil.
**2.** Place salmon on a lightly oiled rack, skin side up. Grill, covered, over high heat or broil 3-4 in. from heat 5 minutes. Turn; grill 4-6 minutes longer or until fish just begins to flake easily with a fork.

**1 fillet:** 295 cal., 18g fat (3g sat. fat), 85mg chol., 385mg sod., 2g carb. (1g sugars, 0 fiber), 29g pro. **Diabetic exchanges.** 5 lean meat, ½ fat.

## PEACH BRUSCHETTA

*As a starter or light snack, this bruschetta is a wonderful way to savor the season with just a bite of fresh peach amid a medley of lively flavors.*
—Nikiko Masumoto, Del Ray, CA

**Prep:** 35 min. • **Cook:** 15 min.
**Makes:** 2 dozen

- ¼ cup chopped walnuts
- 1 garlic clove
- 1½ cups fresh arugula
- ¼ cup extra virgin olive oil
  Salt and pepper to taste

**BRUSCHETTA**
- 1 Tbsp. olive oil plus additional for brushing bread, divided
- 1 large red onion, thinly sliced (1½ cups)
- 1 tsp. minced fresh rosemary
- 24 slices French bread baguette (⅜ in. thick)
- 1 to 2 garlic cloves, halved
- 2 small ripe peaches, cut into ¼-in. slices
  Shaved Parmesan cheese
  Coarse salt

**1.** For pesto, place walnuts and garlic in a small food processor; pulse until finely chopped. Add arugula; process until blended. Continue processing while gradually adding oil in a steady stream. Season with salt and pepper to taste.
**2.** For bruschetta, in a large skillet, heat 1 Tbsp. oil over medium heat. Add the onion and rosemary; cook until onion is softened, 15-20 minutes, stirring occasionally.
**3.** Brush both sides of bread slices with additional oil. Grill, covered, over medium heat or broil 4 in. from heat until golden brown, 1-2 minutes on each side.
**4.** Rub garlic halves on both sides of toasts; discard garlic. Spread toasts with pesto. Top with the onion mixture, peach slices and cheese. If desired, sprinkle with coarse salt. Serve immediately.

**1 appetizer:** 69 cal., 5g fat (1g sat. fat), 0 chol., 37mg sod., 5g carb. (1g sugars, 0 fiber), 0 pro.

**GRILLED KIWI-CHICKEN KABOBS WITH HONEY-CHIPOTLE GLAZE**

## GRILLED KIWI-CHICKEN KABOBS WITH HONEY-CHIPOTLE GLAZE

*When guests bite into these juicy grilled kabobs, their eyes always widen with satisfaction. Our four children are crazy about the spicy-sweet sauce.*
—Joni Hilton, Rocklin, CA

- - - - - - - - - - - - - - - - - - - - - - - - - - -

**Prep:** 20 min. + marinating • **Grill:** 10 min.
**Makes:** 8 kabobs

6 garlic cloves, minced
2 Tbsp. lime juice
1 Tbsp. olive oil
1 tsp. salt
1 lb. boneless skinless chicken breasts, cut into 1-in. cubes
8 medium kiwifruit, peeled and halved
3 Tbsp. honey
1 Tbsp. minced chipotle peppers in adobo sauce
Lime juice, optional
Hot cooked rice, optional

**1.** Combine garlic, lime juice, oil and salt. Add the chicken and kiwi; turn to coat. Refrigerate, covered, up to 30 minutes.
**2.** Mix honey and chipotle peppers. Drain chicken and kiwi, discarding the marinade. On 8 metal or soaked wooden skewers, alternately thread chicken and kiwi.
**3.** Grill, covered, on an oiled rack over medium heat, turning occasionally, until juices run clear, 10-12 minutes. During last 4 minutes, baste frequently with honey-chipotle mixture.
**4.** Serve kabobs with fresh lime juice and rice if desired.

**2 kabobs:** 284 cal., 5g fat (1g sat. fat), 63mg chol., 380mg sod., 37g carb. (27g sugars, 5g fiber), 25g pro.

**TEST KITCHEN TIP**

An enzyme in kiwi breaks down meat proteins, so you'll find this chicken to be very tender. However, too much of a good thing can destroy your chicken, so stick to 30 minutes or less.

## GRILLED SHRIMP & TOMATOES WITH LINGUINE

*This pasta came about one night when I started making up dinner as I went along, using what was on hand. We knew it turned out great with the very first bite.*
—Lisa L. Bynum, Brandon, MS

---

**Takes:** 30 min. • **Makes:** 4 servings

- 8    oz. uncooked linguine
- 16   cherry tomatoes
- 2    Tbsp. olive oil
- 1    lb. uncooked large shrimp, peeled and deveined
- ½    tsp. pepper
- ¼    tsp. salt
- ¼    tsp. garlic powder
- ¼    tsp. Italian seasoning
- 2    Tbsp. butter
- ¼    cup grated Parmesan cheese
- 2    Tbsp. torn fresh basil

**1.** In a large saucepan, cook linguine according to the package directions. Meanwhile, thread tomatoes onto metal or soaked wooden skewers; brush with 1 Tbsp. oil. Thread shrimp onto skewers; brush with remaining oil. Mix seasonings; sprinkle over shrimp.

**2.** Grill shrimp, covered, over medium heat 3-4 minutes on each side or until shrimp turn pink. Grill tomatoes, covered, over medium heat 2-3 minutes or until slightly softened, turning occasionally.

**3.** Drain linguine, reserving ¼ cup pasta water. In same saucepan, melt butter over medium heat. Add linguine, cheese and reserved pasta water, tossing to combine. Remove shrimp and tomatoes from the skewers; serve with the pasta. Sprinkle with basil.

**1 serving:** 445 cal., 17g fat (6g sat. fat), 158mg chol., 416mg sod., 45g carb. (4g sugars, 3g fiber), 29g pro. **Diabetic exchanges:** 3 starch, 3 lean meat, 3 fat.

## GRILLED GREEN BEANS
### (PICTURED ON P. 179)

*I cook almost everything outdoors, including green beans. I prepare this snappy side dish while the entree is cooking. The recipe has won over my picky eaters.*
—Carol Traupman-Carr, Breinigsville, PA

---

**Prep:** 25 min. • **Grill:** 10 min.
**Makes:** 4 servings

- 1    lb. fresh green beans, trimmed
- 2    Tbsp. butter
- 1    small shallot, minced
- 1    garlic clove, minced
- ½    cup grated Parmesan cheese

**1.** In a 6-qt. stockpot, bring 4 qt. water to a boil. Add beans; cook, uncovered, just until crisp-tender, 2-3 minutes. Remove green beans and immediately drop into ice water.

**2.** In a small skillet, melt the butter over medium-high heat. Add shallot; cook and stir until lightly browned, 2-3 minutes. Add the garlic; cook 30 seconds longer. Remove from heat. Drain the beans and pat dry.

**3.** In a large bowl, combine beans, shallot mixture and cheese; toss to coat. Transfer to a piece of heavy-duty foil (about 18 in. square) coated with cooking spray. Fold foil around beans, sealing tightly.

**4.** Grill, covered, over medium heat or broil 4 in. from heat until the cheese is melted, 7-9 minutes. Open foil carefully to allow steam to escape.

**1 cup:** 137 cal., 9g fat (5g sat. fat), 24mg chol., 234mg sod., 12g carb. (3g sugars, 4g fiber), 5g pro. **Diabetic exchanges:** 2 fat, 1 vegetable.

**GRILLED SHRIMP & TOMATOES WITH LINGUINE**

**ZUCCHINI &
CHEESE ROULADES**

## FLAT IRON STEAK SALAD

*This steak salad with avocado and radishes is a big plate of summer deliciousness. I sometimes add dried cranberries and cherry tomatoes, but you can customize it to suit your tastes.*
—Marla Clark, Albuquerque, NM

**Takes:** 30 min. • **Makes:** 4 servings

- ¾ lb. beef flat iron steak or top sirloin steak
- ¾ tsp. salt, divided
- ½ tsp. pepper, divided
- ¼ cup olive oil
- 2 Tbsp. balsamic vinegar
- 2 tsp. lemon juice
- 5 oz. fresh baby spinach (about 6 cups)
- 1 medium beefsteak tomato, sliced
- ½ medium ripe avocado, peeled and sliced
- 4 radishes, thinly sliced
- ¼ cup crumbled blue cheese, optional

**1.** Sprinkle steak with ½ tsp. salt and ¼ tsp. pepper. Grill steak, covered, over medium heat or broil 4 in. from heat 6-8 minutes on each side or until meat reaches desired doneness (for medium-rare, a thermometer should read 135°; medium, 140°; medium-well, 145°). Let stand 5 minutes.
**2.** Meanwhile, in a small bowl, whisk oil, vinegar, lemon juice and the remaining salt and pepper. Divide spinach among 4 plates. Add the sliced tomato, avocado and radishes.
**3.** Cut steak into slices; place over salad. Drizzle with dressing; if desired, sprinkle with cheese.
**1 salad:** 321 cal., 25g fat (6g sat. fat), 55mg chol., 529mg sod., 7g carb. (3g sugars, 3g fiber), 18g pro.
**\* HEALTH TIP \*** Include vitamin C-rich fruits or vegetables, like this recipe's beefsteak tomato, in spinach salads to increase the absorption of iron from the spinach.

## ZUCCHINI & CHEESE ROULADES

*My husband enjoys this recipe so much that he even helps me roll up the roulades! You can change the filling any way you'd like—I have used feta instead of Parmesan, and tried sun-dried tomatoes in the place of the olives.*
—April McKinney, Murfreesboro, TN

**Takes:** 25 min. • **Makes:** 2 dozen

- 1 cup part-skim ricotta cheese
- ¼ cup grated Parmesan cheese
- 2 Tbsp. minced fresh basil or 2 tsp. dried basil
- 1 Tbsp. capers, drained
- 1 Tbsp. chopped Greek olives
- 1 tsp. grated lemon zest
- 1 Tbsp. lemon juice
- ⅛ tsp. salt
- ⅛ tsp. pepper
- 4 medium zucchini

**1.** In a small bowl, mix first 9 ingredients.
**2.** Slice zucchini lengthwise into twenty-four ⅛-in.-thick slices. On a greased grill rack, cook zucchini in batches, covered, over medium heat. Grill until tender, 2-3 minutes on each side.
**3.** Place 1 Tbsp. ricotta mixture on the end of each zucchini slice. Roll up and secure each with a toothpick.
**1 appetizer:** 24 cal., 1g fat (1g sat. fat), 4mg chol., 58mg sod., 2g carb. (1g sugars, 0 fiber), 2g pro.

## GRILLED BASIL CHICKEN & TOMATOES

**(PICTURED ON P. 179)**

*Relax after work with a cold drink while this savory chicken marinates in an herby tomato blend for an hour, then toss it on the grill. It tastes just like summer.*
—Laura Lunardi, West Chester, PA

- - - - - - - - - - - - - - - - - - - - -

**Prep:** 15 min. + marinating • **Grill:** 10 min.
**Makes:** 4 servings

- ¾  cup balsamic vinegar
- ¼  cup tightly packed fresh basil leaves
- 2  Tbsp. olive oil
- 1  garlic clove, minced
- ½  tsp. salt
- 8  plum tomatoes
- 4  boneless skinless chicken breast halves (4 oz. each)

**1.** For marinade, place first 5 ingredients in a blender. Cut 4 tomatoes into quarters and add to blender; cover and process until blended. Halve remaining tomatoes for grilling.
**2.** In a bowl, combine chicken and ⅔ cup marinade; refrigerate, covered, 1 hour, turning occasionally. Reserve remaining marinade for serving.
**3.** Drain chicken, discarding marinade. Place the chicken on an oiled grill rack over medium heat. Grill the chicken, covered, until a thermometer reads 165°, 4-6 minutes per side. Grill the tomatoes, covered, over medium heat until lightly browned, 2-4 minutes per side. Serve the chicken and tomatoes with the reserved marinade.
**1 serving:** 177 cal., 5g fat (1g sat. fat), 63mg chol., 171mg sod., 8g carb. (7g sugars, 1g fiber), 24g pro. **Diabetic exchanges:** 3 lean meat, 1 vegetable, ½ fat.

## GRILLED PORK TENDERLOIN WITH CHERRY SALSA MOLE

*The combination of pork and cherries has long been a favorite of mine. The hint of spice and chocolate in the salsa mole makes the combination even more special.*
—Roxanne Chan, Albany, CA

- - - - - - - - - - - - - - - - - - - - -

**Prep:** 25 min. • **Grill:** 15 min. + standing
**Makes:** 6 servings

- 2  pork tenderloins (¾ lb. each)
- 1  Tbsp. canola oil
- ½  tsp. salt
- ¼  tsp. ground cumin
- ¼  tsp. chili powder
- 1  cup pitted fresh or frozen dark sweet cherries, thawed, chopped
- 1  jalapeno pepper, seeded and minced
- ½  cup finely chopped peeled jicama
- 1  oz. semisweet chocolate, grated
- 2  Tbsp. minced fresh cilantro
- 1  green onion, thinly sliced
- 1  Tbsp. lime juice
- 1  tsp. honey
   Salted pumpkin seeds or pepitas

**1.** Brush the pork tenderloins with oil; sprinkle with the salt, cumin and chili powder. Grill the pork, covered, over medium heat 15-20 minutes or until a thermometer reads 145°, turning occasionally. Let stand 10-15 minutes.
**2.** Meanwhile, combine cherries, jalapeno, jicama, chocolate, cilantro, green onion, lime juice and honey. Slice pork; serve with cherry salsa and pumpkin seeds.
**Note:** Wear disposable gloves when cutting hot peppers; the oils can burn skin. Avoid touching your face.
**3 oz. cooked pork with ¼ cup salsa:**
218 cal., 8g fat (3g sat. fat), 64mg chol., 248mg sod., 11g carb. (9g sugars, 2g fiber), 23g pro. **Diabetic exchanges:** 3 lean meat, ½ starch, ½ fat.

**GRILLED PORK TENDERLOIN WITH CHERRY SALSA MOLE**

GRILLED CHORIZO
& SHRIMP PAELLA

## GRILLED ASPARAGUS

*Tender, with a delicious barbecue flavor, this grilled asparagus recipe makes a perfect side dish for grilled meats. Don't know how to cook asparagus on the grill? Just place asparagus on a double skewer.*
—Taste of Home *Test Kitchen*

**Takes:** 20 min. • **Makes:** 4 servings

- 1 cup water
- 1 lb. fresh asparagus, trimmed
- ¼ cup barbecue sauce

**1.** In a large skillet, bring water to a boil; add asparagus. Cover and cook until crisp-tender, 4-6 minutes; drain and pat dry. Cool slightly.
**2.** Thread several asparagus spears onto 2 parallel soaked wooden skewers. Repeat. Grill, uncovered, over medium heat for 2 minutes, turning once. Baste with barbecue sauce. Grill 2 minutes longer, turning and basting once.

**1 serving:** 43 cal., 0 fat (0 sat. fat), 0 chol., 181mg sod., 9g carb. (7g sugars, 1g fiber), 2g pro. **Diabetic exchanges:** 1 vegetable.

## GRILLED CHORIZO & SHRIMP PAELLA

*This shrimp paella recipe is not only healthy, but it's satisfying, too! There's vitamin C from the sweet red pepper, fiber from the rice, and the chicken sausage is a great source of lean protein.*
Daniel Bartholomay, Fargo, ND

**Prep:** 25 min. • **Grill:** 10 min.
**Makes:** 8 servings

- 1 medium sweet red pepper, chopped
- 1 medium onion, chopped
- 2 Tbsp. olive oil
- 4 cups instant brown rice
- 4 garlic cloves, minced
- 1 chipotle pepper in adobo sauce, chopped
- 6 cups reduced-sodium chicken broth
- 1 can (14½ oz.) no-salt-added diced tomatoes
- 1 tsp. saffron threads or 4 tsp. ground turmeric
- 1 lb. uncooked medium shrimp, peeled and deveined
- 1 pkg. (12 oz.) fully cooked chorizo chicken sausage or flavor of your choice, cut into ¼-in. slices
- 1 medium mango, coarsely chopped
- 2 Tbsp. lime juice
- ¼ tsp. cayenne pepper
- 1 medium lime, cut into wedges
- 2 Tbsp. minced fresh cilantro

**1.** In a Dutch oven, saute red pepper and onion in oil until tender. Add the rice, garlic and chipotle pepper; saute 2 minutes longer. Add the chicken broth, tomatoes and saffron. Bring to a boil. Reduce heat; cover and simmer for 5 minutes or until liquid is absorbed. Let stand for 5 minutes.
**2.** Meanwhile, in a large bowl, combine the shrimp, chicken sausage and mango; sprinkle with the lime juice and cayenne. Transfer mixture to a grill wok or basket. Grill, covered, over medium heat for 5-8 minutes or until shrimp turn pink, stirring occasionally.
**3.** Add shrimp mixture to Dutch oven; toss to combine. Garnish with lime wedges and cilantro.

**1½ cups:** 388 cal., 9g fat (2g sat. fat), 101mg chol., 787mg sod., 55g carb. (11g sugars, 4g fiber), 24g pro.

## WATERMELON PIZZA

*Start with grilled melon slices and layer on the tangy, salty and sweet toppings for a summer-fresh appetizer.*
—Ellen Riley, Murfreesboro, TN

**Prep:** 25 min. • **Grill:** 10 min. + chilling
**Makes:** 8 servings

- 8 wedges seedless watermelon, about 1 in. thick
- 1 cup heirloom cherry tomatoes, sliced
- 1 cup fresh baby arugula
- ½ cup fresh blueberries
- ⅓ cup crumbled feta cheese
- ⅓ cup pitted Greek olives, halved
- 1 Tbsp. olive oil
- ⅛ tsp. kosher salt
- ⅛ tsp. coarsely ground pepper
  Balsamic glaze, optional

**1.** Grill watermelon, covered, on a greased grill rack over medium-high direct heat until seared, 5-6 minutes on each side. Remove from heat; transfer to a platter. Chill.

**2.** To serve, top chilled watermelon with tomatoes, arugula, blueberries, feta and olives. Drizzle with olive oil; season with salt and pepper. If desired, drizzle with balsamic glaze.

**1 wedge:** 91 cal., 4g fat (1g sat. fat), 3mg chol., 169mg sod., 13g carb. (11g sugars, 1g fiber), 2g pro. **Diabetic exchanges:** 1 fruit, 1 fat.

**SIMPLE GRILLED STEAK FAJITAS**

## SIMPLE GRILLED STEAK FAJITAS

*After moving to a new state with two toddlers in tow, I came up with effortless fajitas. They make an easy weeknight meal on the grill or in a cast-iron skillet.*
—Shannen Mahoney, Yelm, WA

**Takes:** 30 min. • **Makes:** 4 servings

- 1 beef top sirloin steak (¾ in. thick and 1 lb.)
- 2 Tbsp. fajita seasoning mix
- 1 large sweet onion, cut crosswise into ½-in. slices
- 1 medium sweet red pepper, halved
- 1 medium green pepper, halved
- 1 Tbsp. olive oil
- 4 whole wheat tortillas (8 in.), warmed
  Sliced avocado, optional
  Minced fresh cilantro, optional
  Lime wedges, optional

**1.** Rub steak with seasoning mix. Brush onion and peppers with oil.

**2.** Grill steak and vegetables, covered, on a greased rack over medium direct heat 4-6 minutes on each side or until meat reaches desired doneness (for medium-rare, a thermometer should read 135°; medium, 140°; and medium-well, 145°) and vegetables are tender. Remove from grill. Let steak stand, covered, 5 minutes before slicing.

**3.** Cut vegetables and steak into strips; serve in tortillas. If desired, top with avocado and cilantro and serve with lime wedges.

**1 serving:** 363 cal., 13g fat (4g sat. fat), 54mg chol., 686mg sod., 34g carb. (6g sugars, 5g fiber), 27g pro. **Diabetic exchanges:** 3 lean meat, 2 starch, 1 vegetable, ½ fat.

## TERIYAKI GLAZED PORK & VEGETABLE KABOBS

*Here's a delicious, pretty and fun-to-eat entree. Be sure to cook down the reserved Asian-style marinade and serve it alongside the kabobs for dipping— it's so yummy.*

—Jane Whittaker, Pensacola, FL

**Prep:** 40 min. + marinating • **Grill:** 10 min.
**Makes:** 16 kabobs

- ⅔ cup unsweetened pineapple juice
- ⅔ cup reduced-sodium teriyaki sauce
- ⅓ cup white wine or chicken broth
- 2 Tbsp. sweet chili sauce
- 4 garlic cloves, minced
- 5 tsp. rice vinegar
- 5 tsp. sesame oil
- 2 pork tenderloin (1 lb. each), cut into 1¼-in. cubes

**KABOBS**
- 4 cups cubed fresh pineapple
- 2 medium zucchini, cut into 1-in. pieces
- 1 large sweet red pepper, cut into 1-in. pieces
- 1 large red onion, cut into 1-in. pieces
- ⅓ cup sesame oil

**1.** In a bowl, whisk the first 7 ingredients until blended. Pour 1 cup marinade into a large bowl and add pork; turn to coat. Cover and refrigerate both the pork and the remaining marinade for 2 hours.

**2.** In a small saucepan, bring reserved marinade to a boil; cook 8-10 minutes or until the liquid is reduced by half. Reserve for serving.

**3.** Drain pork, discarding marinade in bag. On 16 metal or soaked wooden skewers, alternately thread the pork, pineapple and vegetables. Brush kabobs with oil.

**4.** Grill kabobs, covered, over medium heat or broil 4 in. from heat 8-10 minutes or until the pork and zucchini are tender, turning occasionally. Remove from grill. Brush kabobs with some of the glaze; serve with remaining glaze.

**2 kabobs:** 336 cal., 15g fat (3g sat. fat), 64mg chol., 481mg sod., 24g carb. (18g sugars, 2g fiber), 25g pro. **Diabetic exchanges:** 3 lean meat, 3 fat, 1½ starch.

TERIYAKI GLAZED PORK & VEGETABLE KABOBS

**TROPICAL CHICKEN
CAULIFLOWER RICE BOWLS**

## TROPICAL CHICKEN CAULIFLOWER RICE BOWLS

*This tropical favorite is a delicious and healthy dinner with tons of flavor! You can substitute regular rice for the cauliflower rice if desired.*
—Bethany DiCarlo, Harleysville, PA

------------------------------------------------

**Prep:** 40 min. + marinating. • **Grill:** 10 min.
**Makes:** 4 servings

- 1 fresh pineapple, peeled, cored and cubed (about 3 cups), divided
- ½ cup plain or coconut Greek yogurt
- 2 Tbsp. plus ½ cup chopped fresh cilantro, divided
- 3 Tbsp. lime juice, divided
- ¾ tsp. salt, divided
- ¼ tsp. crushed red pepper flakes
- ⅛ tsp. chili powder
- 4 boneless skinless chicken breast halves (6 oz. each)
- 3 cups fresh cauliflower florets (about ½ small cauliflower)
- 1 Tbsp. canola oil
- 1 small red onion, finely chopped
  Optional: Toasted sweetened shredded coconut or lime wedges

**1.** For marinade, place 1 cup pineapple, yogurt, 2 Tbsp. each cilantro and lime juice, ¼ tsp. salt, pepper flakes and chili powder in a food processor; process until blended. In a large bowl, toss chicken with marinade; refrigerate, covered, 1-3 hours.
**2.** In a clean food processor, pulse the cauliflower until it resembles rice (do not overprocess). In a large skillet, heat oil over medium-high heat; saute the onion until lightly browned, 3-5 minutes. Add the cauliflower; cook and stir until lightly browned, 5-7 minutes. Stir in 1 cup pineapple and the remaining lime juice and salt; cook, covered, over medium heat for 3-5 minutes or until cauliflower is tender. Stir in the remaining cilantro. Keep warm.
**3.** Preheat grill or broiler. Drain chicken, discarding marinade. Place chicken on an oiled grill rack over medium heat or in a greased foil-lined 15x10x1-in. pan. Grill, covered, or broil 4 in. from heat until a thermometer reads 165°, 4-6 minutes per side. Let stand 5 minutes before slicing.
**4.** To serve, divide cauliflower mixture among 4 bowls. Top with the chicken, remaining pineapple and, if desired, coconut and lime wedges.
**1 serving:** 325 cal., 10g fat (3g sat. fat), 100mg chol., 529mg sod., 22g carb. (15g sugars, 4g fiber), 38g pro. **Diabetic exchanges:** 5 lean meat, 1 fruit, 1 vegetable, 1 fat.

**TEST KITCHEN TIP**

Save time and buy cauliflower that's already been processed. Look for riced cauliflower in the refrigerated section of the produce department. You'll need 3 cups.

## GRILLED BRUSCHETTA

**(PICTURED ON P. 178)**

*This is my go-to appetizer in the summer when tomatoes and basil are fresh from the garden. The balsamic glaze takes this bruschetta recipe over the top. I like to use a Tuscan herb- or basil-infused olive oil for this. But it works well with plain olive oil, too.*
—Brittany Allyn, Mesa, AZ

**Prep:** 30 min. • **Grill:** 5 min.
**Makes:** 16 servings

- ½ cup balsamic vinegar
- 1½ cups chopped and seeded plum tomatoes
- 2 Tbsp. finely chopped shallot
- 1 Tbsp. minced fresh basil
- 2 tsp. plus 3 Tbsp. olive oil, divided
- 1 garlic clove, minced
- 16 slices French bread baguette (½ in. thick)
  Sea salt and grated Parmesan cheese

**1.** In a small saucepan, bring the vinegar to a boil; cook until liquid is reduced to 3 Tbsp., 8-10 minutes. Remove from heat. Meanwhile, combine tomatoes, shallot, basil, 2 tsp. olive oil and garlic. Cover and refrigerate until serving.

**2.** Brush remaining oil over both sides of baguette slices. Grill, uncovered, over medium heat until bread is golden brown on both sides.

**3.** Top toasts with tomato mixture. Drizzle with balsamic syrup; sprinkle with salt and Parmesan. Serve immediately.

**1 appetizer:** 58 cal., 3g fat (0 sat. fat), 0 chol., 49mg sod., 7g carb. (3g sugars, 0 fiber), 1g pro. **Diabetic exchanges:** ½ starch, ½ fat.

### TEST KITCHEN TIP

To quickly seed a tomato, cut it into wedges. Swipe your index finger over each wedge to remove the gel pockets and its seeds. Then chop tomato as desired. This is a nice technique for when you don't need perfectly seeded tomatoes.

## MOJITO-STYLE YELLOW TOMATO SALSA

*With grilled tomatoes, crunchy peppers and a sprinkle of mint, this fresh salsa is good on just about everything. Try it in fish tacos, on tortilla chips or by the spoonful!*
—Patterson Watkins, Philadelphia, PA

**Prep:** 20 min. • **Grill:** 10 min. + chilling
**Makes:** 4 cups

- 2 lbs. large yellow tomatoes, halved
- 1 Tbsp. olive oil
- 2 garlic cloves, minced
- 1 tsp. chopped shallot
- ¾ tsp. salt, divided
- 3 medium limes
- 2 tsp. coarse sugar
- 12 fresh mint leaves
- ¼ cup chopped Cubanelle or banana peppers

**1.** Grill tomatoes, uncovered, on an oiled rack over high heat (or broil 3-4 in. from the heat) until skin is slightly charred, 3-4 minutes on each side. Cool to room temperature. Meanwhile, combine oil, garlic, shallot and ¼ tsp. salt. When the tomatoes are cool enough to handle, finely chop; stir in garlic mixture until well combined.

**2.** Finely grate zest of each lime; set aside. Peel limes and discard white membranes; section limes. In a food processor, pulse lime sections, sugar, mint and remaining salt until finely chopped. Combine with tomatoes; add the peppers and lime zest. Mix well.

**3.** Refrigerate at least 1 hour. Serve with chips or grilled meats.

**¼ cup:** 23 cal., 1g fat (0 sat. fat), 0 chol., 161mg sod., 4g carb. (1g sugars, 1g fiber), 1g pro. **Diabetic exchanges:** 1 vegetable.

**MOJITO-STYLE YELLOW TOMATO SALSA**

**FRESH ARTICHOKES
WITH LEMON-YOGURT DIP**

## GRILLED CAULIFLOWER WEDGES

*This meal is incredibly easy, yet is packed with flavor and looks like a dish from a five-star restaurant. The grill leaves the cauliflower cooked but crisp, and the red pepper flakes add bite.*
—Carmel Hall, San Francisco, CA

- - - - - - - - - - - - - - - - - - - - - - - - - - - -

**Takes:** 30 min. • **Makes:** 8 servings

 1 large head cauliflower
 1 tsp. ground turmeric
 ½ tsp. crushed red pepper flakes
 2 Tbsp. olive oil
   Optional: Lemon juice, additional
   olive oil and pomegranate seeds

**1.** Remove leaves and trim stem from cauliflower. Cut the cauliflower into 8 wedges. Mix turmeric and pepper flakes. Brush wedges with oil; sprinkle with turmeric mixture.
**2.** Grill, covered, over medium-high heat or broil 4 in. from heat until cauliflower is tender, 8-10 minutes on each side. If desired, drizzle with lemon juice and additional oil, and serve with the pomegranate seeds.

**1 wedge:** 57 cal., 4g fat (1g sat. fat), 0 chol., 32mg sod., 5g carb. (2g sugars, 2g fiber), 2g pro. **Diabetic exchanges:** 1 vegetable, 1 fat.

## FRESH ARTICHOKES WITH LEMON-YOGURT DIP

*Artichokes are at their best when you prepare them simply, without a lot of fuss or seasonings to overdress them. Many people dip the petals in melted butter or mayonnaise, but I think you'll love my tangy lemon-yogurt dip.*
—Jill Haapaniemi, Brooklyn, NY

- - - - - - - - - - - - - - - - - - - - - - - - - - - -

**Prep:** 15 min. • **Cook:** 45 min.
**Makes:** 12 servings (1½ cups dip)

 6 medium artichokes
 3 Tbsp. olive oil
   Sea salt and coarsely ground
   pepper to taste
 1½ cups plain yogurt
 1 tsp. lemon juice
 ¼ tsp. salt
 ¼ tsp. pepper
   Lemon wedges

**1.** Using a sharp knife, cut 1 in. from top of each artichoke and trim stem so it will stand upright. Using kitchen scissors, cut off tips of outer leaves. Place artichokes upright in a Dutch oven; cover with water and bring to a boil. Reduce heat; simmer, covered, until a leaf in the center pulls out easily, 35-40 minutes. Invert artichokes to drain. Cool slightly; cut each artichoke in half lengthwise. With a spoon, carefully scrape and remove the fuzzy centers of artichokes.
**2.** In a cast-iron skillet or grill pan, heat oil over medium-high heat. Place artichokes in pan, cut side down. Cook until lightly browned, 5-7 minutes. Sprinkle with salt and pepper. In a small bowl, mix yogurt, lemon juice, salt and pepper. Serve with artichokes and lemon wedges.

**½ artichoke with 2 Tbsp. dip:** 81 cal., 5g fat (1g sat. fat), 4mg chol., 99mg sod., 9g carb. (2g sugars, 3g fiber), 3g pro. **Diabetic exchanges:** 1 vegetable, 1 fat.

SHRIMP & SCALLOPS
TROPICAL SALAD

## SHRIMP & SCALLOPS
## TROPICAL SALAD

*A fruity dressing makes this seafood salad shine. Served on a bed of greens, the scrumptious combination of grilled seafood, veggies and macadamia nuts is the perfect way to celebrate a special summer occasion.*
—Jackie Pressinger, Stuart, FL

**Prep:** 35 min. • **Cook:** 5 min.
**Makes:** 2 servings

- 2 Tbsp. diced peeled mango
- 1 Tbsp. diced fresh pineapple
- 1½ tsp. mango chutney
- 1½ tsp. olive oil
- 1 tsp. rice vinegar
- ¾ tsp. lime juice
- Dash salt
- Dash crushed red pepper flakes
- 3 cups torn Bibb or Boston lettuce
- 1 cup chopped peeled cucumber
- ½ medium ripe avocado, peeled and sliced
- 2 Tbsp. coarsely chopped macadamia nuts, toasted
- 1 Tbsp. finely chopped red onion
- 1 Tbsp. minced fresh cilantro
- 2 Tbsp. canola oil
- 1½ tsp. Caribbean jerk seasoning
- 6 uncooked large shrimp, peeled and deveined
- 6 sea scallops, halved

**1.** Place first 8 ingredients in a blender. Cover and process until blended; set aside. Divide the lettuce, cucumber, avocado, nuts, onion and cilantro between 2 serving plates.
**2.** In a small bowl, combine oil and jerk seasoning. Thread shrimp and scallops onto 2 metal or soaked wooden skewers; brush with oil mixture.
**3.** Grill skewers, covered, over medium heat until shrimp turn pink and scallops are firm and opaque, 2-3 minutes on each side. Place on salads; drizzle with dressing.

**1 salad:** 413 cal., 32g fat (4g sat. fat), 96mg chol., 523mg sod., 16g carb. (6g sugars, 5g fiber), 19g pro.

## BEEF SUYA

*My Nigerian brother-in-law introduced me to beef suya, a very spicy street food that's popular in western Africa. I was intrigued when I found out the spice rub is made from ground peanuts and a savory blend of different seasonings. After lots of experimenting, I came up with my own version.*
—Elena Iorga, Helena, MT

**Prep:** 30 min. + marinating • **Grill:** 15 min.
**Makes:** 8 servings

- 1   cup salted peanuts
- 1   Tbsp. paprika
- 2   tsp. onion powder
- 2   tsp. ground ginger
- 1   tsp. crushed red pepper flakes
- 1   tsp. garlic powder
- 1   beef tri-tip roast or beef top sirloin steak (2 lbs.), thinly sliced against the grain
- 2   Tbsp. canola oil
- 1   tsp. salt
- 1   medium onion, cut into wedges
- 1   large tomato, cut into wedges
     Fresh cilantro leaves

**1.** Place peanuts in a food processor; process until finely chopped. Add paprika, onion powder, ginger, pepper flakes and garlic powder; pulse until combined.
**2.** Place beef in a large bowl or shallow dish. Drizzle with oil; sprinkle with salt. Toss to coat. Add peanut mixture; turn to coat. Refrigerate, covered, for 2 hours. Drain beef, discarding marinade.
**3.** Thread beef onto metal or soaked wooden skewers. Grill, covered, over medium-high heat until beef reaches desired doneness, 10-15 minutes, turning occasionally. Serve with onion, tomato and cilantro.

**1 kabob:** 329 cal., 21g fat (5g sat. fat), 68mg chol., 405mg sod., 7g carb. (2g sugars, 3g fiber), 29g pro.

> **DID YOU KNOW?**
>
> Popular side dish options for beef suya that we can easily pull off in the West include hot cooked noodles, sweet potato fries and potato chips.

## SPINACH & MUSHROOM SMOTHERED CHICKEN

**(PICTURED ON P. 178)**
*Chicken breasts stay nice and moist tucked under a blanket of melted cheese. It's extra special to serve but is not tricky to make.*
—Katrina Wagner, Grain Valley, MO

**Takes:** 30 min. • **Makes:** 4 servings

- 1½   tsp. olive oil
- 1¾   cups sliced fresh mushrooms
- 3   green onions, sliced
- 3   cups fresh baby spinach
- 2   Tbsp. chopped pecans
- 4   boneless skinless chicken breast halves (4 oz. each)
- ½   tsp. rotisserie chicken seasoning
- 2   slices reduced-fat provolone cheese, halved

**1.** Preheat grill or broiler. In a large skillet, heat oil over medium-high heat; sauté the mushrooms and green onions until tender. Stir in spinach and pecans until spinach is wilted. Remove from heat; keep warm.
**2.** Sprinkle the chicken with seasoning. Grill, covered, on an oiled grill rack over medium heat or broil 4 in. from heat on a greased broiler pan until a thermometer reads 165°, 4-5 minutes per side. Top with cheese; grill or broil until cheese is melted. Spoon mushroom mixture over the top.

**1 serving:** 203 cal., 9g fat (2g sat. fat), 68mg chol., 210mg sod., 3g carb. (1g sugars, 2g fiber), 27g pro. **Diabetic exchanges:** 3 lean meat, 1 vegetable, 1 fat.
* HEALTH TIP * This low-carb main dish is also gluten-free.

**BEEF SUYA**

## GRILLED BROCCOLI

*I started using this recipe in 1987, when I began cooking light, and it's been a favorite side dish ever since. With its lemon and Parmesan flavors, it once took second place in a cooking contest.*
—Alice Nulle, Woodstock, IL

**Prep:** 5 min. + standing • **Grill:** 10 min.
**Makes:** 6 servings

- 6 cups fresh broccoli spears
- 2 Tbsp. plus 1½ tsp. lemon juice
- 2 Tbsp. olive oil
- ¼ tsp. salt
- ¼ tsp. pepper
- ¾ cup grated Parmesan cheese
  Optional: Grilled lemon slices and red pepper flakes

1. Place broccoli in a large bowl. Combine lemon juice, oil, salt and pepper; drizzle over broccoli and toss to coat. Let stand for 30 minutes.
2. Toss the broccoli; drain broccoli, discarding marinade. Place cheese in a small shallow bowl. Add the broccoli, a few pieces at a time, toss to coat.
3. Prepare grill for indirect heat using a drip pan. Place broccoli over drip pan on an oiled grill rack. Grill, covered, over indirect medium heat for 8-10 minutes on each side or until crisp-tender. If desired, garnish with grilled lemon slices and red pepper flakes.

**1 cup:** 107 cal., 8g fat (3g sat. fat), 8mg chol., 304mg sod., 5g carb. (2g sugars, 2g fiber), 6g pro. **Diabetic exchanges:** 1½ fat, 1 vegetable.

CASHEW MANGO GRILLED CHICKEN

## CASHEW MANGO GRILLED CHICKEN

*This sweet and nutty chicken hits all the right spots for taste, speed and family appeal. On a rainy day, you can bake it, then finish it under the broiler.*
—Trisha Kruse, Eagle, ID

**Takes:** 25 min. • **Makes:** 8 servings

- ¼ cup mango chutney, chopped
- ¼ cup cashew butter
- 2 Tbsp. reduced-sodium soy sauce
- 2 Tbsp. rice vinegar
- 8 boneless skinless chicken thighs
- ½ tsp. salt
- ½ tsp. crushed red pepper flakes
- 1 large mango, peeled and thinly sliced
- ⅓ cup lightly salted cashews, chopped
  Additional mango chutney, optional

1. Mix together the first 4 ingredients until blended.
2. Sprinkle chicken with salt and pepper flakes; place on an oiled grill rack over medium heat. Grill chicken, covered, until a thermometer reads 170°, 6-8 minutes per side, brushing with chutney mixture during the last 5 minutes. Serve with the mango; top with cashews and, if desired, additional chutney.

**1 serving:** 308 cal., 16g fat (4g sat. fat), 76mg chol., 537mg sod., 18g carb. (12g sugars, 1g fiber), 24g pro. **Diabetic exchanges:** 3 lean meat, 2½ fat, 1 starch.

## HONEY-GARLIC PORK CHOPS

*These chops are so simple to prepare yet taste really special. Honey, lemon and garlic are a classic combination that tastes even better on grilled pork. I like that I can marinade the chops the night before or even the morning I'd like to serve. At dinner, just start up the grill and dinner's ready in no time.*

—Helen Carpenter, Albuquerque, NM

**Prep:** 5 min. + marinating • **Grill:** 15 min.
**Makes:** 4 servings

- ¼ cup lemon juice
- ¼ cup honey
- 2 Tbsp. soy sauce
- 2 garlic cloves, minced
- 4 boneless pork loin chops (6 oz. each and 1¼ to 1½ in. thick)

1. In a bowl or shallow dish, combine the lemon juice, honey, soy sauce and garlic. Add the pork chops and turn to coat. Cover and refrigerate for 4-8 hours. Drain pork, discarding marinade.
2. Grill, covered, over medium heat for 6-8 minutes on each side or until a thermometer reads 145°. Let meat stand for 5 minutes before serving.

**1 pork chop:** 271 cal., 10g fat (4g sat. fat), 82mg chol., 324mg sod., 11g carb. (11g sugars, 0 fiber), 33g pro. **Diabetic exchanges:** 5 lean meat, ½ starch.

## EGGPLANT SALAD WITH TOMATO & GOAT CHEESE

(PICTURED ON P. 178)

*Tender grilled eggplant helps make this light summer salad feel like a meal. The balsamic dressing adds depth and a burst of bright flavor.*

—Susan Leiser, Hammonton, NJ

**Prep:** 25 min. • **Grill:** 10 min.
**Makes:** 8 servings

- 1 large eggplant, cut into 8 slices
- ¼ cup extra virgin olive oil, divided
- 1¼ tsp. salt, divided
- ½ tsp. pepper, divided
- 4 plum tomatoes, chopped
- ¼ cup chopped red onion
- 2 Tbsp. chopped fresh basil
- 2 Tbsp. chopped fresh parsley
- 4 tsp. balsamic vinegar
- 4 cups fresh arugula or baby spinach
- ½ cup crumbled goat cheese

1. Brush both sides of the eggplant with 2 Tbsp. oil. Sprinkle with ¾ tsp. salt and ¼ tsp. pepper.
2. Broil eggplant 3-4 in. from heat or grill, covered, over medium heat, until tender, 4-5 minutes per side.
3. Meanwhile, in a small bowl, combine tomatoes, onion, basil, parsley, vinegar, 1 Tbsp. oil and remaining salt and pepper. Toss arugula with remaining oil and divide among 8 plates. Top each with eggplant, tomato mixture and goat cheese.

**1 serving:** 115 cal., 9g fat (2g sat. fat), 9mg chol., 410mg sod., 8g carb. (5g sugars, 3g fiber), 3g pro. **Diabetic exchanges:** 2 fat, 1 vegetable.

**TEST KITCHEN TIP**

Try this salad with portobello mushrooms instead of eggplant. Serve with toasted flatbread or pita chips.

HONEY-GARLIC PORK CHOPS

# SLOW-COOKED SUPPERS

"This recipe has regularly appeared on my family menus for more than 40 years, and it's never failed to please at potlucks and bring-a-dish gatherings. Sometimes I turn it into soup by adding a can of beef broth."

—Marie Posavec, Berwyn, IL

**Slow-Cooked Sweet & Sour Pork** (p.206) **Greek Garlic Chicken** (p. 203) **Vegetarian Stuffed Peppers** (p. 212)
**Slow-Cooked Herbed Turkey** (p. 200) **Chili Mac** (p. 202) **Slow-Cooker BBQ Chicken** (p. 211)

## SLOW-COOKED HERBED TURKEY

(PICTURED ON P. 198)

*I prepare this when herbs are plentiful in my garden. The turkey stays moist in the slow cooker and bursts with herb flavors. Everyone in our Bible study potluck group wanted the recipe!*
—Sue Jurack, Mequon, WI

**Prep:** 15 min. + marinating
**Cook:** 4 hours + standing
**Makes:** 16 servings

- 1 can (14½ oz.) chicken broth
- ½ cup lemon juice
- ¼ cup packed brown sugar
- ¼ cup minced fresh sage
- ¼ cup minced fresh thyme
- ¼ cup lime juice
- ¼ cup cider vinegar
- ¼ cup olive oil
- 1 envelope onion soup mix
- 2 Tbsp. Dijon mustard
- 1 Tbsp. minced fresh marjoram
- 1½ tsp. paprika
- 1 tsp. garlic powder
- 1 tsp. pepper
- ½ tsp. salt
- 2 boneless skinless turkey breast halves (3 lbs. each)

**1.** In a blender, combine the first 15 ingredients; cover and process until blended. Pour half the marinade into a bowl; cover and refrigerate. Place turkey breasts in a large, shallow bowl; add remaining marinade. Turn turkey to coat. Cover and refrigerate overnight, turning occasionally.

**2.** Drain turkey, discarding marinade. Transfer turkey breasts to a 5-qt. slow cooker. Add reserved marinade; cover and cook on high until a thermometer reads 165°, 4-5 hours. Let stand for 10 minutes before slicing.

**5 oz. cooked turkey:** 232 cal., 5g fat (1g sat. fat), 97mg chol., 369mg sod., 4g carb. (3g sugars, 0 fiber), 40g pro. **Diabetic exchanges:** 5 lean meat, ½ fat.

## SIRLOIN ROAST WITH GRAVY

*This recipe is perfect for my husband, who is a meat-and-potatoes kind of guy. The peppery roast combined with rich gravy creates a tasty centerpiece for any meal.*
—Rita Clark, Monument, CO

**Prep:** 20 min. • **Cook:** 3½ hours
**Makes:** 8 servings

- 1 beef sirloin tip roast (3 lbs.)
- 2 garlic cloves, minced
- 1 to 2 Tbsp. coarsely ground pepper
- ¼ cup reduced-sodium soy sauce
- 3 Tbsp. balsamic vinegar
- 1 Tbsp. Worcestershire sauce
- 2 tsp. ground mustard
- 2 Tbsp. cornstarch
- ¼ cup cold water

**1.** Rub roast with the garlic and pepper; place in a 3-qt. slow cooker. Mix the soy sauce, vinegar, Worcestershire sauce and mustard; pour over roast. Cook, covered, on low until tender, 3½-4 hours.

**2.** Remove the roast; keep warm. Strain cooking juices into a small saucepan; skim fat. Mix the cornstarch and water until smooth; stir into cooking juices. Bring to a boil; cook and stir until thickened, 1-2 minutes. Cut roast into slices; serve with gravy.

**1 serving:** 241 cal., 8g fat (3g sat. fat), 108mg chol., 358mg sod., 5g carb. (2g sugars, 0 fiber), 35g pro. **Diabetic exchanges:** 5 lean meat.

**SIRLOIN ROAST WITH GRAVY**

## SLOW-COOKER BURGUNDY BEEF

*When my adult children are coming over for dinner, this is their most-requested dish. All three of them, and their significant others, love this dish.*
—Urilla Cheverie, Andover, MA

**Prep:** 10 min. • **Cook:** 8¼ hours
**Makes:** 10 servings

- 4 lbs. beef top sirloin steak, cut into 1-in. cubes
- 3 large onions, sliced
- 1 cup water
- 1 cup burgundy wine or beef broth
- 1 cup ketchup
- ¼ cup quick-cooking tapioca
- ¼ cup packed brown sugar
- ¼ cup Worcestershire sauce
- 4 tsp. paprika
- 1½ tsp. salt
- 1 tsp. minced garlic
- 1 tsp. ground mustard
- 2 Tbsp. cornstarch
- 3 Tbsp. cold water
  Hot cooked noodles

**1.** In a 5-qt. slow cooker, combine the first 12 ingredients. Cook, covered, on low until meat is tender, 8-9 hours.
**2.** Combine cornstarch and water until smooth; stir into the pan juices. Cook, covered, on high until gravy is thickened, about 15 minutes. Serve with noodles.
**1 cup:** 347 cal., 8g fat (3g sat. fat), 74mg chol., 811mg sod., 24g carb. (15g sugars, 1g fiber), 40g pro.

## THAI SHRIMP & RICE

*Raisins and coconut milk add a lovely hint of sweetness to shrimp, while fresh lime and ginger give it a wonderful aroma. This dish adds flair to weeknight menus.*
—Paula Marchesi, Lenhartsville, PA

**Prep:** 30 min. • **Cook:** 3¼ hours
**Makes:** 8 servings

- 2 cans (14½ oz. each) chicken broth
- 2 cups uncooked converted rice
- 1 large carrot, shredded
- 1 medium onion, chopped
- ½ cup each chopped green and sweet red pepper
- ½ cup water
- ½ cup coconut milk
- ⅓ cup lime juice
- ¼ cup sweetened shredded coconut
- ¼ cup each raisins and golden raisins
- 8 garlic cloves, minced
- 1 Tbsp. grated lime zest
- 1 Tbsp. minced fresh gingerroot
- 1 tsp. salt
- 1 tsp. each ground coriander and cumin
- ½ tsp. cayenne pepper
- 1 lb. cooked medium shrimp, peeled and deveined
- ½ cup fresh snow peas, cut into thin strips

**1.** In a 5-qt. slow cooker, combine the broth, rice, vegetables, water, coconut milk, lime juice, coconut, raisins, garlic, lime zest and seasonings. Cover and cook on low for 3 hours or until rice is tender.
**2.** Stir in shrimp and peas. Cover and cook 15-20 minutes longer or until heated through.
**1¼ cups:** 336 cal., 6g fat (4g sat. fat), 88mg chol., 845mg sod., 54g carb. (10g sugars, 3g fiber), 17g pro.

## MUSHROOM PORK RAGOUT

*Savory slow-cooked pork is luscious draped in a delightful tomato gravy and served over noodles. It's a nice change from regular pork roast. I serve it with broccoli or green beans on the side.*
—Connie McDowell, Greenwood, DE

- - - - - - - - - - - - - - - - - - - - - - - - - - - - - -

**Prep:** 20 min. • **Cook:** 3 hours
**Makes:** 2 servings

- 1   pork tenderloin (¾ lb.)
- ⅛   tsp. salt
- ⅛   tsp. pepper
- 1   Tbsp. cornstarch
- ¾   cup canned crushed tomatoes, divided
- 1   Tbsp. chopped sun-dried tomatoes (not packed in oil)
- 1¼  tsp. dried savory
- 1½  cups sliced fresh mushrooms
- ⅓   cup sliced onion
- 1½  cups hot cooked egg noodles

**1.** Rub pork with salt and pepper; cut in half. In a 1½-qt. slow cooker, combine the cornstarch, ½ cup crushed tomatoes, sun-dried tomatoes and savory. Top with mushrooms, onion and pork. Pour the remaining tomatoes over pork. Cover and cook on low 3-4 hours or until the meat is tender.

**2.** Remove meat and cut into slices. Stir cooking juices until smooth; serve with pork and noodles.

**1 serving:** 360 cal., 7g fat (2g sat. fat), 122mg chol., 309mg sod., 32g carb. (3g sugars, 3g fiber), 40g pro. **Diabetic exchanges:** 5 lean meat, 2 vegetable, 1 starch.

## CHILI MAC

**(PICTURED ON P. 199)**

*This recipe has regularly appeared on my family menus for more than 40 years, and it's never failed to please at potlucks and bring-a-dish gatherings. Sometimes I turn it into soup by adding a can of beef broth.*
—Marie Posavec, Berwyn, IL

- - - - - - - - - - - - - - - - - - - - - - - - - - - - - -

**Prep:** 15 min. • **Cook:** 6 hours
**Makes:** 6 servings

- 1   lb. lean ground beef (90% lean), cooked and drained
- 2   cans (16 oz. each) hot chili beans, undrained
- 2   large green peppers, chopped
- 1   large onion, chopped
- 4   celery ribs, chopped
- 1   can (8 oz.) no-salt-added tomato sauce
- 2   Tbsp. chili seasoning mix
- 2   garlic cloves, minced
- 1   pkg. (7 oz.) elbow macaroni, cooked and drained
  Salt and pepper to taste
  Optional: Shredded pepper jack cheese and sliced jalapeno pepper

In a 5-qt. slow cooker, combine the first 8 ingredients. Cover and cook on low for 6 hours or until heated through. Stir in macaroni. Season with salt and pepper. If desired, top servings with cheese and sliced jalapenos.

**1 serving:** 348 cal., 8g fat (3g sat. fat), 47mg chol., 713mg sod., 49g carb. (8g sugars, 12g fiber), 27g pro. **Diabetic exchanges:** 3 starch, 3 lean meat.

## SLOW-COOKED LENTIL STEW

*This vegetarian stew is perfect when you want to take a break from meat. Adding the cream at the end gives it a smooth, rich texture.*
—Michelle Collins, Suffolk, VA

**Prep:** 45 min. • **Cook:** 6 hours
**Makes:** 8 servings (2¾ qt. stew)

- 2 large onions, thinly sliced, divided
- 2 Tbsp. canola oil
- 2 Tbsp. minced fresh gingerroot
- 3 garlic cloves, minced
- 8 plum tomatoes, chopped
- 2 tsp. ground coriander
- 1½ tsp. ground cumin
- ¼ tsp. cayenne pepper
- 3 cups vegetable broth
- 2 cups water
- 2 cups dried lentils, rinsed
- 1 can (4 oz.) chopped green chiles
- ¾ cup heavy whipping cream
- 2 Tbsp. butter
- 1 tsp. cumin seeds
- 6 cups hot cooked basmati or jasmine rice
  Optional: Sliced green onions or minced fresh cilantro

**1.** In a large skillet, saute half of the onions in oil until tender. Add ginger and garlic; saute for 1 minute. Add the tomatoes, coriander, cumin and cayenne; cook and stir 5 minutes longer.
**2.** In a 4-or 5-qt. slow cooker, combine the vegetable broth, water, lentils, green chiles, tomato mixture and remaining onion. Cover and cook on low until lentils are tender, 6-8 hours.
**3.** Just before serving, stir cream into slow cooker. In a small skillet, heat butter over medium heat. Add cumin seeds; cook and stir until golden brown, for 1-2 minutes. Add to lentil mixture.
**4.** To serve, spoon over rice. If desired, sprinkle with green onions or cilantro.

**1⅓ cups stew with ¾ cup rice:** 499 cal., 16g fat (7g sat. fat), 38mg chol., 448mg sod., 72g carb. (5g sugars, 17g fiber), 17g pro.

## GREEK GARLIC CHICKEN

(PICTURED ON P. 198)
*Lively flavors of the Greek Isles come through in this chicken entree. I created it so my husband and I could have a nice dinner after a busy day out and about.*
—Margee Berry, White Salmon, WA

**Prep:** 20 min. • **Cook:** 3½ hours
**Makes:** 6 servings

- ½ cup chopped onion
- 1 Tbsp. plus 1 tsp. olive oil, divided
- 3 Tbsp. minced garlic
- 2½ cups chicken broth, divided
- ¼ cup pitted Greek olives, chopped
- 3 Tbsp. chopped sun-dried tomatoes (not packed in oil)
- 1 Tbsp. quick-cooking tapioca
- 2 tsp. grated lemon zest
- 1 tsp. dried oregano
- 6 boneless skinless chicken breast halves (6 oz. each)
- 1¾ cups uncooked couscous
- ½ cup crumbled feta cheese

**1.** In a small skillet, saute onion in 1 Tbsp. oil until crisp-tender. Add the garlic; cook 1 minute longer.
**2.** Transfer to a 5-qt. slow cooker. Stir in ¾ cup broth, olives, tomatoes, tapioca, lemon zest and oregano. Add chicken. Cover and cook on low for 3½-4 hours or until chicken is tender. If desired, cut chicken into pieces.
**3.** In a large saucepan, bring remaining oil and broth to a boil. Stir in couscous. Cover and remove from the heat; let stand for 5 minutes or until the broth is absorbed. Serve with chicken; sprinkle with feta cheese.

**5 oz. cooked chicken with ¼ cup sauce and ¾ cup couscous:** 475 cal., 11g fat (3g sat. fat), 101mg chol., 683mg sod., 48g carb. (3g sugars, 3g fiber), 44g pro.

**SLOW-COOKED LENTIL STEW**

SPICY SEAFOOD STEW

### CHICKEN MERLOT WITH MUSHROOMS

*A dear friend who liked cooking as much as I do shared this recipe with me, and I think of her every time I make it. Friends and family love it and request it often.*
—Shelli McWilliam, Salem, OR

**Prep:** 15 min. • **Cook:** 5 hours
**Makes:** 8 servings

- ¾ lb. sliced fresh mushrooms
- 1 large onion, chopped
- 2 garlic cloves, minced
- 3 lbs. boneless skinless chicken thighs
- 1 can (6 oz.) tomato paste
- ¾ cup chicken broth
- ¼ cup merlot or additional chicken broth
- 2 Tbsp. quick-cooking tapioca
- 2 tsp. sugar
- 1½ tsp. dried basil
- ½ tsp. salt
- ¼ tsp. pepper
- 2 Tbsp. grated Parmesan cheese
 Hot cooked pasta, optional

**1.** Place the mushrooms, onion and garlic in a 5-qt. slow cooker. Top with chicken.
**2.** In a small bowl, combine the tomato paste, broth, wine, tapioca, sugar, basil, salt and pepper. Pour over chicken. Cover and cook on low for 5-6 hours or until the chicken is tender.
**3.** Sprinkle with cheese. Serve with pasta if desired.

**Freeze option:** Freeze cooled chicken mixture in freezer containers. To use, partially thaw mixture in refrigerator overnight. Heat through in a saucepan, stirring occasionally; add broth or water if necessary.

**5 oz. cooked chicken with ½ cup sauce:**
310 cal., 13g fat (4g sat. fat), 115mg chol., 373mg sod., 11g carb. (5g sugars, 1g fiber), 35g pro. **Diabetic exchanges:** 5 lean meat, ½ starch.

### SPICY SEAFOOD STEW

*The hardest part of this quick and easy recipe is peeling and dicing the potatoes— and you can even do that the night before. Just place the potatoes in water and store them in the refrigerator overnight to speed up assembly the next day.*
—Bonnie Marlow, Ottoville, OH

**Prep:** 30 min. • **Cook:** 4¾ hours
**Makes:** 9 servings (about 2 qt.)

- 2 lbs. potatoes, peeled and diced
- 1 lb. carrots, sliced
- 1 jar (24 oz.) pasta sauce
- 2 jars (6 oz. each) sliced mushrooms, drained
- 1½ tsp. ground turmeric
- 1½ tsp. minced garlic
- 1 tsp. cayenne pepper
- ¼ tsp. salt
- 1½ cups water
- 1 lb. sea scallops
- 1 lb. uncooked shrimp (31-40 per lb.), peeled and deveined

In a 5-qt. slow cooker, combine the first 8 ingredients. Cook, covered, on low until potatoes are tender, 4½-5 hours. Stir in the water, scallops and shrimp. Cook, covered, until scallops are opaque and shrimp turn pink, 15-20 minutes longer.
**1 cup:** 229 cal., 2g fat (0 sat. fat), 73mg chol., 803mg sod., 34g carb. (10g sugars, 6g fiber), 19g pro.

CHICKEN MERLOT
WITH MUSHROOMS

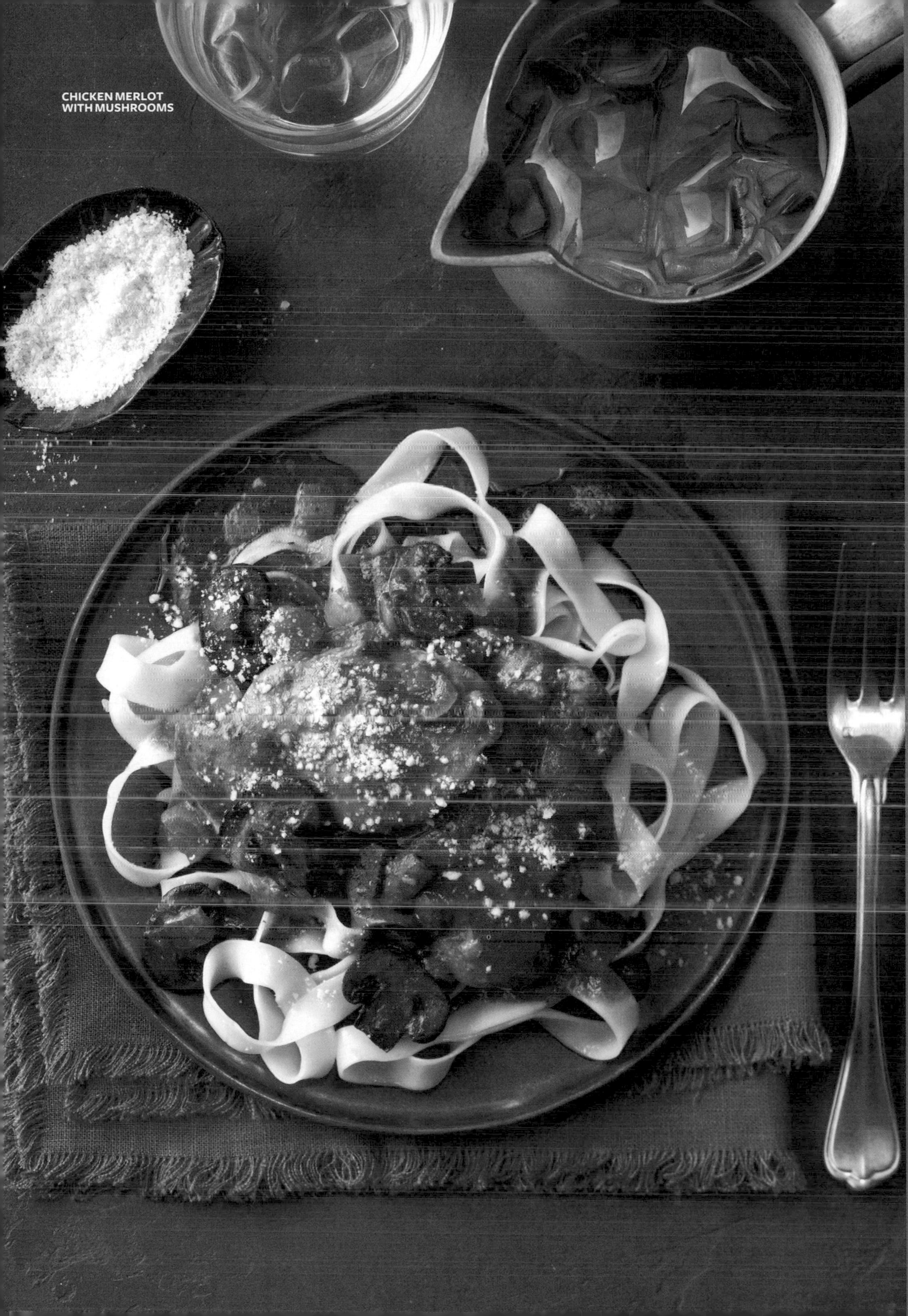

## SLOW-COOKED SWEET & SOUR PORK

**(PICTURED ON P. 198)**

*Even though a co-worker gave me this recipe more than 20 years ago, my family still enjoys it today.*

—Martha Nickerson, Hancock, ME

**Prep:** 20 min. • **Cook:** 6½ hours
**Makes:** 6 servings

- 2 Tbsp. plus 1½ tsp. paprika
- 1½ lbs. boneless pork loin roast, cut into 1-in. strips
- 1 Tbsp. canola oil
- 1 can (20 oz.) unsweetened pineapple chunks
- 1 medium onion, chopped
- 1 medium green pepper, chopped
- ¼ cup cider vinegar
- 3 Tbsp. brown sugar
- 3 Tbsp. reduced-sodium soy sauce
- 1 Tbsp. Worcestershire sauce
- ½ tsp. salt
- 2 Tbsp. cornstarch
- ¼ cup cold water
  Thinly sliced green onions, optional
  Hot cooked rice, optional

**1.** Place paprika in a shallow bowl. Add pork, a few pieces at a time, and turn to coat. In a nonstick skillet, brown pork in oil in batches over medium-high heat. Transfer to a 3-qt. slow cooker.

**2.** Drain pineapple, reserving juice; refrigerate the pineapple. Add the pineapple juice, onion, green pepper, cider vinegar, brown sugar, soy sauce, Worcestershire sauce and salt to slow cooker. Cover and cook on low until meat is tender, 6-8 hours.

**3.** Combine cornstarch and water until smooth; stir into the pork mixture. Add pineapple. Cover and cook 30 minutes longer or until the sauce is thickened. If desired, sprinkle with green onions and serve over rice.

**1 cup:** 281 cal., 8g fat (2g sat. fat), 57mg chol., 551mg sod., 27g carb. (20g sugars, 2g fiber), 24g pro.

## SOUTHERN BARBECUE SPAGHETTI SAUCE

*I revamped our favorite sloppy joe recipe into this thick, tasty spaghetti sauce that simmers in the slow cooker. The flavor is jazzy enough to be interesting to adults, yet mild enough for the kids to enjoy.*

—Rhonda Melanson, Sarnia, ON

**Prep:** 20 min. • **Cook:** 4 hours
**Makes:** 12 servings

- 1 lb. lean ground turkey
- 2 medium onions, chopped
- 1½ cups sliced fresh mushrooms
- 1 medium green pepper, chopped
- 2 garlic cloves, minced
- 1 can (14½ oz.) diced tomatoes, undrained
- 1 can (12 oz.) tomato paste
- 1 can (8 oz.) tomato sauce
- 1 cup ketchup
- ½ cup beef broth
- 2 Tbsp. Worcestershire sauce
- 2 Tbsp. brown sugar
- 1 Tbsp. ground cumin
- 2 tsp. chili powder
- 12 cups hot cooked spaghetti

**1.** In a large nonstick skillet, cook the turkey, onions, mushrooms and green pepper over medium heat until meat is no longer pink. Add garlic; cook 1 minute longer. Drain.

**2.** Transfer to a 3-qt. slow cooker. Stir in the tomatoes, tomato paste, tomato sauce, ketchup, broth, Worcestershire sauce, brown sugar, cumin and chili powder. Cover and cook on low for 4-5 hours or until vegetables are tender. Serve with spaghetti.

**⅔ cup sauce:** 336 cal., 4g fat (1g sat. fat), 26mg chol., 516mg sod., 57g carb. (14g sugars, 5g fiber), 18g pro.

**\* HEALTH TIP \*** Even if you don't follow a gluten-free diet, it's worth checking out alternative pastas. Most have more fiber, vitamins and minerals than pasta made with refined wheat. Look for spaghetti made from ingredients like chickpeas, brown rice, quinoa or corn.

**SOUTHERN BARBECUE SPAGHETTI SAUCE**

**SO-EASY COQ AU VIN**

## SOUTHWEST SHREDDED PORK WITH BEANS

*A friend gave me this recipe, which my sons say is a keeper. For a change of pace, spoon the mouthwatering filling into warm, soft tortillas.*
—Sarah Johnston, Lincoln, NE

- - - - - - - - - - - - - - - - - - - - - - - - - -

**Prep:** 20 min. • **Cook:** 8 hours
**Makes:** 12 servings

- 3 lbs. pork tenderloin, cut into 3-in. lengths
- 2 cans (15 oz. each) black beans, rinsed and drained
- 1 jar (24 oz.) picante sauce
  Hot cooked rice, optional

In a 5-qt. slow cooker, place the pork, beans and picante sauce. Cover and cook on low for 8 hours or until pork is tender. Shred pork; return to slow cooker. Serve with rice if desired.

**1 cup without rice:** 207 cal., 4g fat (1g sat. fat), 64mg chol., 595mg sod., 14g carb. (2g sugars, 3g fiber), 26g pro. **Diabetic exchanges:** 3 lean meat, 1 starch.

## SO-EASY COQ AU VIN

*Here's my adaptation of the beloved French dish. I substituted boneless skinless chicken breasts for a lighter version that still showcases the traditional and memorable taste.*
—Sonya Labbe, West Hollywood, CA

- - - - - - - - - - - - - - - - - - - - - - - - - -

**Prep:** 20 min. • **Cook:** 5 hours
**Makes:** 4 servings

- 4 boneless skinless chicken breast halves (4 oz. each)
- 3 bacon strips, chopped
- ½ lb. sliced fresh mushrooms
- 1 medium onion, chopped
- 4 garlic cloves, minced
- 1 bay leaf
- ⅓ cup all-purpose flour
- ½ cup red wine
- ½ cup chicken broth
- ½ tsp. dried thyme
- ¼ tsp. pepper
  Hot cooked noodles, optional

**1.** In large skillet, cook bacon over medium heat until crisp, stirring occasionally. Remove with a slotted spoon; drain on paper towels. Brown chicken on both sides in drippings over medium heat. Transfer chicken to a 3-qt. slow cooker.
**2.** Add the mushrooms, onion and garlic to skillet; cook and stir just until tender, 1-2 minutes. Spoon over chicken; add the bay leaf.
**3.** In a small bowl, whisk the flour, wine, broth, thyme and pepper until smooth; pour over chicken.
**4.** Cover; cook on low until chicken is tender, 5-6 hours. Discard bay leaf. If desired, serve with noodles.

**1 chicken breast half with ½ cup mushroom sauce:** 299 cal., 11g fat (3g sat. fat), 75mg chol., 324mg sod., 16g carb. (4g sugars, 2g fiber), 28g pro. **Diabetic exchanges:** 3 lean meat, 1½ fat, 1 vegetable, ½ starch.

## RED PEPPER CHICKEN

*We love this flavorful, simple dish served with rice cooked in chicken broth.*
—Piper Spiwak, Vienna, VA

**Prep:** 15 min. • **Cook:** 6 hours
**Makes:** 4 servings

- 4 **boneless skinless chicken breast halves (4 oz. each)**
- 1 **can (15 oz.) no-salt-added black beans, rinsed and drained**
- 1 **can (14½ oz.) Mexican stewed tomatoes, undrained**
- 1 **jar (12 oz.) roasted sweet red peppers, drained and cut into strips**
- 1 **large onion, chopped**
  **Pepper to taste**
  **Hot cooked rice**

Place the chicken in a 3-qt. slow cooker. In a bowl, combine the beans, tomatoes, red peppers, onion and pepper. Pour over the chicken. Cover and cook on low until chicken is tender, about 6 hours. Serve with rice.

**1 serving:** 288 cal., 3g fat (1g sat. fat), 63mg chol., 657mg sod., 28g carb. (8g sugars, 7g fiber), 30g pro. **Diabetic exchanges:** 3 lean meat, 1½ starch, 1 vegetable.

**POT ROAST WITH ASIAN BLACK BEAN SAUCE**

## POT ROAST WITH ASIAN BLACK BEAN SAUCE

*I love stir-fry with black bean sauce. This recipe takes the delicious flavor of black bean sauce and joins it with fork-tender pot roast.*
—Judy Lawson, Chelsea, MI

**Prep:** 25 min. • **Cook:** 5½ hours
**Makes:** 10 servings

- 1 **boneless beef chuck roast (3 to 4 lbs.)**
- ½ **tsp. salt**
- ½ **tsp. pepper**
- 1 **Tbsp. olive oil**
- 1 **medium onion, cut into 1-in. pieces**
- ¾ **cup Asian black bean sauce**
- ¼ **cup reduced-sodium beef broth**
- ½ **lb. sliced fresh mushrooms**
- 8 **oz. fresh snow peas, trimmed**
- 1 **Tbsp. cornstarch**
- 1 **Tbsp. cold water**
  **Hot cooked rice**
- 4 **green onions, sliced**

**1.** Sprinkle roast with salt and pepper. In a large skillet, heat oil over medium-high heat. Brown roast 3-4 minutes on each side. Transfer to a 6-qt. slow cooker. Add onion. Whisk together black bean sauce and broth; pour over the roast. Cook, covered, on low 5-6 hours.
**2.** Add mushrooms and snow peas; continue cooking on low until meat is tender, about 30 minutes.
**3.** Remove the roast and vegetables to a serving platter; keep warm. Transfer the cooking juices to a small saucepan; skim fat. Bring the cooking juices to a boil. In a small bowl, mix cornstarch and cold water until smooth; stir into the cooking juices. Return to a boil; cook and stir 1-2 minutes or until thickened. Serve roast with hot cooked rice and sauce. Sprinkle with green onions.

**1 serving:** 281 cal., 14g fat (5g sat. fat), 89mg chol., 602mg sod., 8g carb. (4g sugars, 1g fiber), 29g pro. **Diabetic exchanges:** 3 lean meat, ½ starch.

## SLOW-COOKER SHREDDED BEEF LETTUCE CUPS

*The slow cooker is our summertime go-to for cool kitchen cooking. After swim lessons and outdoor activities, it's so nice to come back to a wonderful light dinner. If you can't find Bibb or Boston, green leaf lettuce is less sturdy but can work in a pinch.*
—Elisabeth Larsen, Pleasant Grove, UT

**Prep:** 20 min. • **Cook:** 6¼ hours
**Makes:** 8 servings

1   boneless beef chuck roast (2 lbs.)
3   medium carrots, peeled and chopped
2   medium sweet red peppers, chopped
1   medium onion, chopped
1   can (8 oz.) unsweetened crushed pineapple, undrained
½   cup reduced-sodium soy sauce
2   Tbsp. packed brown sugar
2   Tbsp. white vinegar
1   garlic clove, minced
½   tsp. pepper
3   Tbsp. cornstarch
3   Tbsp. water
24  Bibb or Boston lettuce leaves
    Sliced green onions, optional

**1.** In a 4- or 5-qt. slow cooker, combine roast, carrots, peppers and onion. Stir together next 6 ingredients in small bowl; pour over roast. Cook, covered, on low until roast is tender, 6-8 hours.
**2.** Remove roast from slow cooker. Cool slightly; shred roast with 2 forks.
**3.** Skim fat from cooking juices; transfer juices and vegetables to a small saucepan. Bring to a boil over high heat. In a small bowl, combine cornstarch and water. Gradually stir cornstarch mixture into juices; cook until sauce is thickened, 3-4 minutes. Return beef, sauce and vegetables to slow cooker; cook until heated through, 10-15 minutes.
**4.** Serve beef in lettuce leaves. If desired, sprinkle with green onions.

**3 lettuce cups:** 271 cal., 11g fat (4g sat. fat), 74mg chol., 642mg sod., 18g carb. (11g sugars, 2g fiber), 24g pro. **Diabetic exchanges:** 3 lean meat, 1 starch.

**TEST KITCHEN TIP**
Water chestnuts are a great addition to this recipe and hold up well in the slow cooker. For more crunch, top with some shredded carrots and radishes.

**SLOW-COOKER SHREDDED BEEF LETTUCE CUPS**

**PORK & GREEN CHILE STEW**

## PORK & GREEN CHILE STEW

*As an easily adaptable stew, this dish is ready in 4 hours if cooked on high in a slow cooker, or in 8 hours if cooked low and slow.*
—Paul Sedillo, Plainfield, IL

- - - - - - - - - - - - - - - - - - - - - - - - - - - -

**Prep:** 40 min. • **Cook:** 7 hours
**Makes:** 8 servings (2 qt.)

- 2 lbs. boneless pork shoulder butt roast, cut into ¾-in. cubes
- 1 large onion, cut into ½-in. pieces
- 2 Tbsp. canola oil
- 1 tsp. salt
- 1 tsp. coarsely ground pepper
- 4 large potatoes, peeled and cut into ¾-in. cubes
- 3 cups water
- 1 can (16 oz.) hominy, rinsed and drained
- 2 cans (4 oz. each) chopped green chiles
- 2 Tbsp. quick-cooking tapioca
- 2 garlic cloves, minced
- ½ tsp. dried oregano
- ½ tsp. ground cumin
- 1 cup minced fresh cilantro
  Sour cream, optional

**1.** In a large skillet, brown pork and onion in oil in batches. Sprinkle with salt and pepper. Transfer to a 5-qt. slow cooker.
**2.** Stir in the potatoes, water, hominy, chiles, tapioca, garlic, oregano and cumin. Cover and cook on low until meat is tender, 7-9 hours, stirring in cilantro during the last 30 minutes of cooking. If desired, serve stew with sour cream and additional cilantro.

**1 cup:** 322 cal., 15g fat (4g sat. fat), 67mg chol., 723mg sod., 25g carb. (3g sugars, 3g fiber), 21g pro. **Diabetic exchanges:** 3 medium-fat meat, 1½ starch, ½ fat.

## SLOW-COOKER BBQ CHICKEN

**(PICTURED ON P. 199)**
*Of all the recipes I make in my slow cooker, this is my favorite. If you like your BBQ sweet with a little spice, this will be your new go-to dish as well.*
—Yvonne McKim, Vancouver, WA

- - - - - - - - - - - - - - - - - - - - - - - - - - - -

**Prep:** 15 min. • **Cook:** 5 hours
**Makes:** 12 servings

- 6 chicken leg quarters, skin removed
- ¾ cup ketchup
- ½ cup orange juice
- ¼ cup packed brown sugar
- ¼ cup red wine vinegar
- ¼ cup olive oil
- 4 tsp. minced fresh parsley
- 2 tsp. Worcestershire sauce
- 1 tsp. garlic salt
- ½ tsp. pepper
- 2 Tbsp. plus 2 tsp. cornstarch
- ¼ cup water

**1.** Using a sharp knife, cut through the joint of each leg quarter to separate into 2 pieces. Place the chicken pieces in a 4-qt. slow cooker.
**2.** In a small bowl, mix ketchup, orange juice, brown sugar, vinegar, oil, parsley, Worcestershire sauce, garlic salt and pepper; pour over the chicken. Cook, covered, on low until meat is tender, 5-6 hours.
**3.** Remove chicken to a serving platter; keep warm. Skim fat from cooking juices; pour into a measuring cup to measure 2 cups. Transfer to a small saucepan; bring to a boil. In a small bowl, mix cornstarch and water until smooth; stir into cooking juices. Return to a boil, stirring constantly; cook and stir until thickened, 1-2 minutes. Serve with the chicken.

**1 serving:** 179 cal., 9g fat (2g sat. fat), 45mg chol., 392mg sod., 12g carb. (9g sugars, 0 fiber), 13g pro. **Diabetic exchanges:** 2 lean meat, 1 starch, 1 fat.

## VEGETARIAN STUFFED PEPPERS

(PICTURED ON P. 199)

*These flavorful peppers are an updated version of my mom's stuffed peppers, which were a favorite when I was growing up in upstate New York. Whenever I make them, I'm reminded of home.*
—Melissa McCabe, Victor, NY

**Prep:** 30 min. • **Cook:** 3½ hours
**Makes:** 6 servings

- 2 cups cooked brown rice
- 3 small tomatoes, chopped
- 1 cup frozen corn, thawed
- 1 small sweet onion, chopped
- ¾ cup cubed Monterey Jack cheese
- ⅓ cup chopped ripe olives
- ⅓ cup canned black beans, rinsed and drained
- ⅓ cup canned red beans, rinsed and drained
- 4 fresh basil leaves, thinly sliced
- 3 garlic cloves, minced
- 1 tsp. salt
- ½ tsp. pepper
- 6 large sweet peppers
- ¾ cup meatless spaghetti sauce
- ½ cup water
- 4 Tbsp. grated Parmesan cheese, divided

**1.** Place the first 12 ingredients in a large bowl; mix lightly to combine. Cut and discard tops from sweet peppers; remove seeds. Fill peppers with rice mixture.
**2.** In a small bowl, mix spaghetti sauce and water; pour half of the mixture into an oval 5-qt. slow cooker. Add filled peppers. Top with remaining sauce. Sprinkle with 2 Tbsp. Parmesan cheese.
**3.** Cook, covered, on low 3½-4 hours or until heated through and peppers are tender. Sprinkle with remaining Parmesan cheese.

**1 stuffed pepper:** 261 cal., 8g fat (4g sat. fat), 18mg chol., 815mg sod., 39g carb. (9g sugars, 7g fiber), 11g pro. **Diabetic exchanges:** 2 starch, 1 vegetable, 1 lean meat, 1 fat.

## PORK CHOPS & BEANS

*This hearty combination of tender pork chops and two kinds of beans makes a satisfying supper from the slow cooker, no matter what time of year.*
—Dorothy Pritchett, Wills Point, TX

**Prep:** 15 min. • **Cook:** 5 hours
**Makes:** 4 servings

- 4 pork loin chops (½ in. thick)
- ¼ tsp. salt
- ¼ tsp. pepper
- 1 Tbsp. canola oil
- 2 medium onions, chopped
- 2 garlic cloves, minced
- ¼ cup chili sauce
- 1½ tsp. brown sugar
- 1 tsp. prepared mustard
- 1 can (16 oz.) kidney beans, rinsed and drained
- 1¾ cups frozen lima beans, thawed

**1.** Sprinkle the pork chops with salt and pepper. In a large skillet, heat the oil over medium-high heat. Brown chops on both sides. Transfer to a 3-qt. slow cooker. Discard the drippings, reserving 1 Tbsp. drippings in skillet. Add onions; cook and stir until tender. Add garlic; cook and stir 1 minute. Stir in chili sauce, brown sugar and mustard. Pour over chops.
**2.** Cook, covered, on low 4 hours or until meat is almost tender. Stir in lima beans. Cook, covered, 1-2 hours longer or until heated through.

**1 serving:** 297 cal., 5g fat (1g sat. fat), 14mg chol., 607mg sod., 45g carb. (10g sugars, 11g fiber), 19g pro. **Diabetic exchanges:** 3 starch, 3 lean meat.

**PORK CHOPS & BEANS**

**MUSHROOM MEAT LOAF**

## MUSHROOM MEAT LOAF

*Although I don't consider myself much of a cook, I'm really proud of this recipe. The meat loaf is tender and moist, and the sauce has a nice, subtle spiciness to it. The mushrooms and ground turkey are an unexpected yet delicious combination.*
—Tyler Sherman, Williamsburg, VA

**Prep:** 30 min. • **Cook:** 3¼ hours
**Makes:** 6 servings

- 2 large eggs, lightly beaten
- 1⅓ cups soft bread crumbs
- ½ lb. large portobello mushrooms, stems removed, finely chopped
- 1 small onion, finely chopped
- 2 garlic cloves, minced
- ¾ tsp. salt
- ½ tsp. dried thyme
- ¼ tsp. pepper
- 1 lb. lean ground turkey
- ¼ cup chili sauce
- 2 tsp. stone-ground mustard
- ⅛ tsp. cayenne pepper

**1.** Cut three 20x3-in. strips of heavy-duty foil; crisscross so they resemble spokes of a wheel. Place strips on the bottom and up the sides of a 4- or 5-qt. slow cooker. Coat strips with cooking spray.
**2.** In a large bowl, combine the eggs, bread crumbs, mushrooms, onion, garlic, salt, thyme and pepper. Crumble the turkey over mixture and mix lightly but thoroughly. Shape into a 7½x4-in. loaf.
**3.** Place meat loaf in the center of the strips. Cover and cook on low until no pink remains and a thermometer reads 160°, 3-4 hours.
**4.** Combine the chili sauce, mustard and cayenne; pour over meat. Cover and cook until heated through, about 15 minutes. Using foil strips as handles, remove the meat loaf to a platter.
**1 slice:** 194 cal., 8g fat (2g sat. fat), 130mg chol., 648mg sod., 12g carb. (4g sugars, 1g fiber), 17g pro. **Diabetic exchanges:** 2 lean meat, 1 starch, 1 vegetable.

**HOW TO**

### Make a Foil Sling

A sling helps you easily lift meat loaf and layered foods out of the crock. To make, fold one or more pieces of heavy-duty foil into strips. Place on bottom and up sides of the slow cooker; coat with cooking spray.

NEW ZEALAND ROSEMARY
LAMB SHANKS

## NEW ZEALAND ROSEMARY LAMB SHANKS

*When I was young my family lived in New Zealand for two years after the war. One item that was always available was lamb shanks. Mother cooked them all the time with root vegetables, and to this day I love lamb!*

—Nancy Heishman, Las Vegas, NV

**Prep:** 25 min. • **Cook:** 6 hours
**Makes:** 8 servings

- 1 tsp. salt
- ¾ tsp. pepper
- 4 lamb shanks (about 20 oz. each)
- 1 Tbsp. butter
- ½ cup white wine
- 3 medium parsnips, peeled and cut into 1-in. chunks
- 2 large carrots, peeled and cut into 1-in. chunks
- 2 medium turnips, peeled and cut into 1-in. chunks
- 2 large tomatoes, chopped
- 1 large onion, chopped
- 4 garlic cloves, minced
- 2 cups beef broth
- 1 pkg. (10 oz.) frozen peas, thawed
- ⅓ cup chopped fresh parsley
- 2 Tbsp. minced fresh rosemary

**1.** Rub salt and pepper over lamb. In a large skillet, heat butter over medium-high heat; brown meat. Transfer meat to a 6- or 7-qt. slow cooker. Add wine to skillet; cook and stir 1 minute to loosen brown bits. Pour over lamb. Add the parsnips, carrots, turnips, tomatoes, onion, garlic and broth. Cook, covered, on low 6-8 hours or until meat is tender.
**2.** Remove lamb; keep warm. Stir in peas, parsley and rosemary; heat through. Serve lamb with vegetables.

**½ lamb shank with 1 cup vegetables:**
350 cal., 15g fat (6g sat. fat), 103mg chol., 668mg sod., 22g carb. (8g sugars, 6g fiber), 31g pro. **Diabetic exchanges:** 4 lean meat, 1 starch, 1 vegetable, ½ fat.

## GROUND BEEF SPAGHETTI SAUCE WITH MUSHROOMS

*I got the recipe for this sauce in a recipe exchange and wish I could credit the person who gave it to me. My children love it! I added mushrooms, but if you'd like it even chunkier, toss in some bell pepper and other veggies, too.*
—Meg Fisher, Marietta, GA

**Prep:** 20 min. • **Cook:** 6 hours
**Makes:** 12 servings (6 cups)

- 1 lb. lean ground beef (90% lean)
- ½ lb. sliced fresh mushrooms
- 1 small onion, chopped
- 2 cans (14½ oz. each) diced tomatoes, undrained
- 1 can (12 oz.) tomato paste
- 1 can (8 oz.) tomato sauce
- 1 cup reduced-sodium beef broth
- 2 Tbsp. dried parsley flakes
- 1 Tbsp. brown sugar
- 1 tsp. dried basil
- 1 tsp. dried oregano
- 1 tsp. salt
- ¼ tsp. pepper
  Hot cooked whole wheat spaghetti
  Shredded Parmesan cheese, optional

**1.** In a large nonstick skillet, cook the beef, mushrooms and onion over medium heat until the meat is no longer pink; drain. Transfer to a 3-qt. slow cooker.
**2.** Stir in the tomatoes, tomato paste, tomato sauce, broth, parsley, brown sugar, basil, oregano, salt and pepper. Cover and cook on low for 6-8 hours. Serve with spaghetti. Sprinkle with cheese if desired.

**½ cup:** 115 cal., 3g fat (1g sat. fat), 19mg chol., 493mg sod., 12g carb. (0g sugars, 3g fiber), 10g pro. **Diabetic exchanges:** 2 vegetable, 1 lean meat.

## SUNDAY POT ROAST

*This wonderful pork roast turns out tender and savory every time.*
—Brandy Schaefer, Glen Carbon, IL

**Prep:** 10 min. + chilling • **Cook:** 8 hours
**Makes:** 14 servings

- 1 tsp. dried oregano
- ½ tsp. onion salt
- ½ tsp. caraway seeds
- ½ tsp. pepper
- ¼ tsp. garlic salt
- 1 boneless pork loin roast (3½ to 4 lbs.), trimmed
- 6 medium carrots, peeled and cut into 1½-in. pieces
- 3 large potatoes, peeled and quartered
- 3 small onions, quartered
- 1½ cups beef broth
- ⅓ cup all-purpose flour
- ⅓ cup cold water
- ¼ tsp. browning sauce, optional

**1.** Combine first 5 ingredients; rub over roast. Cover; refrigerate overnight.
**2.** Place vegetables in a 6-qt. slow cooker; add broth. Place the roast on top. Cook, covered, on low until meat and vegetables are tender, 8-10 hours.
**3.** Transfer roast and vegetables to a serving platter; tent with foil. Pour the cooking juices into a small saucepan. Mix flour and water until smooth; stir into pan. Bring to a boil; cook and stir until thickened, about 2 minutes. If desired, add browning sauce. Serve with roast.

**1 serving:** 217 cal., 5g fat (2g sat. fat), 57mg chol., 230mg sod., 17g carb. (3g sugars, 2g fiber), 24g pro. **Diabetic exchanges:** 3 lean meat, 1½ starch.

> **READER REVIEW**
>
> *"Absolutely delicious! We were so hungry I forgot to make the gravy, but the roast and vegetables with the broth spooned over top was amazing. This is a keeper."*
>
> —PAJAMAANGEL, TASTEOFHOME.COM

**GROUND BEEF SPAGHETTI SAUCE WITH MUSHROOMS**

## TENDER STEAK FAJITAS

*Flank steak turns out tender, juicy and flavorful in the slow cooker to create these tempting fajitas. I like to serve them with a side of Spanish rice.*

—Twila Burkholder, Middleburg, PA

**Prep:** 20 min. • **Cook:** 6 hours
**Makes:** 6 servings

- 1 beef flank steak (1½ lbs.)
- 1 medium onion, sliced
- 1 cup tomato juice
- 1 jalapeno pepper, seeded and chopped
- 2 garlic cloves, minced
- 1 Tbsp. minced fresh cilantro
- 1 tsp. ground cumin
- 1 tsp. chili powder
- ¼ tsp. salt
- 1 medium green pepper, julienned
- 1 medium sweet red pepper, julienned
- 6 flour tortillas (8 in.), warmed
  Optional: Shredded cheddar cheese, sour cream and guacamole

**1.** Thinly slice steak across the grain into strips; place in a 5-qt. slow cooker. Add the onion, tomato juice, jalapeno, garlic, cilantro, cumin, chili powder and salt. Cover and cook on low for 5 hours.
**2.** Add green and red peppers. Cover and cook 1 hour longer or until the meat and vegetables are tender.
**3.** Using a slotted spoon, spoon the meat mixture down the center of each tortilla. Sprinkle with cheese if desired. Fold sides of tortilla over filling. Serve with sour cream and guacamole if desired.
**Note:** Wear disposable gloves when cutting hot peppers; the oils can burn skin. Avoid touching your face.
**1 fajita:** 340 cal., 12g fat (4g sat. fat), 48mg chol., 549mg sod., 33g carb. (4g sugars, 2g fiber), 25g pro. **Diabetic exchanges:** 3 lean meat, 2 starch, 1 vegetable.

## HERBED SLOW-COOKER CHICKEN

*I use my slow cooker to prepare these well-seasoned chicken breasts that cook up moist and tender. My daughter, who has two young sons to keep up with, shared this great recipe with me several years ago. I've since made it repeatedly.*

—Sundra Hauck, Bogalusa, LA

**Prep:** 5 min. • **Cook:** 4 hours
**Makes:** 4 servings

- 1 Tbsp. olive oil
- 1 tsp. paprika
- ½ tsp. garlic powder
- ½ tsp. seasoned salt
- ½ tsp. dried thyme
- ½ tsp. dried basil
- ½ tsp. pepper
- ½ tsp. browning sauce, optional
- 4 bone-in chicken breast halves (8 oz. each)
- ½ cup chicken broth

In a small bowl, combine the first 7 ingredients and, if desired, browning sauce; rub over chicken. Place in a 5-qt. slow cooker; add broth. Cover and cook on low until chicken is tender, 4-5 hours.
**1 chicken breast half:** 211 cal., 7g fat (2g sat. fat), 91mg chol., 392mg sod., 1g carb. (0 sugars, 0 fiber), 33g pro. **Diabetic exchanges:** 5 lean meat, 1 fat.

---

**TEST KITCHEN TIP**

Good cooks like to keep a few go-to meals on hand that don't require a special trip to the store. Keep chicken breasts in the freezer and you'll always be ready to make this dish.

**TENDER STEAK FAJITAS**

## MOM'S CELERY SEED BRISKET

*Warning: Keep a close eye on this tangy pot of goodness. Because it's been fine-tuned to perfection, it tends to vanish at gatherings.*
—Aysha Schurman, Ammon, ID

- - - - - - - - - - - - - - - - - - - - - - - - - - - -

**Prep:** 20 min. • **Cook:** 8 hours
**Makes:** 8 servings

- 1 fresh beef brisket (3 to 4 lbs.)
- 1 can (28 oz.) Italian crushed tomatoes
- 1 large red onion, chopped
- 2 Tbsp. red wine vinegar
- 2 Tbsp. Worcestershire sauce
- 4 garlic cloves, minced
- 1 Tbsp. brown sugar
- 1 tsp. celery seed
- 1 tsp. pepper
- ½ tsp. salt
- ½ tsp. ground cumin
- ½ tsp. liquid smoke
- 4 tsp. cornstarch
- 3 Tbsp. cold water

**1.** Place brisket in a 5-qt. slow cooker. In a large bowl, combine the tomatoes, onion, vinegar, Worcestershire sauce, garlic, brown sugar, celery seed, pepper, salt, cumin and liquid smoke. Pour over beef. Cover and cook on low for 8-10 hours or until meat is tender.

**2.** Remove the meat to a serving platter; keep warm. In a large saucepan, combine the cornstarch and water until smooth. Gradually stir in 4 cups cooking liquid. Bring to a boil; cook and stir for 2 minutes or until thickened. Slice brisket across the grain; serve with gravy.

**5 oz. cooked meat with ½ cup gravy:**
262 cal., 7g fat (3g sat. fat), 72mg chol., 425mg sod., 10g carb. (5g sugars, 1g fiber), 36g pro. **Diabetic exchanges:** 5 lean meat, 1 vegetable.

## GARLIC CHICKEN & BROCCOLI

*This simple riff on Chinese chicken proves you can savor the takeout taste you crave while still eating right.*
—Connie Krupp, Racine, WI

- - - - - - - - - - - - - - - - - - - - - - - - - - - -

**Prep:** 15 min. • **Cook:** 3 hours
**Makes:** 8 servings

- 2 lbs. boneless skinless chicken breasts, cut into 1-in. pieces
- 4 cups fresh broccoli florets
- 4 medium carrots, julienned
- 1 can (8 oz.) sliced water chestnuts, drained
- 6 garlic cloves, minced
- 3 cups reduced-sodium chicken broth
- ¼ cup reduced-sodium soy sauce
- 2 Tbsp. brown sugar
- 2 Tbsp. sesame oil
- 2 Tbsp. rice vinegar
- ½ tsp. salt
- ½ tsp. pepper
- ⅓ cup cornstarch
- ⅓ cup water
  Hot cooked rice

**1.** In a 4- or 5-qt. slow cooker, combine the chicken, broccoli, carrots, water chestnuts and garlic. In a large bowl, mix next 7 ingredients; pour over the chicken mixture. Cook, covered, on low until chicken and broccoli are tender, 3-4 hours.

**2.** Remove chicken and vegetables; keep warm. Strain cooking juices into a small saucepan; skim fat. Bring juices to a boil. In a small bowl, mix cornstarch and water until smooth; stir into cooking juices. Return to a boil; cook and stir until thickened, 1-2 minutes. Serve with chicken, vegetables and hot cooked rice.

**Freeze option:** Place the chicken and vegetables in freezer containers; top with sauce. Cool and freeze. To use, partially thaw in refrigerator overnight. Microwave, covered, on high in a microwave-safe dish until heated through, stirring gently; add broth or water if necessary.

**1¼ cups:** 241 cal., 6g fat (1g sat. fat), 63mg chol., 798mg sod., 19g carb. (8g sugars, 3g fiber), 26g pro. **Diabetic exchanges:** 3 lean meat, 1 vegetable, ½ starch, ½ fat.

GARLIC CHICKEN & BROCCOLI

**MANCHESTER STEW**

## FAVORITE BEEF ROAST DINNER

*This is our family's favorite slow-cooked beef roast. My two children love it and always want seconds. I love putting together new flavor combinations in the kitchen.*
—Sheryl Padilla, Peyton, CO

**Prep:** 15 min. • **Cook:** 6 hours
**Makes:** 8 servings

- 4   medium potatoes, peeled and quartered
- ½   lb. fresh baby carrots
- 1   boneless beef chuck roast (3 to 4 lbs.)
- 4½  tsp. dried minced onion
- 3   garlic cloves, minced
- 1   Tbsp. Worcestershire sauce
- 1   tsp. garlic salt
- 1   tsp. celery seed
- 1   tsp. dried oregano
- 1   tsp. dried thyme
- 1   tsp. pepper

**1.** Place the potatoes, carrots and roast in a 6-qt. slow cooker. Sprinkle with the remaining ingredients. Cover and cook on low for 6-8 hours or until meat and vegetables are tender.
**2.** Skim fat from cooking juices; serve with roast and vegetables.
**5 oz. cooked beef with ¾ cup vegetables and 3 Tbsp. cooking juices:** 368 cal., 16g fat (6g sat. fat), 111mg chol., 342mg sod., 19g carb. (3g sugars, 2g fiber), 35g pro. **Diabetic exchanges:** 5 lean meat, 1 starch.

## MANCHESTER STEW

*While in college, I studied abroad at the University of Manchester in England. At the time, I was a vegetarian and was pleasantly surprised at how delicious and diverse vegetarian food in Britain could be. My favorite meal, served at my favorite restaurant, was Deans Burgundy, and after returning to the States I created this version. As it simmers in the slow cooker and the enticing aroma fills the kitchen, I'm reminded of my time in England!*
—Kimberly Hammond, Kingwood, TX

**Prep:** 25 min. • **Cook:** 8 hours
**Makes:** 6 servings (2½ qt.)

- 2   Tbsp. olive oil
- 2   medium onions, chopped
- 2   garlic cloves, minced
- 1   tsp. dried oregano
- 1   cup dry red wine
- 1   lb. small red potatoes, quartered
- 1   can (16 oz.) kidney beans, rinsed and drained
- ½   lb. sliced fresh mushrooms
- 2   medium leeks (white portions only), sliced
- 1   cup fresh baby carrots
- 2½  cups water
- 1   can (14½ oz.) no-salt-added diced tomatoes
- 1   tsp. dried thyme
- ½   tsp. salt
- ¼   tsp. pepper
    Fresh basil leaves

**1.** In a large skillet, heat oil over medium-high heat. Add onions; cook and stir until tender, 2-3 minutes. Add the garlic and oregano; cook and stir 1 minute longer. Stir in wine. Bring to a boil; cook until liquid is reduced by half, 3-4 minutes.
**2.** Transfer to a 5- or 6-qt. slow cooker. Add the potatoes, beans, mushrooms, leeks and carrots. Stir in water, tomatoes, thyme, salt and pepper. Cook, covered, on low 8-10 hours or until potatoes are tender. Top with basil.
**1⅔ cups:** 221 cal., 5g fat (1g sat. fat), 0 chol., 354mg sod., 38g carb. (8g sugars, 8g fiber), 8g pro. **Diabetic exchanges:** 2 starch, 1 vegetable, 1 fat.

## SLOW-COOKER STUFFED SHELLS

*There's no need to precook the pasta shells in this simple pasta dish. It's almost like magic to lift the lid and find such deliciousness ready to serve. Add garlic bread and you're golden!*
—Sherry Day, Pinckney, MI

**Prep:** 30 min. • **Cook:** 4 hours
**Makes:** 10 servings

- 1  carton (15 oz.) part-skim ricotta cheese
- 1  pkg. (10 oz.) frozen chopped spinach, thawed and squeezed dry
- 2½  cups shredded Italian cheese blend
- ½  cup diced red onion
- ½  tsp. garlic powder
- 2  tsp. dried basil
- ½  tsp. dried oregano
- ½  tsp. dried thyme
- 2  jars (24 oz. each) roasted garlic Parmesan pasta sauce
- 2  cups water
- 1  pkg. (12 oz.) jumbo pasta shells
   Optional: Additional shredded Italian cheese blend and sliced fresh basil

**1.** Mix first 8 ingredients (mixture will be stiff). In a greased 6-qt. slow cooker, mix 1 jar pasta sauce with water. Fill shells with ricotta mixture; layer in slow cooker. Top with remaining jar of pasta sauce.
**2.** Cook, covered, on low until pasta is tender, 4-5 hours. If desired, serve with additional cheese and fresh basil.
**4 stuffed shells:** 303 cal., 10g fat (6g sat. fat), 34mg chol., 377mg sod., 34g carb. (4g sugars, 3g fiber), 17g pro. **Diabetic exchanges:** 2 starch, 2 medium-fat meat.
**\* HEALTH TIP \*** Relative to other cheeses, ricotta is especially high in calcium. Just ¼ cup provides almost 20% of the recommended daily intake.

SPICY LIME CHICKEN

## SPICY LIME CHICKEN

*I've been turning this spicy lime chicken into tacos for years, but it was my son Austin who put it on cooked rice with all his favorite taco toppings. A family favorite was created out of leftovers!*
—Christine Hair, Odessa, FL

**Prep:** 10 min. • **Cook:** 3 hours
**Makes:** 6 servings

- 1½  lbs. boneless skinless chicken breast halves (about 4)
- 2  cups chicken broth
- 3  Tbsp. lime juice
- 1  Tbsp. chili powder
- 1  tsp. grated lime zest
   Fresh cilantro leaves

**1.** Place chicken in a 3-qt. slow cooker. Combine the broth, lime juice and chili powder; pour over the chicken. Cook, covered, on low until chicken is tender, about 3 hours.
**2.** Remove chicken. When cool enough to handle, shred meat with 2 forks; return to slow cooker. Stir in lime zest. Serve with fresh cilantro.
**1 serving:** 132 cal., 3g fat (1g sat. fat), 64mg chol., 420mg sod., 2g carb. (1g sugars, 1g fiber), 23g pro. **Diabetic exchanges:** 3 lean meat.

### TEST KITCHEN TIP

It's easy to turn this into a burrito bowl. Simply mix shredded chicken with hot cooked rice and any combination of rinsed and drained black beans, cooked fresh corn, quartered cherry tomatoes, cotija cheese, chopped avocado, fresh cilantro leaves and chunky salsa.

## SLOW-COOKER CHICKEN & BLACK BEAN TACOS

*My husband and I love Mexican food, and these tacos have become one of our favorite meals. Try setting out the toppings in different bowls on the table so dinner guests and kids can make their own tacos.*
—Laura Rodriguez, Willoughby, OH

**Prep:** 20 min. • **Cook:** 4¼ hours
**Makes:** 6 servings

1    can (8 oz.) crushed pineapple
½    cup salsa
2    green onions, sliced
1    tsp. grated lime zest
¼    cup lime juice
½    tsp. chili powder
¼    tsp. garlic powder
¼    tsp. ground cumin
⅛    tsp. each salt, cayenne pepper and pepper
1    lb. boneless skinless chicken thighs
1    can (15 oz.) black beans, rinsed and drained
12    flour tortillas (6 in.), warmed
Toppings: Shredded Mexican cheese blend, shredded lettuce, peeled medium ripe avocado and hot sauce

**1.** In a small bowl, combine the first 5 ingredients; stir in seasonings. Place the chicken in a 3-qt. slow cooker; add pineapple mixture. Cook, covered, on low 4-5 hours or until chicken is tender.
**2.** Remove chicken; cool slightly. Shred meat with 2 forks; return to slow cooker. Stir in beans. Cook, covered, on low until heated through, 15-20 minutes longer. Using a slotted spoon, serve the chicken mixture in tortillas with toppings.
**2 tacos:** 387 cal., 12g fat (2g sat. fat), 50mg chol., 757mg sod., 47g carb. (9g sugars, 3g fiber), 24g pro. **Diabetic exchanges:** 3 starch, 3 lean meat.

SLOW COOKER CHICKEN & BLACK BEAN TACOS

## APPLE BUTTER PORK WITH WHITE BEANS

*This enticing dish is an entire dinner—perfect to come home to after I've run the kids around to activities all afternoon. The apple butter with the pork roast is wonderful for fall!*
—Elisabeth Larsen, Pleasant Grove, UT

**Prep:** 20 min. • **Cook:** 4 hours
**Makes:** 10 servings

- 12 oz. fresh baby carrots, coarsely chopped
- 1 small onion, chopped
- 1 boneless pork loin roast (3 lbs.)
- 1½ tsp. salt, divided
- ½ tsp. pepper, divided
- 1 Tbsp. olive oil
- 1 cup apple butter
- 2 Tbsp. apple cider vinegar
- 1 Tbsp. Dijon mustard
- 3 garlic cloves, minced
- 2 cans (15 oz. each) great northern beans, rinsed and drained

**1.** Place carrots and onion in a 6-qt. slow cooker. Sprinkle roast with 1 tsp. salt and ¼ tsp. pepper. In a large skillet, heat oil over medium-high heat; brown roast on all sides. Transfer to slow cooker.
**2.** In a small bowl, combine apple butter, vinegar, mustard, garlic, and remaining salt and pepper; pour over the pork and vegetables. Cook, covered, on low for 3½-4½ hours or until the vegetables are tender and a thermometer inserted into pork reads 145°.
**3.** Remove roast from slow cooker; tent with foil. Add beans to slow cooker; cook, covered, on high until heated through, about 30 minutes. Serve sliced pork with bean mixture.

**4 oz. cooked pork with ½ cup bean mixture:** 314 cal., 8g fat (3g sat. fat), 68mg chol., 579mg sod., 28g carb. (12g sugars, 5g fiber), 31g pro.

## SAUCY RASPBERRY CHICKEN

*I first had this dish as a teenage babysitter, when the children's mom prepared it for us to eat while she was out. The kids loved it, and so did I! Now I make it for my own kids.*
—Melissa Wales, Elephant Butte, NM

**Prep:** 15 min. • **Cook:** 5 hours
**Makes:** 5 servings

- 5 chicken leg quarters, skin removed
- ⅓ cup seedless raspberry spreadable fruit
- 3 Tbsp. reduced-sodium soy sauce
- 1 tsp. spicy brown mustard
- ¼ tsp. pepper
- 2 Tbsp. cornstarch
- 2 Tbsp. cold water

**1.** Place chicken in a 3-qt. slow cooker. In a small bowl, combine the spreadable fruit, soy sauce, mustard and pepper; pour over chicken. Cover and cook on low for 5-6 hours or until meat is tender.
**2.** Remove chicken to a serving platter; keep warm. Skim fat from cooking juices; transfer to a small saucepan. Bring to a boil. Combine cornstarch and water until smooth; gradually stir into the pan. Bring to a boil; cook and stir for 2 minutes or until thickened. Serve with chicken.

**1 chicken leg quarter with ⅓ cup sauce:** 337 cal., 16g fat (4g sat. fat), 105mg chol., 468mg sod., 14g carb. (9g sugars, 0 fiber), 31g pro.

**APPLE BUTTER PORK WITH WHITE BEANS**

**BEEF DAUBE PROVENCAL**

## BEEF DAUBE PROVENCAL

*This dish is perfect on cold winter days, especially after we have been out cutting wood or white-tail hunting. If you are lucky enough to have venison, try it here for melt-in-your-mouth goodness.*
—Brenda Ryan, Marshall, MO

- - - - - - - - - - - - - - - - - - - - - - - - - - - - - -

**Prep:** 30 min. • **Cook:** 5 hours
**Makes:** 8 servings

2 tsp. olive oil
1 boneless beef chuck roast or venison roast (about 2 lbs.), cut into 1-in. cubes
1½ tsp. salt, divided
½ tsp. coarsely ground pepper, divided
2 cups chopped carrots
1½ cups chopped onion
12 garlic cloves, crushed
1 Tbsp. tomato paste

1 cup dry red wine
1 can (14½ oz.) diced tomatoes
½ cup beef broth
1 tsp. chopped fresh rosemary
1 tsp. chopped fresh thyme
1 bay leaf
Dash ground cloves
Hot cooked pasta or mashed potatoes
Fresh thyme leaves, optional

**1.** In a large skillet, heat oil over medium-high heat. Sprinkle the meat with ½ tsp. salt and ¼ tsp. pepper; brown the meat in batches. Transfer the beef to 4-qt. slow cooker.
**2.** Add the carrot, onion, garlic and the remaining salt and pepper to skillet; cook and stir until golden brown, 4-6 minutes. Add the tomato paste; cook and stir until fragrant, about 1 minute. Add red wine, stirring to loosen browned bits from pan; bring to a boil.

**3.** Transfer meat mixture, tomatoes, broth and seasonings to slow cooker. Cook, covered, on low 5-7 hours or until tender. Discard bay leaf. Serve with hot cooked pasta or mashed potatoes. If desired, sprinkle with fresh thyme.
**1 cup beef mixture:** 237 cal., 12g fat (4g sat. fat), 74mg chol., 651mg sod., 8g carb. (3g sugars, 2g fiber), 23g pro. **Diabetic exchanges:** 3 lean meat, 1 vegetable.

**DID YOU KNOW?**

Daube is a traditional braised French stew made with beef (often an inexpensive cut), vegetables, garlic and red wine.

## SLOW-COOKER CHICKEN CHOP SUEY

*If you're in for a busy evening, here's a great way to ensure you can still have a healthful supper. It's tasty and traditional, and easy, too!*
—Melody Littlewood, Royal City, WA

**Prep:** 20 min. • **Cook:** 5½ hours
**Makes:** 9 servings

- 1½ lbs. boneless skinless chicken thighs, cut into 2-in. pieces
- 8 oz. sliced fresh mushrooms
- 2 celery ribs, sliced
- 1 medium onion, chopped
- 1 can (14 oz.) bean sprouts, rinsed and drained
- 1 can (8 oz.) bamboo shoots, drained
- 1 can (8 oz.) sliced water chestnuts, drained
- 1 can (14½ oz.) reduced-sodium chicken broth
- ½ cup reduced-sodium soy sauce
- 1 Tbsp. minced fresh gingerroot
- ¼ tsp. crushed red pepper flakes
- 2 Tbsp. cornstarch
- 2 Tbsp. cold water
- ½ cup frozen shelled edamame
  Hot cooked rice

**1.** Place the chicken in a 4- or 5-qt. slow cooker. Top with the mushrooms, celery, onion, bean sprouts, bamboo shoots and water chestnuts. In a small bowl, combine the broth, soy sauce, ginger and pepper flakes. Pour over chicken and vegetables. Cover and cook on low until chicken is tender, 5-6 hours.
**2.** Combine cornstarch and water until smooth, gradually stir into chop suey. Add edamame, cover and cook on high until thickened, about 30 minutes. Serve with rice.

**1 cup:** 178 cal., 6g fat (2g sat. fat), 50mg chol., 739mg sod., 12g carb. (3g sugars, 3g fiber), 19g pro. **Diabetic exchanges:** 2 lean meat, 1 vegetable.

**SLOW-COOKER CHICKEN CHOP SUEY**

## ASIAN-STYLE ROUND STEAK

*My friend gave me this recipe two decades ago. All I added was a little more meat, the celery and mushrooms. My family loves it!*
—Marilyn Wolfe, Des Moines, IA

**Prep:** 20 min. • **Cook:** 7 hours
**Makes:** 8 servings

- 2 lbs. beef top round steak, cut into 3-in. strips
- 2 Tbsp. canola oil
- 3 celery ribs, chopped
- 1 cup chopped onion
- ¼ cup reduced-sodium soy sauce
- 1 tsp. sugar
- ½ tsp. minced garlic
- ¼ tsp. ground ginger
- ¼ tsp. pepper
- 2 medium green peppers, julienned
- 1 can (15 oz.) tomato sauce
- 1 can (14 oz.) bean sprouts, rinsed and drained
- 1 can (8 oz.) sliced water chestnuts, drained
- 1 jar (4½ oz.) sliced mushrooms, drained
- 1 Tbsp. cornstarch
- ½ cup cold water
  Hot cooked rice
  Minced chives, optional

**1.** In a large skillet, brown meat in oil on all sides. Transfer meat and drippings to a 5-qt. slow cooker. Combine the celery, onion, soy sauce, sugar, garlic, ginger and pepper; pour over meat. Cover and cook on low for 5½-6 hours or until the meat is tender.
**2.** Add green peppers, tomato sauce, bean sprouts, water chestnuts and mushrooms; cover and cook on low 1 hour longer.
**3.** Combine cornstarch and water until smooth; stir into beef mixture. Cover and cook on high for 30 minutes or until sauce is thickened. Serve with rice; if desired, sprinkle with chives.

**1 cup:** 237 cal., 8g fat (2g sat. fat), 63mg chol., 659mg sod., 14g carb. (4g sugars, 4g fiber), 29g pro. **Diabetic exchanges:** 3 meat, 1 starch, 1 fat.

# TREAT YOURSELF

"You can whip up this classic dessert on short notice if you keep cooked rice on hand. Cooked rice can be frozen in an airtight container for up to three months. Just thaw it in the refrigerator or microwave when you're ready to use it."

—Margaret DeChant, Newberry, MI

**Peach-Blueberry Crumble Tart** (p. 239) **Pumpkin Bars with Browned Butter Frosting** (p. 228) **Apple Fritter Cake** (p. 236)
**Peanut Butter Chocolate Chip Zucchini Cake** (p. 234) **Grandma's Rice Pudding** (p. 241) **Blueberry Rhubarb Country Tart** (p. 231)

## PUMPKIN BARS WITH BROWNED BUTTER FROSTING

(PICTURED ON P. 226)

*I based this recipe on one my grandmother used to make, so sweet memories are baked into every bar. When preparing the frosting, carefully watch the butter and remove it from the heat as soon as it starts to brown. Do not use margarine.*
—Mary Wilhelm, Sparta, WI

**Prep:** 30 min. • **Bake:** 20 min. + cooling
**Makes:** 2 dozen

- 1½ cups sugar
- 1 cup canned pumpkin
- ½ cup orange juice
- ½ cup canola oil
- 2 large eggs, room temperature
- 2 tsp. grated orange zest
- 2 cups all-purpose flour
- 2 tsp. baking powder
- 2 tsp. pumpkin pie spice
- 1 tsp. baking soda
- ¼ tsp. salt

FROSTING‡‡
- ⅔ cup butter, cubed
- 4 cups confectioners' sugar
- 1 tsp. vanilla extract
- 4 to 6 Tbsp. 2% milk

**1.** Preheat the oven to 350°. Grease a 15x10x1-in. baking pan. In a large bowl, beat the first 6 ingredients until well blended. In another bowl, whisk flour, baking powder, pie spice, baking soda and salt; gradually beat into pumpkin mixture.
**2.** Transfer to prepared pan. Bake until a toothpick inserted in center comes out clean, 18-22 minutes. Cool completely in pan on a wire rack.
**3.** In a small heavy saucepan, melt butter over medium heat. Heat 5-7 minutes or until golden brown, stirring constantly. Transfer to a large bowl. Gradually beat in confectioners' sugar, vanilla and enough milk to reach desired consistency. Spread over bars; let stand until set.
**1 bar:** 265 cal., 10g fat (4g sat. fat), 29mg chol., 166mg sod., 42g carb. (33g sugars, 1g fiber), 2g pro.

## COOKIES & CREAM BERRY DESSERTS

*This sweet berry dessert makes for an especially pretty final course. With berries, a creamy topping and a sprinkle of meringue cookies, it always earns raves.*
—Lily Julow, Lawrenceville, GA

**Prep:** 10 min. + standing
**Makes:** 6 servings

- 2 cups quartered fresh strawberries
- 1¼ cups fresh raspberries
- 1¼ cups fresh blackberries
- ⅔ cup fresh blueberries
- 4 Tbsp. sugar, divided
- 2 tsp. lemon juice
- 4 oz. reduced-fat cream cheese
- 1½ cups fat-free whipped topping
  Dash ground cinnamon
- 6 meringue cookies

**1.** In a large bowl, combine the berries, 2 Tbsp. sugar and lemon juice; let stand at room temperature for 30 minutes.
**2.** In a small bowl, beat cream cheese until smooth. Beat in the whipped topping, cinnamon and remaining sugar until combined. Just before serving, divide berry mixture among 6 dessert dishes. Dollop with topping and add a meringue cookie to each dish.
**1 serving:** 170 cal., 5g fat (3g sat. fat), 13mg chol., 93mg sod., 26g carb. (20g sugars, 5g fiber), 3g pro. **Diabetic exchanges:** 1 starch, 1 fruit, 1 fat.

**COOKIES & CREAM BERRY DESSERTS**

**PEAR OLIVE OIL CAKE**

## BUTTERNUT APPLE CRISP

*Someone brought this crisp to a parish dinner at my church. I asked for the recipe, and now I take this yummy dessert to every potluck I attend.*
—Therese Butler, Ijamsville, MD

- - - - - - - - - - - - - - - - - - - -

**Prep:** 15 min. • **Bake:** 1¼ hours
**Makes:** 9 servings

¾ cup packed brown sugar, divided
1 tsp. ground cinnamon
½ tsp. salt
2 lbs. butternut squash, peeled, seeded and thinly sliced (about 4 cups)
1 can (21 oz.) apple pie filling
2 Tbsp. lemon juice
½ cup all-purpose flour
½ cup quick-cooking oats
6 Tbsp. cold butter, cubed

**1.** In a large bowl, combine ½ cup brown sugar, cinnamon and salt. Add squash, pie filling and lemon juice.
**2.** Pour the mixture into a greased 9-in. square baking dish. Cover and bake at 350° for 30 minutes.
**3.** In a small bowl, combine the flour, oats and remaining brown sugar. Cut in butter until mixture resembles coarse crumbs. Sprinkle over squash mixture.
**4.** Bake 45-50 minutes longer or until the topping is golden brown and the squash is tender.

**1 piece:** 285 cal., 8g fat (5g sat. fat), 20mg chol., 248mg sod., 54g carb. (33g sugars, 4g fiber), 2g pro.

## PEAR OLIVE OIL CAKE

*This moist, flavorful seasonal cake complements any holiday meal. Apples can be used instead of pears if you'd like.*
—Andrea Potischman, Menlo Park, CA

- - - - - - - - - - - - - - - - - - - -

**Prep:** 15 min • **Bake:** 55 min + cooling
**Makes:** 12 servings

1¼ cups plus 2 tsp. packed brown sugar, divided
½ cup olive oil
3 large eggs, room temperature
2 Tbsp. 2% milk
2 tsp. vanilla extract
1 cup all-purpose flour
¾ cup almond flour
2 tsp. baking powder
Dash salt
3 medium red pears, peeled and thinly sliced
¼ tsp. ground cinnamon
Sweetened whipped cream, optional

**1.** Preheat oven to 325°. Grease a 10-in. springform pan. Place pan on a baking sheet. In a large bowl, beat 1¼ cups brown sugar, oil, eggs, milk and vanilla until well blended. In another bowl, whisk flours, baking powder and salt; gradually beat into sugar mixture.
**2.** Transfer the batter to prepared pan. Arrange pear slices over top; sprinkle with the remaining 2 tsp. brown sugar and cinnamon. Bake until a toothpick inserted in center comes out clean, 55-60 minutes. Cool completely in pan on a wire rack. If desired, serve with whipped cream.
**1 piece:** 294 cal., 14g fat (2g sat. fat), 47mg chol., 121mg sod., 40g carb. (28g sugars, 2g fiber), 4g pro.
**\* HEALTH TIP \*** Olive oil keeps this cake tender and moist, and it's rich in healthy unsaturated fat. If this cake was made with the same amount of butter instead of olive oil, it would add nearly 5 grams of saturated fat per serving.

**HOLIDAY MERINGUE
MINIATURES**

## HOLIDAY MERINGUE MINIATURES

*My kids love these light melt-in-your-mouth cookies, and we have fun making them. These were always on our Christmas cookie plate when I was a kid, and now the tradition continues.*

—Susan Marshall, Colorado Springs, CO

- - - - - - - - - - - - - - - - - - - - - - - - - - - -

**Prep:** 20 min. • **Bake:** 1 hour + cooling
**Makes:** about 7 dozen

- 2 **large egg whites,
  room temperature**
- ½ **tsp. white vinegar
  Dash salt**
- ½ **tsp. almond extract**
- ½ **tsp. vanilla extract**
- ½ **cup sugar
  Red gel food coloring**

**1.** Preheat oven to 225°. Beat egg whites with vinegar and salt on medium speed until foamy and doubled in volume. Beat in extracts. Gradually add sugar, 1 Tbsp. at a time, beating on high after each addition until sugar is dissolved. Continue beating until stiff glossy peaks form (this may take 10 minutes).

**2.** Insert a ½-in. round tip into a pastry bag. Paint 5 stripes of red food coloring inside the length of pastry bag. Transfer the meringue to pastry bag; pipe dollops of meringue 1 in. apart onto parchment-lined baking sheets.

**3.** Bake for 1 hour or until set and dry. Turn off oven (do not open oven door); leave meringues in oven 1 hour. Remove and cool completely on baking sheets. Remove the meringues from the paper; store meringues in an airtight container at room temperature.

**1 meringue:** 5 cal., 0 fat (0 sat. fat), 0 chol., 19mg sod., 1g carb. (1g sugars, 0 fiber), 0 pro.
**Diabetic exchanges:** 1 free food.

## BANANA-PINEAPPLE ICE

*My family loves dessert and fruit, but we're trying to make healthier food choices. This refreshing five-ingredient summer treat is always a hit with us.*

—Myra Hughes, Malvern, AR

- - - - - - - - - - - - - - - - - - - - - - - - - - - -

**Prep:** 15 min. + freezing
**Makes:** 10 servings

- 2 **cups unsweetened apple juice**
- 2 **cups mashed ripe bananas**
- 1 **can (8 oz.) unsweetened crushed
  pineapple, undrained**
- 2 **Tbsp. lemon juice**
- 1 **tsp. vanilla extract**

**1.** In a large bowl, combine all ingredients. Pour into an 8-in. square dish. Cover and freeze 1½-2 hours or until almost firm.
**2.** Transfer to a large bowl. Beat until smooth and creamy, 1-2 minutes. Return mixture to dish; freeze until firm. Remove from freezer 30 minutes before serving.
**½ cup:** 79 cal., 0 fat (0 sat. fat), 0 chol., 2mg sod., 20g carb. (14g sugars, 1g fiber), 1g pro.
**Diabetic exchanges:** 1 fruit.
**\* HEALTH TIP \*** Substitute this for your usual scoop of ice cream and save about 100 calories and 5 grams of saturated fat per serving. If you're still craving the decadence of real ice cream, mix some of your favorite flavor into this frozen treat—you'd still save big!

## EASY PUMPKIN PIE

*Pumpkin pie does not have to be difficult to make. This recipe has a wonderful taste and will be a hit at your holiday meal.*
—Marty Rummel, Trout Lake, WA

**Prep:** 10 min. • **Bake:** 50 min. + cooling
**Makes:** 8 servings

- 3  large eggs
- 1  cup canned pumpkin
- 1  cup evaporated milk
- ½  cup sugar
- ¼  cup maple syrup
- 1  tsp. ground cinnamon
- ½  tsp. salt
- ½  tsp. ground nutmeg
- ½  tsp. maple flavoring
- ½  tsp. vanilla extract
- 1  frozen deep-dish pie crust (9 in.)
   Pastry for a single-crust pie, optional
   Whipped cream, optional

**1.** In a large bowl, beat first 10 ingredients until smooth; pour into pie crust. Cover edge loosely with foil.
**2.** Bake at 400° for 10 minutes. Reduce heat to 350°; bake 40-45 minutes longer or until a knife inserted in the center comes out clean. Remove foil. Cool on a wire rack.
**3.** If decorative cutouts are desired, roll pie dough to ⅛-in. thickness; cut out with 1-in. to 1½-in. leaf-shaped cookie cutters. With a sharp knife, score leaf veins on crust cutouts.
**4.** Place on an ungreased baking sheet. Bake at 400° for 6-8 minutes or until golden brown. Remove to a wire rack to cool. Arrange around edge of pie. Garnish with whipped cream if desired.
**1 piece:** 275 cal., 11g fat (5g sat. fat), 94mg chol., 306mg sod., 38g carb. (24g sugars, 1g fiber), 6g pro.

## BLUEBERRY RHUBARB COUNTRY TART

**(PICTURED ON P. 227)**

*When the rhubarb comes in, mix it with blueberries for a rustic and bubbly tart. Offer it to a friend with a warm cup of tea.*
—Jeanne Ambrose, Milwaukee, WI

**Prep:** 15 min. • **Bake:** 40 min.
**Makes:** 8 servings

   Pastry for single-crust pie
- ¾  cup sugar
- ¼  cup all-purpose flour
- 4  cups chopped fresh or frozen rhubarb, thawed
- 1  cup fresh or frozen blueberries, thawed
- 2  Tbsp. 2% milk
- 1  Tbsp. coarse sugar

**1.** Preheat oven to 400°. On a lightly floured surface, roll dough into a 14-in. circle. Transfer to a parchment-lined baking sheet.
**2.** In a large bowl, mix the sugar and flour. Add the rhubarb and blueberries; toss to coat. Spoon filling over crust to within 2 in. of edge. Fold crust edge over filling, pleating as you go and leaving a 4-in. opening in the center. Brush folded crust with milk; sprinkle with coarse sugar. Bake 40-45 minutes or until the crust is golden and filling is bubbly. Transfer the tart to a wire rack to cool.
**1 piece:** 290 cal., 12g fat (7g sat. fat), 30mg chol., 159mg sod., 44g carb. (23g sugars, 2g fiber), 3g pro.
**Pastry for single-crust pie (9 in.):** Combine 1¼ cups all-purpose flour and ¼ tsp. salt; cut in ½ cup cold butter until crumbly. Gradually add 3-5 Tbsp. ice water, tossing with a fork until dough holds together when pressed. Wrap and refrigerate for 1 hour.

**EASY PUMPKIN PIE**

**PEACH CRUMBLE DESSERT**

## CHERRY CRANBERRY PINWHEELS

*With the combination of cranberries, cherries, orange zest and cinnamon, these festive cookies are as fragrant as they are flavorful.*
—Deb Perry, Bluffton, IN

**Prep:** 1 hour + chilling
**Bake:** 10 min./batch • **Makes:** 4½ dozen

1½ cups dried cranberries
1 jar (10 oz.) cherry spreadable fruit
¼ cup water
½ tsp. ground cinnamon
DOUGH
¼ cup butter, softened
1¼ cups sugar
3 large egg whites, room temperature
3 Tbsp. canola oil
2 Tbsp. fat-free milk
2 tsp. vanilla extract
1½ tsp. grated orange zest
3⅓ cups all-purpose flour
¾ tsp. baking powder
½ tsp. ground cinnamon
⅛ tsp. baking soda

**1.** For filling, combine first 4 ingredients in a small saucepan. Cook and stir over medium heat for 8 minutes or until liquid is absorbed and cranberries are softened. Remove from heat; cool slightly. Transfer to a blender; cover and process until smooth. Transfer to a bowl; cover and refrigerate until chilled.
**2.** For dough, in a large bowl, beat butter and sugar for 2 minutes or until crumbly. Beat in the egg whites, oil, milk, vanilla and zest. Combine flour, baking powder, cinnamon and baking soda; gradually add to sugar mixture and mix well.
**3.** Divide the dough in half. On a floured surface, roll 1 portion of dough into a 14x9-in. rectangle. Spread with half of the filling. Roll up jelly-roll style, starting with a long side. Repeat with remaining dough and filling. Wrap each roll in waxed paper; refrigerate for at least 4 hours.
**4.** Unwrap dough; cut into ½-in. slices. Place slices 2 in. apart on greased baking sheets. Bake at 375° for 10-12 minutes or until bottoms are lightly browned (do not overbake). Remove to wire racks to cool.
**1 cookie:** 83 cal., 2g fat (1g sat. fat), 2mg chol., 21mg sod., 16g carb. (9g sugars, 0 fiber), 1g pro. **Diabetic exchanges:** 1 starch, ½ fat.

## PEACH CRUMBLE DESSERT
*We save our forks after dinner so we can enjoy this yummy, old-fashioned dessert. It's delicious and so easy to make—and wonderful with ice cream.*
—Nancy Horsburgh, Everett, ON

**Prep:** 15 min. • **Bake:** 35 min.
**Makes:** 12 servings

6 cups sliced peeled ripe peaches
¼ cup packed brown sugar
3 Tbsp. all-purpose flour
1 tsp. lemon juice
½ tsp. grated lemon zest
½ tsp. ground cinnamon
TOPPING
1 cup all-purpose flour
1 cup sugar
1 tsp. baking powder
¼ tsp. salt
¼ tsp. ground nutmeg
1 large egg, room temperature, lightly beaten
½ cup butter, melted and cooled
Vanilla ice cream, optional

**1.** Preheat oven to 375°. Place peaches in a greased shallow 2½-qt. Dutch oven, cast-iron pan or 2½-qt. ovenproof baking dish. In a small bowl, combine the brown sugar, flour, lemon juice, lemon zest and cinnamon; sprinkle over the peaches.
**2.** Combine flour, sugar, baking powder, salt and nutmeg. Stir in the egg until the mixture resembles coarse crumbs. Sprinkle over the peaches. Pour butter evenly over topping.
**3.** Bake 35-40 minutes. If desired, serve with ice cream.
**1 serving:** 237 cal., 8g fat (5g sat. fat), 38mg chol., 167mg sod., 40g carb. (28g sugars, 2g fiber), 2g pro.

> **TEST KITCHEN TIP**
>
> Go for freshly squeezed lemon juice when preparing this recipe. Bottled lemon juice, which is from concentrate, won't provide the same bright, fresh flavor.

CHERRY CRANBERRY
PINWHEELS

## PEANUT BUTTER CHOCOLATE CHIP ZUCCHINI CAKE

(PICTURED ON P. 226)

*Years ago, I added some zucchini to a peanut butter bar I had created, and this time I wanted to try it with a cake. The zucchini make the cake super moist, but doesn't get in the way of the chocolate and peanut butter goodness.*
—Marilyn Blankschien, Clintonville, WI

**Prep:** 20 min. • **Bake:** 20 min.
**Makes:** 10 servings

- ⅓ cup creamy peanut butter
- ¼ cup butter, softened
- 1 cup packed brown sugar
- 1½ cups all-purpose flour, divided
- ½ tsp. salt
- ½ tsp. baking soda
- 1 large egg, room temperature
- 1 tsp. vanilla extract
- ¼ cup buttermilk
- 1 cup shredded zucchini
- ¼ tsp. ground cinnamon
- ½ cup semisweet chocolate chips

**1.** Preheat oven to 350°. In a large bowl, cream peanut butter, butter and brown sugar until blended. In another bowl, whisk 1¼ cups flour, salt and baking soda; add to creamed mixture. Beat just until mixture is sandy. Remove ½ cup crumb mixture for topping.

**2.** To remaining mixture, beat in remaining flour, egg, vanilla and buttermilk. Stir in the zucchini. Spread into a greased 9-in. round baking pan. Stir cinnamon into reserved topping. Sprinkle over batter; top with chocolate chips.

**3.** Bake 20-25 minutes or until a toothpick inserted in center comes out with moist crumbs. Cool in pan on a wire rack.

**1 piece:** 297 cal., 12g fat (6g sat. fat), 31mg chol., 281mg sod., 44g carb. (28g sugars, 2g fiber), 5g pro.

> **TEST KITCHEN TIP**
> If you like a chunky streusel topping, squeeze it into clumps as you sprinkle it over the batter.

## GINGERED APRICOT-APPLE CRUMBLE

*Hot or cold, plain or topped with ice cream, this crumble is tasty. If you'd like, leave out the apricots to make traditional apple crisp instead.*
—Sylvia Rice, Didsbury, AB

**Prep:** 15 min. • **Bake:** 50 min.
**Makes:** 12 servings

- 1 cup apricot nectar
- ¾ cup finely chopped dried apricots
- ⅓ cup honey
- ¼ cup maple syrup
- 2 Tbsp. lemon juice
- 8 cups sliced peeled tart apples (about 8 large)
- 3 Tbsp. all-purpose flour
- 1 tsp. ground cinnamon
- ½ tsp. ground ginger
- ½ tsp. ground cardamom

**TOPPING**

- ¾ cup all-purpose flour
- ½ cup quick-cooking oats
- ½ cup chopped pecans, optional
- ¼ cup canola oil
- ¼ cup maple syrup

**1.** In a large bowl, combine the first 5 ingredients; set aside. Arrange apples in an ungreased 13x9-in. baking dish.

**2.** Combine flour, cinnamon, ginger and cardamom; stir into the apricot mixture. Spoon over apples.

**3.** Combine topping ingredients; sprinkle over fruit. Bake at 350° for 50-60 minutes or until topping is golden brown and fruit is tender.

**1 serving:** 228 cal., 5g fat (1g sat. fat), 0 chol., 8mg sod., 46g carb. (32g sugars, 3g fiber), 2g pro.

GINGERED APRICOT-APPLE CRUMBLE

## NO-FRY FRIED ICE CREAM

*This ice cream has a crispy cinnamon coating just like the fried ice cream served at Mexican restaurants, but minus the oily mess. Make it ahead of time and freeze until serving.*
—Tim White, Windsor, ON

----

**Prep:** 15 min. + freezing
**Bake:** 5 min. + freezing • **Makes:** 8 servings

1   qt. vanilla ice cream
¼   cup packed brown sugar
1   Tbsp. butter, melted
1   tsp. ground cinnamon
2   cups crushed cornflakes
     Optional: Whipped cream and
     caramel ice cream topping

**1.** Preheat oven to 350°. Using a ½-cup ice cream scoop, place 8 scoops of ice cream on a baking sheet. Freeze until firm, about 1 hour. Meanwhile, combine brown sugar, butter and cinnamon. Stir in cornflakes. Transfer to an ungreased 15x10x1-in. baking pan. Bake until lightly browned, 4-6 minutes. Cool completely.
**2.** Roll ice cream balls in crumb mixture. Cover and freeze until firm, at least 1 hour. If desired, serve with toppings.
**½ cup:** 216 cal., 8g fat (5g sat. fat), 32mg chol., 168mg sod., 33g carb. (20g sugars, 1g fiber), 3g pro.

## TRIPLE FRUIT FREEZE

*These pops won't turn your tongue blue or neon green like many store-bought pops because they're made with fresh grapes, blueberries and kiwifruit. What could be better?*
—Colleen Ludovice, Wauwatosa, WI

----

**Prep:** 20 min. + freezing • **Makes:** 10 pops

1   cup sliced peeled kiwifruit (about 3 medium)
1   cup water, divided
2   Tbsp. sugar, divided
10  wooden pop sticks and 10 freezer pop molds or 10 paper cups (3 oz. each)
1   cup fresh blueberries or frozen unsweetened blueberries
½   cup seedless red grapes
½   cup red grape juice

**1.** Place kiwi, ½ cup water and 1 Tbsp. sugar in a food processor; pulse until combined. Pour into molds or paper cups. Top molds or paper cups with foil and insert sticks through foil. Freeze until firm, about 2 hours.
**2.** Place blueberries and the remaining water and sugar in food processor; pulse until combined. Spoon over the kiwi layer. Freeze, covered, until firm, about 2 hours.
**3.** Wipe food processor clean. Repeat with grapes and grape juice. Spoon over blueberry layer. Freeze, covered, until firm.
**1 pop:** 50 cal., 0 fat (0 sat. fat), 0 chol., 3mg sod., 12g carb. (10g sugars, 1g fiber), 0 pro.
**Diabetic exchanges:** 1 starch.

## APPLE FRITTER CAKE
(PICTURED ON P. 227)

*I was experimenting with a beer bread to make it into a dessert when I came up with this delectable cake. It tastes just like our favorite apple fritters.*
—Ann Marie Eberhart, Gig Harbor, WA

- - - - - - - - - - - - - - - - - - - - - - - - -

**Prep:** 10 min. • **Bake:** 40 min. + cooling
**Makes:** 12 servings

- 3   cups all-purpose flour, sifted
- ¼   cup sugar
- 2   Tbsp. ground cinnamon
- 3   tsp. baking powder
- 1   tsp. salt
- 2   medium apples, peeled and chopped (about 2 cups)
- 1   bottle (12 oz.) beer or unsweetened apple juice, room temperature
- ¼   cup butter, melted

ICING
- 2   cups confectioners' sugar
- 3   to 5 Tbsp. 2% milk
- ½   tsp. vanilla extract

**1.** Preheat oven to 350°. Line an 8-in. square baking pan with parchment, letting ends extend up sides.
**2.** Whisk together the first 5 ingredients. Add the apples and beer; mix just until blended (do not overmix; batter will be thick). Transfer to prepared pan. Bake until a toothpick inserted in center comes out clean, 40-45 minutes.
**3.** Lifting with parchment, immediately remove the cake from pan. Brush all sides with melted butter. Cool. Meanwhile, combine all icing ingredients. Spread or drizzle over cooled cake.

**1 piece:** 261 cal., 4g fat (3g sat. fat), 10mg chol., 350mg sod., 52g carb. (27g sugars, 2g fiber), 4g pro.

**WINTER FRUIT WITH PROSECCO SABAYON**

## WINTER FRUIT WITH PROSECCO SABAYON

*This recipe is special to me because it allows me to treat my dinner guests to a special, unusual dessert. The bright, vivid colors are perfect for the holidays. Substitute sparkling grape juice when serving to children.*
—Jerry Gulley, Pleasant Prairie, WI

- - - - - - - - - - - - - - - - - - - - - - - - -

**Takes:** 25 min.
**Makes:** 6 servings (¾ cup sauce)

- 6   medium blood oranges, peeled and cut into ¼-in. slices
- 1   vanilla bean, split
- ¼   cup sugar plus 3 Tbsp. sugar, divided
- ½   cup Prosecco or other sparkling wine, divided
      Dash salt
- 3   large egg yolks

**1.** Arrange orange slices on a serving platter or individual plates. Scrape the vanilla bean seeds into a small bowl. Add ¼ cup sugar, ¼ cup Prosecco and salt; combine and drizzle over oranges. Refrigerate until serving.
**2.** In a double boiler or metal bowl over simmering water, constantly whisk the egg yolks and remaining sugar and Prosecco until mixture reaches 160° and coats the back of a spoon. Drizzle over oranges. Serve immediately.

**1 sliced orange with 2 Tbsp. sauce:**
151 cal., 3g fat (1g sat. fat), 92mg chol., 249mg sod., 26g carb. (24g sugars, 2g fiber), 2g pro.
**Diabetic exchanges:** 1 starch, 1 fruit, ½ fat.

**TEST KITCHEN TIP**

With a bright rosy color, blood oranges can make a stunning dessert, but they are available for only a short amount of time. Grab them when you can, but feel free to substitute navel oranges, tangerines or pink grapefruit when the season is over.

# PUMPKIN BAKED ALASKA

*For years, I was a flop at making pumpkin pies. So I pulled out this recipe, which I got at a cooking class. It's been dazzling people ever since.*
—Linda Sanner, Portage, WI

**Prep:** 50 min. + freezing • **Bake:** 5 min.
**Makes:** 12 servings

- 1   qt. vanilla ice cream, softened
- 2   tsp. pumpkin pie spice
  Confectioners' sugar
- 2   large eggs, room temperature
- 1¼ cups sugar, divided
- 3   Tbsp. plus 5 tsp. water, divided
- ½   tsp. vanilla extract
- ⅔   cup cake flour
- ½   tsp. baking powder
- ⅛   tsp. salt
- 5   large egg whites
- ½   tsp. cream of tartar
- 1   tsp. rum extract
- 2   Tbsp. sliced almonds, toasted

**1.** In a large bowl, combine the ice cream and pumpkin pie spice. Transfer to a 1½-qt. bowl lined with plastic wrap; freeze until set.

**2.** Line a greased 9-in. round baking pan with waxed paper; grease paper and set aside. Place a clean kitchen towel over a wire rack; dust towel with confectioners' sugar; set aside.

**3.** In a large bowl, beat eggs, ½ cup sugar, 3 Tbsp. water and vanilla until thick and lemon-colored. Combine the flour, baking powder and salt; fold into egg mixture. Pour into prepared pan.

**4.** Bake at 375° for 12-14 minutes or until cake springs back when lightly touched. Immediate run a knife around the edge of the pan; invert onto prepared kitchen towel. Gently peel off the waxed paper; cool completely.

**5.** Place cake on an ungreased freezer to oven-safe platter or foil-lined baking sheet. Unmold ice cream onto cake; remove plastic wrap. Return to freezer.

**6.** In a heavy saucepan, combine the egg whites, cream of tartar and remaining sugar and water; beat on low speed with a portable mixer for 1 minute. Continue beating over low heat until the mixture reaches 160°, about 10 minutes. Remove from the heat. Add extract; beat until stiff peaks form, about 4 minutes.

**7.** Spread meringue over frozen ice cream and cake, sealing meringue to the platter; sprinkle with almonds. Freeze until ready to serve, up to 24 hours.

**8.** Just before serving, broil on the lowest oven rack position for 3-5 minutes or until the meringue is light browned. Serve immediately.

**1 piece:** 225 cal., 6g fat (3g sat. fat), 55mg chol., 110mg sod., 38g carb. (28g sugars, 0 fiber), 5g pro.

PUMPKIN BAKED ALASKA

TREAT YOURSELF

## HOMEMADE RHUBARB UPSIDE-DOWN CAKE

*This light and airy yellow cake is not too sweet, and the caramelized rhubarb topping adds tangy flavor and eye appeal. We like it with a scoop of strawberry ice cream.*
—Joyce Rowe, Stratham, NH

**Prep:** 30 min. • **Bake:** 40 min. + cooling
**Makes:** 12 servings

- ⅔ cup packed brown sugar
- 3 Tbsp. butter, melted
- 2¼ cups diced fresh or frozen rhubarb
- 4½ tsp. sugar
- BATTER
- 6 Tbsp. butter, softened
- ¾ cup sugar
- 2 large eggs, separated, room temperature
- 1 tsp. vanilla extract
- 1 cup plus 2 Tbsp. all-purpose flour
- 1½ tsp. baking powder
- ½ tsp. salt
- ¼ cup milk
- ¼ tsp. cream of tartar
  Optional: Whipped cream or vanilla ice cream

**1.** In a small bowl, combine brown sugar and butter. Spread into a greased 10-in. cast-iron or other ovenproof skillet. Layer with rhubarb and sprinkle with sugar. Set aside.
**2.** In a large bowl, cream butter and sugar until light and fluffy, 5-7 minutes. Beat in egg yolks and vanilla. Combine the flour, baking powder and salt; add to creamed mixture alternately with milk, beating well after each addition.
**3.** In a small bowl, beat egg whites and cream of tartar on medium speed until stiff peaks form. Gradually fold into the creamed mixture, about ½ cup at a time. Gently spoon over rhubarb.
**4.** Bake at 325° until cake springs back when lightly touched, 40-50 minutes. Cool for 10 minutes before inverting onto a serving plate. If desired, serve warm with whipped cream or ice cream.
**1 piece:** 240 cal., 10g fat (6g sat. fat), 59mg chol., 254mg sod., 36g carb. (27g sugars, 1g fiber), 3g pro.

## PEACH-BLUEBERRY CRUMBLE TART

**(PICTURED ON P. 226)**
*This easy tart is a family favorite, fresh out of the oven or at room temperature with a scoop of vanilla ice cream.*
—James Schend, Pleasant Prairie, WI

**Prep:** 30 min. • **Bake:** 35 min. + cooling
**Makes:** 12 servings

- 1⅓ cups all-purpose flour
- ¼ cup sugar
- ¼ tsp. ground cinnamon
- ½ cup butter, melted
- 2 cups frozen unsweetened blueberries, thawed
- 2 cups frozen unsweetened sliced peaches, thawed
- 1 Tbsp. honey
- CRUMB TOPPING
- ¼ cup all-purpose flour
- ¼ cup packed brown sugar
- ¼ cup old-fashioned oats
- ¼ cup chopped pecans
- ⅛ tsp. ground cloves
- 2 Tbsp. butter, melted

**1.** Preheat oven to 350°. In a small bowl, mix flour, sugar and cinnamon; stir in the butter just until blended. Press into a 9-in. fluted tart pan with removable bottom. Bake for 15-20 minutes or until lightly browned. Cool on a wire rack.
**2.** Meanwhile, in a large bowl, combine blueberries, peaches and honey; toss to coat. In a small bowl, combine first 5 topping ingredients; stir in butter.
**3.** Spoon fruit mixture into crust; sprinkle with topping. Bake at 350° 35-40 minutes or until topping is golden brown and filling is bubbly. Cool on a wire rack for at least 15 minutes before serving.
**1 piece:** 229 cal., 12g fat (6g sat. fat), 25mg chol., 70mg sod., 30g carb. (15g sugars, 2g fiber), 3g pro.

**READER REVIEW**

*"Delicious and easy to prepare. My peaches weren't the sweetest, so I added an extra 2 Tbsp. of brown sugar and 1 more Tbsp. of melted butter to the topping."*
—IV712LN, TASTEOFHOME.COM

## APPLE PANDOWDY

*This apple pandowdy, which comes from a very old cookbook, is tangy and delicious.*
—Doreen Lindquist, Thompson, MB

**Prep:** 25 min. • **Bake:** 55 min.
**Makes:** 9 servings

- 1 cup packed brown sugar
- 1¼ cups all-purpose flour, divided
- ½ tsp. salt, divided
- 1 cup water
- 1 tsp. lemon juice
- 2 tsp. baking powder
- 5 Tbsp. butter, divided
- ¾ cup 2% milk
- 5 cups sliced peeled apples
- ½ tsp. plus ⅛ tsp. ground cinnamon, divided
- ½ tsp. ground nutmeg
- 1 tsp. vanilla extract
- 1 Tbsp. coarse sugar
  Whipped cream, optional

**1.** In a saucepan, combine brown sugar, ¼ cup flour and ¼ tsp. salt. Add water and lemon juice; cook and stir over medium heat until thick. Cover and set aside.

**2.** In a bowl, combine baking powder and remaining flour and salt. Cut in 3 Tbsp. butter. Add the milk and mix just until moistened (a few lumps will remain); set aside.

**3.** Arrange apples in a 1½-qt. baking dish; sprinkle with ½ tsp. cinnamon. Add the nutmeg, vanilla and remaining butter to sauce; pour over apples. Drop dough by spoonfuls over sauce. Combine remaining cinnamon and coarse sugar; sprinkle over dough. Bake at 350° until top is brown and apples are tender, about 55 minutes. Serve pandowdy warm, with whipped cream if desired.

**1 serving:** 260 cal., 7g fat (4g sat. fat), 20mg chol., 304mg sod., 47g carb. (33g sugars, 2g fiber), 3g pro.

## TUSCAN ORANGE CRANBERRY CAKE

*This recipe came to be through much trial and error. Growing up, my family used farina flour in desserts, and I thought it would lend a nice texture to this cake. It's an Old-World Italian-style cake—delicious but not too sweet. The combination of orange and cranberry is perfect!*
—Ninette Holbrook, Orlando, FL

**Prep:** 25 min. • **Bake:** 20 min. + cooling
**Makes:** 8 servings

- ⅓ cup sugar
- ⅓ cup canola oil
- 2 large eggs, room temperature
- 1 Tbsp. grated orange zest
- 1 Tbsp. orange juice
- ⅓ cup all-purpose flour
- ⅓ cup cream of wheat or farina flour
- ½ tsp. salt
- ¼ tsp. baking powder
- ⅓ cup dried cranberries, chopped
- ¼ cup sliced almonds

### ORANGE GLAZE

- ¾ cup confectioners' sugar
- 1 Tbsp. orange juice
- 2 tsp. 2% milk
  Grated orange zest, optional

**1.** Preheat oven to 350°. Grease an 8-in. round baking pan.

**2.** In a large bowl, beat sugar, oil, eggs, orange zest and juice until well blended. In another bowl, whisk flour, cream of wheat, salt and baking powder; gradually beat into oil mixture. Stir in cranberries.

**3.** Transfer to prepared pan; sprinkle with almonds. Bake until a toothpick inserted in center comes out clean, 20-25 minutes.

**4.** Combine glaze ingredients; pour over warm cake. Cool for 10 minutes before serving. If desired, sprinkle the cake with orange zest.

**1 slice:** 263 cal., 12g fat (1g sat. fat), 47mg chol., 182mg sod., 36g carb. (25g sugars, 1g fiber), 4g pro.

**TUSCAN ORANGE CRANBERRY CAKE**

**BLACKBERRY
DAIQUIRI SHERBET**

## GRANDMA'S RICE PUDDING

*You can whip up this classic dessert on short notice if you keep cooked rice on hand. Cooked rice can be frozen in an airtight container for up to three months. Just thaw it in the refrigerator or microwave when you're ready to use it.*
—Margaret DeChant, Newberry, MI

**Prep:** 10 min. • **Bake:** 45 min.
**Makes:** 6 servings

- 1½ cups cooked rice
- ¼ cup raisins
- 2 large eggs
- 1½ cups whole milk
- ½ cup sugar
- ½ tsp. ground nutmeg
  Additional milk, optional

**1.** Place rice and raisins in a greased 1-qt. casserole. In a small bowl, whisk the eggs, milk, sugar and nutmeg; pour over rice.
**2.** Bake, uncovered, at 375° until a knife inserted in the center comes out clean, 45-50 minutes. Cool. Pour milk over each serving if desired. Refrigerate leftovers.
**1 cup:** 197 cal., 4g fat (2g sat. fat), 79mg chol., 52mg sod., 36g carb. (23g sugars, 0 fiber), 5g pro.

## BLACKBERRY DAIQUIRI SHERBET

*This summer I decided to try making sherbet, which is one of my favorites. Blackberries were in season in my mom's garden, and I love the flavor of daiquiris. The two blend together beautifully!*
—Shelly Bevington, Hermiston, OR

**Prep:** 15 min. • **Process:** 30 min. + freezing
**Makes:** 1¼ qt.

- 3 cups fresh or frozen blackberries, thawed
- 1 cup sugar
- ¼ tsp. salt
- 1 can (12 oz.) evaporated milk
- 2 Tbsp. lime juice
- 1 tsp. rum extract
- ½ tsp. citric acid

**1.** Place blackberries, sugar and salt in a food processor; process until smooth. Press through a fine-mesh strainer into a bowl; discard the seeds and pulp. Stir remaining ingredients into puree.
**2.** Fill the cylinder of ice cream maker no more than two-thirds full; freeze according to the manufacturer's directions. Transfer sherbet to freezer containers, allowing headspace for expansion. Freeze until firm, 8 hours or overnight.
**½ cup:** 147 cal., 3g fat (2g sat. fat), 12mg chol., 96mg sod., 28g carb. (26g sugars, 2g fiber), 3g pro.

**DID YOU KNOW?**

Using real rum instead of extract might seem like a fun idea, but the alcohol will keep your dessert from freezing solid. Better to stick with extract, which delivers highly concentrated rum flavor.

ROASTED STRAWBERRY
SHEET CAKE

## ROASTED STRAWBERRY SHEET CAKE

*My Grandma Gigi loved summer berry cakes. Almost any time I'd call her during the warmer months, she'd invite me over to taste her latest masterpiece. This cake is an ode to her.*
—Kristin Bowers, Rancho Palos Verdes, CA

- - - - - - - - - - - - - - - - - - - - - - - - - - - - -

**Prep:** 1 hour • **Bake:** 30 min. + cooling
**Makes:** 24 servings

- 4 **lbs. halved fresh strawberries**
- ½ **cup sugar**

CAKE

- 1 **cup butter, softened**
- 1½ **cups sugar**
- 2 **large eggs, room temperature**
- 2 **tsp. almond extract**
- 3 **cups all-purpose flour**
- 3 **tsp. baking powder**
- 2 **tsp. salt**
- 1 **cup 2% milk**
- ¼ **cup turbinado (washed raw) sugar**

**1.** Preheat oven to 350°. Place the strawberries on a parchment-lined rimmed baking sheet. Sprinkle with sugar and toss to coat. Bake until just tender, 35-40 minutes. Cool slightly.
**2.** Meanwhile, grease a 15x10x1-in. baking pan. In a large bowl, cream butter and sugar until light and fluffy, 5-7 minutes. Add 1 egg at a time, beating well after each addition. Beat in extract. In another bowl, whisk flour, baking powder and salt; add to creamed mixture alternately with milk, beating well after each addition (batter may appear curdled).

**3.** Transfer to the prepared pan. Top with 3 cups roasted strawberries; sprinkle with turbinado sugar. Reserve the remaining strawberries for serving. Bake until a toothpick inserted in center comes out clean, 30-35 minutes. Cool completely in pan on a wire rack. Serve with reserved roasted strawberries.
**1 piece:** 235 cal., 9g fat (5g sat. fat), 37mg chol., 329mg sod., 37g carb. (23g sugars, 2g fiber), 3g pro.

**TEST KITCHEN TIP**

It's important to just halve the strawberries, not quarter them. If they're too small, they will sink into the cake. When roasting the berries, use a rimmed baking sheet to capture all the juices that will be released.

## PEAR RASPBERRY CRISP

*We grow our own luscious red raspberries and feast on them fresh and freeze them for winter. This simple recipe combines the berries with fresh pears and a crunchy cereal topping.*
—Fancheon Resler, Albion, IN

**Prep:** 15 min. • **Bake:** 25 min. + cooling
**Makes:** 6 servings

- 2 cups sliced peeled fresh pears
- 2 cups fresh or frozen raspberries
- ¾ cup packed brown sugar, divided
- 1 tsp. ground cinnamon, divided
- ½ cup all-purpose flour
- 3 Tbsp. cold butter
- 1 cup cranberry almond whole grain cereal, lightly crushed
  Vanilla ice cream, optional

**1.** In a large bowl, combine the pears, raspberries, ¼ cup brown sugar and ½ tsp. cinnamon. Spoon into a greased 9-in. pie plate.

**2.** In a small bowl, combine the flour and remaining brown sugar and cinnamon; cut in butter until the mixture resembles coarse crumbs. Stir in the cereal. Sprinkle over fruit.

**3.** Bake at 375° until filling is bubbly and topping is golden brown, 25-30 minutes. Cool for 10 minutes. Serve with ice cream if desired.

**1 serving:** 282 cal., 7g fat (4g sat. fat), 15mg chol., 102mg sod., 55g carb. (37g sugars, 5g fiber), 2g pro.

PEAR RASPBERRY CRISP

## FRUIT JUICE POPS

*I've used this recipe for years as a refreshing treat. My children enjoyed these pops more than any store-bought ones I ever brought home. They taste great with either pineapple or orange juice. Try freezing and serving them in cups made from hollowed-out oranges.*
—Barbara Stewart, Garland, TX

**Prep:** 25 min. + freezing • **Makes:** 1 dozen

- 2 cups water
- 1½ cups sugar
- 4 cups unsweetened apple juice
- 1 cup unsweetened pineapple or orange juice
- ½ cup lemon juice
- 12 freezer pop molds or 12 paper cups (3 oz. each) and wooden pop sticks

**1.** In a large saucepan, combine water and sugar; bring to a boil. Reduce heat; simmer, uncovered, for 3-4 minutes or until sugar is dissolved, stirring occasionally. Remove from the heat; stir in juices.

**2.** Fill molds or cups with ¼ cup juice mixture. Top the molds with holders. If using cups, top with foil and insert sticks through foil. Freeze until firm.

**1 pop:** 149 cal., 0 fat (0 sat. fat), 0 chol., 3mg sod., 38g carb. (36g sugars, 0 fiber), 0 pro.

CREAMY COCONUT
RICE PUDDING PARFAITS

## HONEY CINNAMON BARS

*My Aunt Ellie gave us the recipe for these sweet bar cookies with cinnamon and walnuts. Drizzle with icing, and serve with coffee or tea.*
—Diane Myers, Star, ID

**Prep:** 25 min. • **Bake:** 10 min. + cooling
**Makes:** 2 dozen

- 1 cup sugar
- ¾ cup canola oil
- ¼ cup honey
- 1 large egg, room temperature
- 2 cups all-purpose flour
- 1 tsp. baking soda
- 1 tsp. ground cinnamon
- ¼ tsp. salt
- 1 cup chopped walnuts, toasted

GLAZE
- 1 cup confectioners' sugar
- 2 Tbsp. mayonnaise
- 1 tsp. vanilla extract
- 1 to 2 Tbsp. water
  Additional toasted chopped walnuts, optional

**1.** Preheat oven to 350°. In a large bowl, beat sugar, oil, honey and egg until well blended. In another bowl, whisk flour, baking soda, cinnamon and salt; gradually beat into the sugar mixture. Stir in 1 cup of walnuts.
**2.** Spread into a greased 15x10x1-in. baking pan. Bake until golden brown (edges will puff up), 10-12 minutes. Cool completely on a wire rack.
**3.** For the glaze, in a small bowl, mix confectioners' sugar, mayonnaise, vanilla and enough water to reach the desired consistency; spread over top. If desired, sprinkle with additional walnuts. Let stand until set. Cut into bars. Refrigerate the leftovers.
**1 bar:** 206 cal., 11g fat (1g sat. fat), 8mg chol., 86mg sod., 25g carb. (16g sugars, 1g fiber), 2g pro.

## CREAMY COCONUT RICE PUDDING PARFAITS

*When my daughter's friends come over for lunch, she treats them to her tropical parfaits made with brown rice and coconut milk. They're fresh, creamy and comforting.*
—Suzanne Clark, Phoenix, AZ

**Prep:** 15 min. • **Cook:** 45 min.
**Makes:** 6 servings

- 2 cups 2% milk
- 1½ cups coconut milk
- 1½ cups cold cooked brown rice
- ¼ cup maple syrup
- ¼ tsp. salt
- 2 tsp. vanilla extract
- ¼ tsp. almond extract
- 2 medium oranges, peeled and sectioned
- 2 medium kiwifruit, peeled and sliced
- ¼ cup sliced almonds, toasted
  Toasted sweetened shredded coconut

**1.** In a large heavy saucepan, combine the first 5 ingredients; bring to a boil over medium heat. Reduce the heat to maintain a low simmer. Cook, uncovered, 35-45 minutes or until rice is soft and milk is almost absorbed, stirring occasionally.
**2.** Remove from heat; stir in extracts. Cool slightly. Serve warm or refrigerate, covered, and serve cold. To serve, spoon pudding into dishes. Top with fruit; sprinkle with almonds and coconut.
**1 serving:** 291 cal., 13g fat (10g sat. fat), 7mg chol., 157mg sod., 37g carb. (19g sugars, 3g fiber), 7g pro.
**Note:** To toast nuts and coconut, spread individually in a dry nonstick skillet and heat over low heat until lightly browned, stirring occasionally.

**HONEY CINNAMON BARS**

## JUMBLEBERRY CRUMBLE

*A friend brought this delicious down-home dessert to church, and everyone enjoyed it so much they showered her with compliments! She was kind enough to share the recipe. It's especially wonderful served warm with a dollop of creamy whipped topping.*
—Mary Ann Dell, Phoenixville, PA

**Prep:** 10 min. + standing • **Bake:** 45 min.
**Makes:** 8 servings

- 3 cups halved fresh strawberries
- 1½ cups fresh raspberries
- 1½ cups fresh blueberries
- ⅔ cup sugar
- 3 Tbsp. quick-cooking tapioca
- ½ cup all-purpose flour
- ½ cup quick-cooking oats
- ½ cup packed brown sugar
- 1 tsp. ground cinnamon
- ⅓ cup butter, melted
- Optional: Vanilla ice cream or sweetened whipped cream

**1.** In a large bowl, combine strawberries, raspberries and blueberries. Combine the sugar and tapioca; sprinkle over the berries and toss gently. Pour into a greased 11x7-in. baking dish; let stand for 15 minutes.

**2.** Meanwhile, in a small bowl, combine flour, oats, brown sugar and cinnamon. Stir in melted butter; sprinkle over the berry mixture.

**3.** Bake at 350° until filling is bubbly and topping is golden brown, 45-50 minutes. Serve warm and, if desired, with vanilla ice cream or sweetened whipped cream.

**1 piece:** 290 cal., 8g fat (5g sat. fat), 20mg chol., 84mg sod., 54g carb. (36g sugars, 4g fiber), 2g pro.

## NO-CRUST PUMPKIN PIE

*Baked in a water bath, this pie has a texture that's more like a custard than a traditional pumpkin pie. In place of canned or fresh pumpkin, I sometimes use cushaw, a type of crookneck squash.*
—Linda McClung, Robbinsville, NC

**Prep:** 5 min. • **Bake:** 50 min.
**Makes:** 8 servings

- 1¼ cups sugar
- 3 Tbsp. all-purpose flour
- 3 large eggs
- 2 cups canned pumpkin
- ¾ cup evaporated milk
- 1½ tsp. vanilla extract
- ¼ tsp. ground cinnamon, optional

In a bowl, combine the sugar and flour. Add eggs; mix well. Stir in the pumpkin, milk, vanilla and, if desired, cinnamon; mix until well blended. Pour into a greased 9-in. pie plate. Place the pie plate in a 15x10x1-in. baking pan; add ½ in. of hot water to pan. Bake at 350° until a knife inserted in the center comes out clean, 50-55 minutes. Cool on a wire rack.

**1 piece:** 211 cal., 4g fat (2g sat. fat), 87mg chol., 49mg sod., 40g carb. (35g sugars, 3g fiber), 5g pro.

JUMBLEBERRY CRUMBLE

**MAPLE-APPLE CLAFOUTI**

—Carol Klein, Franklin Square, NY

## QUICK MANGO SORBET

*Last summer, I decided to try my hand at making a passion fruit and mango sorbet. But fresh fruits require more prep and are difficult to find ripened at the same time. So I experimented using frozen fruit and juice, and voila! Both are readily available and inexpensive, too.*

**Takes:** 5 min. • **Makes:** 2½ cups

- 1 pkg. (16 oz.) frozen mango chunks, slightly thawed
- ½ cup passion fruit juice
- 2 Tbsp. sugar

Place all the ingredients in a blender; cover and process until smooth. Serve immediately. If desired, for a firmer texture, cover and freeze at least 3 hours.
**½ cup:** 91 cal., 0 fat (0 sat. fat), 0 chol., 2mg sod., 24g carb. (21g sugars, 2g fiber), 1g pro.

## MAPLE-APPLE CLAFOUTI

*This fruit pudding could not be easier to make! A traditional comfort food in France, it is often made with cherries. I use apples and maple syrup to give it real midwestern flair.*

—Bridget Klusman, Otsego, MI

**Prep:** 20 min. • **Bake:** 40 min.
**Makes:** 8 servings

- 4 medium tart apples, thinly sliced
- 2 Tbsp. lemon juice
- 4 large eggs
- 1¼ cups 2% milk
- ½ cup maple syrup
- 1 tsp. vanilla extract
- ½ cup all-purpose flour
- ½ tsp. ground cinnamon
  Dash salt
  Additional maple syrup, optional

**1.** Preheat oven to 375°. Toss the apples with lemon juice; place in a greased 2-qt. baking dish. In a large bowl, whisk eggs, milk, syrup and vanilla until combined. In another bowl, combine flour, cinnamon and salt; add to egg mixture. Pour batter over apples.
**2.** Bake until puffed and lightly browned, 40-50 minutes. Serve warm, or cool on a wire rack. If desired, serve with additional maple syrup.
**1 piece:** 177 cal., 3g fat (1g sat. fat), 96mg chol., 75mg sod., 32g carb. (22g sugars, 2g fiber), 5g pro. **Diabetic exchanges:** 1½ starch, ½ fruit, ½ fat.

> **TEST KITCHEN TIP**
> When it's pulled right out of the oven, this is a showstopping masterpiece, all puffed up and golden brown. However, when it sits, it will deflate a little bit. So if you're looking to impress folks, serve it hot out of the oven.

## CARAMEL-PECAN APPLE SLICES

*Here's a warm, decadent dish that's great for winter brunch. Ready to eat in only 15 minutes, the apples are good alongside waffles, pancakes, or simply spooned over vanilla ice cream.*
—Carol Gillespie, Chambersburg, PA

**Takes:** 15 min. • **Makes:** 6 servings

- ⅓ cup packed brown sugar
- 2 Tbsp. butter
- 2 large apples, cut into ½-in. slices
- ¼ cup chopped pecans, toasted

In a large skillet, cook and stir the brown sugar and butter over medium heat until the sugar is dissolved. Add the apples; cook, uncovered, over medium heat until tender, 5-7 minutes, stirring occasionally. Stir in pecans. Serve warm.

**½ cup:** 155 cal., 8g fat (3g sat. fat), 10mg chol., 43mg sod., 23g carb. (21g sugars, 2g fiber), 1g pro.

**ORANGE CORNMEAL CAKE**

## ORANGE CORNMEAL CAKE

*This cake bakes up tender and light with a subtle orange taste. It tastes rich but is comparatively low in saturated fat. Serve the cake as is, or dress it up with a dollop of whipped cream and strawberries or raspberries. It is wonderful warm, but the flavor improves as it sits, so make it a day or two before you plan to serve it. Store the cake at room temperature.*
—Leigh Rys, Herndon, VA

**Prep:** 25 min. • **Bake:** 40 min. + cooling
**Makes:** 12 servings

- 1 cup sugar
- ½ cup canola oil
- 3 large eggs, room temperature
- 1 cup fat-free plain yogurt
- ¼ cup orange juice
- 4 tsp. grated orange zest
- 1¼ cups all-purpose flour
- ½ cup yellow cornmeal
- 1 tsp. baking powder
- ½ tsp. salt
- ¼ tsp. baking soda

**GLAZE**
- ½ cup sugar
- ½ cup orange juice
- 1 Tbsp. butter

Sweetened whipped cream
Grated orange zest, optional

1. Preheat oven to 350°. In a large bowl, beat sugar and oil until blended. Beat in eggs, yogurt, orange juice and zest. In another bowl, whisk flour, cornmeal, baking powder, salt and baking soda; gradually beat into sugar mixture. Pour into a greased 9-in. springform pan. Place pan on a baking sheet.
2. Bake until cake is golden brown and a toothpick inserted in center comes out with moist crumbs, 40-45 minutes.
3. For glaze, in a microwave-safe bowl, combine sugar, orange juice and butter; microwave on high 2-3 minutes, stirring every 30 seconds. Place cake on a wire rack. Slowly drizzle ½ cup glaze over warm cake; let stand 5 minutes. Slowly drizzle remaining glaze over cake; loosen sides from pan with a knife. Cool cake completely in pan. Cover and let stand overnight. Remove rim from pan. Serve with whipped cream and, if desired, orange zest.

**1 piece:** 294 cal., 12g fat (2g sat. fat), 49mg chol., 202mg sod., 44g carb. (28g sugars, 1g fiber), 4g pro.

# BLUEBERRY ZUCCHINI SQUARES

*I saw a bar recipe using apple and lemon zest on a muffin mix box. I tried it from scratch with shredded zucchini and fresh blueberries instead. It's a nifty combo.*
—Shelly Bevington, Hermiston, OR

**Prep:** 30 min. • **Bake:** 30 min. + cooling
**Makes:** 2 dozen

- 2 **cups shredded zucchini (do not pack)**
- ½ **cup buttermilk**
- 1 **Tbsp. grated lemon zest**
- 3 **Tbsp. lemon juice**
- 1 **cup butter, softened**
- 2½ **cups sugar**
- 2 **large eggs, room temperature**
- 3¼ **cups plus 2 Tbsp. all-purpose flour, divided**
- 1 **tsp. baking soda**
- ½ **tsp. salt**
- 2 **cups fresh or frozen blueberries**

### GLAZE
- 2 **cups confectioners' sugar**
- ¼ **cup buttermilk**
- 1 **Tbsp. grated lemon zest**
- 2 **tsp. lemon juice**
- ⅛ **tsp. salt**

**1.** Preheat the oven to 350°. Grease a 15x10x1-in. baking pan.

**2.** In a small bowl, combine the first 4 ingredients; toss to combine. In a large bowl, cream the butter and sugar until light and fluffy, 5-7 minutes. Beat in the eggs, 1 at a time. In another bowl, whisk 3¼ cups flour, baking soda and salt; gradually add to the creamed mixture alternately with zucchini mixture, mixing well after each addition. Toss blueberries with remaining flour; fold into batter.

**3.** Transfer the batter to prepared pan, spreading evenly (pan will be full). Bake 30-35 minutes or until light golden brown and a toothpick inserted in center comes out clean. Cool completely in pan on a wire rack.

**4.** In a small bowl, mix glaze ingredients until smooth; spread over top. Let stand until set.

**1 piece:** 270 cal., 8g fat (5g sat. fat), 36mg chol., 197mg sod., 47g carb. (33g sugars, 1g fiber), 3g pro.

### HOW-TO
## Make Buttermilk
If you don't have buttermilk, make your own by mixing 1 to 2 Tbsp. of lemon juice or vinegar with enough milk to measure 1 cup. Let sit 5-10 minutes.

BLUEBERRY
ZUCCHINI
SQUARES

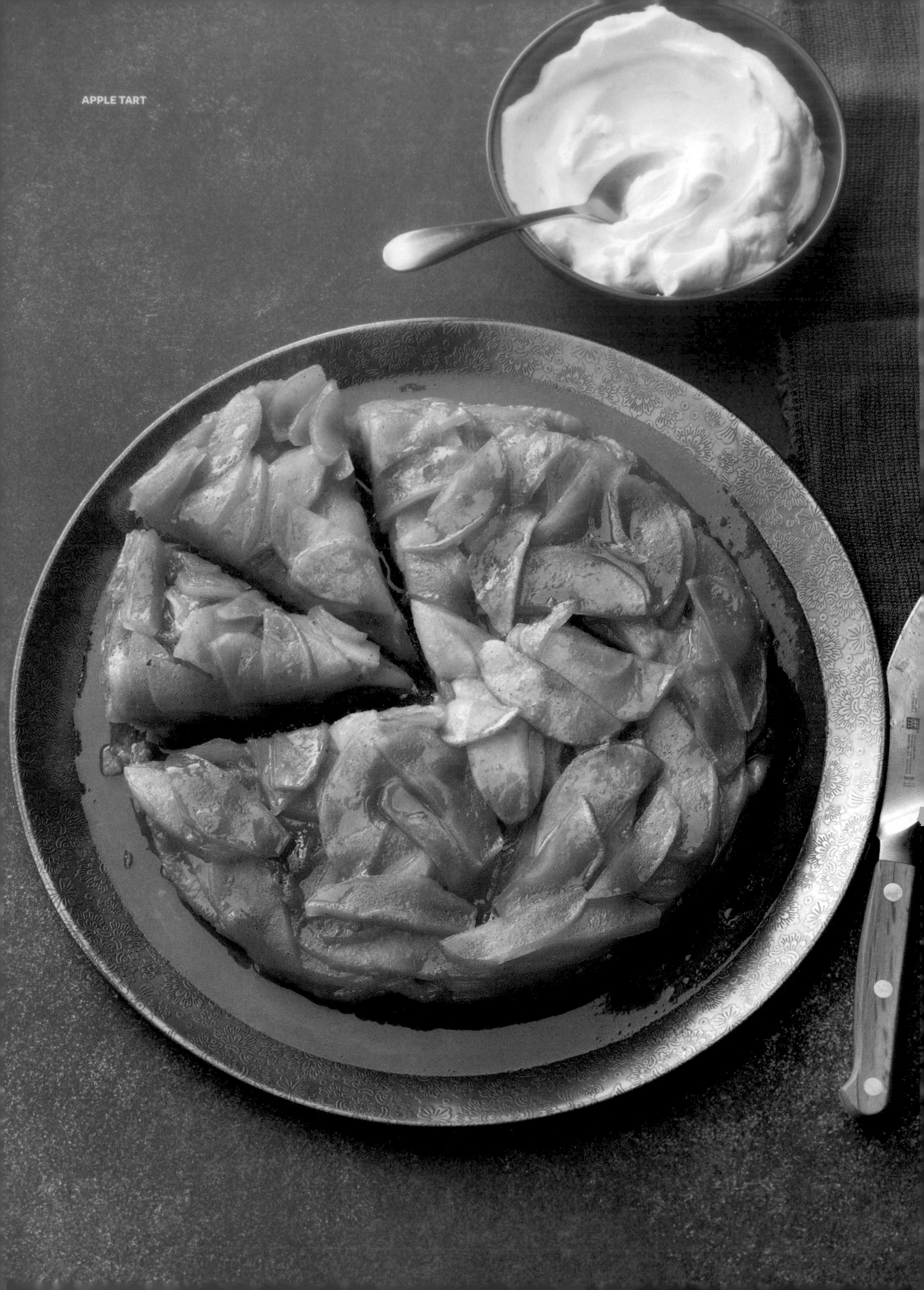
APPLE TART

## APPLE TART

*For 15 years my husband, daughter and I owned and operated an apple orchard, where we raised 27 variations of apples on 2,200 trees. This recipe is my personal favorite. My family even prefers this wonderful tart over traditional apple pie. I hope you enjoy it, too.*
—Marilyn Begres, Dexter, MI

- - - - - - - - - - - - - - - - - - - - - - - -

**Prep:** 25 min. • **Bake:** 50 min. + cooling
**Makes:** 8 servings

| | |
|---|---|
| 1 | cup sugar, divided |
| 2 | Tbsp. all-purpose flour |
| ½ | tsp. ground cinnamon |
| 6 | medium tart apples, peeled and thinly sliced |
| 1 | Tbsp. butter |
| | Pastry for a single-crust pie |

**1.** In a 10-in. cast-iron or other ovenproof skillet, heat ¾ cup sugar, stirring constantly until it is liquefied and golden brown. Remove from the heat.
**2.** In a small bowl, combine the flour, cinnamon and remaining sugar. Arrange half the apples in a single layer in skillet. Sprinkle with half the sugar mixture. Arrange half the remaining apples in circular pattern over sugar; sprinkle with remaining sugar mixture. Place remaining apples over all, keeping the top as level as possible. Dot with butter.
**3.** Roll out the dough to 11-in. circle; place over apples, pressing gently to completely cover. Do not flute. Bake at 400° until apples are tender and golden brown, about 50 minutes. Cool 5 minutes before inverting onto a serving plate.
**1 piece:** 284 cal., 9g fat (4g sat. fat), 9mg chol., 115mg sod., 52g carb. (35g sugars, 2g fiber), 1g pro.
**Pastry for single-crust pie (9 in.):**
Combine 1¼ cups all-purpose flour and ¼ tsp. salt; cut in ½ cup cold butter until crumbly. Gradually add 3-5 Tbsp. ice water, tossing with a fork until dough holds together when pressed. Wrap and refrigerate 1 hour.

**CHERRY GRUNT**

## CHERRY GRUNT

*My husband and two sons really enjoy this old-time dessert. Besides cooking for them, I'm a hot lunch cook and prepare the main dish for about 1,300 students!*
—Judy Meikle, Cherokee, IA

- - - - - - - - - - - - - - - - - - - - - - - -

**Prep:** 15 min. • **Cook:** 30 min.
**Makes:** 10 servings

| | |
|---|---|
| 1 | can (16 oz.) pitted tart red cherries, undrained |
| 1½ | cup water |
| ¾ | cup sugar, divided |
| ¼ | cup butter, divided |
| 1 | cup all-purpose flour |
| 1½ | tsp. baking powder |
| | Pinch salt |
| ¼ | cup 2% milk |
| ½ | tsp. vanilla extract |

**1.** Place cherries and juice in a straight-sided skillet or Dutch oven along with water, ½ cup sugar and 2 Tbsp. butter. Simmer for 5 minutes.
**2.** Meanwhile, sift together flour, baking powder, salt and remaining sugar; place in a bowl. Cut in remaining butter with a pastry blender. Add milk and vanilla.
**3.** Drop by teaspoonfuls over cherry mixture; cover and simmer until the dumplings are cooked through, about 20 minutes.
**½ cup:** 183 cal., 5g fat (3g sat. fat), 13mg chol., 128mg sod., 34g carb. (24g sugars, 1g fiber), 2g pro.

## CHERRY PUDDING CAKE

*A cross between a cake and a cobbler, this cherry dessert is awesome. Add it to your list of trusty potluck recipes, because this one is sure to go fast.*
—Brenda Parker, Kalamazoo, MI

**Prep:** 10 min. • **Bake:** 40 min.
**Makes:** 12 servings

- 2 cups all-purpose flour
- 2½ cups sugar, divided
- 4 tsp. baking powder
- 1 cup 2% milk
- 2 Tbsp. canola oil
- 2 cans (14½ oz. each) water-packed pitted tart red cherries, well drained
- 2 to 3 drops red food coloring, optional
- ⅛ tsp. almond extract
- Optional: Whipped cream or ice cream

**1.** In a bowl, combine flour, 1 cup sugar, baking powder, milk and oil; pour into a greased shallow 3-qt. baking dish. In a bowl, combine cherries, food coloring, extract if desired, and remaining sugar; spoon over batter.

**2.** Bake at 375° for 40-45 minutes or until a toothpick inserted in the cake portion comes out clean. Serve warm, with whipped cream or ice cream if desired.

**1 serving:** 296 cal., 3g fat (1g sat. fat), 3mg chol., 147mg sod., 65g carb. (48g sugars, 1g fiber), 3g pro.

## PEANUT BUTTER POPCORN BARS

*If you're looking for a fun snack for kids, try these chewy popcorn treats that have a mild peanut butter taste. They're easy to stir up and can be pressed into a pan to form bars, or shaped into balls.*
—Kathy Oswald, Wauzeka, WI

**Takes:** 30 min. • **Makes:** 2 dozen

- 10 cups popped popcorn
- ½ cup sugar
- ½ cup light corn syrup
- ½ cup creamy peanut butter
- ½ tsp. vanilla extract

**1.** Place popcorn in a large bowl; set aside. In a saucepan over medium heat, bring sugar and corn syrup to a boil, stirring constantly. Boil for 1 minute. Remove from the heat.

**2.** Stir in the peanut butter and vanilla; mix well. Pour over popcorn and stir until well coated. Press into a buttered 13x9-in. pan. Cool slightly before cutting.

**1 bar:** 90 cal., 4g fat (1g sat. fat), 0 chol., 74mg sod., 13g carb. (8g sugars, 1g fiber), 2g pro.

CHERRY PUDDING CAKE

MANGO GLACE
WITH PINEAPPLE
POMEGRANATE SALSA

## SUMMER STRAWBERRY SHORTCAKE SOUP

*When folks are longing for something sweet and refreshing, this soup is sure to hit the spot. To serve it with dinner or as an appetizer, simply omit the shortcake.*
—Joan Hallford, North Richland Hills, TX

- - - - - - - - - - - - - - - - - - - - - - -

**Prep:** 15 min. + chilling • **Makes:** 4 cups

- 2 **cups fresh or frozen strawberries, hulled**
- 1½ **cups unsweetened pineapple juice**
- ½ **cup white grape juice**
- ⅓ **cup confectioners' sugar**
- ½ **cup moscato wine or additional white grape juice**
- ½ **cup sour cream**
- 6 **individual round sponge cakes**
   **Whipped cream and additional strawberries**

**1.** Place strawberries in a blender; cover and process until pureed. Add juices and confectioners' sugar; cover and process until smooth. Transfer to a bowl; whisk in wine and sour cream. Refrigerate, covered, until chilled, 1-2 hours. Stir.
**2.** Serve with sponge cakes, whipped cream and additional strawberries.
**¾ cup:** 227 cal., 6g fat (3g sat. fat), 32mg chol., 191mg sod., 37g carb. (27g sugars, 1g fiber), 3g pro.

## MANGO GLACE WITH PINEAPPLE POMEGRANATE SALSA

*I'd like to say this dish was a brilliant idea that came from expert planning. But the truth is that between the quickly ripening fruit on my counter and the 100-degree heat, it pretty much invented itself! Very ripe fruit eliminates the need for added sugar.*
—Jodi Taffel, Altadena, CA

- - - - - - - - - - - - - - - - - - - - - - -

**Prep:** 45 min. + freezing • **Makes:** 1 dozen

- 4 **medium ripe mangoes, peeled and chopped**
- 1 **fresh ripe pineapple, peeled and cut into ½-in. pieces**
- 2 **Tbsp. lime juice**
SALSA
- 4 **cups finely chopped fresh pineapple**
- ½ **cup pomegranate seeds**
- ¼ **cup minced fresh mint**

**1.** Combine mangoes, pineapple and lime juice in a blender. Cover and process until smooth. Strain the mixture through a fine-mesh strainer into a large bowl. Pour into 1¾-in. silicone ice cube trays. Freeze until firm, 8 hours or overnight.
**2.** Combine salsa ingredients; cover and refrigerate overnight.
**3.** Remove cubes from freezer 10 minutes before serving. Run a small spatula around the edge of each fruit cube to loosen; remove from trays. Serve glace with salsa.
**1 cube with 4 tsp. salsa:** 137 cal., 1g fat (0 sat. fat), 0 chol., 3mg sod., 35g carb. (29g sugars, 4g fiber), 2g pro.

# INDEX

*•Table-ready in 30 minutes or less.*

NUTTY STUFFED MUSHROOMS, P. 35

INDEX